D1598393

The American
New Woman
Revisited

The American
New Woman
Revisited

A Reader, 1894–1930

EDITED BY
MARTHA H. PATTERSON

RUTGERS UNIVERSITY PRESS
NEW BRUNSWICK, NEW JERSEY, AND LONDON

Library of Congress Cataloging-in-Publication Data

The American new woman revisited : a reader, 1894–1930 / [edited by] Martha H. Patterson.
    p.   cm.
  Includes bibliographical references and index.
  ISBN 978–0-8135–4295–9 (hardcover : alk. paper)
  ISBN 978–0-8135–4296–6 (pbk. : alk. paper)
  1. Women—United States—History.   2. Minority women—United States—History.
  3. Feminism—United States—History.   4. Women's rights—United States—History.
  I. Patterson, Martha H., 1966–
  HQ1410.A44 2008
  305.48′800973—dc22

                                            2007029662

A British Cataloging-in-Publication record for this book is available from the British Library.

Visit our Web site: http://rutgerspress.rutgers.edu

Manufactured in the United States of America

Dedicated to my grandmothers,

Helen Long Patterson
and
Haidee Hersey Hansen

Contents

Acknowledgments

This project could not have been completed without the help of many individuals and institutions.

Numerous individuals at libraries, archives, or educational institutions helped me with research. I thank Carolina Villarroel, project manager, Recovering the U.S. Hispanic Literary Heritage Project; Stephen Greenberg, History of Medicine Division, National Library of Medicine; Andrea J. Bainbridge, archivist II, Records Management and Archives, American Medical Association; Zalman Alpert, reference librarian, Mendel Gottesman Library, Yeshiva University; Paul Anderson, associate professor and archivist, and Lilla Vekerdy, librarian, Bernard Becker Memorial Library; Jana Lonberger U.S. history librarian, Emory University; Michael Luther, collections assistant, Division of Rare and Manuscript Collections, Cornell University Library; Kevlin C. Haire, archives assistant, Ohio State University Archives; Jennifer Comins, archives assistant, Columbia University Archives; the reference desk at the Milstein Division of U.S. History, Local History, and Genealogy, as well as the Schomburg Center for Research in Black Culture, New York Public Library; and Trish Cunningham, Ohio State University.

The staff at the St. Louis Public Library could not have been more helpful. I am especially grateful to Jean E. Meeh Gosebrink, special collections specialist, and Katherine A. LaBarbera for help with reproducing images.

I thank McKendree University and more specifically Dennis Ryan and Gerald Duff for steadfastly supporting the research time and travel necessary to assemble this collection. The McKendree library staff provided invaluable assistance with research and gathering materials. I also thank Jill Campbell, Michael Artime, Liz Vogt, LeAnn Noland, Bill Harroff, Debbie Houk, and, most recently, Meseret Gebremichael.

My research assistants Nell Novara, Valerie Morrese, Emily Gonzalez, Elizabeth Sherman, and Kendra Sigafoos did wonderful work scanning microfilm, proof-reading copy, and, in the cases of Nell Novara and Emily Gonzalez, providing rough translations from the Spanish to help guide my research.

xiv ACKNOWLEDGMENTS

For their professional translations, I thank Paul Coltrin; Edward Cook, reference librarian, St. Louis Area Studies; Peter Conolly-Smith; and Carol Wallace. Two scholars in particular provided assistance that enriched the manuscript tremendously. María Teresa Vera Rojas offered generous advice as I embarked on interpreting the material from *Gráfico*. And Peter Conolly-Smith provided patient, detailed e-mails and translations, without which I could not have included the German material.

I am indebted to Leslie Mitchner of Rutgers University Press for her support and adroit advice in steering the project toward publication. Alicia Nadkarni and Marilyn Campbell expertly guided me through the manuscript preparation process, while Kathryn Gohl was a most patient and careful copyeditor. My reader, Ann Ardis, has provided invaluable suggestions for revision to the manuscript. I am particularly indebted to her advice about shaping the manuscript and, more precisely, for prompting me to look more closely at the periodical history during this era.

Friends and colleagues read drafts of the manuscript or offered helpful suggestions or a much-needed break. I am especially indebted to Debra Blake, Michael Tavel Clark, John Greenfield, Mark Hernandez, Michael McClintock, Michael Pfiefer, Michele Stacey-Doyle, Nancy Beck Young, and Carol Wallace.

My family members have given more help than they realize. Marge, Karen, and Dick Hansen combed through numerous boxes of family records to find information for me. My sister-in-law, Colleen, helped at a crucial junction to care for my children. My mother, with unstinting love, has acted as a sounding board and source of support in so many forms. My siblings, Cheryl, Steve, and John, have listened, encouraged, and wondered if I would ever finish. My husband, Bill Thomas, continues to be my most generous, thoughtful, and supportive critic, while my children, Mark and Walter, bring joy and meaning to what I do. Thank you, Mark, for starting your own New Woman book, stapled and in crayon.

The American
New Woman
Revisited

Introduction

Although scholars disagree as to when the phrase New Woman was coined, the 1894 exchange between British writers Sarah Grand and Ouida in the *North American Review* certainly brought it into general circulation. Immediately, the New Woman sparked debate on both sides of the Atlantic and around the world. Who was she and where did she come from? What did she represent? Would she last? Was she to be celebrated as the agent and sign of progress or reviled as a traitor to the traditional family and by extension her race? Whether the American New Woman signified a suffragist, progressive reformer, prohibitionist, or flapper, her emergence signaled a tidal change in women's roles. Although women of previous generations had seemed to be comfortingly fixed as abundant, selfless Nature, by the turn of the twentieth century, as increasing numbers of women demanded a public voice and private fulfillment through work, education, and political engagement, women, like their male counterparts, seemed to be evolving. The rise of the American New Woman represents one of the most significant cultural shifts of the late nineteenth and twentieth centuries, and in this anthology I have striven to represent the variable web of her development through print culture artifacts published from 1894 to 1930. These texts reveal the sometimes paradoxical but always impassioned appeals inspired by the New Woman during one of the most important eras in the history of the feminist movement.

But evolving to what? Was woman realizing her distinctiveness from man by developing her inherent altruism, or was she demonstrating her similarity to man in her desire for meaningful work? Was she more concerned with the goals of mass political movements or her own personal self-expression? Was she invested in progressive social change, revolutionary upheaval, self-indulgence, personal freedom, or what to our contemporary perspective appear as frightening programs of social engineering? In the documents I have assembled here, the New Woman represents all of these contradictory positions and more: suffragist, prohibitionist, clubwoman, college girl, American girl, socialist, capitalist, anarchist, pickpocket, bicyclist, barren spinster, mannish woman, outdoor girl, birth-control advocate, modern girl, eugenicist, flapper, blues woman, lesbian, and vamp. She is conceived differently in the South, North, East, and West—in working-class newspapers and highbrow monthly magazines, in socialist and sensationalist newspapers, in Marcus Garvey's the *Negro World* and the nationally circulated black newspaper the *Chicago Defender*, in the Puerto Rican *Gráfico*, and in the Mexican American *La Crónica*. Indeed, although we most often think of the American New Woman in the dominant narrative— featuring the bloomer-wearing bicyclist or slogan-wielding suffragist—the story of the New Woman's emergence is far more complex, varying according to region, class, politics, race, and ethnicity, while changing through time and depending greatly on historical conditions. All of the writers in this anthology agreed that women were changing, but they contested the direction that change should take as well as its meaning. Signifying at once a character type and a cultural phenomenon, the term New Woman described women more broadly than suffragist or settlement worker, while connoting a distinctly modern ideal of self-refashioning. Not simply shorthand for a commitment to greater female liberation, the term could signal multiple and contradictory positions on the most pressing issues of the day. My aim in this book is not only to offer a precise understanding of the New Woman and, by extension, the Progressive era in general, but also, in the words of Daylanne English, to provide an "inclusive cultural context" for studies in the U.S. modern period. Even as the writers of these selections often worked in distinct communities, depending on their race, class, gender, region, and political perspective, they all saw the New Woman as a crucial modern social development.[1]

Defining the New Woman in the Periodical Press

The New Woman emerged from the periodical press, from which she also gained her name. The period between 1880 and 1920 witnessed a decline in books as a mass medium and the spectacular growth in the number, variety, and circulation of periodicals. Rapid increases in the literacy rate, the extension of second-class bulk mailing privileges and free rural delivery service, combined with tremendous advances in printing technologies and the expansion of telegraph, railroad, and later telephone networks all enabled periodical publishers to appeal to ever larger audiences. The number of magazines jumped from approximately 2,400 in 1880 to 5,100 in 1895, but circulation grew by even greater strides. Earlier in the nineteenth century, magazines had been largely purchased by upper-middle-class audiences, but by the late nineteenth century, with new inexpensive printing and illustrating technologies, fierce competition exacerbated by the depressions of 1893 and 1897, and an advertising bonanza devoted to selling new mass-manufactured objects, many magazines lowered their price and consequently attracted a much larger readership. Indeed, in the 1880s most of the few magazines whose circulation was greater than 100,000 were priced from twenty-five to thirty-five cents, but by the 1890s ten-cent magazines had arrived, and magazine readership surged, reaching the tens of millions by 1900. Circulation for monthly magazines rose from 18 million in 1890 to 64 million in 1905 or about four magazines per household, greater than the combined circulation of weekly periodicals and newspapers, which rose during the same period from 36 million to 57 million. In the 1890s Joseph Pulitzer and William Hearst, rival pioneers in "yellow" journalism, made their newspapers entertainment vehicles by offering readers titillating, heavily illustrated articles on crime and vice even as they crusaded for social reforms and spearheaded philanthropic ventures. Savvy publishers such as Edward Willis Scripps, meanwhile, offered one-cent, pro-labor, antimonopoly daily newspapers to the under-served, urban working class in the Midwest and West. Bolstered by increased literacy and rising income rates among African Americans and spurred by proliferating Jim Crow abuses, the black press grew rapidly in the 1880s and 1890s. Immigrants also started their own newspapers for those newly arrived and trying to adjust to a foreign culture. From 1900 to 1930 the immigrant press in the United States flourished, reaching a peak in 1917 when more than 1,300 foreign-language newspapers were published, with German and Jewish newspapers enjoying the largest circulation.[2]

Enticing readers visually while entertaining them with sensational stories became critical to a periodical's success. Increasing amounts of serialized fiction—of which the "New Woman romance" was a prominent part—spurred the growth of the major women's magazines. After 1900, color images became increasingly popular, and photography, in the form of halftone prints, came to dominate magazine illustrations. Advertising—for products ranging from Columbia bicycles, Eastman Kodak cameras, and Quaker Oats cereals to Lydia E. Pinkham's patent medicines—was at first text heavy, but it became increasingly visual as the industry professionalized. Rather than depending primarily on newsstand or subscription sales, periodical publishers increasingly relied on advertising revenue for profits, which in turn allowed them to cut prices, expand their market, and attract more advertising dollars. To help them compete with magazines, newspapers, beginning in the 1890s, developed Sunday editions with comics, illustrations, and more advertising. Magazines, such as B. O. Flower's *Arena*, adopted Pulitzer and Hearst's approach of advocating various social reforms, while the best-selling *Munsey's Magazine* adopted aspects of the yellow press's Sunday supplements. Even though many magazines and papers regularly lampooned the yellow press, they adopted some of the same tactics as the dailies.[3]

The new emphasis on illustration in both magazines and newspapers depended heavily on featuring attractive women. In the late nineteenth century and through the first decade of the twentieth, the image of the American woman as drawn by Charles Dana Gibson and others whose work was in the same vein—Howard Chandler Christy, James Montgomery Flagg, and Harrison Fisher—dominated the marketplace. Tall, distant, elegant, and white, with a pert nose, voluminous upswept hair, corseted waist, and large bust, the Gibson Girl offered a popular version of the New Woman that both sanctioned and undermined women's desires for progressive sociopolitical change and personal freedom at the turn of the century. Charlotte Perkins Gilman, for example, lauded the Gibson Girl as a New Woman representing women's legal, social, mental, and physical progress, a symbol of their growing freedom from what she termed the "sexuo-economic" relationship with men:

The Gibson Girl and the Duchess of Towers,—these are the new women; and they represent a noble type, indeed. The heroines of romance and drama to-day are of a different sort from the Evelinas and Arabellas of the last century. . . . The false sentimentality, the false delicacy, the false modesty, the utter falseness of elaborate compliment and servile gallantry which went with the other falsehoods—all these are disappearing. Women are growing honester, braver, stronger, more healthful and skillful and able and free, more human in all ways.[4]

Gilman may have embraced the Gibson Girl and the George du Maurier heroine the Duchess of Towers because they seemed to be the best mainstream alternatives to the caricatures of the New Woman that abounded in the periodical press. The popular tabloid the *National Police Gazette*, for example, regularly featured New Women in bloomers or tights who were boxing, drinking, smoking, or committing crimes. At least one proponent of women's suffrage pilloried the sensational press for using the term New Woman to conflate the frivolous hoyden with the serious suffragist. In a column titled "Very Cheap Wit," written for her suffrage journal *Woman's Era*, Agnes Hudson Young wrote in 1895:

If by the "new woman" is meant that class of women who attend the races, keep saloons, tend bar, smoke cigarettes, etc., the term is not out of place. But when a newspaper so far forgets itself and its calling as to apply the term to women whose intelligence is unquestioned and whose characters are above reproach, and all because their sense of justice will not allow them to be classed with idiots, imbeciles and criminals, it is carrying the joke, if it is a joke, a little too far.[5]

After World War I, new images of American beauty and social transgression emerged that seemed to turn the Gibson Girl on her head. John Held Jr.'s illustrations for *Life, College Humor,* and many other magazines popularized a gangly, pliable female figure who could dance the Charleston, pull the cork on a bottle of liquor during Prohibition, or crack up a car with equal nonchalance. Although dress lengths varied somewhat, according to the occasion and the fashion, they were definitely getting shorter—sometimes revealing roll-top silk stockings—and showed no signs of returning to the ankle-length propriety of the Gibson Girl's. Even the chemise, the "oldest female garment," was now a visually advertised fashion, coming in multiple colors, lacey and embroidered, suggesting that it too would be open to view. Critics of the new vogue decried the flappers "sunken chests and round shoulders," which evoked fatigue rather than beauty. Celebrants of the new fashion emphasized that it required "the 'ideal modern figure . . . , the acrobat's dream of fitness. . . . A really supple and muscular young body, with no spare flesh on the well-made frame.'" Calorie counting, the bathroom scale, and ads for reducing diets and cigarettes played on this new obsession with thinness. Ads for Lucky Strike urged women to "reach for a Lucky instead of a sweet." Girdle bras further reduced the female form by binding the breasts and streamlining the hips, creating a prepubescent figure. Achieving the new ideal not only required dieting and a willingness to put much more of the body on display but also purchasing the ever-increasing range of products that defined a woman's leisured lifestyle. In the process, in the words of journalism historian Carolyn Kitch, the New Woman as flapper "became the New Girl who was a new product." As such, she was an international phenomenon.[6]

By the 1920s, New Women films, performers, advertising, and products crisscrossed international boundaries, creating a vast market for the New Woman as visual icon. But even from the New Woman's inception, American magazines borrowed New Woman iconography mostly from European, especially British, sources and charted the status of the New Woman around the world. The intellectual dimensions of this struggle are so many and so complex that I enumerate only a few to foreshadow the selections in this anthology and the way they reveal how international feminist art, theory, and practice shaped the American concept of the New Woman. In *A Doll's House* (1879), for example, the Norwegian Henrik Ibsen inspired New Woman writers and activists throughout Europe and the United States with his scathing indictment of conventional gender roles within Victorian marriage. American radical and New Woman proponent Emma Goldman visited Paris in 1900 to learn more about birth control from the neo-Malthusians, who believed that population control could improve society. As a term denoting the advocacy of women's rights, "feminism" had its origins in nineteenth-century France, then appeared in England in the 1890s, before being widely adopted in the United States after 1910 as a signifier of a larger, modern quest for women's complete emancipation. Meanwhile, the Mexican Revolution, begun in 1910, helped spur demands for greater women's rights in the borderlands. The fact that the National Woman's Party, founded in 1913 by Alice Paul and Lucy Burns, adopted some of the militant tactics of the British Emmeline Pankhurst, her daughters Christabel and Sylvia, and their Women's Social and Political Union, demonstrates the transatlantic nature of the suffrage movement. Given that American magazines regularly published international perspectives on women's changing roles and that many of the writers included in this volume engaged in this international women's rights dialogue, understanding the evolution of the American New Woman necessarily means crossing international boundaries as much as disciplinary or ideological ones.[7]

At the same time, even though New Women figures such as Jane Addams were widely known for their antimilitarist stance, the American New Woman, like her British counterpart, served as an icon of both imperialist conquest and racist ambivalence over the success of those conquests. Spurred by the Spanish-American War of 1898, the New Woman appeared in popular magazines and literature to sanction imperialism as overseas "adventures" or patriotic nation-building imperatives. As a result of the Spanish-American War, the United States acquired a number of Spanish colonies—Guam, Puerto Rico, and the Philippines—and Cuba came under new American influence as a virtual protectorate. In addition, the United States formally annexed the Hawaiian Islands in 1898 and gained control of a section of the isthmus of Panama in preparation for building the transoceanic canal. Under a policy of what has been termed dollar diplomacy, the administration of William Howard Taft (1909–1913) sought to protect U.S. sugar interests in Cuba, promote banking interests in China, and bolster the Nicaraguan government. Under President Woodrow Wilson's administration (1913–1921), the United States briefly occupied

Vera Cruz, Mexico, in 1914; began a nineteen-year occupation of Haiti in 1915 and an eight-year occupation of the Dominican Republic in 1916; and sent an expeditionary force into Mexico in 1916. Despite the relative "success" of U.S. interventionism, however, many Americans balked at the idea of having what they saw as so many poor, ethnically inferior populations under U.S. control. The dominant Anglo-Saxon, middle-class image of the New Woman represented this anxiety as well. As a symbol of the nation, Howard Chandler Christy's girl would bear an equal share with her mate of the "Titanic labor of carrying forward into the wilds the standard of civilization," even as Charles Dana Gibson's girl wondered in 1898 if, in regard to these new "foreign relations," or European imperial powers, she wanted "to go in with that crowd."[8]

WOMEN'S SUFFRAGE AND POLITICAL PARTICIPATION

If you were to ask most Americans before 1919 what the New Woman stood for, chances are they would have said women's suffrage. At one time or another, all the leaders of the mainstream suffrage movement, the National American Woman Suffrage Association (NAWSA), were called New Women, including Elizabeth Cady Stanton, Susan B. Anthony, Carrie Chapman Catt, and Anna Howard Shaw. With the merging of the National Woman Suffrage Association and the American Woman Suffrage Association in 1890 until the ratification of the Nineteenth Amendment in 1920, the influence of the movement steadily grew; from 1893 to 1917, membership in NAWSA increased from 13,000 to 2 million. Drawing on an egalitarian strain of Enlightenment thinking, one that found expression in the Declaration of Independence's assertion that all men are created equal, early suffragists maintained that that equality applied to women. Some early suffragists argued that the Declaration also applied to African Americans and argued for abolition as well. Eager to make more substantial political headway, however—by 1894 only Wyoming and Colorado had granted women the right to vote and to serve on juries—key leaders in the movement changed tactics, and many more adopted expedient arguments. By the mid-1890s, leaders of NAWSA bolstered the natural rights argument with the pragmatic one that allowing women to vote would help eliminate many of the social ills—such as child labor, contaminated food, and unsanitary housing—that progressive reformers, regardless of gender, railed against. The advent of the "new immigration," meanwhile, caused growing anxiety among native-born, middle-class white suffragists. The tremendous number of immigrants from eastern and southern Europe who settled in urban areas in the late nineteenth and early twentieth century generated fears that these newcomers would corrupt American politics.

The northern leadership of NAWSA also faced increasing pressure from southern suffragists to exclude African Americans from the rights of citizenship. Bowing to these pressures, NAWSA often abandoned explicit natural rights arguments in favor of xenophobic and racist ones. Granting women the right to vote, so a popular argument went, would ensure white control because there would be more native-born, white female rather than black male or ethnic "other" voters. More explicitly racist actions also accompanied the new expediency. In 1899, for example, the NAWSA convention refused to endorse a resolution, forwarded by black suffragists, to oppose Jim Crow cars on railroads, and in 1913, black suffragists were asked not to march in the Washington suffrage parade. African American civil rights leaders deplored racism within the women's movement. In 1907, for example, W.E.B. Du Bois complained that "the Negro race has suffered more from the antipathy and narrowness of women both South and North than from any other single source."[9]

Partially in response to white exclusionary practices, African American women formed their own suffrage associations, often as part of women's clubs, and broadened the suffrage appeal to include increasingly disenfranchised black men. Thousands of black women joined clubs for which women's suffrage and, by extension, the reenfranchisement of black men were a key goal. Socialist groups, likewise, fought discrimination by demanding that the foreign-born be considered essential to any democratic movement such as women's suffrage. And a few isolated leaders in NAWSA, such as Jane Addams, who had been deeply moved by her work with immigrants in Chicago, maintained that the women of this group needed the vote if they were to prevent the degradation of their families in the often deplorable conditions of the urban ghetto.[10]

After the vote was won, a few women managed to get elected to public office, and women's groups could claim a few notable legislative successes. In 1920 eight women's organizations, including the League of Women Voters, the National Congress of Mothers, and the Parent-Teachers Association, organized the Women's Joint Congressional Committee (WJCC). The committee's founders crafted an agenda featuring the six Ps: prohibition, public schools, protection of infants, physical education in the public schools, peace through international arms reduction, and protection of women in industry. With the passage in 1921 of the Sheppard-Towner Act, promoting maternal and infant welfare and hygiene, the WJCC achieved its first, albeit short-lived (the act terminated in 1929), substantial victory. Facing a political shift to the right in the 1920s, the WJCC grew most frustrated in its failure to get a child-labor amendment passed. In addition, many public observers decried what seemed a low voter turnout among women and puzzled over voting trends suggesting that women did not vote as a bloc.[11]

The National Woman's Party (NWP), widely considered the more radical wing of the suffrage movement, also faced discouraging setbacks for its initiatives in the 1920s. Under the leadership of Alice Paul, the NWP lobbied for passage of the Equal Rights Amendment (ERA) to fight remaining discrimination in American society. Writing for the *Nation* in 1924, socialist Crystal Eastman defended the Equal Rights Amendment on the grounds that "the battle for 'equal rights' . . . must be fought and it will be fought by a free-handed, non-partisan minority of energetic feminists to whom politics in general, even 'reform' politics, will continue to be a matter of indifference so long as women are classed with children and minors in industrial legislation, so long as even in our most advanced States a woman can be penalized by the loss of her job when she marries."[12]

Women running for political office faced tremendous hurdles, beginning with winning the nomination, and most female political officeholders were widows or daughters of incumbent politicians. In 1928, a high point of women's representation in Congress, 7 women served in the U.S. House of Representatives, 119 in state assemblies, and 12 in state senates. Although, on the national level, women representatives were mostly appointed to committees focusing on education, Indian and veterans' affairs, and the District of Columbia, California Republican Florence Prag Kahn won appointment to the Military Affairs Committee and New Jersey Democrat Mary Norton eventually chaired the Committee on Labor. At the state level, two women, Nellie Tayloe Ross of Wyoming and Miriam "Ma" Ferguson of Texas, succeeded their husbands and served as governors.[13]

TEMPERANCE, SOCIAL PURITY, AND MATERNALISM

The fight for women's suffrage drew some of its greatest support from the prohibition movement, in part because the groups shared a common foe. The liquor interests, fearing that women would more likely support prohibition, funded both antisuffrage and antiprohibition campaigns. Having long blamed poverty, domestic violence, and family abandonment on male drunkenness, prohibition advocates, organized under Frances Willard's Woman's Christian Temperance Union (WCTU), drew many women into politics for the first time. By the end of the 1890s, the WCTU was the largest women's organization in the United States and promoted a host of progressive causes in addition to temperance. Speaking before a convention of the World's Woman's Christian Temperance Union in 1893, Willard declared that the larger mission of the organization was to support various facets of women's emancipation including women's suffrage: "There are three sets of slaves that we women are working to emancipate. They are, white slaves, that is, degraded women; wage slaves, that is, the working classes; and whiskey slaves, that is, the product furnished by brewers and distillers."[14]

Advocates for social or sexual purity—which included the sociologist Lester Ward, Christian Science founder Mary Baker Eddy, Elizabeth Cady Stanton, and Frances Willard—believed that society and the race would improve if the ethics of pure, altruistic, rational woman prevailed rather than those of lustful, competitive man. Masculine desire, social purity proponents argued, led not only to massive economic inequalities and corruption, but also to marital rape, prostitution, sexual promiscuity, and unwanted pregnancies—moral evils that a commitment to social purity would help remedy. Missionary women might use this rationale to convert "heathens," temperance advocates to fight alcohol consumption, clubwomen to emphasize the elevating effects of literacy, and charity organizations to fight poverty. Personal transformation could occur, advocates argued, if people better understood the mind's capacity for self-transformation. The dominant early version of the period's New Thought literature (from 1875 until 1905) urged readers to discover the creative potential of the mind and its ability to control reality. And whereas later advocates of New Thought focused far more on how adopting a different mental

attitude could bring masculinized material success, early turn-of-the-century proponents urged followers to focus on the feminine spiritual rather than the masculine
material reality around them if they were to reach an evolved consciousness.[15]

Indeed, for many conservative social purity reformers, the struggle against alcohol
was part of an even larger struggle of altruistic women motivated by their "mother-
heart" against selfish masculinity and its incumbent vice, including alcoholism,
prostitution, and worker exploitation. As Molly Ladd-Taylor notes, motherhood,
which was "inextricably tied to state-building and public policy," became a dominant
theme in Progressive-era politics, and the discourse of its activists ranged from sentimental to progressive to feminist. Settlement house reformers such as Jane Addams
and Lillian Wald, figures designated as New Women, argued for what Ladd-Taylor
notes was a kind of progressive maternalism. On the one hand, professional mater-
nalists "assumed that women had a special capacity for nurture by virtue of being
women, stressed women's political obligation to raise the nation's citizens, held
privileged women responsible for all children's welfare, and insisted on the virtues
of an Anglo-American family structure that defined men as breadwinners and kept
women and children at home." On the other hand, they emphasized that women
had a right and responsibility to participate in the public world because they relied
on professional expertise, rather than intuitive or emotional arguments, to justify
their child-rearing advice. Accordingly, the settlement house leader Florence Kelley
campaigned for better work-place conditions but opposed not only health-insurance
measures that provided wage-earning women with maternity benefits but also compulsory maternity leave from work because she feared that such initiatives would
prompt more women to remain in the labor force rather than attend to their primary
role as mothers.[16] In the work of African American writers, maternal rights and
responsibilities in large part define the New Negro Woman's authority. Because
under slavery black women had had no rights to their children, maternal rights held
special resonance for the New Negro Woman and would be central to defining both
her ambition and her purview, which would extend to uplift the entire race.

Most white feminists' arguments of the period, by contrast, emphasized women's
need to be economically independent and their right to be fulfilled as individuals,
even as they stressed women's duties to the race as mothers. Charlotte Perkins Gilman,
the period's leading feminist voice, railed against the typical middle-class courtship
in which the woman must develop her consumer abilities. The woman must adorn
herself to attract a mate, whereas the man, by virtue of his sex alone, could perform
productive labor. This "sexuo-economic" relationship between men and women
was both unnatural and destructive. To free women to work more productively, the
duties of the home—cleaning, cooking, and child care—should be performed col-
lectively. And because the best child rearing, according to Gilman, demanded not
only love and inclination but also some measure of professional expertise, traditional conceptions of motherhood had to be reformulated in the best interest of the
race. For Gilman a commitment to the New Motherhood meant first realizing "the
fullest development of the woman, in all her powers, that she may be the better
qualified for her duties of transmission by inheritance," then picking a mate based

on "his fitness for fatherhood," and finally recognizing the "high specialization" needed in the art of "child culture."[17]

The Women's Club Movement and Women's Education

Women who may have eschewed working directly for a political movement such as prohibition or suffrage often participated in the women's club movement. Membership in women's clubs, especially among middle-class women, grew exponentially from 1880 to 1900, peaking at two million clubwomen at the turn of the last century. Organized generally along racial, class, religious, or political lines, such clubs appeared in every region of the country. Two of the most significant coalitions of club members were formed in the late nineteenth century: the General Federation of Women's Clubs in 1890 and the National Association of Colored Women (NACW) in 1896. The focus of most white women's clubs was to encourage a better understanding of social, political, or cultural issues, thereby enabling greater engagement in issues of national importance, whereas black women's clubs tended to be more service oriented. Mary White Ovington, a white women who was active in both the settlement house movement and the black women's club movement, noted that "the National Association of Colored Women, as I saw it, was not working along cultural lines but along social service lines. It was starting kindergartens and day nurseries and looking after old people." Regardless of race, clubwomen engaged in activities aimed at both self-improvement and community enrichment. They hosted speakers on current topics ranging from women's suffrage to the uses of electricity, offered opportunities for immigrant and working-class women to read about and write on conditions in factories and tenement houses, and worked to improve housing and employment conditions. Although native-born white women often faced derision for their membership in women's clubs, black women seemed to encounter less community opposition, a difference perhaps due to the cross-gendered appeal of their racial uplift agenda. Often inspired by a Christian commitment to social and personal uplift, African American clubwomen advocated a kind of progressive maternalism that sanctioned their advocacy of governmental reform and remediation of social ills, such as providing homes for dependent and delinquent children. Their approach to social reform was in keeping with both Booker T. Washington's industrial education model and W.E.B. Du Bois's "talented tenth" leadership ideal.[18]

With the ratification of the Nineteenth Amendment in 1920, many younger women abandoned women's organizations, hoping that now they would be seen on equal footing with men. Accompanying a desire for cross-gender working alliances was a growing conviction that the older generation's women's clubs were outdated. Mary White Ovington described this generational divide: "My mother joined the Brooklyn Woman's Club. . . . Women had few opportunities then for education and the club was intended to keep up their reading and study, to give them something beside the daily household round. My generation, that had more opportunity for education, looked down on these clubs and made fun of the papers that discussed Roman history in half an hour." Indeed, when younger women began attending

college and working in settlement houses and reform movements, many also struggled for autonomy, a struggle for personal freedom that estranged them from the
women's club movement of their mothers' generation. Both white and black women's
club leaders wanted no part of the "new morality" that was associated with flappers
and female blues performers. At the National Association of Colored Women in 1927,
honorary president Hallie Q. Brown, for example, warned black women to stay fast
to the mission of uplift and not become "obsessed with fashion and things of pleasure
only."[19]

Eventually, civil rights and social welfare organizations such as the National
Association for the Advancement of Colored People (NAACP) took up many of the
National Association of Colored Women's initiatives, making the NACW seem less
relevant.[20] The NAACP, founded in 1909 by a group that included Mary White
Ovington and turn-of-the-century journalist, anti-lynching crusader, and NACW
member Ida B. Wells-Barnett, continued the NACW's impassioned anti-lynching
campaigns and civil rights initiatives.

Access to formal higher education for women in general, but particularly for
middle-class women, increased, and attendance rose exponentially during this period.
In 1870 the percentage of college-age American women who attended college was
0.7 percent; by 1900 the rate had increased to just under 3 percent, and by 1920 to just
under 8 percent, numbers proportionally small but signifying a substantial social
change. Between 1900 and 1930, women's attendance at colleges and universities
tripled, and although women comprised only 35 percent of the college population
in 1890, by 1920 they made up just over 47 percent of it. Better-educated women
enjoyed greater opportunities in the paid workforce, and before the 1920s at least,
such women tended to delay marriage and childbearing, a practice that provoked
alarm among many prominent social critics. The British evolutionary theorist Herbert
Spencer argued in 1899, for example, that the "deficiency of reproductive power
among" upper-class girls may be "reasonably attributed to the overtaxing of their
brains." Psychologist G. Stanley Hall's 1904 study of adolescence likewise maintained that academically ambitious women would "become functionally castrated,
unwilling to accept the limitations of married life," and would resent being called
to perform "the functions peculiar to their sex."[21]

College was also opening up, albeit in limited ways, to a female student body
that was more diverse. According to a 1911 report from the Immigration Commission,
of female students attending sixty-three colleges across the country, 23.8 percent had
immigrant parents, and black women comprised 0.3 percent of the female student
population. With bigotry against Jews, southern Europeans, African Americans,
and Native Americans prevalent in the United States, members of these groups saw
higher education as a personal pursuit with profound communal ramifications. In
her autobiography *The Promised Land* (1912), Mary Antin describes her frustration
with patriarchal privileges enjoyed by men in Russian Jewish culture. Although all
Russian Jewish boys were sent to Hebrew school and could be Torah scholars or
rabbis, girls could not: "A girl's real schoolroom was her mother's kitchen. . . . And
while her hands were busy, her mother instructed her in the laws regulating a pious

Jewish household and in the conduct proper for a Jewish wife, for, of course, every girl hoped to be a wife. A girl was born for no other purpose."[22] Antin presents American educational opportunities not only as the means to her own success, but also as the ultimate remedy for the gender, ethnic, and class inequities afflicting the nation.

By contrast Dakota Sioux writer Zitkala-Ša (Gertrude Simmons Bonin) presents a more ambivalent assessment of educational opportunity. Competing in an otherwise all-white, all-male college oratorical contest in 1896, she delivered a stirring address advocating indigenous rights; in response, the opposing team displayed a large white flag with a caricature of an Indian girl under which was printed "squaw." Although she ended up winning second place in the contest, symbolically defeating bigotry, and left feeling vindicated, she also felt profoundly alienated and unable to connect her academic success with her Dakota heritage. Disapproving of her "attempt to learn the white man's ways," her mother, writes Zitkala-Ša, was "far away on the Western plains . . . [holding] a charge against me."[23]

WORK AND THE LABOR MOVEMENT

Women's access to higher education contributed to what perhaps was the most demonstrable change in many women's lives—a change that the New Woman represents: greater involvement in the paid workforce. By 1900, an estimated five million, or one out of every five women, were employed in a number of mostly low-paying fields, such as textile manufacturing, secretarial work, sales, housekeeping, primary education, nursing, agriculture, and domestic service, the last of which employed the largest percentage of women. Approximately 10 percent of the total number of employed women held professional positions as teachers and another 10 percent as clerks. For single and married women, however, and for women of different ethnic and racial groups, work patterns were strikingly different. In 1890, 40 percent of all single white women performed some sort of paid labor, compared to 60 percent of single nonwhite women and 70 percent of single foreign-born women. In 1900, 3.3 percent of married white women earned wages, and in 1920 the census recorded 9 percent as wage earners. Despite this threefold increase, white women overall tended to stop working after they married. By the end of the 1920s, however, married women's participation in the workforce had increased by more than 25 percent. In 1900 and 1920, approximately 40 percent of all black women, however, were paid employees, and they would remain employed for their entire adult lives, relegated, for the most part, to jobs as domestic laborers in white households. Facing far greater employment discrimination than white women did, "black women as a group continued to make beds and wash dishes while white women were being hired as switchboard operators, stenographers, and sales clerks." Although, in the 1920s, Chicago stores hired both white and black women, the former worked as salesclerks and ate on the first floor, whereas the latter served as maids and ate in the basement. Facing endemic discrimination, well-educated African American women often were not able to find work in the paid workforce. Those few who were able to find employment as teachers, journalists, or secretaries were usually employed within the black community. Puerto Rican women, meanwhile, faced both language barriers and racial discrimination in their efforts to find clerical employment. In 1925 only 3.4 percent of Puerto Rican women held clerical positions. Married Puerto Rican women in New York City worked for textile companies, making lace, clothing, and other goods in their homes. Overall, married immigrant women had the lowest rates of paid employment.[24]

For most women—and especially for immigrant and African American women—working conditions were poor to abysmal, opportunities for advancement few, safety measures almost nonexistent, and hours long, with wages far lower than those paid to their male counterparts. To alleviate poor working conditions, tens of thousands of women joined labor organizations. Although less than 7 percent of wage-earning women were in trade unions by 1920, they proved to be tenacious and successful union members. Between 1905 and 1915, 100,000 women in garment factories went on strike demanding higher wages, an end to subcontracting, and better working conditions, including an end to sexual harassment by male supervisors. During "the first great strike of women" in 1909, 20,000 women organized under the auspices of the Women's Trade Union League (WTUL). Striking women endured bitter cold, arrests for vagrancy, and beatings by hired strikebreakers, prompting one observer of the events to remark: "There was never any thing like it. . . . An equal number of men would never hold together under what these girls are enduring." Meanwhile, settlement house leaders such as Jane Addams and Florence Kelley campaigned for a wide range of workplace reforms, including a ban on child labor, an eight-hour work day for women, and an end to sweatshop labor conditions.[25] Whereas foreign-born socialist women tended to favor more traditional gender roles, native-born women forged a distinct socialist vision apart from that of their male counterparts. Appealing to the conservative gender politics of its readers, the German-language socialist newspaper the *New Yorker Volkszeitung*, for example, was careful to distance itself from the middle-class American suffrage movement; cooperation with it would have been considered "tantamount to class treason." Although the newspaper eventually came out in support of women's suffrage, it also bristled at what it deemed New Woman transgressions in dress, declaring that "even for the most festive of occasions, working women never wear anything but buttoned, even highnecked dresses." Some of the more radical foreign-born activists who protested the tremendous wealth inequities within capitalism tended to favor a greater degree of gender equality, but their belief in the ineffectualness of voting meant that they had less interest in supporting women's suffrage.[26]

WORLD WAR I AND ITS AFTERMATH

World War I split the women's movement. During the period of American neutrality (1914–1917), American women's rights activists, many of whom were closely allied with the suffrage movement, worked for peace under the banner of the Woman's Peace Party (WPP). Led by Jane Addams, the WPP, which began in 1915 and claimed

40,000 members in 1916, based its argument for peace in "pacifist maternalism"—
the idea that women's ability to give life made them more concerned with protecting it. As the United States' entry into the war appeared imminent, some suffragist
leaders, including NAWSA leader Carrie Chapman Catt, offered President Woodrow
Wilson a pledge of war service from women's suffrage advocates across the nation,
a commitment that angered some NAWSA members. After the United States declared
war in April 1917, the WPP, under intense pressure from the federal government and
the mass media to demonstrate "loyalty," now fell virtually silent, and membership
dropped precipitously. In the end, NAWSA expressed support for the war, while the
National Woman's Party under Alice Paul was noncommittal.[27]

World War I was the first conflict in which American women were mobilized on
a large scale. Despite the divisions among the various women's groups, many saw
the war as an opportunity to demonstrate women's willingness to sacrifice for the
nation and hence their readiness for the demands of equal citizenship. In addition,
even as some stereotypical gender roles were reinforced by the war rhetoric—
especially those of the female nurturer versus the masculine aggressor—others were
destabilized, creating yet other variations of the American New Woman. As demand
for workers on the home front increased dramatically after the United States entered
the war in 1917, women were able to secure jobs in steel and lumber mills, the arma-
ments industry, and chemical and electrical plants. Pressured by the Women's
Trade Union League, the National War Labor Board also took the unprecedented
step of trying to garner greater pay equity for female workers. The U.S. military,
however, employed far fewer women than its European counterparts did and, given
the intense racism and anti-Semitism of the period, almost no African American or
Jewish women. Over 16,000 women served overseas, under the umbrella of the
American Expeditionary Force (AEF), as members of the Army Nurse Corps, ambu-
lance drivers, clerks, telephone operators, and auxiliary or welfare workers. Women
in the AEF, however, weren't accorded the same status as their male colleagues. The
one exception to this inequity in the military was the U.S. Navy, which enlisted over
12,000 women on an "equal footing" with men mostly in stateside positions. Through
the YMCA, YWCA, the American Red Cross, the Salvation Army, and other private
social service groups, thousands of women went overseas to work. Many more
thousands, including African American and Jewish women, worked at home as
volunteers in war service organizations. Female service arguably created a new conviction among many men that women had earned the right to vote. Having opposed
women's suffrage before the United States' entrance into the war, Woodrow Wilson
now changed course decisively. In a speech before the U.S. Senate in 1918, Wilson
urged support of the women's suffrage amendment to the Constitution: "Shall we
admit them only to a partnership of sacrifice and suffering and toil and not to a
partnership of privilege and of right?"[28]

After World War I, with demobilization and new economic strains, most women
were pushed out of "men's jobs." By the 1920s the dominant image of the New
Woman shifted dramatically, a shift reflected both by a change in historical conditions and by the growing disaffection of young women with the organizations of

their mothers' generation. With the Russian Bolshevik Revolution in November 1917 and waves of strikes and race riots throughout the United States in 1919, antiradical and socialist sentiment coupled with virulent xenophobia reached a fever pitch. The rise of anti-immigrant feeling in the United States after World War I led to a surge in Ku Klux Klan membership as well as the passage of legislation that drastically curtailed immigration from southern and eastern Europe and ended Japanese immigration entirely. Pressures from right-wing political groups that feared communist influence and conflicts over an increasingly unpopular Prohibition amendment also splintered women's groups.[29]

Prohibition and Sexuality

With the passage of the Eighteenth Amendment in 1919 outlawing the manufacture, sale, or transportation of alcoholic beverages, drinking became a daring act claimed by young people already challenging other social mores. To be sure, some New Women had advocated drinking as a kind of defiant assertion of self before World War I, but such assertions were much more central to the flapper-styled New Woman after Congress enacted nationwide Prohibition and drinking increasingly became socially, if not legally, acceptable.

Indeed, at the peak of the Jazz Age, "public drinking became so fashionable that both decent and indecent women went to the speak-easy, even though the old-time saloon had been a male preserve, only spotted by the occasional prostitute. For women, too, liquor became a flag of their new freedom." Many college students in the 1920s viewed Prohibition as a joke and saw nothing wrong with enjoying a cocktail or sharing a hip flask with the opposite sex. And although excessive drinking seemed to be a signature of modern masculinity, epitomized by the desultory drunks of Ernest Hemingway's *The Sun Also Rises* and the phantasmagoric binges depicted in *The Great Gatsby,* female artists of the 1920s increasingly claimed the right to drink as a sign of either postwar anomie or feminist New Woman defiance. Writing the nightclub column for the *New Yorker* in 1925, the signature flapper Lois Long expressed her "girlish delight in barrooms" and her excitement when the speakeasy was raided, like "one of those movie affairs, where burly cops kick down the doors, and women fall fainting on the tables, and strong men crawl under them, and waiters shriek and start throwing bottles out of windows." Reflecting back on those days, when "you were thought to be good at holding your liquor . . . if you could make it to the ladies' room before throwing up," Long explained the new trend: "We women had been emancipated and weren't sure what we were supposed to do with all the freedom and equal rights, so we were going to hell laughing and singing."[30]

The blues lyrics of Bessie Smith and Gertrude "Ma" Rainey linked alcohol consumption with more suffering and sexual assertiveness suggestive of a working-class variant of black feminism, even as they signaled a similar defiant indulgence. In "Dead Drunk Blues," Rainey laments, "Daddy, I'm going to get drunk just one more time / Where's the whiskey bottle? / Honey, I'm going to get drunk, papa, just one more time / 'Cause when I'm drunk, nothing's gonna worry my mind." And in

Bessie Smith's recording of "Me and My Gin," she declares, "Any bootlegger sho' is a pal of mine / 'Cause a good ol' bottle of gin will get it all the time."[31]

For most writers in African American journals of the twenties and for the editorialists and health columnists of black newspapers, however, alcohol consumption was a dangerous modern trend. On May 9, 1925, the *New York Age* offered Maybelle McAdoo's column titled "The Girl Who Drinks May Be Modern, But She Is Foolish as Well," in which a young woman describes the pressure to drink that she and her friends face during New York social functions, when "Prohibition is put under the table and liquor on top. If we insist on something like ginger ale or soda our friends poke fun and call us old-fashioned or a prude." Arguments against drinking in the black press ranged from fears that advocating social drinking would reinforce stereotypes to concerns that it would undermine larger goals of racial uplift. Writing for the *Crisis* in March 1928, Allison Davis chastised the "College Girl": "You spent every week-end / In all-night liquor parties with your 'man'; / You spent the money your mother / Feared to borrow on her home."[32]

The transgression of drinking alcohol also went hand in hand with the growing demand by many women, especially younger women, for greater sexual autonomy. In 1922, Ohio State University's student newspaper published the reflections of a "representative co-ed," who declared: "We do all the things that our mothers, fathers, aunts and uncles do not sanction, and we do them knowingly. . . . The slogan of the present college generation is 'getting by' or 'getting away with it.' We are 'playing the game' . . . smoking, dancing like Voodoo devotees, dressing decollete, 'petting' and drinking. We do these things because we honestly enjoy the attendant physical sensations. . . . College girls thrive on thrills." Describing the "reckless atmosphere" of New York nightclubs in the 1920s, Lois Long recalled, "We wore wishbone diaphragms that weren't always reliable. There was a woman doctor who handled abortions for our crowd." For most of the nineteenth century, however, most Americans believed that white women should be insulated from sexual knowledge because their highest calling was a spiritual and domestic one. Even in the early twentieth century, some physicians believed that the sex drive was far weaker if not absent in women, but advocates of the "new morality" disputed such claims. Drawing on the arguments of European sex theorists, including Swedish feminist Ellen Key (1849–1926), who argued that sexual love made marriages durable, and of Sigmund Freud (1856–1939), who maintained that sexuality was a crucial determinant of the self, many "sex radicals" on both sides of the Atlantic argued that sexuality if repressed was liable to emerge in destructive ways. Although not making a hedonist argument per se, advocates of the new morality maintained that sexuality was an "irresistible drive" and that its most healthy expression among (white middle-class) women occurred if it was not strictly governed. Their criticism of sexual repression was part of a larger feminist critique of male supremacy and a commitment to ensuring that women would be able to lead full self-actualized lives. Mabel Dodge Luhan, host to many of New York City's most famous radicals, perhaps best embodied this sentiment when, on the advice of birth-control pioneer Margaret Sanger, she learned ways of "heightening . . . pleasure and of prolonging it . . . the spreading out and sexualizing of the whole body until it should become sensitive and alive throughout, and complete."[33]

With growing public acceptance of at least some measure of the new morality's emphasis on a woman's right to experience sexual pleasure came new expectations that marriage should be pleasurable as well. Increasing numbers of unmarried women were having sexual experiences, and increasing numbers of married women were seeking a divorce if their marriage was unhappy. According to Alfred Kinsey's study undertaken during the 1950s, although only 14 percent of women born before 1900 admitted to having had premarital sexual intercourse, among those born between 1900 and 1910 the number rose to 36 percent. By the 1920s, increasing numbers of social theorists rejected the idea that marriage meant an emotionally detached father exerting his right to familial control and a submissive mother dutifully tending the house and children, in favor of one in which emotional intimacy and sexual expression created a companionate bond. Feminists, meanwhile, increasingly defended a woman's right to seek a divorce if she and her spouse had become irrevocably estranged. This changing perspective, coupled with other post–Civil War changes in American society—a greater willingness to take advantage of liberalized divorce laws, more options for women to support themselves through paid labor if they left a marriage, the falling birth rate (with fewer dependents it was probably easier to obtain a divorce)—led observers to decry what seemed a disturbing trend. Before the Civil War, most women married young and very few divorced, but by 1890 only 47 percent of women aged twenty to twenty-four had married, and the divorce rate had increased dramatically, from 1.2 for every 1,000 marriages in 1860, to 3.0 in 1890, 4.5 in 1910, and 7.7 in 1920.[34]

At the same time that many women, especially married women, were encouraged to express heterosexual desire, homosexuality was pathologized in ways never before seen, and lesbianism was increasingly viewed as one of the pernicious effects of the women's movement. Edward Carpenter, a leading British sex researcher and free love advocate, wrote in 1897 that the "Modern Woman" "with her clubs, her debates, her politics, her freedom of action and costume, . . . seems to be preparing to 'spank' and even thump the Middle-class Man in real earnest." Lacking a maternal and a sexual instinct, such women are "rather mannish in temperament; some are 'homogenic,' that is inclined to attachments to their own sex rather than the opposite, sex; some are ultra-rationalizing and brain-cultured; to many, children are more or less a bore; to others, man's sex-passion is a mere impertinence, which they do not understand, and whose place they consequently misjudge." The rise of women's colleges prompted fears that "mannish lesbians" would ruin many young women for childbearing. The leading European sexologist of the time, Richard von Krafft-Ebing, described the "Mannish Lesbian" this way: "The masculine soul, heaving in the female bosom, finds pleasure in the pursuit of manly sports, and in manifestations of courage and bravado. There is a strong desire to imitate the male fashion in dressing the hair and in general attire, under favorable circumstances even to don male attire and impose in it." By creating the new term "Mannish Lesbian," Krafft-Ebing, as Carroll Smith-Rosenberg notes, "linked women's rejection of traditional gender roles and their demands for social and economic equality to cross-dressing, sexual perversion, and borderline hermaphroditism. . . . physical disease again bespoke social disorder." Although more ambivalent in his conclusions, English sexologist Havelock Ellis likewise suggested that female gender crossing was an indication of lesbianism. For Ellis, a wide range of "masculine habits" associated with the New Woman signaled the "psychic abnormality" of inversion: "the brusque energetic movements, the attitude of the arms, the direct speech . . . the masculine straightforwardness and sense of honor, and especially the attitude towards men, free from any suggestion either of shyness or audacity." By the 1920s, with the continual linking of feminist assertiveness with possible "abnormal" sexual expression, overt critiques of marriage by those hoping to advance the cause of women's rights sharply declined.[35]

Despite the hostile environment, some women led openly lesbian lives during this period, especially if their incomes were substantial enough to grant them a degree of autonomy. One of the highest-paid African American performers of the 1920s, Bessie Smith, began her affairs with women in late 1926 while on tour singing the blues. Many college-educated women who had found well-paying jobs in the late nineteenth century established Boston marriages, committed relationships between two women who shared a household. Carrie Chapman Catt and Mollie Garrett Hay, for example, loved and lived with each other as they worked tirelessly in support of suffrage; after Mollie's death in 1928, Carrie purchased a double plot in New York's Woodlawn Cemetery, which they now share. Dr. Martha May Eliot, denied entrance to Harvard because of her sex, earned a medical degree from Johns Hopkins Medical School in 1918, where she met her longtime romantic partner, Ethel Dunham. Together they attended Johns Hopkins as two of the eleven women in a class of ninety-five; together they would perform pioneering work in the field of children's health.[36]

CONSUMER CULTURE, LEISURE CULTURE, AND TECHNOLOGY

The larger historical developments that had the most pronounced impact on the concept of the New Woman were the growing dominance of consumer capitalism, evolutionary and eugenic discourse, and changing technologies emphasizing speed and efficiency. The period between 1895 and 1930 witnessed a revolution in the display and marketing of manufactured goods in American culture. New, more aggressive advertising strategies were developed to create new desires among primarily female consumers. Indeed, in 1901 James H. Collins wrote in *Printers' Ink,* the foremost advertising journal of the period, that woman, compared to man, is without reason, common sense, thrift, or foresight, yet "she does all of his buying and the whole world is built pretty much to her tastes, whims and prejudices." Consequently, the wise advertiser should "take her into strict account when he deals with her in space and dollars and cents." Department stores worked to seduce women into purchasing. Large plate glass windows encouraged customers to gaze at sumptuously decorated displays; main doorsteps were removed and revolving doors were installed to invite customers in; floodlights, spotlights, prismatic lights, electric lights of all sorts saturated interior shopping spaces; elevators and later escalators moved customers closer to goods; air conditioning was introduced; and a growing number of female store clerks graciously helped their customers navigate the increasingly complex but sensuous purchasing process. Orientalism, with its notion of a feminized, primitive Asia and its accompanying "exotic" products—Indian silks, Turkish carpets, Japanese ceramics, and Chinese florals—became a favorite aesthetic of department stores.[37]

Through consumption women could appropriate different identities. Despite the prevailing racist images within advertising of the period, transformation through consumption seemed to bypass the more reified hierarchies within evolutionary theory or eugenics. One means of demonstrating a willingness to assimilate was to buy those goods that signified a commitment to the demands of bourgeois culture. Yet the fact that the "consuming" practices of Americans deemed "other" were viewed as highly suspect—either these individuals were seen as attempting to forge crass imitations of white originals or they were revealing their reversion to the primitive—suggests, in part, why we find in this volume's essays such ambivalent images of the New Woman as the consummate purchaser of new goods.

By the mid-1920s, advertising had taken a distinct shift, concentrating less on describing the merits of the product and far more on appealing to the desires and anxieties of, again, primarily the female consumer. People rather than products increasingly filled ads that now included "participatory" anecdotes and illustrations, with copy such as "Are You Sure You Know Your Type?" Advertisements featured advice-giving friends, an authoritative doctor, or a trusted movie star. "Scare copy" invented new social shames requiring new products—halitosis, bromodosis (sweaty foot odors), homotosis (lack of attractive home furnishings), and dandruff. Fearing the economic consequences of overproduction, advertisers emphasized a consumption ethic based on keeping up with the current style, a concern deemed to be of particular interest to women, whether in fashion, cameras, or automobiles. And if money were a problem, buying on installment provided an easy remedy. By the end of the 1920s, Americans bought 60 percent of automobiles, radios, and furniture on the installment plan.[38]

Most urban families by the mid-1920s, regardless of wealth, had indoor plumbing and gas or electric lighting, and over 35 percent had telephones. Although electricity had yet to reach many rural areas, it was widespread in urban ones—enough both to be integral to lavish department store displays designed to entice female consumers and to be celebrated as a new force for, among other things, female independence. An editorialist writing for the *Independent* in 1902 proclaimed that rather than fighting for the ballot, women should fight to control the "new power": "Woman must now become an electrician. This achieved, and she passes into control of the force that not only does house work and farm work, but the force that controls the age." In a 1912 article for *Good Housekeeping,* Thomas A. Edison made even greater claims for the power of electricity to transform women's lives. He described the "housewife of the future" as more a "domestic engineer than a domestic laborer, with the greatest of all handmaidens, electricity, at her service." With a bevy of new electric appliances at her command, woman was developing a "real sex independence" and was newly free to exercise her mental energy, which would in turn build "new fibers, new involutions, and new folds" in the brain.[39]

If most people at the turn of the century viewed electricity as a mysterious, gendered force of modern economic progress, by the 1910s social observers and advertisers heralded the automobile as the new agent and sign of modern success. By the end of the 1920s, more than 20 percent of Americans owned a car. For many, driving a car was a signature New Woman activity, akin to riding a bicycle in the previous generation and even more liberating in that women could now travel farther from home. Indeed, as the rural-dwelling Christine McGaffey Frederick exclaimed in *Suburban Life* in 1912, "Spark, throttle, cylinders, gear, magneto and steering wheel have yielded their secrets to me. . . . learning to handle the car has wrought my emancipation, my freedom. I am no longer a country-bound farmer's wife; I am no longer dependent on tricksome trains, slow-buggies, the 'old mare,' or the almanac." At the same time, by emphasizing how much easier owning a car made performing a woman's household tasks, automobile advertisers in popular American women's magazines increasingly tried to reconcile conventional gender roles with the potentially destabilizing technology.[40]

Although popular opinion traditionally viewed aviation as a feat of "intrepid airmen," by the late 1920s an emergent aviation industry, hoping to sell planes and air travel to a wary public, tried to assure the public that flying was safe. And according to Louise Thaden, winner of the first women's air derby in 1929, "nothing impresses the safety of aviation on the public quite so much as to see a woman flying an airplane." Such a notion depended on a belief in women's mechanical incompetence, and women faced pervasive discrimination in aviation training and employment. Nonetheless, for many women, taking to the skies in an airplane promised an even greater feeling of liberation. As Thaden wrote, "flying is the only real freedom we are privileged to possess."[41]

Most women, however, regarded the new technologies and the cultural shifts that accompanied them with ambivalence. Under the new "scientific" methods of labor management, a process pioneered in the manufacturing of automobiles, workers' time and motion were monitored so that the work process could be reduced to its simplest steps, which in the end made for grueling, repetitive work. Telephone operators, for example, deemed modern women by occupation, complained bitterly of headaches, backaches, and stress—"always nervous, always on edge"—as a result of the relentless pace of work. Yet scientific management's new emphasis on providing workers with monetary incentive also meant some women had greater opportunity for higher wages and upward mobility. Indeed, for women who traditionally had been relegated to unskilled factory work, the new system of scientific management offered tremendous stress but also better economic opportunities and more personal freedom.[42]

Young people of the 1920s, regardless of class, found it easier to escape parental supervision than they had in previous generations. With the lower birthrate, children tended to receive more attention and to have more opportunities to pursue their own interests rather than fulfill family obligations. Jobs away from home, disposable income, and coeducational opportunities all provided the younger generation greater freedom to embrace the values of a mass-market leisure culture, a trend that only confirmed the fears of the older generation's women's club movement. Between 1890 and 1925, dating had trumped courting to become an almost universal practice in the United States. Instead of a ritual of courtship whereby a man hoped to be invited to call on a woman at her home, where watchful parents waited, young men now increasingly invited women on dates away from home for which they paid. Amusement parks, theaters, and movie houses provided public places where working-class women especially might feel greater freedom to express themselves sexually with men, free from chaperones. But women also lost a measure of control when they, often by necessity, relied on men to pay. The growing popularity of auto-mobiles only accelerated the trend. Men and women now enjoyed petting in the privacy of the back seat, but it was in the man's car, which he generally drove.[43]

The professionally produced and marketed mass culture that young people consumed in their leisure time acted as a powerful homogenizing and sometimes transgressive force. During the 1920s, spending on leisure activities increased threefold. Weekly attendance at movies doubled, with audience members reaching 100–115 million, and by 1930 surveys indicated that young people admired movie stars more than leaders in politics, business, or the arts. Stars such as Clara Bow and Mae West freely asserted themselves as resourceful, sexual heroines even as their roles indicated that their primary job was to attract male attention. Although the golden age of radio wouldn't arrive until the 1930s, by the late 1920s, after the formation of the National Broadcast Company in 1926, millions of Americans tuned in at the same time to listen to the same news, entertainment, and advertising. Twenties radio exposed many white people in urban centers such as Chicago and New York to the work of black jazz performers, music they wouldn't ordinarily have sought out. As the African American newspaper the *New York Amsterdam News* reported in 1926, "then all the dear white radiolanders settle back in their easy chairs, in the perfect illusion of a universally white world, and listen to this dark brown girl entertain them through the colorless air."[44]

Evolution, Birth Control, and Eugenics

To legitimize the New Woman and the new social stratification her ascendancy necessarily created, many of her proponents relied on evolutionary discourse. Considering the dismal prospects that most evolutionary theorists offered for women's advancement, the strategy was, in some respects, unlikely. As Cynthia Eagle Russett notes, the overwhelming consensus among evolutionary theorists was that women were fundamentally different from men, not only anatomically and physiologically but also emotionally and intellectually. Childlike in body and mind, women lagged behind the more courageous and intellectually sophisticated men, much as the "primitive" peoples lagged behind Europeans. Indeed, in *Descent of Man and Selection in Relation to Sex,* Charles Darwin writes: "The chief distinction in the intellectual powers of the two sexes is shewn by man's attaining to a higher eminence in whatever he takes up, than can woman—whether requiring deep thought, reason, or imagination, or merely the use of the sense and hands." Although Darwin claimed that evidence of the highest state of evolution was altruism, a trait women were more likely to possess, women had a host of other qualities associated with the "lower races." For women the "powers of intuition, of rapid perception, and perhaps of imitation, are more strongly marked than in man; but some, at least, of these faculties are characteristic of the lower races, and therefore of a past and lower state of civilization."[45]

Charlotte Perkins Gilman argued in *Women and Economics* (1898) that the appearance of the New Woman was a definitive sign of overall race progress. Less a sudden apparition than a logical product of improved family and social conditions, this "stronger and healthier" New Woman reflected a generally positive vision of technological and social change at the turn of the century. To legitimate their desires for progressive reform, many feminist writers before World War I seem to have favored a neo-Lamarckian approach to evolutionary change in which natural selection was a secondary force in evolution and characteristics acquired during one's lifetime might be inherited by the next generation.[46]

Proponents of "voluntary motherhood," including suffragists, free love advocates, and moral reformers, shared a similar perspective, both in their fears that undesirable characteristics would be inherited and in their hopes for progressive social change. Involuntary motherhood, then, was likely to produce a legacy of vice because a woman distraught either at the time of intercourse or during her pregnancy would pass along her disquietude to her unborn child, fundamentally impairing his or her physical, emotional, and moral well-being. According to birth-control historian Linda Gordon, "it would be hard to find a single piece of writing on voluntary motherhood between 1890 and 1910 that did not assert that unwanted children were likely to be morally and/or physically defective." If free to determine when to bear children, the happy and naturally more altruistic woman, so the argument went, would improve the race.[47]

Voluntary motherhood advocates, however, did not promote artificial means of birth control. Even before the birth-control movement achieved a wide following in the 1920s, birth rates had been declining. Whereas in the mid-eighteenth century it was common for women to have eight to ten children, by 1900 the average number of children per household was close to three. Although the lower birth rate, especially among native-born, middle-class, urban white women, was the result of a number of factors, including greater concern for children's welfare and aspirations for a middle-class lifestyle, it clearly demonstrates that men, and women especially, were intent on limiting reproduction. Even after passage of the Comstock law in 1873, which made it illegal to send items deemed "obscene, lewd or lascivious" through the U.S. mail, including contraceptive devices and information, birth control was commonly practiced (albeit most often in the form of douches and withdrawal).[48]

Not until after 1910 and the advent of the new morality in the form of female sexual freedom did the birth-control movement gain popular legitimacy. In its earliest stages, the socialist and anarchist movements defended birth control as a means of liberating working-class women. Emma Goldman played a crucial role in popularizing birth-control ideology, and a student of Goldman's, Margaret Sanger, became its leading advocate, in part because of her ability to build a sustained grass-roots movement. Sanger did her best to downplay the radical, and hence controversial, origins of the birth-control movement and instead emphasized the victimization of poor women grappling with unplanned pregnancies. After witnessing the suffering of Mrs. Jake Sachs, a slum dweller who died from the effects of a self-induced abortion, Sanger describes a vision that inspired her devotion to the cause of birth control as a fundamental human right:

> a moving picture rolled before my eyes with photographic clearness: women writhing in travail to bring forth little babies; the babies themselves naked and hungry, wrapped in newspapers to keep them from the cold; six-year-old children with pinched, pale, wrinkled faces, old in concentrated wretchedness, pushed into gray and fetid cellars, crouching on stone floors, their small scrawny hands scuttling through rags, making lamp shades, artificial flowers; white coffins, black coffins, coffins, coffins interminably passing in never-ending succession.

Sanger established her first clinic in 1916, and by the 1920s the demand for birth-control information was so great that she had received approximately a million letters from mothers asking for advice. When birth-control clinics opened for the first time in the United States in the 1920s and 1930s, their statistical research confirmed that birth-control use, the most popular methods being male withdrawal and condoms, was widespread. In 1922, Katherine Bement Davis interviewed a thousand married women, all either college graduates or women's club members, and almost 75 percent reported using contraceptives. Most public organizations and popular magazines, however, were reticent to discuss the issue, and most medical literature throughout the 1920s warned of the danger of the practice.[49]

Sanger, however, not only was committed to the feminist necessity of birth control, but she increasingly advocated for what she saw as its racial importance. In *Woman and the New Race* (1920), she appealed to eugenic fears by offering statistics that showed nonnative whites had higher birthrates and much higher illiteracy rates, which, when combined with the high birthrates of the feebleminded, threatened the development of a "greater American race." Indeed, many intellectuals of the period had long been concerned about the rise of divorce and the drop in the birthrate among white, native-born, Protestant women, particularly in light of the higher birthrate among new immigrants and African Americans, and these concerns frequently served as the basis for anti–New Woman attacks. Social commentators such as economist R. R. Kuczynski expressed widespread nativist fears when he reported in 1902 that the immigrant birthrate was 70–80 percent higher than the native birthrate and that it was "probable that the native population can not hold its own. It seems to be dying out." Fearing "race suicide" as a result of the confluence of increased immigration and new calls for women's rights, Theodore Roosevelt urged women to see their greatest calling as wives and mothers. By the 1920s, however, the notion of who was fit to reproduce had become more specific.[50]

From its peak in the late 1910s and throughout the 1920s, eugenics, the "science" of selectively breeding better human beings, became commonplace in American politics, literature, higher education, and popular culture, and many leading feminist intellectuals, most notably Charlotte Perkins Gilman and Margaret Sanger, expressed support for it. Drawing on popular interpretations of Charles Darwin's theories of natural selection and Herbert Spencer's "survival of the best fitted," eugenics was codified by Sir Francis Galton, who introduced the term and "scientifically" hierarchized the races, with white, northern Europeans on the top. Soon the science of eugenics became the most popular argument used to counter the reform initiatives of those trying to combat poverty or reduce the spread of disease. By weeding out the unfit, eugenics offered the promise of increased efficiency and competitiveness to a nation grappling with vast numbers of new immigrants and African American migrants to urban areas, and with increasing urbanization and industrialization. Between 1907 and 1930, according to American cultural historian Daylanne English, twenty-four states legalized "compulsory sterilization of the feeble-minded or otherwise dysgenic state residents," and between 1907 and 1964, at least 60,000 compulsory sterilizations were performed for explicitly eugenic reasons. From 1910 to 1918, the Eugenic Record Office employed college-educated New Women who had training in biology, sociology, or social work and sent them traveling throughout the United States to find incriminating evidence of dysgenic families. Once such families were identified, members were targeted for compulsory institutionalization or sterilization.[51]

Critics and celebrants of the New Woman throughout the period voiced this fear of the reproductive potential of ethnic or underclass Others, even as they explored the psychological burdens of motherhood and celebrated the autonomy afforded by limited reproduction or childlessness. Kate Chopin's *The Awakening* (1899) is a revealing example. On the one hand, Edna Pontellier rejects her husband and sees her children as "antagonists . . . who had overpowered and sought to drag her into the soul's slavery for the rest of her days." On the other hand, as recent scholars have pointed out, the novel also reveals Chopin's "eugenic anxiety about the repercussions of white middle-class feminism" in her depiction of women of color in the novel as unfazed by their "natural" reproductive purpose. Ellen Glasgow's work suggests more comfort with the white New Woman's triumph because that triumph is linked with a concomitant reappraisal of the "true woman" and the Old South ideal with which she is associated. Even though in *Virginia* (1913) Glasgow contrasts the enervating selfless child-laden "true woman" with the self-assured dynamism of the childless New Woman, she rewards the "true woman" with filial loyalty.[52]

White writers were not the only proponents of eugenics, however. Black intellectuals also saw the new science as a vehicle of empowerment. For W.E.B. Du Bois, eugenics offered a means of racial uplift, whereas for Marcus Garvey it promised a way of purifying what he saw as a mongrelized black population. Whatever the rationale, this outlook put the New Negro Woman in an untenable position. Even as Du Bois maintained that "only at the sacrifice of intelligence and the chance to do their best work can the majority of modern women bear children," he urged "families of the better class" to rear more children. A number of black women writers of the period resisted such eugenic injunctions. Through her anti-lynching drama *Rachel* (1916), Angelina Weld Grimké, for example, dismissed eugenicist reasoning by showing that eugenics and even black motherhood ceased to make sense, given the prevailing racial hostility within the United States.[53]

Other intellectuals rejected evolutionary and eugenic arguments to embrace cultural anthropology and Freudian psychology, which offered new theories to help rethink the relations among gender roles, race, and civilization. In her landmark *Coming of Age in Samoa* (1928), for example, Margaret Mead challenged evolutionism in favor of a kind of cultural relativism. Mead showed the degree of variation in gender roles that occurred within different cultures regardless of race. In doing so, she disputed the racism and sexism characteristic of eugenic and evolutionary anthropological arguments and shifted the debate about male and female behavior from biology to culture. Although Gilman's work had argued for the elimination of the "primitive" dynamic in American gender relations, Mead's work enabled feminists to develop new arguments whereby "primitive" cultures might offer alternative, more liberating gender roles.[54]

The intertwined histories of the New Woman, New Negro Woman, New Negro, "new immigration," New South, New Psychology, New Morality, and New Empire suggest how the trope of the New Woman worked to define American identity during a period of dramatic technological and social change. The New Woman in all of her incarnations—degenerate highbrow, evolved type, race leader or race traitor, brow-beating suffragette, farmer, prohibitionist, mannish lesbian, college girl, eugenicist, savvy professional woman, barren spinster, clubwoman, saleswoman, restless woman, bicyclist, anarchist, or insatiable shopper—was an evolving, fiercely contested icon. Amid the controversy, millions of women with dogged persistence, dramatic flare, or sheer necessity went about the business of changing their lives and their society.

PART I

Defining the New Woman
in the Periodical Press

"The New Aspect of the Woman Question"

Sarah Grand

The literary exchange between British New Woman novelist Sarah Grand (1854–1943) and Ouida, a popular antifeminist novelist, made the New Woman into a cultural phenomena. Born with the name Frances Bellenden-Clarke, married at sixteen, and soon thereafter a mother, Grand, after twenty years of marriage, made a startling life change. With the proceeds she earned from sales of her first novel *Ideala* (1888), she moved to London, became a full-time writer, and changed her name to Madame Sarah Grand. Her best-selling novel, *The Heavenly Twins* (1893), gained notoriety for its frank discussion of unhappy marriages, the sexual double standard, and the ravages of venereal disease. In addition to writing novels, Grand advocated rational dress, lobbied for suffrage, and lectured on women's issues in England and the United States, where she became friends with leaders of the women's suffrage and social purity movements. In addition to writing for the *North American Review*, she contributed to a number of other American magazines, including *Cosmopolitan*, the *Independent*, and *Harper's Bazaar*.[1]

Grand's essay "New Aspect of the Woman Question" was published by the *North American Review*, a periodical begun in Boston in 1815 and for many years considered the most important intellectual magazine in the United States. Indeed, it was the first U.S. journal to achieve international prestige. The *Review* featured articles on government, economics, and religion but favored Boston intellectual debates until Allen Thorndike Rice purchased the journal in 1878 and moved it to New York, made it a monthly, and began publishing articles on the most contentious topics in the country, including labor demands, divorce, evolution, and agnosticism. But it was the *Review*'s longstanding contribution to literature and literary

North American Review, Mar. 1894, 270–276.

criticism that earned it lasting acclaim. Even as it published the work of some
of the most significant American writers—including Ralph Waldo Emerson and
Mark Twain—and called for a unique American literary voice, it also published
reviews of and introductions to foreign literature. By 1891, with an annual subscription price of five dollars, the *Review* achieved a peak circulation of 76,000 but later
lost circulation with the depressions of the 1890s.[2] The *Review*'s debate in late
1894 and 1895 between Sarah Grand and Ouida resulted in a surge of American
press coverage, both laudatory and satiric, on the topic of the New Woman.

It is amusing as well as interesting to note the pause which the new aspect of the
woman question has given to the Bawling Brothers who have hitherto tried to howl
down every attempt on the part of our sex to make the world a pleasanter place
to live in. That woman should ape man and desire to change places with him was con-
ceivable to him as he stood on the hearth-rug in his lord-and-master-monarch-of-all-
I-survey attitude, well inflated with his own conceit; but that she should be content to
develop the good material which she finds in herself and be only dissatisfied with the
poor quality of that which is being offered to her in man, her mate, must appear to him
to be a thing as monstrous as it is unaccountable. "If women don't want to be men,
what do they want?" asked the Bawling Brotherhood when the first misgiving of the
truth flashed upon them; and then, to reassure themselves, they pointed to a certain
sort of woman in proof of the contention that we were all unsexing ourselves.

It would be as rational for us now to declare that men generally are Bawling
Brothers or to adopt the hasty conclusion which makes all men out to be fiends on
the one hand and all women fools on the other. We have our Shrieking Sisterhood,
as the counterpart of the Bawling Brotherhood. The latter consists of two sorts of
men. First of all is he who is satisfied with the cow-kind of woman as being most
convenient; it is the threat of any strike among his domestic cattle for more consideration that irritates him into loud and angry protests. The other sort of Bawling
Brother is he who is under the influence of the scum of our sex, who knows nothing
better than women of that class in and out of society, preys upon them or ruins
himself for them, takes his whole tone from them, and judges us all by them. Both
the cow-woman and the scum-woman are well within range of the comprehension
of the Bawling Brotherhood, but the new woman is a little above him, and he never
even thought of looking up to where she has been sitting apart in silent contemplation all these years, thinking and thinking, until at last she solved the problem
and proclaimed for herself what was wrong with Home-is-the-Woman's-Sphere,
and prescribed the remedy.

What she perceived at the outset was the sudden and violent upheaval of the suffering sex in all parts of the world. Women were awaking from their long apathy,
and, as they awoke, like healthy hungry children unable to articulate, they began to
whimper for they knew not what. They might have been easily satisfied at that time
had not society, like an ill-conditioned and ignorant nurse, instead of finding out
what they lacked, shaken them and beaten them and stormed at them until what

was once a little wail became convulsive shrieks and roused up the whole human household. Then man, disturbed by the uproar, came upstairs all anger and irritation, and, without waiting to learn what was the matter, added his own old theories to the din, but, finding they did not act rapidly, formed new ones, and made an intolerable nuisance of himself with his opinions and advice. He was in the state of one who cannot comprehend because he has no faculty to perceive the thing in question, and that is why he was so positive. The dimmest perception that you may be mistaken will save you from making an ass of yourself.

We must look upon man's mistakes, however, with some leniency, because we are not blameless in the matter ourselves. We have allowed him to arrange the whole social system and manage or mismanage it all these ages without ever seriously examining his work with a view to considering whether his abilities and his motives were sufficiently good to qualify him for the task. We have listened without a smile to his preachments, about our place in life and all we are good for, on the text that "there is no understanding a woman." We have endured most poignant misery for his sins, and screened him when we should have exposed him and had him punished. We have allowed him to exact all things of us, and have been content to accept the little he grudgingly gave us in return. We have meekly bowed our heads when he called us bad names instead of demanding proofs of the superiority which alone would give him a right to do so. We have listened much edified to man's sermons on the subject of virtue, and have acquiesced uncomplainingly in the convenient arrangement by which this quality has come to be altogether practised for him by us vicariously. We have seen him set up Christ as an example for all men to follow, which argues his belief in the possibility of doing so, and have not only allowed his weakness and hypocrisy in the matter to pass without comment, but, until lately, have not even seen the humor of his pretensions when contrasted with his practices nor held him up to that wholesome ridicule which is a stimulating corrective. Man deprived us of all proper education, and then jeered at us because we had no knowledge. He narrowed our outlook on life so that our view of it should be all distorted, and then declared that our mistaken impression of it proved us to be senseless creatures. He cramped our minds so that there was no room for reason in them, and then made merry at our want of logic. Our divine intuition was not to be controlled by him, but he did his best to damage it by sneering at it as an inferior feminine method of arriving at conclusions; and finally, after having had his own way until he lost his head completely, he set himself up as a sort of a god and required us to worship him, and, to our eternal shame be it said, we did so. The truth has all along been in us, but we have cared more for man than for truth, and so the whole human race has suffered. We have failed of our effect by neglecting our duty here, and have deserved much of the obloquy that was cast upon us. All that is over now, however, and while on the one hand man has shrunk to his true proportions in our estimation, we, on the other, have been expanding to our own; and now we come confidently forward to maintain, not that this or that was "intended," but that there are in ourselves, in both sexes, possibilities hitherto suppressed or abused, which, when properly developed, will supply to either what is lacking in the other.

The man of the future will be better, while the woman will be stronger and wiser. To bring this about is the whole aim and object of the present struggle, and with the discovery of the means lies the solution of the Woman Question. Man, having no conception of himself as imperfect from the woman's point of view, will find this difficult to understand, but we know his weakness, and will be patient with him, and help him with his lesson. It is the woman's place and pride and pleasure to teach the child, and man morally is in his infancy. There have been times when there was a doubt as to whether he was to be raised or woman was to be lowered, but we have turned that corner at last; and now woman holds out a strong hand to the child-man, and insists, but with infinite tenderness and pity, upon helping him up.

He must be taught consistency. There are ideals for him which it is to be presumed that he tacitly agrees to accept when he keeps up an expensive establishment to teach them: let him live up to them. Man's faculty for shirking his own responsibility has been carried to such an extent in the past that, rather than be blamed himself when it did not answer to accuse woman, he imputed the whole consequence of his own misery-making peculiarities to God.

But with all his assumption man does not make the most of himself. He has had every advantage of training to increase his insight, for instance, but yet we find him, even at this time of day, unable to perceive that woman has a certain amount of self-respect and practical good sense—enough at all events to enable her to use the proverb about the bird in the hand to her own advantage. She does not in the least intend to sacrifice the privileges she enjoys on the chance of obtaining others, especially of the kind which man seems to think she must aspire to as so much more desirable. Woman may be foolish, but her folly has never been greater than man's conceit, and the one is not more disastrous to the understanding than the other. When a man talks about knowing the world and having lived and that sort of thing, he means something objectionable; in seeing life he generally includes doing wrong; and it is in these respects he is apt to accuse us of wishing to ape him. Of old if a woman ventured to be at all unconventional, man was allowed to slander her with the imputation that she must be abandoned, and he really believed it because with him liberty meant license. He has never accused us of trying to emulate him in any noble, manly quality, because the cultivation of noble qualities has not hitherto been a favorite pursuit of his, not to the extent at least of entering into his calculations and making any perceptible impression on public opinion; and he never, therefore, thought of considering whether it might have attractions for us. The cultivation of noble qualities has been individual rather than general, and the person who practised it is held to be one apart, if not actually eccentric. Man acknowledges that the business of life carried on according to his methods corrodes, and the state of corrosion is a state of decay; and yet he is fatuous enough to imagine that our ambition must be to lie like him for our own benefit in every public capacity. Heaven help the child to perceive with what travail and sorrow we submit to the heavy obligation, when it is forced upon us by our sense of right, of showing him how things ought to be done.

We have been reproached by Ruskin for shutting ourselves up behind park palings and garden walls, regardless of the waste world that moans in misery without, and that has been too much our attitude; but the day of our acquiescence is over. There is that in ourselves which forces us out of our apathy; we have no choice in the matter. When we hear the "Help! help! help!" of the desolate and the oppressed, and still more when we see the awful dumb despair of those who have lost even the hope of help, we must respond. This is often inconvenient to man, especially when he has seized upon a defenceless victim whom he would have destroyed had we not come to the rescue; and so, because it is inconvenient to be exposed and thwarted, he snarls about the end of all true womanliness, cants on the subject of the Sphere, and threatens that if we do not sit still at home with cotton-wool in our ears so that we cannot be stirred into having our sympathies aroused by his victims when they shriek, and with shades over our eyes that we may not see him in his degradation, we shall be afflicted with short hair, coarse skins, unsymmetrical figures, loud voices, tastelessness in dress, and an unattractive appearance and character generally, and then he will not love us any more or marry us. And this is one of the most amusing of his threats, because he has said and proved on so many occasions that he cannot live without us whatever we are. O man! man! you are a very funny fellow now we know you! But take care. The standard of your pleasure and convenience has already ceased to be our conscience. On one point, however, you may reassure yourself. True womanliness is not in danger, and the sacred duties of wife and mother will be all the more honorably performed when women have a reasonable hope of becoming wives and mothers of *men*. But there is the difficulty. The trouble is not because women are mannish, but because men grow ever more effeminate. Manliness is at a premium now because there is so little of it, and we are accused of aping men in order to conceal the side from which the contrast should evidently be drawn. Man in his manners becomes more and more wanting until we seem to be near the time when there will be nothing left of him but the old Adam, who said, "It wasn't me."

Of course it will be retorted that the past has been improved upon in our day; but that is not a fair comparison. We walk by the electric light: our ancestors had only oil-lamps. We can see what we are doing and where we are going, and should be as much better as we know how to be. But where are our men? Where is the chivalry, the truth, and affection, the earnest purpose, the plain living, high thinking, and noble self-sacrifice that make a man? We look in vain among the bulk of our writers even for appreciation of these qualities. With the younger men all that is usually cultivated is that flippant smartness which is synonymous with cheapness. There is such a want of wit amongst them, too, such a lack of variety, such monotony of threadbare subjects worked to death! Their "comic" papers subsist upon repetitions of those three venerable jests, the mother-in-law, somebody drunk, and an edifying deception successfully practised by an unfaithful husband or wife. As they have nothing true so they have nothing new to give us, nothing either to expand the heart or move us to happy mirth. Their ideas of beauty threaten always to be satisfied with the ballet dancer's legs, pretty things enough in their way, but not worth mentioning as an aid to the moral, intellectual, and physical strength that make a man. They are sadly deficient in imagination, too; that old fallacy to which they cling, that because an evil thing has always been, therefore it must always continue, is as much the result of want of imagination as of the man's trick of evading the responsibility of seeing right done in any matter that does not immediately affect his personal comfort. But there is one thing the younger men are specially good at, and that is giving their opinion; this they do to each other's admiration until they verily believe it to be worth something. Yet they do not even know where we are in the history of the world. One of them only lately, doubtless by way of ingratiating himself with the rest of the Bawling Brotherhood, actually proposed to reintroduce the Acts of the Apostles-of-the-Pavements; he was apparently quite unaware of the fact that the mothers of the English race are too strong to allow themselves to be insulted by the reimposition of another most shocking degradation upon their sex.[3] Let him who is responsible for the economic position which forces women down be punished for the consequence. If any are unaware of cause and effect in that matter, let them read *The Struggle for Life* which the young master wrote in *Wreckage*. As the working-man says with Christ-like compassion: "They wouldn't be there, poor things, if they were not driven to it."

There are upwards of a hundred thousand women in London doomed to damnation by the written law of man if they dare to die, and to infamy for a livelihood if they must live; yet the man at the head of affairs wonders what it is that we with the power are protesting against in the name of our sex. But *is* there any wonder we women wail for the dearth of manliness when we find men from end to end of their rotten social system forever doing the most cowardly deed in their own code, striking at the defenceless woman, especially when she is down?

The Bawling Brotherhood have been seeing reflections of themselves lately which did not flatter them, but their conceit survives, and they cling confidently to the delusion that they are truly all that is admirable, and it is the mirror that is in fault. Mirrors may be either a distorting or a flattering medium, but women do not care to see life any longer in a glass darkly. Let there be light. We suffer in the first shock of it. We shriek in horror at what we discover when it is turned on that which was hidden away in dark corners; but the first principle of good housekeeping is to have no dark corners, and as we recover ourselves we go to work with a will to sweep them out. It is for us to set the human household in order, to see to it that all is clean and sweet and comfortable for the men who are fit to help us to make home in it. We are bound to raise the dust while we are at work, but only those who are in it will suffer any inconvenience from it, and the self-sufficing and self-supporting are not afraid. For the rest it will be all benefits. The Woman Question is the Marriage Question, as shall be shown hereafter.

"The New Woman"

Ouida

Born to an English mother and French father, Marie Louise de La Ramée (1839–1908) adopted the pen name Ouida with her first published story in 1859. Most of Ouida's extensive body of short stories and romantic novels, including *Under Two Flags* (1867), her most popular, were published in Britain and the United States. Later in life she published a series of essays critical of women's suffrage, animal cruelty, the British book trade, and British imperialism. By the late nineteenth century, she was a regular contributor to a number of American magazines, including Philadelphia's *Lippincott's Magazine*, Boston's *Living Age*, the *North American Review*, and *Cosmopolitan*. As Ouida cultivated the life of a grande dame in Italy, she became increasingly known for her flamboyance, cynicism, and risqué subject matter, prompting one critic to call her an "apostle for insidious immorality." Acknowledging that her florid writing style had inspired parody, the renowned English writer G. K. Chesterton quipped: "It's impossible not to laugh at Ouida; and equally impossible not to read her."[1]

It can scarcely be disputed, I think, that in the English language there are conspicuous at the present moment two words which designate two unmitigated bores: The Workingman and the Woman. The Workingman and the Woman, the New Woman, be it remembered, meet us at every page of literature written in the English tongue; and each is convinced that on its own especial W hangs the future of the world. Both he and she want to have their values artificially raised and rated, and a status given to them by favor in lieu of desert. In an age in which persistent clamor is generally crowned by success they have both obtained considerable attention; is it offensive to say much more of it than either deserves? Your contributor avers that the Cow-Woman and the Scum-Woman, man understands; but that the New Woman is above him. The elegance of these appellatives is not calculated to recommend them to readers of either sex; and as a specimen of style forces one to hint that the New Woman who, we are told, "has been sitting apart in silent contemplation all these years" might in all these years have studied better models of literary composition. We are farther on told "that the dimmest perception that you may be mistaken, will save you from making an ass of yourself." It appears that even this dimmest perception has never dawned upon the New Woman.

We are farther told that "thinking and thinking" in her solitary sphynx-like contemplation she solved the problem and prescribed the remedy (the remedy to a problem!); but what this remedy was we are not told, nor did the New Woman apparently disclose it to the rest of womankind, since she still hears them in "sudden and violent upheaval" like "children unable to articulate whimpering for they know not what." It is sad to reflect that they might have been "easily satisfied at that time" (at what time?), "but society stormed at them until what was a little wail became convulsive shrieks"; and we are not told why the New Woman who had "the remedy for the problem," did not immediately produce it. We are not told either in what country or at what epoch this startling upheaval of volcanic womanhood took place in which "man merely made himself a nuisance with his opinions and advice," but apparently did quell this wailing and gnashing of teeth since it would seem that he has managed still to remain more masterful than he ought to be.

We are further informed that women "have allowed him to arrange the whole social system and manage or mismanage it all these ages without ever seriously examining his work with a view to considering whether his abilities and his methods were sufficiently good to qualify him for the task."

There is something deliciously comical in the idea, thus suggested, that man has only been allowed to "manage or mismanage" the world because woman has graciously refrained from preventing his doing so. But the comic side of this pompous and solemn assertion does not for a moment offer itself to the New Woman sitting aloof and aloft in her solitary meditation on the superiority of her sex. For the New Woman there is no such thing as a joke. She has listened without a smile to her enemy's "preachments"; she has "endured poignant misery for his sins," she has "meekly bowed her head" when he called her bad names; and she has never asked for "any proof of the superiority" which could alone have given him a right to use such naughty expressions. The truth has all along been in the possession of woman; but strange and sad perversity of taste! she has "cared more for man than for truth, and so the whole human race has suffered!"

"All that is over, however," we are told, and "while on the one hand man has shrunk to his true proportions" she has, all the time of this shrinkage, been herself expanding, and has in a word come to "fancy herself" extremely. So that he has no longer the slightest chance of imposing upon her by his game-cock airs.

Man, "having no conception of himself as imperfect," will find this difficult to understand at first; but the New Woman "knows his weakness," and will "help him with his lesson." *Man morally is in his infancy.* There have been times when there was a doubt as to whether he was to be raised to her level, or woman to be lowered to his, but we "have turned that corner at last and now woman holds out a strong hand to the child-man and insists upon helping him up." The child-man (Bismarck? Herbert Spencer? Edison? Gladstone? Alexander III? Lord Dufferin? the Duc d'Aumale?) the child-man must have his tottering baby steps guided by the New Woman, and he must be taught to live up to his ideals. To live up to an ideal, whether our own or somebody else's, is a painful process; but man must be made to do it. For, oddly enough, we are assured that despite "all his assumption he does not make the best of himself," which is not wonderful if he be still only in his infancy; and he has the incredible stupidity to be blind to the fact that "woman has self-respect and good sense," and that "she does not in the least intend to sacrifice the privileges she enjoys on the chance of obtaining others."

I have written amongst other *pensées éparses* which will some day see the light, the following reflection:

> The new school of liberated women forgets that one cannot fight men on their own territory and at the same time expect from them acts of politeness, tenderness, and gallantry. One should not at the same time take from a man his chair at the University and his seat on the bus. If one takes away his livelihood, one cannot demand that he offer you also his umbrella.[2]

The whole kernel of the question lies in this. Your contributor says that the New Woman will not surrender her present privileges; *i.e.*, she will still expect the man to stand that she may sit; the man to get wet through that she may use his umbrella. But if she retain these privileges she can only do so by an appeal to his chivalry, *i.e.*, by a confession that she is weaker than he. But she does not want to do this: she wants to get the comforts and concessions due to feebleness, at the same time as she demands the lion's share of power due to superior force alone. It is this overweening and unreasonable grasping at both positions which will end in making her odious to man and in her being probably kicked back roughly by hint into the seclusion of a harem.

Before me lies an engraving in art illustrated journal of a woman's meeting; whereat a woman is demanding in the name of her sovereign sex the right to vote at political elections. The speaker is middle-aged and plain of feature; she wears an inverted plate on her head tied on with strings under her double-chin; she has balloon-sleeves, a bodice tight to bursting, a waist of ludicrous dimensions in proportion to her portly person; she is gesticulating with one hand, of which all the fingers are stuck out in ungraceful defiance of all artistic laws of gesture. Now, why cannot this orator learn to gesticulate and learn to dress, instead of clamoring for a franchise? She violates in her own person every law, alike of common-sense and artistic fitness, and yet comes forward as a fit and proper person to make laws for others. She is an exact representative of her sex.

Woman, whether new or old, has immense fields of culture untilled, immense areas of influence wholly neglected. She does almost nothing with the resources she possesses, because her whole energy is concentrated on desiring and demanding those she has not. She can write and print anything she chooses; and she scarcely ever takes the pains to acquire correct grammar or elegance of style before wasting ink and paper. She can paint and model any subjects she chooses, but she imprisons herself in men's *atéliers* to endeavor to steal their technique and their methods, and thus loses any originality she might possess. Her influence on children might be so great that through them she would practically rule the future of the world; but she delegates her influence to the vile school boards if she be poor, and if she be rich to governesses and tutors; nor does she in ninety-nine cases out of a hundred ever attempt to educate or control herself into fitness for the personal exercise of such influence. Her precept and example in the treatment of the animal creation might be of infinite use in mitigating the hideous tyranny of humanity over them, but she does little or nothing to this effect; she wears dead birds and the skins of dead creatures; she hunts the hare and shoots the pheasant, she drives and rides with more brutal recklessness than men; she watches with delight the struggles of the dying salmon, of the gralloched deer; she keeps her horses standing in snow and fog for hours with the muscles of their heads and necks tied up in the torture of the bearing rein; when asked to do anything for a stray dog, a lame horse, a poor man's donkey, she is very sorry, but she has so many claims on her already; she never attempts by orders to her household, to her *fournisseurs*, to her dependents, to obtain some degree of mercy in the treatment of sentient creatures and in the methods of their slaughter.

The immense area which lies open to her in private life is almost entirely uncultivated, yet she wants to be admitted into public life. Public life is already overcrowded, verbose, incompetent, fussy, and foolish enough without the addition of her in her sealskin coat with the dead humming bird on her hat. Woman in public life would exaggerate the failings of men, and would not have even their few excellencies. Their legislation would be, as that of men is too often, the offspring of panic or prejudice; and she would not put on the drag of common-sense as man frequently does in public assemblies. There would be little to hope from her humanity, nothing from her liberality; for when she is frightened she is more ferocious than he, and when she has power more merciless.

"Men," says your contributor, "deprived us of all proper education and then jeered at us because we had no knowledge." How far is this based on facts? Could not Lady Jane Grey learn Greek and Latin as she chose? Could not Hypatia lecture? Were George Sand or Mrs. Somerville withheld from study? Could not in every age every woman choose a Corinna or Cordelia as her type? become either Helen or Penelope? If the vast majority have not either the mental or physical gifts to become either, that was Nature's fault, not man's. Aspasia and Adelina Patti were born, not made. In all eras and all climes a woman of great genius or of great beauty has done what she chose; and if the majority of women have led obscure lives, so have the majority of men. The chief part of humanity is insignificant, whether it be male or female. In most people there is very little character indeed, and as little mind. Those who have much never fail to make their marks, be they of which sex they may.

The unfortunate idea that there is no good education without a college curriculum is as injurious as it is erroneous. The college education may have excellencies for men in its *frottement*, its preparation for the world, its rough destruction of personal conceit; but for women it can only be hardening and deforming. If study be delightful to a woman, she will find her way to it as the hart to water brooks. The author of *Aurora Leigh* was not only always at home, but she was an invalid; yet she became a fine classic, and found her path to fame. A college curriculum would have done nothing to improve her rich and beautiful mind; it might have done much to debase it.

The perpetual contact of men with other men may be good for them, but the perpetual contact of women with other women is very far from good. The publicity of a college must be odious to a young girl of refined and delicate feeling.

The "Scum-woman" and the " Cow-woman," to quote the elegant phraseology of your contributor, are both of them less of a menace to humankind than the New Woman with her fierce vanity, her undigested knowledge, her over-weening estimate of her own value and her fatal want of all sense of the ridiculous.

When scum comes to the surface it renders a great service to the substance which it leaves behind it; when the cow yields pure nourishment to the young and the suffering, her place is blessed in the realm of nature; but when the New Woman splutters blistering wrath on mankind she is merely odious and baneful.

The error of the New Woman (as of many an old one) lies in speaking of women as the victims of men, and entirely ignoring the frequency with which men are the victims of women. In nine cases out of ten the first to corrupt the youth is the woman. In nine cases out of ten also she becomes corrupt herself because she likes it.

It is all very well to say that prostitutes were at the beginning of their career victims of seduction; but it is not probable and it is not provable. Love of drink and of finery, and a dislike to work, are the more likely motives and origin. It never seems to occur to the accusers of man that women are just as vicious and as lazy as he is in nine cases out of ten, and need no invitation from him to become so.

A worse prostitution than that of the streets, *i.e.*, that of loveless marriages of convenience, are brought about by women, not by men. In such unions the man always gives much more than he gains, and the woman in almost every instance is persuaded or driven into it by women—her mother, her sisters, her acquaintances. It is rarely that the father interferes to bring about such a marriage.

In even what is called a well-assorted marriage, the man is frequently sacrificed to the woman. As I wrote long ago, Andrea del Sartre's wife has many sisters. Correggio dying of the burden of the family, has many brothers. Men of genius are often dragged to earth by their wives. In our own day a famous statesman is made very ridiculous by his wife; frequently the female influences brought to bear on him render a man of great and original powers and disinterested character, a time-server, a conventionalist, a mere seeker of place. Woman may help man sometimes, but she certainly more often hinders him. Her self-esteem is immense and her self-knowledge very small. I view with dread for the future of the world the power which modern inventions place in the hands of woman. Hitherto her physical weakness has restrained her in a great measure from violent action; but a woman can make a bomb and throw it, can fling vitriol, and fire a repeating revolver as well as any man can. These are precisely the deadly, secret, easily handled modes of warfare and revenge, which will commend themselves to her ferocious feebleness.

Jules Ruchard has written:

I have taught anatomy for many years and I have spent a large part of my life in
lecture halls, but I have nonetheless experienced a painful feeling when I find in
all educational establishments skeletons of animals and anatomical mannequins
in the hands of young girls.[3]

I suppose this passage will be considered as an effort "to withhold knowledge
from women," but it is one which is full of true wisdom and honorable feeling.
When you have taken her into the physiological and chemical laboratories, when
you have extinguished pity in her, and given weapons to her dormant cruelty which
she can use in secret, you will be hoist with your own petard—your pupil will be
your tyrant, and then she will meet with the ultimate fate of all tyrants.

In the pages of this REVIEW a physician has lamented the continually increasing
unwillingness of women of the world to bear children, and the consequent increase
of ill-health, whilst to avoid child-bearing is being continually preached to the
working classes by those who call themselves their friends.

The elegant epithet of Cow-woman implies the contempt with which maternity is
viewed by the New Woman who thinks it something fine to vote at vestries, and shout
at meetings, and lay bare the spines of living animals, and haul the gasping salmon
from the river pool, and hustle male students off the benches of amphitheatres.

Modesty is no doubt a thing of education or prejudice, a conventionality artificially stimulated; but it is an exquisite grace, and womanhood without it loses its most
subtle charm. Nothing tends so to destroy modesty as the publicity and promiscuity
of schools, of hotels, of railway trains and sea voyages. True modesty shrinks from
the curious gaze of other women as from the coarser gaze of man.

Men, moreover, are in all except the very lowest classes more careful of their talk
before young girls than women are. It is very rarely that a man does not respect real
innocence; but women frequently do not. The jest, the allusion, the story which sullies
her mind and awakes her inquisitiveness, will much oftener be spoken by women
than men. It is not from her brothers, nor her brother's friends, but from her female
companions that she will understand what the grosser laugh of those around her
suggests. The biological and pathological curricula complete the loveless disflowering
of her maiden soul.

Everything which tends to obliterate the contrast of the sexes, like your mixture
of boys and girls in your American common schools, tends also to destroy the charm
of intercourse, the savor and sweetness of life. Seclusion lends an infinite seduction
to the girl, as the rude and bustling publicity of modern life robs woman of her grace.
Packed like herrings in a railway carriage, sleeping in odious vicinity to strangers
on a shelf, going days and nights without a bath, exchanging decency and privacy
for publicity and observation, the women who travel, save those rich enough to still
purchase seclusion, are forced to cast aside all refinement and delicacy.

It is said that travel enlarges the mind. There are many minds which can no more
be enlarged, by any means whatever, than a nut or a stone. The fool remains a fool,
though you carry him or her about over the whole surface of the globe, and it is

certain that the promiscuous contact and incessant publicity of travel, which may not hurt the man, do injure the woman.

Neither men nor women of genius are, I repeat, any criterion for the rest of their sex; nay, they belong, as Plato placed them, to a third sex which is above the laws of the multitude. But even whilst they do so they are always the foremost to recognize that it is the difference, not the likeness, of sex which makes the charm of human life. Barry Cornwall wrote long ago:

> As the man beholds the woman,
> As the woman sees the man;
> Curiously they note each other,
> As each other only can.
>
> Never can the man divest her
> Of that mystic charm of sex;
> Ever must she, gazing on him,
> That same mystic charm annex.

That mystic charm will long endure despite the efforts to destroy it of orators in tight stays and balloon sleeves, who scream from platforms, and the beings so justly abhorred of Mrs. Lynn Lynton, who smoke in public carriages and from the waist upward are indistinguishable from the men they profess to despise.

But every word, whether written or spoken, which urges the woman to antagonism against the man, every word which is written or spoken to try and make of her a hybrid, self-contained, opponent of men, makes a rift in the lute to which the world looks for its sweetest music.

The New Woman reminds me of an agriculturist who, discarding a fine farm of his own, and leaving it to nettles, stones, thistles, and wire-worms, should spend his whole time in demanding neighboring fields which are not his. The New Woman will not even look at the extent of ground indisputably her own, which she leaves unweeded and untilled.

Not to speak of the entire guidance of childhood, which is certainly already chiefly in the hands of woman (and of which her use does not do her much honor), so long as she goes to see one of her own sex dancing in a lion's den, the lions being meanwhile terrorized by a male brute; so long as she wears dead birds as millinery and dead seals as coats; so long as she goes to races, steeplechases, coursing and pigeon matches; so long as she "walks with the guns"; so long as she goes to see an American lashing horses to death in idiotic contest with velocipedes; so long as she courtesies before princes and emperors who reward the winners of distance-rides; so long as she receives physiologists in her drawing-rooms, and trusts to them in her maladies; so long as she invades literature without culture and art without talent; so long as she orders her court-dress in a hurry; so long as she makes no attempt to interest herself in her servants, in her animals, in the poor slaves of her tradespeople; so long as she shows herself as she does at present without scruple at every brutal and debasing spectacle which is considered fashionable; so long as she understands nothing of the beauty of meditation, of solitude, of Nature; so long as she is utterly incapable of keeping her sons out of the shambles of modern sport, and lifting her daughters above the pestilent miasma of modern society—so long as she does not, can not, or will not either do, or cause to do, any of these things, she has no possible title or capacity to demand the place or the privilege of man.

"The Campaign Girl"

Kate Masterson

Journalist Kate Masterson (1871?–1927) was raised in Brooklyn and began her career by writing poems for *Judge* and *Puck*. She published under a number of sobriquets, including Kittie Kelly, Lady Kate, and Little Kate, and was known for her poetry and humor pieces, which circulated in a number of newspapers and magazines, including the *Smart Set, Life,* and *Lippincott's Magazine.* In 1894 she argued that the women most likely to succeed in journalism weren't those with a college degree but rather those with a "good common-school education," a "modicum of common sense," "an ability to push," "a physical strength that will brave all weathers and conditions," and a willingness to start at the lowest rung as proofreaders. In 1900, she published the novel *The Dobleys* about a bohemian couple in the suburbs.[1]

Masterson's poem "The Campaign Girl" originally appeared in the *New York Herald* but was reprinted by the *Washington Post* in November 1894. The *Post* had been founded in the nation's capital as a Democratic daily paper by Stilson Hutchins in 1877, the year that marked the official end of Reconstruction with the withdrawal of federal troops from the South. In 1889, Frank Hatton and Beriah Wilkins purchased the paper and soon afterward announced that they would deliver the news "without personal or partisan bias." Under their leadership, the *Post* grew steadily more influential and successful. By 1890 it claimed to sell about 16,300 daily and 19,900 Sunday papers regularly. By 1905, when the *Post* changed ownership again, the figures had increased to 33,967 daily and about 45,000 on Sundays; the price continued at three cents daily and five cents on Sundays. While under Hatton and Wilkins, the paper criticized Theodore Roosevelt in his post as a member of the U.S. Civil Service Commission, but it supported his call, as

___

Washington Post, Nov. 7, 1894, 10.

3

New York police commissioner, for imperial expansion before the war of 1898. The paper opposed the federal income tax, unrestricted immigration, and what the editorial writers considered the "anarchist" impulse of striking labor unions. It supported, however, the eight-hour day and women's suffrage. In 1895, when a "fashionable young woman" was caught smoking on Pennsylvania Avenue and sent to the workhouse for fifteen days, the *Post* conceded that the young woman was foolish—like the "organ-grinders' monkeys hoping to attract a crowd"—but the police were even more so for arresting her.[2]

Although Masterson claims in "The Campaign Girl" that the New Woman's quest for reform has overridden her desire for suffrage, she displays the often-used suffrage argument that politically empowered women would clean up politics.

> You will know if you have seen her
> Through these fierce election days
> By her positive demeanor
> And her captivating ways.
> She is working really, truly,
> And of course she's bound to win,
> In the fight with rings unruly,
> And with Tammanistic sin![3]
> She has ceased to care for fashion,
> All her hair is out of curl,
> Politics is now the passion
> Of this dear Election Girl;
> Neath the mantle all unheeded
> And forgotten sticks her gum;
> Now for higher things she's needed,
> And the nation wants her some!
> Put away the "rights" petition,
> Vanished is her wish to vote,
> For reform is now her mission,
> She must have the Tiger's coat.
> Difficulties, dangers, maybe,
> But there's no such word as "fail,"
> And papa can mind the baby
> While its mother's on the trail!
> She can out-talk any speaker,
> And her word will be the last,
> Though her sex is called the "weaker,"
> She can make mere men aghast;
> "Parkhurst," "Lexow" on her banner,[4]
> "Goff" she cheers for with a will,[5]

And not for a moment can her
Patriotic tongue be still.
Oh, the "Future Woman" coming,
All the poets love to sing,
And their lyres they're fond of strumming,
Garlands at her feet to fling,
But for even a single minute,
Though the harps for her may play,
The "New Woman" isn't in it
With the woman of to-day.

⟨≋≋≋≋⟩

"Here Is the New Woman"

In 1860, Philadelphia journalist Alexander Cummings founded the *New York World* as a religious Republican penny paper. When in 1883 Joseph Pulitzer purchased the paper, which included a valuable Associate Press franchise, the paper was struggling. With staffers he brought from St. Louis, Pulitzer immediately revamped the style and sensationalized the content of the paper to focus on crime, disasters, the tawdry, and the bizarre. Pulitzer introduced many more illustrations and ads, which were key to profits, and by 1893 the two-cent *World* included nearly 100,000 ads a month and boasted that its circulation was 400,000. (When William Randolph Hearst purchased the *New York Morning Journal* in 1895, Pulitzer, hoping to fend off the competition, dropped the price of the *World* to one cent.) Declaring itself a paper for the workingman, the *World* tried to appeal to recent immigrants, but most of its readers were likely native born, lower middle class, with some schooling—salespeople, clerks, and secretaries. Known for its cautious commitment to a wide range of reforms, the *World* published muckraking articles. Nellie Bly (Elizabeth Cochrane) reported first hand on the struggles of workingwomen and the dreadful conditions in the city's hospitals, asylums, and prisons. The *World* did its best to appeal to female readers not only by hiring female reporters but also by including articles on fashion, social events, and women's clubs and by offering an advice column and a Sunday supplement for women. Although Pulitzer himself did not support women's suffrage, he recognized women's economic clout.[1]

A great deal has been said about the new woman, but nobody, until today, has had the opportunity of looking her in the face. The above picture is a composite of the new woman. It is faithfully made up of twelve excellent likenesses of the twelve most prominent new women in the world. It will be observed that the term "new" woman is used here in a sort of Pickwickian sense, as none of these ladies is what

---

New York World, Aug. 18, 1895, n.p.

46

"Here is the New Woman. As She Looks in a Composite Made from the Photographs of Twelve of the Most Advanced Women of the Day."

might be called new, merely judging from the lapse of years. They are new, however, in the sense of representing the most advanced ideas of the present progressive movement of womankind. These women believe that nature fully intended the female sex to be equal in all respects with the male, and they have devoted lifetimes in the effort to make others, especially the men, believe so, too. These women believe that, as they constitute quite an essential element in a world which is kept peopled by a reproduction of the species, they should have just as much to say about governing themselves, just as many opportunities for mental advancement and for earning a living, as men. They do not totally disapprove of the "old" woman, the woman who nursed you when you didn't know where on earth you were or what business you had there, the woman who soothed you when you were consumed with the agony of cutting your first teeth, the woman who has been and will be your refuge all through life. The above ladies stand ready to mete out to that woman due approval, but they believe that women as a class have a higher, a more noble duty in life than the mere bearing and nursing of children and the comforting and encouraging of men. They believe that after the incidental business of the household has been performed women should go out into the world, work side by side with the men, fight when they are oppressed, vote, insist upon their rights and make themselves generally agreeable.

It will be seen at once that the composite new woman has a strong face. It is an intellectual face, and—it is said with some regret—possibly a stern, unyielding face. Yet it is a face that indicates character and progression. The most utter novice in composite matters of this sort will detect at once the intellectual features that make the countenance of Mrs. Stanton instantly attractive, mingled with the resolution and enterprise of that forcefully Western citizen Mrs. Lease.[2] It is a most excellent thing about this particular composite picture that the peculiar traits of all the originals have been preserved, which is most difficult to accomplish and reflects great credit on the photographer and artist.

The old man (again used in a Pickwickian sense) may well ask himself whether he would like to marry the woman he sees pictured here. Undoubtedly that is a matter of taste, and there are some men who, were they matrimonially inclined, might perhaps prefer a face which gave greater promise of masculine independence after the ceremony. But, after all, the question of matrimony has no concern here. The picture is printed only to show what an intellectual-looking person the new woman is, and what little chance there is, judging from facial indications, that she will ever languish in the royal struggle for the liberty of her sex.

"Bloomers at the Bar"

By the late nineteenth century, the *National Police Gazette* was the most popular tabloid of its day. Begun by George Wilkes in 1845, it profiled New York's most wanted criminals and exposed their methods. In 1878 an Irish journalist, Richard K. Fox, with borrowed money, turned the debt-burdened paper into a sixteen-page quarto printed on pale pink paper and aggressively expanded its distribution. In 1888 Fox began distributing his paper in England, and in 1893 he published a Spanish-language edition for Mexican, Cuban, Spanish, and South and Central American readers. Throughout the 1880s and 1890s, the *Gazette* sold about 150,000 newspapers daily (in 1894 it sold for ten cents an issue), but that number would shoot up dramatically when the paper excited interest in a boxing match. To attract primarily male working-class readers, Fox reduced the subscription rate for saloonkeepers, barbershops, and hotel owners and gradually changed the pictorial focus away from lurid crime to sports, women, and popular theater. Woodcuts and later halftone engravings of buxom women, chorus girls, and prize fighters, along with sensational headlines—"Would-Be Voters: A Bevy of Strong-Minded Amazons Make a Sensation at a New York Polling Place," "Noose Notes," "Crimes of the Clergy"—sent circulation skyrocketing and made Fox a millionaire.[1] During the period 1879 to 1906, approximately 90 percent of the covers of the *Gazette* featured women, mostly white, often engaged in some kind of "unwomanly" activity. Images of women drinking appeared on about 15 percent of the covers, 7 percent depicted fighting between women, and about 6 percent showed women defending themselves against men. In 1880 the *Gazette* featured sexually suggestive illustrations on an average of 2.25 pages per issue; by 1895 that number had risen to 2.9, and sexually charged images appeared most frequently on the covers. Stories of the New Woman's supposed escapades appeared in a number of issues. According to historian Guy Reel, the *Gazette* was "filled with

---

National Police Gazette, Oct. 5, 1895, 6.

seeming contradictions—it championed the underclass, but was an outlet for bigotry; it cheered strong, independent women, but illustrated them as sex objects; it decried crime, but celebrated vice."[2]

Fannie Dee is a bloomer girl. Fannie is also a new woman. For several hours one night recently she monopolized the attention of the citizens of the town of Lake and Englewood, Ill., by a practical demonstration of her ideas of what a new woman should be.

The spectacular exhibition that Fannie made of herself will not soon be forgotten. It was something fearful, startling and wonderful, and caused a smile to flit over the

"Bloomers at the Bar. Daring Fannie Dee, an Englewood, Ill., New Woman, Waltzes into a Saloon and Takes Her Tipple Just Like a Man."

faces of the old men, a blush to mantle the cheek of the maid and matron and a huge grin to disfigure the countenance of the small boy.

Early in the evening Fannie left her place of abode at 510 Forty-second place, mounted her wheel and scorched down the street. She was attired in bloomers, bloomers that were bloomers, bloomers seldom seen in Chicago's intensely proper thoroughfares. And as she spun along pedestrians stopped and gazed in silent admiration.

But a mere ride on a wheel in bloomers was too pacific for Fannie. The old man had more liberties. He could stand up at the bar and drink. Why not also the new woman? Fannie settled the question, and although "I will" was not emblazoned on the front of that phenomenal bloomer suit, Fannie did act as her thoughts inclined.

She stood her wheel against the saloon door, walked to the bar, planked down the necessary price and asked for whisky, casually remarking that she took hers straight. She was served.

The result was exhilarating to the fair bloomer girl. The next saloon on her route was visited, and then another. Repetition increased the pleasures, and after a dozen drink stores had been patronized Fannie proceeded to the residence of Mrs. Carey, at the corner of Forty-fifth and Atlantic streets.

Mr. Carey was not at home, and as a result, when the new woman entered, Mrs. Carey was seized with a great desire, likewise thirst, to emulate her. Several bottles of whisky were purchased, and when Mr. Carey arrived he was speechless.

Fannie was singing and screaming, in fact, Fannie was hilarious. Without waiting to discuss the ethics of the emancipation of women the "old man" called in two policemen. In the meantime the noise which had almost reached the dignity of a riot, had attracted the attention of a crowd of the neighbors of the Carey family. When the bluecoats arrived they placed both women under arrest.

"The New-Woman
Santa Claus"

Hoping to capitalize on the success of the comic magazine *Puck*, a group of artists
lead by James Albert Wales left *Puck* and formed *Judge* in 1881, a weekly, sixteen-
page quarto satirical magazine filled with chromolithographs—brightly colored,
inexpensive illustrations—and selling for a dime. Shortly thereafter, Philadelphia
author Albert H. Smyth and Harry Hart took over the magazine. William J. Arkell
purchased the magazine in 1885 and enticed two more leading caricaturists,
Eugene Zimmerman and Bernard Gillam, away from *Puck*. As a supporter of the
Republican Party, Arkell persuaded his cartoonists to attack the Democratic
administration of President Grover Cleveland. William McKinley, the Republican
president who succeeded Cleveland, in fact called *Judge* cartoons "the greatest single factor" in his successful bid for the presidency. *Judge* boomed during the 1880s
and 1890s, surpassing *Life* in advertising and circulation. By the early 1890s, the
magazine's circulation had reached 50,000; in 1898 it charged ten cents an issue.[1]

"Mrs. Santa Claus—'Now Santa, take care of the babies: I'll attend to this toy distribution myself!'"

"The New Negro Woman"

Mrs. Booker T. Washington

Born in Macon, Mississippi, Margaret James Murray (1865–1925) earned her college degree from Fisk University in 1889. Upon graduation, she began teaching at Booker T. Washington's Tuskegee Institute, where she was employed as lady principal and director of the Department of Domestic Service. She married Booker T. Washington in 1892. As an educator, clubwoman, and essayist, Washington stressed the importance of female-led home maintenance and domestic science, land ownership, and prison reform, a mission parallel to her husband's model of industrial education for the black underclass. For M. M. Washington, the crucial race work was to be done in the South, a place that needed to be identified less with the degradations of slavery and more with the possibilities of reform. In an 1896 letter to Ednah Cheney, a frustrated Margaret Washington asserts that even though she did not belong to the "aggressive class" of female reformers, she wished that women such as Frances Willard, Ellen Henrotin, and Mary Dickinson would "show a little less fear of their southern sisters" and speak out in support of colored women, thousands of whom "live a living death": "The women who live north object to coming south to hold a meeting because of the travel. This is where work must be done for this is where the great mass of the colored women are."[1]

In "The New Negro Woman" (1895) Margaret Murray Washington appears to have coined that variant of the term. The paper was read at the First National Conference of Colored Women, held in Boston in August 1895, and then published in Edward Everett Hale's Boston monthly *Lend a Hand*, a journal committed to reform, philanthropy, and uplift. The publication had been started as an extension of Hale's Lend-a-Hand and Ten-Times-One clubs and published articles on "Negroes, Indians, and immigrant groups."[2]

Lend a Hand, Oct. 1895, 254–260.

Our world is made up of nations. The nations are made up of races, which, in their turn, are formed of classes or clans. There are, in each of these, the masses who, in their immensity, ought to not only attract the greatest attention in the way of criticism, but ought to receive the most thorough and systematic care from the rest of the world.

It is to the masses of negro women that I wish to call your attention for a few minutes. We certainly have no time to be idle in reference to these sisters of ours, for sisters they surely are. Not many days ago I was talking with a Northern white lady who told me this story: She said that, sitting beside a colored woman in a street car, she turned and said to her, "I am greatly interested in your people. I have for a number of years taught in the South," when all to the surprise of this good woman, the younger one turned, and, with a contemptuous sneer, said: "Oh, we don't have anything to do with those folks down there; they are none of us." The North, the South, the East, the West, must be one united whole in this great uplifting of our women—there can be no separation of interests, and the sooner each of us recognizes this fact, the sooner will the work be accomplished.

I repeat, we cannot be slow. We are the children of parents who were not the architects of their destiny, and perhaps we should not to-day be censured for having handed down to us a womanhood not equalling in strength that of our Caucasian sisters. But in the years that are to come we will be held responsible if the manhood, the womanhood, of the race is not higher, nobler, and stronger than it is today. In the words of Dr. Hale, let us "Look up and not down; look out and not in; look forward and not back, and lend a hand" to this mass of women who, in their helplessness, appeal to us, their older sisters—if not older in years, certainly in advantages and the things which go to make life happier and more hopeful. Women of all races had a friend in George Eliot, and it is she who says to us:

For they, the royal-hearted women are,
Who nobly love the noble,
Yet have grace
For needy suffering lives in lowliest place;
Carrying a choicer sunlight in their smile,
The heavenliest ray, that pitieth the vile.

Though I were happy, throned beside the king,
I should be tender to each little thing,
With hurt-warm breast that had no speech to tell
Its inward pangs; and I would sooth it well with tender touch,
And with a low, soft moan for company.

We are a race of servants, not in the low sense of this word, but in the highest and purest sense, and, in our serving, let us keep these beautiful lines of the servant of all women as our guide.

In the struggle for money, for power, for intellectual attainment, for growth of any sort, there is always, and must always be, a starting-point. Thus it is with the struggle to uplift the negro woman there is a starting-point, and this I believe to be the home. The two words, home and woman, are so closely connected that I could not, even if I desired, separate one from the other.

Someone has said, "No race can rise above its women." This is just as true as the fact that no river can rise above its source; are we not the source of the home life, and if our influence upon this life is not good, how can the home be better? History will bear us out in all we say in reference to woman and home. Our own Emerson says, "A sufficient measure of civilization is the influence of good women." Plato, the Athenian philosopher, when he stood at the height of his intellectual attainments, gave to the ancient and modern world his great "Republic," which he had thought it worth the while to write to show to the world his regard for woman in the home. He held that women are a very important factor in the human race, and that, holding out to her the help she so much needed, she will raise the standard of the home and thus from the home will come stronger men to execute the nation's plan.

In every race there are many societies, and these societies are higher or lower as the case may be. But, for convenience, I shall divide the negro race of women into two classes, viz., that class which has had opportunity to improve and develop themselves mentally, physically, morally, spiritually, and financially, and that class who, because of the lack of these advantages, because of their unblamed-for ignorance, who, because of the cruelty of the master for more than two centuries—the master who, thirty years ago, turned his slave mothers away without giving them a single idea of the beauty of home life, a single idea of the responsibility of womanhood, wifehood, or citizenship—are our inferiors. This latter class is overwhelming in its numbers, mighty in its strength if only these numbers and this strength can be lifted up, can be inspired, taught and sustained. Is there no bond between these two classes of the same race? Yes, there is a tie which no attempt on our part can sever.

I sometimes fear that we are too slow in doing for others because we are, as we think, doing well. Individuals here and there among our men and women are climbing the ladder in almost all of the avenues of life, but this is not race progress; it is the lifting up as we climb which means growth to the race.

Thirty years ago the negro slaves were declared free. The most helpless members of the race at that time, as now, were its women. During all the black days of slavery they had come and gone only as commanded by the man and woman who called themselves master and mistress.

The negro woman had been given in marriage as the whim of the master's family saw fit; she had been sold from her husband as the master's financial interests demanded, with no more pity than was exhibited at the selling of a hog. Was it possible that she should know or think very strongly of the cultivation of the sacredness of the marital relations which are at the very root of the home? Was there anything in these lessons to inspire morality, or even a respect for it? And yet these same people, with all their boasted chivalry for their own women, are ever ready to thrust the sword at this race of which these poor women, their own pupils, are members. In this time of the master and slave, it was not the mother who taught the responsibility of motherhood. The children came, and as soon as possible the mother went to the field or elsewhere to work, and the children were left practically alone. There was no time to bathe the babies, even once a day. There was no time to dress the children, to comb their hair, to see that they were getting clean, wholesome habits in order to become clean, wholesome men and women. It was not the slave mother who said how her children should be dressed, whether they should wear shoes or go bare-footed, and thus have inculcated within themselves respect for personal appearance and decency of dress. It was not the chattel-mother who said the baby was sick enough to need medical aid. These things and more in reference to the children were decided by the master and mistress. Was there anything in a lesson like this to teach responsibility of motherhood? Was there a single thing in a lesson like this to bring about the sanctity of family life? Was there anything in a life like this to establish confidence between mother and daughter, father and son, which is absolutely necessary in the home, in a truly happy family life?

In the awful days gone by, the word "home," the word "woman" was a mockery, so far as we are concerned; in fact, there was no home, there was no manhood. All were chattel, bought, used, and sold at the master's will.

The log cabin of one room, with perhaps no hole to let in sunlight and air, holding the household goods, cooking utensils, furnishing room for cooking, sleeping, eating, and living, was a substitute for home. Could anything good and healthy come out of this? Was it at all probable that these mothers could hand down to their daughters and sons correct ideas of home-making, pure ideas of family life? Was it at all probable that there should have come from homes like these women strong to fight disease, strong to fight the tempter who stands in the South as a sentinel by day and by night? Was there anything in this sort of living to instil purity of thought, and purity of action?

The women of this class are to-day needing our aid, needing our sympathy. We will answer as Cain answered the Master, "Am I my brother's keeper?" Surely we are the keepers of these women, and will answer, "Here am I; use me."

Let us not suppose that although more than thirty years have gone by, there is a very great change in the condition of the masses of the women of whom I speak. Turned loose with no knowledge of these things, she has groped the way but slowly. In the country districts of the Southern states in which slaves were held, a condition of affairs exists to-day that would touch the heart of any woman. Look for a moment into a log cabin in Alabama. There is only one room, 12 × 10, with a little hole in the side for a window, which in winter time is kept tightly closed. In this hut live the father and mother, and in here their eight or ten children are born and reared and die. I draw the curtain. I could show you other pictures more pathetic in their hopelessness, but I refrain.

Lessons in making home neat and attractive; lessons in making family life stronger, sweeter, and purer by personal efforts of the woman; lessons in tidiness of appearance among women; lessons of clean and pure habits of everyday life in the home, and thus bringing to the women self-respect and getting for them the respect of others; how to keep the girls near the mother, and many other kindred subjects, need to be given to this class of women to-day.

In the village of Tuskegee, in the state of Alabama, a little more than a year ago, a few of us women undertook this kind of work for this class of women. To us it was not a very inviting work, but we could not rid ourselves of the recognition of the bond which linked us to these women. We knew that as they were lifted up, so might we rise. We meet the women in a hall in the central part of the town on Saturday afternoon, when they usually flock to the town from the neighboring plantations and country districts and congregate on the street corners to gossip and eat peanuts. Our meetings are very informal, and hence, I believe, very helpful; for the women would not come if the meetings were not informal. During the past few months we have talked in a simple way on home-getting, home-making, cultivating confidence between the parent and the child, how to protect our girls, plain and simple dress for the children, kinds of food best for the home, and many like subjects tending to better them along all lines. We have emphasized the respect that comes to a woman because of her neatness of dress, and upon the disrespect that comes to her by reason of her love for gaudy and extravagant dress. We have tried to get our women to substitute the neat calico dress of to-day for the slave homespun of the past. We have tried to teach them the self-respect which comes from wearing shoes instead of going bare-footed as the master taught them; the lack of self-respect and the physical injury incident to wrapping the hair. These are only a few of the crude things which these women will do. They have been taught these lessons by people who have had hundreds of years of advantages and experience, and they would naturally be loth to give up these habits. But we do not feel discouraged.

In addition to the work we are trying to do for the women, we have also each week a meeting for young girls, to whom we give lessons in simple sewing, in house-cleaning, in street and church manners, and in every line which goes to make young womanhood purer and nobler. Much of the social purity literature is given out to these girls, and here and there a seed is being sown which will bring forth a better wifehood and motherhood.

We only want women who will, everywhere that is needed, take up this cause of the large class of negro women who have not had the same opportunity which you and I have had. Are we not all of one race? Are not the interests of this class our interests? There is a hearty response in the efforts of the women to rise and shake off the terrible habits which, for two hundred and fifty years, were being fastened upon them. It is not rapid work, but I believe that it is sure work. I believe that in this kind of work is the salvation of the negro women, and all will agree with me that just in proportion as the women rise will the race rise. Work for these masses and you work for the race.

But this lamentable condition of affairs is not confined to any particular section of our country; but is it not true that right here, under the shadow of the Cradle of Liberty, as it were, and where a "man's a man for a' that and a' that," there are to be found parallel cases? In picturing to you the condition of affairs at the South, and pleading for my Southern sisters, I do not wish to withdraw your interest in and for the needy ones nearer home, but my heart goes out with a great longing in the interest of the Southern negro woman who is what she is because of force of circumstances, and not because of a lack of desire to be otherwise.

Let us all rise, shine and push right along in the work of helping our women in the South, in the North, everywhere that it is needed—and it is needed everywhere; let us rise with our money, though it be little; let us rise with our voices even though they be weak, with our hands even though they be feeble, and do this all-important work. Then only will there be fewer thrusts at the immorality of the race; there will be less lynchings of negro men and women; then only will the white man who hates everything that is black, and the black man who despises everything white, recognize in the broadest and truest sense the brotherhood of man and the fatherhood of God, and more readily accept the doctrine that of one blood hath he made the nations of the earth.

"Woman in Another
New Role"

Frank A. Munsey, the son of a poor farmer-carpenter, grew up to become a leader in the field of low-cost, high-profit American magazine publishing at the turn of the century. His publication *Munsey's Weekly*, begun in 1889 as a ten-cent, thirty-six-page magazine modeled on the satirical *Life*, changed its size, price, and periodicity in 1891 to become the twenty-five-cent, ninety-six-page monthly titled *Munsey's Magazine*. As a weekly the periodical had struggled, so when it continued to do so as a monthly, Munsey lowered the price back to ten cents in 1893, advertised the magazine heavily, and included much more advertising; issues then contained about 160 pages of text and 80–100 pages of advertising. He also began to publish more heavily illustrated articles about famous public figures and performers, as well as serial fiction and poetry. And using a hook from lowbrow entertainment, he initially offered a significant number of halftone images of semi-nude women. Munsey repeatedly offered his lower-middle-class readers visions of success that could be obtained through a Horatio Alger–like work ethic (Munsey was, in fact, an early publisher of Alger's rags-to-riches stories). Although not considered a progressive reformer, Munsey published a number of stories and articles that implicitly endorsed many of the changes associated with the New Woman. By 1895, circulation had shot up to approximately 500,000, and to about 700,000 by 1897, making *Munsey's Magazine* the leader in circulation after *Ladies' Home Journal*. Advertising revenue totaled between $25,000 and $35,000 a month.[1]

Is it not time to stop calling woman the weaker sex, and alleging that she is naturally disqualified for callings that demand physical strength? The Chicago press recently reported a remarkable instance of her triumphant success in a field hitherto monopolized by tyrant man—that of burglary. It seems that there has been something of

Munsey's Magazine, Dec. 1896, 384.

an epidemic of this particular form of industry in the Lake City, two specialists, whose identity is veiled under the titles of "the long man" and "the short man," having won a prestige seldom equaled in criminal annals since the Whitechapel celebrity of Jack the Ripper. But the boldest feat of these two gentlemen was outdone by a lady housebreaker who, single handed, attacked a suburban residence containing seven inmates and defended by a ferocious dog. Her success was artistic and complete, and a brief campaign resulted in her driving away with the choicest contents of the dwelling packed in her buggy, and the ferocious dog tied under the seat. It may be noted that among the spoils seized by this eminently new woman was a pair of masculine nether integuments. On second thought, however, she rejected the garment in question, and threw it out upon the lawn, as if in deliberate scorn of an article long regarded as the special token of the other sex. After this, let us hear no more of the exploded myth of "woman's weakness."

"The New Woman"

An Address by Emma Goldman before the
Liberal Progressive Society

Born in Lithuania, a part of the Russian Empire, Emma Goldman (1869–1940)
arrived in the United States in 1885 and took a number of jobs in the garment
industry before meeting Alexander Berkman, who would become a lifelong comrade and mentor, and growing committed to the anarchist cause. As an anarchist,
Goldman espoused a political philosophy that advocated individual freedom and
voluntary association while rejecting all forms of governmental control. Applying
anarchist philosophy to a wide range of social issues, Goldman endorsed homosexuality, birth control, and free love but denounced the suffrage movement, in
part because proponents predicated their arguments on women's supposed moral
superiority: "When she has learned to be as self-centred and as determined as he,
when she gains the courage to delve into life as he does and pay the price for it, she
will achieve her liberation, and incidentally also help him become free." To achieve
meaningful freedom, Goldman argued, woman must begin by "asserting herself as
a personality, and not as a sex commodity. Second, by refusing the right to anyone
over her body; by refusing to bear children, unless she wants them; by refusing to
be a servant to God, the State, society, the husband, the family, etc. by making her
life simpler, but deeper and richer." By the time the transcript of her speech "The
New Woman" appeared in the Chicago-based anarchist newspaper *Free Society* in
February 1898, Goldman was traveling extensively around the United States giving
talks on anarchism, free love, revolution, and the New Woman.[1]

The bible story of woman's inequality and inferiority is based on the declaration of her
being created from the rib of man. Woman cannot without equal opportunity ever
rise to equality with him, and hence women are slaves to society as a consequence,

---

Free Society: A Periodical of Anarchist Thought, Work, and Literature, Feb. 1898.

and intensified under the marriage code. Despotic rule causes people to revolt, and they will do so as a necessity. Woman is bred to be seen and for outside show, and hence the sham in society. Her only mission is to marry and to be a wife and mother, and to cater to a husband who for this will support her. She thus degrades herself. The present mothers are not so much to be blamed for this condition, this comes about by copying their mothers. The mother who is thus raised cannot have any conception of the true knowledge of the rearing of the children, i.e., of raising children as a profession, and she never can bring up the child as she ought to under this system. Mothers are conquered by the child, the exception being a good mother.

The duty of a wife is considered as an impure subject of consideration to the young, unmarried woman, and thus the ignorant girl is forced in the battle unprepared for life consequences. Another great error in the ideal new woman, and one is that to be condemned, is that of aping the male, seeking to become masculine, considering that man is superior to woman. No decent woman can emulate them. We must first have the New Man. In all things women are the equal of men, even in the productive field. Even radicals do not differ from the christians; they do not wish their wives to become radical; even they deem themselves necessary to her protection. So long as she needs protection she is not on equal footing, we need only to protect weaklings. One of the invasive points in the character of man is, that he is too authoritative for the forced progress in woman, and while he has evolved slowly he is making the fatal mistake of securing more liberty for woman through the very thing that was his own enslavement, i.e., authority. Opposition to this will correct this evil.

Contemptible marriage laws and the adherence to them tend to still farther increase the degradation. To assert that freedom of the sex relations is the natural law is interpreted to mean free lust. The law of love governs this as in all matters, love being the fulfillment of the law. Motherhood and its beauty, of which poets have sung and written, is a farce, and cannot be otherwise until we have freedom—economically.

Men are all heroes at home, but cowards abroad. Women, too, would be as unjust at the ballot box as are the men. They are tyrants as well as are the men. Woman, to be free, must be the mutual friend and mate of man. The individual is the ideal liberty. We owe no duty to anyone, save ourselves. When universal woman once comprehends this ideal, then all protective laws, intended for protection, which is indeed her weakness, will disappear, and this adulterous system goes, and with it charity and all its attendant ills. In short, the new woman movement demands and equal advancement by the modern man.

"Women in the Territories:

SOME OF THEIR ACHIEVEMENTS IN FIELDS OF ENERGY GENERALLY FILLED BY MEN—TYPICAL EXAMPLES, INCLUDING A MINING SPECULATOR AND A COWBOY"

The *New York Times* was founded in 1851 as a penny daily, but after Adolph S. Ochs took it over in 1896, he sought to make it the gold standard of American newspapers. While Pulitzer's *New York World* and Hearst's *New York Journal* pursued sensational topics to boost their already thriving circulations, the *Times*, Ochs announced, would take a different path. It would be a "high-standard news-paper, clean, dignified and trustworthy," which would deliver "the news impar-tially, without fear or favor, regardless of any party, sect or interest involved." Two months after Ochs took over, the slogan "All the News That's Fit to Print" appeared on the masthead. According to advertising executive James H. Collins in 1901, the *Times* banned "word contests, prize puzzles, immoral books, diseases of men, female pills, fortune tellers, clairvoyants, palmists, massage, offers of large salaries and things for nothing, guaranteed cures and speculations that guaran-tee large dividends." Under Ochs, the *Times* expanded its coverage of financial news and maintained an overall conservative stance, which appealed to business readers. By 1898, after the paper lowered its price from three cents down to a penny, the *Times* enjoyed a jump in circulation, going from 9,000 in 1896 to 82,000 in 1900 and 121,000 in 1905.[1]

There are several thousands of women on the plains and among the mountains and cañons in the Far West who deserve to be well up toward the top of the catalogue of

---

New York Times, May 10, 1903.

those who are prominent for achievements in those fields of human energy which for years have been occupied exclusively by the sturdiest of men. While the women in the East are making success in professions, business, and trades alongside of their husbands and brothers, there are women in every part of the raw, new West, as it is known to-day, who are not only adapting themselves to a crude and strange environment but are winning fortune and fame by reaching results in pursuits that were thought impossible of entrance by women a dozen years ago.

There is the case of Mrs. Marion Phelps, who has become an excellent gold mining prospector in the Globe mining region in Southwestern Arizona. Ex-Gov. Wolfley of Arizona is authority for saying that she is as good a judge as there is in the Southwest concerning the value of ledges of low-grade gold ore. Her husband was a graduate from a New England scientific school, and, marrying when but twenty-two years of age, he came West with his young wife. He soon sank all his little fortune in a placer mine that had been abundantly salted for his benefit. His wife tramped over the mountains, traveled across burning deserts, lived in lonely cañons, camped on bleak and barren mountain sides, slept in the chaparral, and dwelt with Indians through several years, while young Phelps searched for gold mines. Mrs. Phelps shared every hardship with her husband and in time she developed into as correct and quick an observer of pay rock and became as well versed as any one in that region in the formations of auriferous rocks, the slant, frangibility, and dip of ledges.

When her husband fell from a cliff one day in Williams Cañon and was killed the young woman was left with two small children and a few dollars. During the years that she and her husband had been barely subsisting, while they prospected for mines, neither of them had ever written a relative in the East as to their condition and their struggle with poverty. Not a word did she write now about her distress. Pride is a powerful characteristic in the average new woman of the West.

With the help of several miner friends, Mrs. Phelps built a rude cabin sufficient for comfort in the semi-tropic latitudes of Arizona, and with her own hands cultivated an area of valley land about her cabin. She grew vegetables and made a market for all she could raise at the mining town of Globe, a few miles away. She never lost her interest in seeking mines, and when her children were a year or two older and could be left with others she went forth to prospect through Williams Cañon, where she and her husband had once found evidence of gold-bearing rock. She prospected there for several weeks at a time during the Summer, going back to her cabin home occasionally to look after her children and their Indian squaw nurse and to cultivate anew her vegetable farm. Along in the Fall she located two claims, one of which she sold for $2,000. This gave her the capital she needed, and from the day in March, 1890, that the money was paid her, she has been an assayer and an expert in judging the value of low-grade gold quartz. Her opinions are sought from Yuma to Albuquerque, and, although now not yet over thirty-one years of age, she earns a good competency every year in fees from Eastern people, who have confidence that what she tells them about gold mining is reliable. Her children are in school in Los Angeles, and she has a pretty home at Tucson.

The Case of Miss Dunn

Then there is Miss Amelia Dunn, who is regarded in the region of Prescott as the most capable girl cowboy in the Southwest. Every one in the Territories knows about 'Melia Dunn and her success among cattle, and hardly a fortnight passes that some new story about her broncos and cattle is not started on the rounds of the rural press in Arizona and New Mexico. The Dunns came from the vicinity of Elmira, N.Y. Mr. Dunn, the father, was an invalid with consumption, and settled at Deming and bought cattle, because the care of them would make him money and keep him out of doors at the same time. That was in 1877, when Miss Amelia was a little tot of a girl.

After a long and hard experience with marauding Pimas, who at different times stole three-fourths of the little herd of cattle on the Dunn ranch and intimidated the family so that they died a thousand deaths, barricaded for a week at a time in the dugout cellar under the rude ranch home, Mr. Dunn rounded up some 350 cattle. When Amelia was seventeen years old her father died. She had been with him almost daily for several years in his rides across the mesas, among the foothills, and through the arroyos, so she was as well posted about the cattle business as he had been. It was natural that when he died she became his successor. It took several years for the girl to develop good business sense—to know beef values, when to sell her stock, when to ship, and how to graze her herd most economically. She was apt, and before she was twenty-one years old her opinion was authority among the cattlemen in that region. She knows every detail of the ranch work, and has performed some part of all phases of the career of a cowboy of the Southwest. The past ten years have at times been sorry ones for many an experienced cattle ranchman in the drought-stricken regions of the Southwest, but 'Melia Dunn has had the foresight to drive her beeves to valleys where they have fattened while thousands of other cattle have died of exhaustion and starvation.

The young woman's duties as vaquero and proprietor of some 4,000 cattle often take her 150 and 200 miles from home across sandy wastes and among foothills and mountains, as the cattle must be kept moving to feed well. Frequently some of the cattle become mired in the mud along creeks where they graze, or where they wade in to drink. Then comes the hardest part of the work. With true cowboy skill she throws the lariat over the slender branching horns, while the other end of the long but phenomenally strong rawhide rope is fastened to the saddle. Then a steady pull on the part of the pony draws the imprisoned animal to a place of safety on dry ground. She has a large herd for one person to handle, but with the assistance of two well-trained cattle dogs she does it.

While on the range Miss Dunn dresses in true cowboy fashion—wide-brimmed white felt hat, long gauntlet gloves, a lariat coiled about the saddle horn, and a revolver at her belt—and rides the wildest bronco with thorough ease. When off duty she is a quiet, unassuming young lady, the last one that would be suspected of such masculine accomplishments. "I only regret," said she recently to a newspaper man, "that I have never had an opportunity to gain any of the womanly accomplishments in the way of study, literature, and music. I fear I would be laughed at by the young women in the East if I should go among them. But I have made good money, and some day may have some of the longed-for feminine accomplishments."

Mrs. Daniels's Bravery

The people in the San Joaquin Valley of California have never ceased telling of a deed of rare bravery enacted by Mrs. Victor Daniels, some twenty-five miles southwest from Bakersfield, in the Summer of 1883. The Danielses came from New Jersey and settled on a cattle ranch, fifteen miles from the nearest neighbor. Mrs. Daniels was born and reared in Morristown, N.J., but she soon adapted herself in her new home to the strange environment. Her husband, with great difficulty and constant watchfulness had acquired a bunch of cows, about fifty in all, and was endeavoring to start a little herd in order to rescue his family from the poverty which hung over the claim. Mrs. Daniels had the herding of them as well as the care of the house. One day, when the husband had gone twenty miles to the store, she was compelled to leave the cattle grazing while she looked after a sick baby at home. Suddenly, she saw two men ride from behind the foothills and start the cattle off, full canter, abducting the whole bunch. She wasted not a minute, but, mounting her bronco, was after them.

The men probably thought themselves undiscovered, and in the bustle of hurrying on the stock did not hear the pattering hoofs of the pursuer's pony as she came cantering up behind. Suddenly one of them gave a yell and tumbled backward off his saddle, with the noose of a lariat tight around his throat. Frightened, the other turned to see a furious woman facing him.

"What are you doing?" she demanded.

"Who are you?" he responded, gruffly.

"I own these cattle, and you will help me drive them back where you got them."

As she held a cocked revolver toward his head he decided to submit, and, with her following closely, rode around the scattered herd and turned their heads homeward. For three miles the stock was driven, and then, with a warning not to look backward, the depredator was dismissed. He fled without a backward glance. His companion, choked to death, and with neck broken, was found among the chaparral, but there was never inquiry as to the manner of his taking off. It was enough to know that he had been engaged in cattle stealing, and that summary justice had been visited upon him. The Danielses became in time well-to-do people, and are now residents of Los Angeles.

The women who have gone with their husbands or brothers to make homes down in the famous gold mining region of Tombstone in Southern Arizona, are accounted among the most daring of any in the territories in the last ten years. The Apache Indians, when Geronimo was their Chief, made frequent incursions into that part of the country, and the outrages committed in the homes of settlers and ranchmen among the mountains and foothills are among the most atrocious and horrible ever known by savages. With the conquering of the Apaches some twelve years ago by Gen. Miles the fearful slaughter of settlers' families and cattlemen came to an end,

but the women who still live in that region deserve merit for frequent acts of bravery and coolness in their daily life. . . .

The women of the Western plains are as quick, if not quicker, as their Eastern sisters
to put into practice modern ideas. At the rude little mining camp of San Miguel,
among the copper mines of Cochise County, in the sullen desert wastes of Arizona,
a Bellamy co-operative cooking club that has met with remarkable success, has just
completed its fourth year. It is conducted by some of the first women of the camp,
and the forty-five families on its list include those prominent alike for wealth and
brains in the community.

Weary of the drudgery of cooking and tired of wrestling with the long line of
refractory Mexican hired help, the Bellamy club was organized. A centrally located
residence was rented and turned over to a matron, with a corps of assistants, who
were to have full charge of preparing meals for the club members and do nothing
else. The Executive Committee of three does all the purchasing of supplies, and
meets every Saturday morning to hold a consultation and audit bills. Everything is
paid for on Monday morning, assessments being paid a week in advance on Saturday
by the members. This prevents any debts or bills due at the end of the week, and any
surplus or accidental deficit is easily carried to the end of the next week.

The Executive Committee is all-powerful, and club members are bound to report
grievances only to it and not to one another. The club is run on the family plan, and
so far as possible all bickering and faultfinding are shut out. Any one who is not satisfied can leave at any time, and the fact that the club has lasted so long proves much
for the good sense of the members.

The families have tables for themselves if they wish, and there is a table d'hôte
for unmarried people, if they wish to take advantage of it. The expense has been found
to be remarkably small, the members declaring that it is less than one-half what they
can afford to run a home kitchen and pay and pay for the necessary service. The
women are sole managers and their husbands only foot the bills.

"The 'New Woman' Got the Drop on Him"

When in 1886 Harrison Gray Otis became the president, general manager, and editor in chief of the *Los Angeles Daily Times*, he immediately dropped the "Daily" from its title and built a four-story brick and granite headquarters, called the Fortress, replete with castle-looking stone turrets and containing the most technologically advanced printing presses of the day. Otis sought to make the paper the voice of southern California, and as such it was a staunchly Republican, antiunion, pro-development voice. During a period when Los Angeles experienced dramatic fluctuations in growth—with the real estate boom of 1887, the population had burgeoned to 80,000, up from a scant 11,000 only six years earlier—Otis, founder of the Los Angeles chamber of commerce, spearheaded a media blitz to sell California. Otis's growth-at-any-cost boosterism spurred the paper's bitter attacks against unions. When in 1894 Chicago's Pullman Palace Car Company's employees, faced with a steep wage cut, called a strike, and the American Railroad Union called sympathy strikes across the nation, the *Los Angeles Times* railed against the strikers and their leader, Eugene Debs. Debs later decried the *Times* as the "Los Angeles Daily Liar." In 1895, it advertised its circulation as 14,700 for its daily and 19,500 for its Sunday paper.[1]

The following illustration depicts Mrs. Leva Marshall, who was a night operator at the Baden Station on the Southern Pacific Railroad, allegedly defending the office from "would-be-robbers." A week after the initial story appeared in the *Times*, the paper recanted, stating that railroad officials now thought Mrs. Marshall was shot after having rejected the advances of an acquaintance.

Los Angeles Times, Oct. 12, 1895, 1.

"Mrs. Leva Marshall of Baden Station demonstrates that the modern woman is fully able to protect herself against robbers."

"The Negro Woman—Social and Moral Decadence"

Eleanor Tayleur

In New York in 1867, Henry E. Childs began a Baptist newspaper called the *Church Union*, but soon thereafter the famous Congregationalist minister and social reformer Henry Ward Beecher took over editorship and renamed the newspaper the *Christian Union* to signify a broader religious stance. By 1893, the periodical under the editorship of Lawrence F. Abbott had evolved once again into the weekly *Outlook*, moving away, albeit not entirely, from a religious periodical in favor of a broader family magazine devoted to coverage of the arts and news. By 1894 *Outlook* had reached a circulation of over 30,000. In 1897, it reduced its size while adding illustrations and nearly doubling the length of each month's first issue (about 120 pages as opposed to the usual 68). Abbott declared that the *Outlook* believed "in the immortality of the spirit and in changes of forms, in the old religion and in a new theology, in the old patriotism and in new politics, in the old philanthropy and in new institutions, in the old brotherhood and in a new social order." It published a number of important autobiographies in serial form, including Booker T. Washington's *Up from Slavery* from 1900 to 1902. In 1902, the *Outlook* boasted a circulation of over 100,000.[1]

Eleanor Tayleur's essay "The Negro Woman—Social and Moral Decadence" is informed by the frequent discussions in the white press of the "New Negro Crime," which, by reiterating a narrative of emboldened black men eager to ravish helpless white women, helped to legitimate Jim Crow laws and mob violence. The New Negro Woman in the white press was a degraded imitation of a legitimate original. Tayleur's essay immediately preceded one by Margaret Murray Washington,

Outlook, Jan. 30, 1904, 266–271.

"The Gain in the Life of Negro Woman," in which Washington offered a series of
figures—including the number of black women enrolled in various educational
programs—to prove the gains made by the "superior class of negro women."

The most anomalous and portentous figure in America today is the negro woman. Little account has been taken of her in the discussion of the race problem, yet if the key to that dark riddle is ever found, hers must be the hand that first discovers it.

It is an axiom that no people can rise higher than their source. The measure of its womanhood is the measure of the potentialities of a race. If this be virtuous, clean of mind and body, filled with high ideals and noble aspirations, all things are possible to its sons. If, on the contrary, it be unchaste, diseased physically and morally, with groveling and material desires, the race is doomed, for death and decadence have set their seal upon it. Women mold the character of a people. It is eternally true that the hand that rocks the cradle rules the world. In the great crises of life the thing that determines the action of the great majority of men is not the code of ethics of their mature years, or the system of philosophy that they have reasoned out. It is the teaching that they imbibed at their mother's knee—it is the memory of old prayers they lisped in childhood, old songs and stories, a mother's kiss, a mother's tears that have crystallized into character, and that at the crucial moment decides their action for right or wrong, and whether they shall go forward or backward. Before a mother's influence political decrees are as empty and powerless as sounding brass and tinkling cymbals, and even the education of books and schools falls back impotent and defeated. At the last it is the woman who bears the race who determines its destiny.

It is this that gives a somber interest to the negro woman, for she is the pivot upon which the great race question turns. It is her hand that rocks the cradle in which the little pickaninny sleeps; it is she who sweeps the cabin floor, and makes it a home that is clean and bright or else an abode of disease; it is she who bequeaths to the child that is bone of her bone and flesh of her flesh, soundness of body and soul or else the tendencies that make it a moral and physical leper; it is her hand that sets the little feet about her knee on the road which they are to travel in life. All that the white woman is to the white race, the negro woman is to the black. Her influence is just as potent, and she is the dominant factor that must be reckoned with in every effort to help the negro.

In the Northern cities there are many, and in the South a few, negro women who in intelligence, nobility of character, and refinement would challenge comparison with any women in the world. These are exceptions, and it is not proposed to consider them here, but the great dark, helpless, hopeless mass of the women of their race as they are found leading their lawless and purposeless lives in the cane and cotton field, or herded together in the streets of the cities.

As she exists in the South to-day the negro woman is the Frankenstein product of civilization, a being created out of conditions of sectional hate and revenge, and set in motion by wild experimentalists who knew not what they did; and within the length and breadth of Christendom there is no other figure so forlorn and pathetic as she. Doubly cursed by her color and her sex, on her has fallen alike the heaviest burden of the negro and of womanhood. Shut out by her blood from the privileges of the white woman and by her sex from the opportunities of the negro man, she is the victim of every injustice of society, and she revenges herself upon it by striking at the very foundations of the political and social structure. She has always been a hapless sacrifice to the lust of man, and retribution has made of her a Nemesis who has forged the thunderbolts of the race question for the white man, and who stands a sinister figure behind the black man, forever dragging him downward.

No women in the world ever went through such a radical change as has taken place among the negro women since the Civil War. For them emancipation meant the severing of every association, habit, and custom of their lives, and the inauguration of a new heaven and a new earth; and the negro woman of to-day, in character and thought, in aspiration and ideal, is no more like the negro woman of ante-bellum days than if a thousand generations, instead of one or two, rolled between them. History records no change of the women of a whole race so rapid and so radical; and the sadly significant feature of this change is that it has been for the worse and not for the better.

Many explanations may be offered to account for the decadence of the negro woman. First and foremost is the abolition of the home; for woman's highest virtues, whatever her color or her race, are garden flowers that flourish best about her doorstep, and lacking this congenial soil they wither and die. Whatever the burdens and wrongs of slavery, and they were great and many, it at least gave the negro woman a home in which she was sure of food and warmth and privacy; and when within the four walls of her cabin, or her quarters in the city mansion, she was as truly and completely mistress of her home as the chatelaine of her castle. So much was the slave's unquestioned right; but now, when the negro must pay rent for the roof that shelters him, whole herds of them crowd together in a single room, like rabbits in a warren, without regard to age or sex or consanguinity. Under such conditions all privacy, or even decency, is impossible.

In the country the cabin may still be seen with the gourd vine trained above the door, with its beds covered with gay patchwork, with its floors scrubbed until they shine with glistening whiteness, and these homes furnish the great percentage of the respectable, thrifty, and industrious men and women of the negro race. In the cities the majority of negro women have no homes, but a room which they oftener than not share with strangers. The beds are unmade, the dishes unwashed, the floor unswept. Here children are born to be thrust out into the street as soon as possible to get them out of the way, and thus the mother and the child are deprived of the home influence that is one of the strongest powers for good in the world.

Another reason for the decadence of the negro woman is that she no longer has the uplift of close personal association with white women. Before the war the negro woman was brought into intimate contact with the refined and educated women of the dominant race. Essentially imitative as negroes are, they copied the manners and the morals of the mistress they served. Many a black woman was a grande dame who would have graced a court, and imbued with as high and lofty a sense of loyalty and fealty as any knight; and among the most cherished recollections of the old South are the memories of these women, between whom and their owners existed a bond of affection that only death could sever.

No such conditions prevail to-day, save in the rare instances when a family is fortunate enough to attach to itself some negress whose ideals and traditions were formed in the days of slavery, when, as foster-sister to some white child, or handmaiden to some white woman, she imbibed the precepts of honor and honesty and duty that must alike guide both races. The modern negro woman has no such object-lesson in morality or morals or modesty, and she wants none. She hates the white woman with a hatred born of hopeless envy, and her most exquisite pleasure is in insulting her with childlike brutality. She does this in a thousand little puerile ways—by rudely jostling her in a crowd, by pushing her off the sidewalk, and—favorite method of all—by invariably speaking of her own race as "ladies and gentlemen" and the white as "men and women." Thus the announcement by your maid that a lady wishes to speak to you sends you down the back stairs to interview a dusky charwoman, while, when you are told that there is a strange woman downstairs, you prepare to receive your friend of a most aristocratic lineage and exquisite refinement. When the black woman imitates the white, she only imitates what is worst in her. She copies her extravagance in tawdry finery that is a grotesque exaggeration of fashion, she copies her independence in utter abandon of all restraints, she copies her vices and adds to them frills of her own, and it is as if one saw a vulgar picture ineffably coarsened by being reproduced in hideous and glaring colors that emphasized every unlovely detail.

Before the war the negro women also had the uplifting influence of honest work. They were taught the various branches of domestic labor, and had the pride in their work that comes from skillful craftsmanship. But the Aunt Dinahs, ample of girth, clad in clean cottonade, who boasted that they laid a heavy hand on the seasoning when they compounded dainties, and who at dinner would poke an anxious head through the doorway to hear the compliments bestowed upon their art, are almost as extinct as the dodo. Gone, too, are the neat housemaids in guinea-blue calicoes, starched until they rattled like the best taffeta, who felt a personal pride in keeping the mahogany shining like a mirror, and whose ministrations were benedictions, so filled were they with loving care and solicitude. Gone, also, are the old black mammies on whose broad breasts childish sorrows sobbed themselves to sleep and broken baby hearts were mended.

In their places is an ignorant creature in dirty finery, the first article of whose faith is a settled determination not to work. For the time being this has been shaken by hunger or a desire to buy a sleazy silk dress, and she condescends to preside in your kitchen or make your beds, but she does it under protest. She has no pride in her occupation, or desire to do it well. She does not burden her mind with the insignificant details that go to make good cooking. She dashes a lot of things together, and if they turn out all right, well and good. If not, also well and good. All that she is interested in is in drawing her wages, and carrying back and forth the basket that is the commissary department of a horde of idle and shiftless friends.

In the peculiar code of ethics that governs the new negro woman any way of obtaining a livelihood is more honorable and respectable than working for it.

The colored Mrs. Grundy does not frown on the demi-mondaine, nor does the conviction of theft call forth any social ostracism.[2] Nor is this surprising. It was to have been expected that a childish race, suddenly freed from slavery, would mistake liberty for license, and that the men and women whose own backs had been bowed with toil should wish to save their children from the burdens they had borne. More than that, the masters and mistresses they idealized did not work with their hands, and so the distorted belief prevails among the negroes that the first step toward being a lady or a gentleman is to be idle. In this the young of both sexes are encouraged by their parents; and nothing could be more grotesquely sad than the feeble old black mothers who are bending over washtubs and cooking-stoves earning the money to support strapping sons and daughters, while they boast proudly that their children never did a lick of work!

So far, education has done but little for the great mass of negro women. Here and there a girl achieves the common-school education, and in rare instances one even develops the ability to take a college course; but these latter cases are as unusual as genius is among the whites. Negroes are avid of schooling, and it is nothing uncommon to see a girl go to school, session after session, for eight or ten years, without achieving anything more than the ability to read and write like a child in the second grade, while the superior elegance of saying "have came," and scorning the humble and admiring mother who goes out scrubbing to support her, entitles her to a diploma. It may be that this tentative education, whose uplifting influence is unseen and unfelt as yet, is the little leaven that will eventually leaven the whole lump and raise the entire race to a higher level; but as yet the only visible result has been to teach the girl a scorn of the work she is fitted to do, and to implant in her breast an insatiable ambition to be a schoolteacher—an ambition that must be futile unless the supply of scholars can be miraculously increased, or the Government subsidizes every kinky-headed little coon and farms him out among the several million negro girls in the South who are looking forward to the glorious career of being schoolma'ams. Never was the truth of the old adage that a little learning is a dangerous thing so fully illustrated as by these imperfectly educated women; yet it is this half-awakened intelligence, struggling with problems that it is too ignorant to understand, misreading both the past and the present, drawing false meanings from history and philosophy, that is one of the menaces of our time.

Important, however, as is the relation of the negro woman to the white race, it is not so important as her relations to her own. Among her own people her position is one peculiar among the women of the world, and it is one full of cruel injustice and bitter suffering. No other woman among civilized people is so little protected, so little cherished, and evokes so little chivalry from the men of her race. All the hardships that other women endure she bears, and more. She loves, but no sense of loyalty, no convention of faithfulness, binds her lover to her. She may marry, but with no certainty of the tie being permanent. She bears children, but with oftener than not no husband's sympathy to cheer her, no husband's hand to even provide the food and clothing. When she toils, it is only too frequently to have her meager wage taken from her by a drunken brute.

There are, of course, negro men who are admirable husbands, but among the vast majority of them the responsibility of the marriage relationship as white people understand it does not exist. The wedding ceremony and the divorce decree are held in light esteem as ornaments that one may have, but that are not necessities by any means; and the average negro man manifests absolutely no sense of obligation about providing for his wife and children. That burden falls upon the woman. His wage, if he works, is generally spent upon his own pleasures and vices. On every Saturday afternoon throughout the South pathetic groups of these defrauded wives may be witnessed, waiting humbly with their empty baskets on the outskirts of the cotton-gin, or factory, or sawmill where their husbands work, trying to wheedle a little of their week's salary out of their lords and masters to feed the hungry mouths at home. Often the man does not work at all, but lives in a paradise of ease and luxury on the dainties his wife purloins from the pantry of the white people for whom she cooks. No other race in the world shows such a number of men supported by women as does the negro race. The answer to the question, how the vast idle male negro population in the South lives without work, finds its answer in the basket that the cooks invariably carry back and forth between their home and the kitchen in which they are employed.

As a general thing, the negro woman is of a tropical temperament, and loves madly and passionately. When roused to jealousy, she is a furious demon who not infrequently kills her rival or the lover who forsakes her. Often her love is as brief as it is stormy, but there are innumerable cases where she displays a dog-like devotion, and follows, year after year, the footsteps of the man who beats her, and mistreats her, and is faithless to her, and sometimes even brings another wife to live under the very rooftree that her own hard toil supports. For her children she has a fierce passion of maternity that seems to be purely animal, and that seldom goes beyond their childhood. When they are little, she indulges them blindly when she is in good humor, and beats them cruelly when she is angry; and once past their childhood her affection for them appears to be exhausted. She exhibits none of the brooding mother-love and anxiety which the white woman sends after her children as long as they live. Infanticide is not regarded as a crime among negroes, but it is so appallingly common that if the statistics could be obtained on this subject they would send a shudder through the world. The story of many negro midwives, who are veritable female Herods, is not a thing to be told.

The negro woman also occupies a unique position in this, that of all women she is the one who personally best illustrates the fallacy of the theory of free love and the abolition of all the conventions and laws that hedge about matrimony. She is literally "the woman who did" of Mr. Richard Grant White's dream.[3] All that the most advanced theorists who rail at the bondage of marriage advocate she does, and under ideal conditions. There is no public opinion to be defied, no society to turn the cold shoulder upon her. She loses no caste changing husbands as the whim seizes her, and no odium is attached to the possession of what she graphically and picturesquely described as a "bandanna family"—meaning thereby one in which each child is a different color.

Yet, with all of these advantages of freedom in securing a soul mate, and, if she makes a mistake in selecting the first time, in being able to seek an affinity to the third and fourth and hundredth time if she pleases, the negro woman is the most unanswerable refutation that the imagination could devise to those who believe that love should never be fettered. A forlorn and warning figure, forsaken and deserted, with her own burdens a hundredfold heavier because no man is bound to help her bear them, crushed under the weight of a motherhood that no fatherhood lightens, the negro woman stands at the gate of the garden of free-loveism, and cries out that it is a false paradise—that all of its fruit are apples of Sodom, and that nowhere else is a woman's sorrow so inescapable, and her lot so bitter, as in that mockery of freedom.

Such is the negro woman of to-day, the most unfortunate and sinned-against creature in all the world, the victim of heredity, of social conditions, of environment, the very sport and plaything of destiny, yet holding in her hands the fate of a race. There is something almost sardonically humorous in the thought of this woman, with the brain of a child and the passions of a woman, steeped in centuries of ignorance and savagery, and wrapped about with immemorial vices, playing with the die of fate.

Yet there she sits, unthinking, unknowing, with no desire save of the senses, no ambitions, no aspirations, and the most momentous problem of our day is how to rouse this lethargic giantess to a sense of her responsibilities. In the home all the real progress of a people must begin. You cannot raise a race above its motherhood. Until that is done, until the childhood of the little negro girl is safeguarded, until the negro woman is inspired with ideals of virtue, until the mother teaches the child at her knee the precepts of right and honest living, there can be no real uplift for the negro race, and no solving of the race problem.

The mission of the white woman of this country is to the black woman. If ever there was a God given and appointed task set to the womanhood of any people, it is to the women of America to take these lowly sisters by the hand and lift them out of the pit into which they have fallen. Humanity pleads for it, Christianity prays for it, the very salvation of the country demands it, for be assured unless we succor these Hagars who have been thrust out into the desert of their own ignorance and superstition and sin, they will raise up Ishmaels whose hands shall be against our sons forever.

"Bicycle Number"

This cover from *Judge* appeared shortly after the United States declared war with Spain on April 20, 1898. By the end of the war, the United States had annexed the Hawaiian Islands, gained control of the Panamanian isthmus, and had acquired Guam, Puerto Rico, and the Philippines, while making Cuba a virtual protectorate. In the pages of *Judge*, the bicycle became a symbol of both the New Woman and imperialist conquest. In the April 30, 1898, issue, the magazine declared: "The JUDGE celebrates the bicycle. It has gone into all lands and conquered all peoples. Of the builders of it their name is legion: and of the riders behold they are an innumerable host. It brings health. It gives women and children a freedom of action and an independence they never had before." In the same issue, President McKinley appears riding a motorized three-wheeled canon, "a new ball-bearing" wheel, to destroy the bottle-sucking, bicycle-riding Spaniard. In the September 17, 1898, issue, Victor Gillam drew a free-spirited Uncle Sam, who, having left his Monroe Doctrine horse waiting in the background, now enjoys a speedy bicycle with Eastern and Western Hemisphere globes as wheels. The New Woman on the bicycle appears ready for the fight: "If the Women must fight let us suggest a few bicycle regiments; every wheel to belong to a tandem with a man at the rear to do the propelling, while the women operate the destruction." At the same time, the Spaniards' mistreatment of Cuban civilians, many of whom had been forced to relocate to filthy, disease-ridden camps, and in particular the Spaniards' affronts to the dignity of Cuban women, became a rallying cry in American papers. On the same page, *Judge* declares that this is "a War on Women." As historian Kristin Hoganson notes, "those who fretted about assertive New Women were captivated by reports that Cuban women, 'the most feminine and simple women in the world,' spent their time worshiping their husbands rather than meddling in men's affairs."[1]

For more information about *Judge*, see the introduction to "The New-Woman Santa Claus" earlier in part I.

Judge, Apr. 30, 1898, cover.

"Ise Gwine ter Give You Gals What Straddle"

Edward Kemble

Compared with the humor magazines *Puck* and *Judge*, which were larger, color filled, and raucous, John Ames Mitchell's *Life* offered Americans a more genteel chuckle. Despite a shaky beginning in 1883, Mitchell's *Life* became "the most influential cartoon and literary humor magazine of its time," largely because of the popularity of its black-and-white illustrations by Charles Dana Gibson and other prominent artists. Yet its initial commitment to black-and-white line drawings, rather than the new trend of color, coupled with its insistence on charging the same ten-cent price as its rivals, led many to wonder about the new magazine's viability. Contributor Edward W. Kemble recalled in 1930 that *Life*'s "appearance caused the know-it-alls to stick their tongues in their cheeks and, holding the small publication at arm's length, exclaim, 'Ten cents for that? What gall!'" Instead of using woodblock engravings, Mitchell decided to reproduce line drawings directly using a zinc etching process, and so it was as a "picture paper" that *Life* gained its success. By the 1890s, halftones and wash drawings were common. Having received acclaim for his illustrations of Mark Twain's *The Adventures of Huckleberry Finn* (1884), Kemble became America's foremost racist caricaturist of black Americans and a frequent contributor to *Life*. Charles Dana Gibson sold his first drawing to the magazine in 1886, and the statuesque Gibson Girl appeared regularly in its pages shortly thereafter. Kemble's images, meanwhile, often satirized black women as failed imitators of the Gibson Girl. Although the Gibson Girl's vanity was to be indulged, Kemble's black mammies primping before the mirror prompted knowing derision. By the time John Kendrick Bangs arrived at

---

Life, Sept. 8, 1899, 255.

the magazine as literary editor in 1884, *Life* was beginning to flourish. Around the time that Bangs resigned in 1888, Edward S. Martin started writing editorials and other pieces for the magazine, which, according to Mitchell, had a "civilizing influence" on the publication. Corruption, populists, monopolies, immigrants, Jews, imperialism, Booker T. Washington, and women's suffrage were all subjects for *Life*'s satire. By 1890, circulation had reached a profitable 50,000. By 1902, circulation exceeded 65,000.[1]

" 'Ise Gwine ter Give You Gals What Straddle dem Wheels a Good Talkin' to at Nex' Sunday's Meetin.' 'Indeed! What you call it, de Sermon on de Mount?' "

"St. Valentine's Number"

Charles Dana Gibson

Tall, distant, elegant, and white, with a pert nose, voluminous upswept hair, corseted waist, and large bust, the Gibson Girl, as rendered by Charles Dana Gibson in his pen-and-ink drawings of the American girl, offered a popular version of the New Woman that both sanctioned and undermined women's desires for progressive sociopolitical change and personal freedom at the turn of the century. Although some of Gibson's images pointedly depict the need for progressive reform, he did not endorse women's political organizing. Indeed, he said that "in a mass of women, you lose entirely the irresistible appeal of the individual." Gibson portrayed women who engaged in public politics as humorless, severe, and portly, but by presenting women as interacting with men in an unchaperoned environment or as engaging in physical activity, he promoted a measure of women's personal independence and sexual freedom, which many women used to sanction their own reform efforts. His series *The Education of Mr. Pipp* (1899), in which a diminutive Mr. Pipp is dragged about Europe's clothiers and jewelers by his two statuesque Gibson Girl daughters, proved widely popular. In 1899 Gibson was elected to the American Institute of Arts and Letters and in 1902 to the Society of Illustrators. As it turned out, the period between 1900 to 1905 was arguably his most successful.[1]

Life, Feb. 5, 1903, cover.

VOLUME XLI.   NEW YORK, FEBRUARY 5, 1903.   NUMBER 1058.

Entered at the New York Post Office as Second-Class Mail Matter.
Copyright, 1902, by LIFE PUBLISHING COMPANY.

"The Flapper"

H. L. Mencken

Born in Baltimore, Maryland, Henry Louis Mencken (1880–1956) became known as the Great Iconoclast for his sardonic journalism and literary criticism. In one of his many book reviews for the *Smart Set*, which he began co-editing with George Jean Nathan in 1914, Mencken described himself as "a mocker of all sweet and lovely things, a professional snickerer, a saucy fellow by trade." Commuting from Baltimore to "Sodom and Gomorrah" twice a month, Mencken read manuscript submissions first and then passed along to Nathan those that made "as few compromises to public taste as possible." Prohibition was a prime target for Mencken, but he evinced more support for women's suffrage and for women's desire for greater autonomy. In 1912, he remarked, "Who the deuce wants to be a lady? Certainly no intelligent and healthy woman in these bouncing times! The essential thing about a lady is the public assumption that she has neither legs nor brains. . . . If she bumps her shins and lets loose with a *damn*, then, the argument runs, she ceases to be lady: for it is the theory of civilization that (*a*) a lady doesn't know the word and (*b*) that she has no shins." In 1918, he published the successful and generally sympathetic collection of essays about American sexual politics, *In Defense of Women*.[1]

Marketed to a young, hip, and educated elite, the *Smart Set* was begun in 1900 as a highbrow risqué humor magazine. A typical issue sold for twenty-five cents and contained 160 pages, which generally included a play, short stories, poems, an essay, and vignettes. During its first decade, for example, humor pieces featured Alfred Damon Runyon satirizing the New Woman or the mishaps of "country bumpkins." The magazine gradually declined after 1905, the year it reached its peak circulation of 165,000. When Willard Huntington Wright became editor in

---

Smart Set, Feb. 1915.

1913, he engaged some of the best European and American writers to write for the magazine. D. H. Lawrence, W. B. Yeats, August Strindberg, Theodore Dreiser, and Sarah Teasdale all appeared in its pages, earning the magazine critical acclaim if not financial success.[2]

The American language, curiously enough, has no name for her. In German she is *der Backfisch*, in French she is *l'Ingénue*, in English she is the Flapper. But in American, as I say, she is nameless, for Chicken will never, never do. Her mother, at her age, was a Young Miss; her grandmother was a Young Female. But she herself is no Young Miss, no Young Female. Oh, dear, no! . . .

Observe, then, this nameless one, this American Flapper. Her skirts have just reached her very trim and pretty ankles; her hair, newly coiled upon her skull, has just exposed the ravishing whiteness of her neck. A charming creature! Graceful, vivacious, healthy, appetizing. It is a delight to see her bite into a chocolate with her pearly teeth. There is music in her laugh. There is poetry in her drive at tennis. She is an enchantment through the plate glass of a limousine. Youth is hers, and hope, and romance, and—

Well, well, let us be exact: let us not say innocence. This Flapper, to tell the truth, is far, far, far from a simpleton. An Ingénue to the Gaul, she is actually as devoid of ingenuousness as a newspaper reporter, a bartender, or a midwife. The age she lives in is one of knowledge. She herself is educated. She is privy to dark secrets. The world bears to her no aspect of mystery. She has been taught how to take care of herself.

For example, she has a clear and detailed understanding of all the tricks of white slave traders, and knows how to circumvent them. She is on the lookout for them in matinée lobbies and railroad stations—benevolent-looking old women who pretend to be ill, plausible young men who begin business with "Beg pardon," bogus country girls who cry because their mythical brothers have failed to meet them. She has a keen eye for hypodermic needles, chloroform masks, closed carriages. She has seen all these sinister machines of the devil in operation on the screen. She has read about them in the great works of Elizabeth Robins, Clifford G. Roe, and Reginald Wright Kauffman.[3] She has followed the war upon them in the newspapers.

Life, indeed, is almost empty of surprises, mysteries, horrors to this Flapper of 1915. She knows the exact percentage of lunatics among the children of drunkards. She has learned, from *McClure's Magazine*, the purpose and technique of the Twilight Sleep.[4] She has been converted, by Edward W. Bok, to the gospel of sex hygiene.[5] She knows exactly what the Wassermann reaction is,[6] and has made up her mind that she will never marry a man who can't show an unmistakable negative. She knows the etiology of ophthalmia neatorum.[7] She has read Christobel [*sic*] Pankhurst and Ellen Key,[8] and is inclined to think that there must be something in this new doctrine of free motherhood. She is opposed to the double standard of morality, and favors a law prohibiting it. . . .

This Flapper has forgotten how to simper; she seldom blushes; it is impossible to shock her. She saw "Damaged Goods" without batting an eye, and went away wondering what the row over it was all about.[9] The police of her city having prohibited

"Mrs. Warren's Profession,"[10] she read it one rainy Sunday afternoon, and found it a mass of platitudes. She has heard "Salomé" and prefers it to "Il Trovatore." She has read "Trilby," "Three Weeks," and "My Little Sister,"[11] and thinks them all pretty dull. . . .

As I have said, a charming young creature. There is something trim and trig and confident about her. She is easy in her manners. She bears herself with dignity in all societies. She is graceful, rosy, healthy, appetizing. It is a delight to see her sink her pearly teeth into a chocolate, a macaroon, even a potato. There is music in her laugh. She is youth, she is hope, she is romance—she is wisdom!

"The New Negro Woman"

When in November 1917 A. Philip Randolph and Chandler Owen began the *Messenger*, they marketed it as "the Only Radical Negro Magazine in America." As a critic of World War I and champion of socialism in the wake of the Russian Revolution, the magazine faced harassment and surveillance throughout more than half of its ten-year history. Although Randolph and Owen criticized W.E.B. Du Bois, T. Thomas Fortune, and Fred R. Moore (of the *New York Age*) as economically and politically conservative members of the "Old Crowd," they promoted many other writers of the Harlem Renaissance—including Claude McKay, Langston Hughes, and Wallace Thurman—as representatives of the "New Crowd." The New Crowd, according to the *Messenger*, "would have no armistice with lynch-law; no truce with jim-crowism, and disfranchisement; no peace until the Negro receives complete social, economic and political justice." Members of the New Crowd formed alliances with white radical groups such as the International Workers of the World (IWW), socialists, and the Non-Partisan League to build a new society—a society of equals, without class, race, caste, or religious distinctions. In 1920, Randolph and Owen founded the Friends of Negro Freedom, a group initially formed to promote civil rights and to organize black workers. By 1922 the Friends of Negro Freedom and the *Messenger* editors opposed Marcus Garvey vehemently, and in January 1923 the editors urged the U.S. Department of Justice to prosecute him as a "menace to harmonious race relationships." The paper sold for fifteen cents in 1918, and in 1919, during the height of the red scare, the *Messenger*'s circulation peaked at 26,000. By 1923, however, the magazine was struggling—its circulation was down to roughly 5,000 a month—and when Chandler Owen left the magazine to become managing editor of Chicago's *Bee*, much of its radical fervor diminished. Like the *Chicago Defender*, it circulated well beyond New York to all the major northern and midwestern cities to which blacks migrated and claimed that two-thirds of its readers were black and

Editorial, *Messenger*, July 1923, 757.

one-third white (Mary White Ovington, Clarence Darrow, and Carl Van Vechten were all subscribers at one time). The paper ceased publication in 1928 due to lack of funds.[1]

Yes, she has arrived. Like her white sister, she is the product of profound and vital changes in our economic mechanism, wrought mainly by the World War and its aftermath. Along the entire gamut of social, economic, and political attitudes, the New Negro Woman has effected a revolutionary orientation. In politics, business and labor, in the professions, church and education, in science, art and literature, the New Negro Woman, with her head erect and spirit undaunted is resolutely marching forward, ever conscious of her historic and noble mission of doing her bit toward the liberation of her people in particular and the human race in general. Upon her shoulders rests the big task to create and keep alive, in the breast of black men, a holy and consuming passion to break with the slave traditions of the past; to spurn and overcome the fatal, insidious inferiority complex of the present, which, like Banquo's Ghost, bobs up ever and anon, to arrest the progress of the New Negro Manhood Movement; and to fight with increasing vigor, with dauntless courage, unrelenting zeal and intelligent vision for the attainment of the stature of a *full man*, a free race and a new world.

"A Bit of Life"

Russell

In 1879, African American journalists T. Thomas Fortune and Walter Sampson came to New York and invested in George Parker's struggling tabloid the *Rumor*. Fortune immediately called for a name change to the *Globe*, which subsequently became the *Freeman*, and then the *New York Age* in 1887. For his long career in journalism, including his work at the *Age*, Fortune became known as the "dean of Negro journalists." Although overall the *New York Age*, with influential backing by Booker T. Washington, represented a "moderate" view of African American opinion, it also spoke out vigorously against racism, disenfranchisement, and violence perpetrated against black Americans. After a white mob destroyed her newspaper's offices in Memphis, Tennessee, in 1892, Ida B. Wells went to New York, where Fortune hired her to cover lynchings and black life in the South. In 1907 the *New York Age* publishing company was incorporated, with Fortune as president, Jerome B. Peterson as secretary treasurer, and Fred R. Moore as editor. Although Booker T. Washington held the majority of stock in the company until his death in 1915, his covert influence was not always directly apparent. From 1914 until 1923, James Weldon Johnson, an influential Harlem Renaissance writer and the first African American head of the NAACP, became the leading voice in the newspaper by contributing editorials focusing on racial prejudice and violence, race pride, methods of combating white oppression, and problems of interest to the black community. An adamant supporter of the women's suffrage movement, Johnson maintained that "colored women will be less easily intimidated and kept out of voting than the colored men have been." In 1920, he defended the New Woman against charges that by smoking she was "introducing new vice" and two years later described her as one "who has achieved her economic independence and

---

New York Age, Dec. 20, 1919, 5.

who is ready to compete with men in constructive and creative work." Fearing the
paper's outspoken criticism of racial discrimination and violence, the federal
government monitored its content during World War I. Several months before
the cartoon strip "A Bit of Life" appeared, as members of Congress debated the
suffrage amendment, the paper cautioned "Colored Suffragists and members of
colored women's clubs to be actively on the watch" for "substitute resolutions" to
the amendment that would give white women the vote while denying it to women
of color. In addition to news coverage, the paper featured sports news, reviews of
black theatrical performances, advice columns, and cartoons. In 1920 it charged
five cents and declared on its masthead that it was "The Home Paper/The
National Negro Weekly."[1]

PANEL 1: Boys! The New Woman is too **domineering, intolerable** and
          etc. etc.
PANEL 2: I protest against surrendering our rights and privileges.
PANEL 3: As men, we must organize to protect our rights.
PANEL 4: Yes, dear??
          Josephus! Stop that noise this instant!
PANEL 5: What is it a woman can't do?

PART II

Women's Suffrage and Political Participation

"The New Woman of the New South"

Josephine K. Henry

Kentucky-born Josephine Kirby Williamson Henry (1846–1928) seized the new women's rights discourse to demonstrate that southern women wanted the vote. By 1890 Kentucky had still not granted married women the right to own or inherit property, make a will, or receive wages, making them, according to Henry, virtual nonentities.[1] Working in conjunction with the Kentucky Equal Rights Association, Henry spoke eloquently in support of the "Husband and Wife Bill," which gave married woman "equality with the married man in the possession and control of property." Governor John Young Brown signed the bill into law on March 15, 1894.[2] In 1890, Henry became the first woman in Kentucky to run for state office when she served as the Prohibition Party candidate for clerk of the Kentucky Court of Appeals. In 1895, Henry worked alongside Elizabeth Cady Stanton, as a member of the revising committee, on what would become the *Woman's Bible*.[3]

Henry's "New Woman of the New South" was published by the *Arena*, a monthly magazine founded by Benjamin Orange Flower in Boston in 1889. The *Arena* advocated a wide range of economic, political, and social reforms, many of them related to women, including equal suffrage, dress reform (criticism of tight corsets and long skirts), and a higher "age of consent." Women played prominent roles in editing, writing, and determining the content of *Arena*. To raise circulation, which was about 24,000 in 1895, the magazine lowered its annual subscription rate from five dollars to three that year.[4]

Arena 11 (1895): 353–362.

It is not the purpose of the writer to discuss in this paper woman's right to the ballot or the good or evil results to accrue from her enfranchisement. To argue the question of right is not admissible at this stage of the issue. To forecast results would afford no logical ground to stand on. The article will, therefore, be confined to the limitation of facts and their tendencies as they appear to a Southern woman.

The idea seems to be abroad that Southern women do not desire the ballot. Considering the powerful influences which operate to suppress an open manifestation of opinion among Southern women on this question, as in fact on many others, it is easy to see how those who have given the subject no thought are led to accept such an impression as correct. The true index of existing facts is not always found upon the surface of things. We must probe a little if we would know the truth and its relation to cause and effect. Woman in the South is to such an extent the slave of her environment that it is questionable whether she has any clearly outlined opinion, exclusively her own, on any subject. Chivalry has allotted her sphere, and her soul has been so pressed by social and ecclesiastical rigidity that the average woman dares not transgress the limits. This is an appalling condition of the human mind, and fully accounts for the tendency of women as a mass to crouch under the shelter of silence. But every stronghold of conservatism will fall in line with advancing civilization when it must. The struggle will be fierce. "Broad ideas are hated by partial ideas. This, in fact, is the struggle of progress."

Among our representative women there is a class too ethereal to be troubled with affairs, whose mental lethargy is only disturbed by dreams of *ante-bellum* family legends, and whose thought-power is confined to devising ways and means for retaining their social prestige. With them "the virtue in most request is conformity." They love "names and customs," but shrink from "realities and creators."

Then there is another and quite different class, composed of those who stand on higher intellectual ground, who realize their potentialities, and who have the courage to demand a field of thought and action commensurate with their aspirations. These are the New Women of the New South. To them the drowsy civilization of the age appeals for some invigorating incentive to higher aims and grander achievements. They believe with Emerson that "all have equal rights in virtue of being identical in nature." They realize that liberty regards no sex, and justice bows before no idol. . . .

It may be said of the average woman of the South that she is satisfied with her condition. She loves her church and believes in her preacher. She is Pauline in her ideas and therefore loves the music of her chains. But with all this there is pervading this class a strong under-current of sentiment in the direction of larger liberty. With the downward trend of men, socially and politically, confronting them, and their growing sons and daughters around them, they are beginning to question the wisdom of existing customs. To the writer the widening of Southern women's views is one of the most portentous and vital facts in the history of the South. "Events are more concise but tendencies constitute real history."

One of the first noticeable tendencies is what might be termed the reign of woman club life. Literature has been exhausted and art despoiled to find names and devices suitable to the taste and purposes of the women who compose the membership of these clubs. The framing of constitutions and by-laws, election of officers, discussions on ways and means and all the parliamentary usages which cleverness can bring to the aid of mimicry, go to make up this parody on the exercise of individual liberty. It is not difficult to recognize in these clubs the primary schools which lead to the university of politics.

Another and higher department in which the minds and hearts of advanced Southern women are earnestly enlisted is the investigation and revision of statutory law, regarding its application to the sexes alike. They find in the established codes enacted by men alone, for men alone, a most horrible crucifixion of justice. They see themselves taxed without their consent, their property often confiscated for base uses, their sex arraigned before judges and juries composed of men alone. They see in the barbarous "age of consent" laws young girls exposed to the animal lusts of brutes in human form awaiting their prey under the law's protection. They find all along the avenues of urban life dens of drunkenness and crime, with wide-open doors ready to receive the bodies and souls of their loved ones, and when they ask by what right these modern Gehennas exist, they are told that it is by a right secured from the same source that denies to woman the power to destroy them. They are excluded from town and city councils, from the higher state institutions of learning, and from boards of education of our public schools, all of which they are taxed to support.

Southern women have in the past five years resorted in many states to their constitutional right of petition upon the questions of property rights, "age of consent," and the licensed liquor laws. They have pleaded for admission into state universities, and asked for a division of state funds to establish industrial or reform schools for girls, in states which provide such schools for boys alone. They have asked that women be placed on boards of all public institutions for the benefit of both sexes, and in many cases sought and obtained the county superintendency of public schools. These departures from the line of established customs show that the apparent contentment with present conditions is only on the surface, and that there is a half realized idea among our women that in our social and political organism there is something out of gear.

Rising above the terrorism of popular ridicule, and fortified by the intensity of their convictions, a few leading women in the states of Virginia, South Carolina and Kentucky, directly descended from the founders of the republic, have individually petitioned their legislatures, asking that a power be created to which they can apply and receive their enfranchisement papers, pleading for the restoration of an inalienable right and at the same time testing the honesty of that spirit of chivalry which places much emphasis on the willingness to grant the franchise when women want it. This initiative move of these fearless women marks a crisis in Southern thought. It gave an impulse in a new direction to the active minds of both sexes.

Their petitions were disregarded by the majority, and ridiculed by some, but the thought force which they imparted is irresistible. Their heroism will prove an inspiration to timid souls illumined by visions of a new creation for woman. The monochord of political liberty for women of the South has been touched by the finger of manifest destiny, and no power on earth can silence its refrain. This forecast of opinion may and doubtless will be received with a smile of derision by some, but the laws which govern society are as fixed as the laws of the material world. The light of Neptune had not reached the lenses of Leverrier when he first announced its existence in space, but the planet was there. "Immense and continued impulsions pushing together govern human facts, and lead them all within a given time to the logical state, that is to say, to equilibrium, or in other words, to equity."

The writer of this article has in her possession the most convincing evidence of these immense and continued forces that are driving onward to that logical state, a completely rounded civilization, grounded on equity. She has received thousands of letters from the foremost and best women in the South, and the number increases each day, expressive of their deep solicitude for the success of the one cause that gives promise of release from social and political incarceration. Back of these facts stand in evidence the constitutional conventions of Mississippi and Kentucky, and the legislatures of South Carolina and Arkansas. Whenever the question of woman suffrage was touched by those bodies it met the approval and elicited the applause of thoughtful and intelligent women throughout the entire South.

As a unit of value in summarizing evidence of existing conditions and tendencies, there is not, nor could there be a fact more potent than the recent congressional contest in the Ashland District of Kentucky. The eyes of the world watched this contest with intense interest. The women of Kentucky forced the moral issue in American politics, and hence followed a political struggle the intensity of which stands unequalled in the history of politics. The very atmosphere seemed to darken under the tension of individual hate and partisan rancor. Woman's softening influence was demanded and she responded with all the finer impulses of her nature strained to the highest point. She pushed her way to the front, and with her natural tact and matchless skill in using her limited power to the best advantage, she gave to the world a victory which her enfranchised ally would have lost without her aid.

There is nothing in history so pathetic as woman's struggle for freedom. Men of the Old South, armed with all the implements of war, and supplied with the wealth of states, fought for empire based on slavery, and lost. The women of the New South, armed with clear-cut, unanswerable argument alone, are struggling for liberty based on justice, and will win. The failure of the former left our section in ruin and despair; the triumph of the latter will bring progress and hope. Woman's political coronation depends upon herself. The average woman must be educated in the new school, and man must become possessed by new ideas. "The key to every man is his thought; sturdy and defying though he look, he has a helm which he obeys, which is the idea after which all his facts are classified. He can only be reformed by showing him a new idea which commands his own." The women of the South are impressing men with new ideas, and hence that ancient spirit of protection which has so long retarded human progress by dispossessing woman of her share of the common heritage, is losing its force as an element in our civilization.

In attestation of existing suffrage sentiment in the South I append the following extracts from letters from representative women in the different states, giving their opinions on the subject. These women are of the highest intelligence and social standing, among them being many lineal descendants of the signers of the Declaration of Independence and the patriots of 1776, social leaders, noted house-wives, literary women, teachers and taxpayers.

[Henry now lists a series of testimonials from women in various southern states as to why they want the vote.]

MEMPHIS, TENNESSEE

We, the undersigned women of Tennessee *do* and *should* want the ballot,—

1. Because, being twenty-one years old, we object to being classed with *minors,*
2. Being American born, and loyal to her institutions, we protest, against being made perpetual *aliens.*
3. Costing the treasuries of our respective counties nothing, we protest against acknowledging the *male pauper* of Tennessee as our political superior.
4. Being obedient to law, we protest against the law that classes us with the *unpardoned criminal,* and makes the pardoned criminal and the ex-convict our political superiors.
5. Being sane, we object to being classed with the *lunatic.*
6. Possessing an average amount of intelligence, we protest against classification with the *idiot.*
7. We taxpayers claim the right to representation.
8. We married women want to own our own clothes.
9. We married bread winners want our own earnings.
10. We mothers want an equal partnership in our children.
11. We educated women want the power to offset the illiterate vote of our state.

Lide Meriwether, *President Tennessee W.C.T.U. and W.S.A.*

[A list of members of the Memphis Equal Suffrage Club next appears, followed by additional testimonials by women from other southern states, in support of women's suffrage.]

"Foibles of the New Woman"

Ella W. Winston

In 1886 Isaac Leopold Rice organized the Forum Publishing Company in New York and hired Lorettus Sutton Metcalf to act as editor. Under Metcalf, the *Forum* became recognized for its meticulous editing and its editorial policy, which emphasized the importance of including the opinions of experts on the most timely issues of the day. The monthly magazine offered both sides of controversial political, social, religious, scientific, and educational topics, and varied its tone by offering occasional lighter pieces. University libraries appreciated the *Forum*'s balanced analysis of reform topics—including feminism, divorce, immigration, prisons, socialism, and later birth control—and often included it in their collections. In 1891 Metcalf resigned, and Walter Hines Page took over. Recalling Page's period of editorship, Henry Holt, a former contributor to the *Forum*, remarked that Page was "the best editor that, up to that time, America had had." After Page left the *Forum* to edit the *Atlantic Monthly*, Alfred Ernest Keet became editor until 1897. By 1907, the five-dollar magazine's circulation had fallen to around 10,000 to 15,000.[1]

Little is known about Ella W. Winston. She was born in Wisconsin around 1851 to Canadian immigrant parents, was married prior to November 1894, and by 1910 was living with her family in New Mexico. Shortly before writing "Foibles of the New Woman," she wrote an article opposing the Woman's Christian Temperance Union for the liberal *American Journal of Politics* and one against women's suffrage for the *American Magazine of Civics*.

When woman revolts against her normal functions and sphere of action, desiring instead to usurp man's prerogatives, she entails upon herself the inevitable penalty of

---

Forum, Apr. 1896, 186–192.

such irregular conduct, and, while losing the womanliness which she apparently scorns, fails to attain the manliness for which she strives. But, unmindful of the frowns of her observers, she is unto herself a perpetual delight, calling herself and her kind by the epithets "new," "awakened," and "superior," and speaking disdainfully of women who differ from her in what, to her judgment, is the all-important question of life— "Shall women vote or not?" To enumerate her foibles is a dangerous task, for what she asserts to-day she will deny to-morrow. She is a stranger to logic, and when consistency was given to mortals the New Woman was conspicuously absent. Her egotism is boundless. She boasts that she has discovered herself, and says it is the greatest discovery of the century. She has christened herself the "new," but when her opponent speaks of her by that name she replies with characteristic contrariety that the New Woman, like the sea-serpent, is largely an imaginary creature. Nevertheless, in the next sentence, she will refer to herself by her favorite cognomen. She has made many strange statements, and one question she often asks is, "What has changed woman's outlook so that she now desires that of which her grandmother did not dream?"

Within the past forty years woman has demanded of man much that he has graciously granted her. She wanted equality with him, and it has been given her in all things for which she is fitted and which will not lower the high standard of womanhood that he desires for her. This she accepts without relinquishing any of the chivalrous attentions which man always bestows upon her. The New Woman tells us that "an ounce of justice is of more value to woman than a ton of chivalry." But, when she obtains her "ounce of justice," she apparently still makes rigorous demands that her "ton of chivalry" be not omitted. Woman asked to work by man's side and on his level; and to-day she has the chance of so doing. The fields of knowledge and opportunity have been opened to her; and she still "desires that of which her grandmother did not dream," because, like an over-indulged child, so long as she is denied one privilege, that privilege she desires above all others. She has decided that without the ballot she can do nothing, for, in her vocabulary, ballot is synonymous with power.

The New Woman is oftentimes the victim of strange hallucinations. She persists in calling herself a "slave," despite her high position and great opportunities; and she maintains that, because she cannot vote, she is classed with lunatics and idiots,— until those who are weary of hearing her constant iterations of these themes feel that, if the classification were true, it might not be unjust. Still, it has not been clearly shown that withholding the ballot from woman, in common with lunatics and idiots, necessarily makes her one. Women and cripples are exempt from working on roads; does it follow that all women are cripples? Is a woman a bird because she walks on two legs? This hackneyed cry about lunatics and idiots, which has been uttered by nearly all writers and speakers favoring woman suffrage, appeals to prejudice rather than intelligence. If the would-be female politicians—ignoring woman's great opportunities, especial privileges, and the silent testimony of countless happy wives,—choose to consider themselves "slaves," and to announce whenever they speak that they are classed with lunatics and idiots because they are denied the ballot, they are certainly entitled to all the enjoyment they can get out of the delusion. Sensible people know that such statements are false.

The New Woman says that a "mother's prerogative ends at the garden gate"; but common sense replies that no mother's prerogative ends there. A mother's prerogative is to govern and direct her child; and there is no child that does not carry through life his or her mother's influence. Let that influence be good or bad, it is always present. Any mother can make, if she will, her power over her child "stronger than the seas of earth, and purer than the air of heaven"; and she needs no especial legislative act to accomplish her work. If woman does not make the laws, she trains and educates those who do, and thus is indirectly responsible for all legislation.

The plea which these women make, that they need the ballot for the protection of their homes, is self-contradictory. Has the New Woman never heard that "to teach early is to engrave on marble"? If she would devote some of the time in which she struggles to obtain the ballot to rational reflection on the influence a woman has over the pre-natal life of a child, and would then consider what a mother may do with a plastic human life,—say during the first seven years of its existence and before it goes out to be contaminated by the evil influences of the world,—she would then find that ballots are not what women need for the protection of their homes. But the faculty of logically reasoning from cause to effect has never been characteristic of the New Woman.

She laments because government is deprived, by lack of equal suffrage, of the "keen moral sense that is native to women as a class." Since all the people in the world are born of women and trained by women, it is difficult to see how government, or anything else, lacks woman's "keen moral sense." Can women make no use of their moral sense without the ballot?

It is a chronic grievance with the New Woman that she is taxed without representation. She scorns to be represented by the sons she has reared, or by the men who come under her immediate influence. These she pronounces unworthy and considers incapable of doing her justice. But when she is told that, if women vote, they should also bear the burdens of war in case of necessity, she replies with her usual inconsistency, "She who bears soldiers need not bear arms." She has not the aversion to being represented by men on the field of battle that she has to being represented by them in legislative halls and at the ballot-box. She greatly deprecates man's selfishness and tyranny, as exhibited in human history. But she has come vaunting into the arena with "woman's clubs" and "conventions" and "leagues" and "tribunes" and "signals." If a periodical be not wholly devoted to women, they demand that it must at least have its "woman's column" wherein they may chronicle the most insignificant acts of the sex.

The New Woman tells us that the present century is her own; and, indeed, she approaches the truth in this instance. She has promised us a "Woman's Bible," and she has shown that even the Infinite Father does not escape her jealousy, for she has discovered that we should pray to a "Heavenly Mother" as well as to a Heavenly Father. She informs us that the Pilgrim Fathers are no more, and adds, "There stepped on Plymouth Rock, on the bleak shores of New England, thirty-two women accompanied by sixty-nine men and children." At expositions she must have a "woman's building," wherein she may glorify the work of her brain and hand. No work done by man can be placed beside hers for examination or competition. Surely she furnishes a noteworthy example of modesty and self-abnegation for the benefit of the tyrant man!

An illustration of the New Woman's fallacious judgment is shown by her belief that all opponents of equal suffrage are controlled by brewers and liquor dealers. "Sold to the liquor interest" is the cry she always utters when she detects a note of opposition. Now, it is entirely probable that some may object to the extension of the franchise to women and, at the same time, lead thoroughly temperate lives and work for the promotion of temperance. The word temperance means more than total abstinence from intoxicating drinks, and the New Woman has not yet proved that a vote by a woman means a vote for temperance principles.

"Woman's vote will purify politics." This is her favorite cry. Not long since a prominent equal-suffrage lecturer, while earnestly setting forth this claim, and enlarging on the shameless manner in which men conduct elections, declared that woman's chaste and refined influence was the only thing that could change the present undesirable condition of affairs. She was not ashamed, however, to relate, before the close of her lecture, that, a short time previous, her sister had induced the family's hired man to vote for a certain measure by presenting him, on the eve of election, with a half-dozen new shirts, made by her own hands. The absurdity of this incident reached a climax when it was noticed that, in a large audience of women, few saw anything wrong in female bribery. The fair speaker omitted to inform her audience whether or not this was to be the prevailing mode of political purification, when one half of the burdens of state rest on female shoulders. But, as women never lack expedients, some purifying process, less laborious than shirt-making, may soon be devised. . . .

The New Woman has a mania for reform movements. No sooner does she descry an evil than she immediately moves against it with some sort of an organized force. This is very noble of her,—if she have no other duties to perform. It would be more gratifying if her organizations met with greater success; but alas! her efforts, mighty as they are, usually represent just so much valuable time wasted. The evils remain, and continue to increase. She disdains to inquire into the cause of her numerous failures, and moves serenely on bent upon reforming everything she imagines to be wrong. When she gets the ballot all will be well with the world, and for that day she works and waits. But if the New Woman or any other woman neglects private duties for public works, her reform efforts are not noble, but extremely unworthy of her; for the "duty which lies nearest" is still the most sacred of duties. Possibly the many *Mrs. Jellybys* of the present day and the undue interest in "Borrioboola-gha" may have something to do with so much being wrong in the average home and with the average individual.[2] When we read of women assembling together, parading streets, and entering saloons to create, as they say, "a public sentiment for temperance," it is but natural to ask, What are the children of such mothers doing in the meantime? And it will not be strange if many of them become drunkards for the coming generation of reformers to struggle with. The New Woman refuses to believe that duty, like charity, begins at home, and cannot see that the most effectual way to keep clean is not to allow dirt to accumulate.

The New Woman professes to believe that all women are good and will use their influence for noble ends,—when they are allowed the right of suffrage. This theory is extremely pleasant, if it were only demonstrable; but here, as elsewhere, it is folly to ignore the incontrovertible facts. Woman cannot shirk her responsibility for the sins of the earth. It is easy for her to say that men are bad; that, as a class, they are worse than women. But who trained these bad men? Was it not woman? Herein lies the inconsistency of women—striving for a chance to do good when the opportunity is inherently theirs. It is only when they have neglected to train the saplings aright that the trees are misshapen.

It was the New Woman's earliest, and is her latest, foible that woman is superior to man. Perhaps she is. But the question is not one of superiority or inferiority. There is at bottom of all this talk about women nature's inexorable law. Man is man and woman is woman. That was the order of creation and it must so remain. It is idle to compare the sexes in similar things. It is a question of difference, and the "happiness and perfection of both depend on each asking and receiving from the other what the other only can give."

> For woman is not undevelopt man,
> But diverse: could we make her as the man,
> Sweet Love were slain: his dearest bond is this,
> Not like to like, but like in difference.

Sentimental and slavish as this may sound to many ears, it is as true as any of the unchanging laws governing the universe, and is the Creator's design for the reproduction and maintenance of the race.

"In the Public Eye"

In 1889 Frank A. Munsey began the periodical that would become the leader in low-cost, high-profit American monthlies. By 1893 he charged ten cents for *Munsey's Magazine*, which included extensive advertisements, heavily illustrated articles on famous public figures and performers, as well as serial fiction and poetry. Borrowing an eye-catcher from lowbrow entertainment, he also initially included halftone images of semi-nude women. Munsey repeatedly offered his readers stories of success obtained through a Horatio Alger–like work ethic. Although he was not considered a progressive reformer, Munsey published a number of stories and articles implicitly endorsing many of the changes associated with the New Woman. Circulation was at 700,000 in 1897, making *Munsey's Magazine* the leader in circulation after *Ladies' Home Journal*. Advertising revenue totaled between $25,000 and $35,000 a month.[1]

Mary Elizabeth Lease (1853–1933), renowned for urging economically depressed Kansas farmers to "Raise less corn and more hell," was a lawyer, women's rights activist, Populist Party leader, Union Labor Party member, socialist, and Social Darwinist, but she was best known for her fervid denunciations of big-money interests on behalf of the Populist Party in the late 1880s and 1890s. Like many Populists, Lease promoted Prohibition as well as women's suffrage and political participation, but she drew greater fire in part because of her defiance of conventional gender roles. The anti-Populist press called her a "manwife," "demagogess," and "the people's party Amazon" and denounced her husband as childlike and effeminate. When Lease returns home from a political tour, the *Topeka Daily Capital* taunted, "her husband feels like a new woman." In an interview for *Lucifer: The Light-Bearer*, a Kansas-based libertarian radical journal devoted to sex reform, Lease justified women's political participation on the basis that women were essentially purer than men and would elevate politics.

Munsey's Magazine, Jan. 1897, 457–458.

She defined the New Woman as "a potent verity" whose purpose was to "exercise her God assigned mission to enter men's souls and bring the race to harmony and completeness."[2]

Her speeches in the 1890 senatorial campaign helped unseat Kansas Republican senator John J. Ingalls, who had denounced women's suffrage advocates as "the unsexed of both sexes, the capons and the epicenes of society." In 1896 Lease joined Pulitzer's *New York World* as a political reporter, and by 1900 she had broken with the Populists. The following article was illustrated with a half-page frontal photograph of a serious, imposing Lease seated at a writing desk.[3]

For further information about Munsey, see the introduction to "Women in Another New Role" in part I.

Whether Mrs. Mary E. Lease, the feminine Boanerges of Kansas, is or is not an ideal, she is certainly a type. She is the product of the political and social conditions of a wide and important section of the country. She represents an upheaval which had overturned the politics of several Western States, and which bade fair to sweep over the entire Union. She did more than any one else to overthrow the Republican party in Kansas, where it had been dominant since the war. Her oratory might evoke smiles in the classic halls of Congress, but it is a power upon the prairies. When she first made her pyrotechnic appearance, John James Ingalls sneeringly declared that "women, like the Decalogue, have no place in politics." She retorted by driving the brilliant Senator into private life, where he has since remained.

Mrs. Lease is not a Westerner, or even an American, by birth. She was born in Ireland, and came here as a child with her parents, shortly before the civil war. Her father entered the Union army, and died in the prison pen at Andersonville. Mr. Lease—who may be classed among the "unknown husbands of famous wives"— is a druggist in Wichita, Kansas. He is said to attend strictly to his business of mixing pills and powders, leaving the toils and honors of politics to his aggressive wife.

"Suffragette [to the Bearded Lady]: How Do You Manage It?"

Augustus Smith Daggy

Augustus Smith Daggy (1858–1942) was a Connecticut artist who illustrated for *Harper's Weekly* as well as *Life*.

By the 1910s, as the suffrage debate intensified, *Life's* satiric attacks on suffragists and women seeking careers outside the home became sharper. In September 1910, the humor magazine launched a series of essays from "Miss Priscilla Jawbones as Suffragette Editor." Concurrently, it ran "Life's Suffrage Contest" and offered $300 to the reader who could present "the best reason, or reasons why any man should not marry a suffragette." Here, the suffragette's identification with the freak show suggests the extent to which her desire for the vote was a sign of congenital inversion.[1]

For more information about *Life,* see the introduction to Edward Kemble's "Ise Gwine ter Give You Gals What Straddle" in part I.

Life, Feb. 9, 1911, 315.

"Women's Rights: and the Duties of Both Men and Women"

Theodore Roosevelt

Theodore Roosevelt (1858–1919) served as the police commissioner of New York City, assistant secretary to the navy, governor of New York, vice president of the United States, and the twenty-sixth president of the United States (1901–1909) after the assassination of President William McKinley. A progressive reformer, Roosevelt devoted much of his presidency on the home front to breaking up corporate trusts, regulating railroads, ensuring food safety, and protecting the nation's natural resources. In his speeches and writing, Roosevelt implored (white) American men to adopt a "rugged masculinity," which at home was best expressed by hunting or other vigorous sport or serving the nation abroad in its role as international police officer. Indeed, according to historian Gail Bederman, Roosevelt "yearned to be the virile leader of a manly race and to inspire his race to wage an international battle for racial supremacy." By the same token, he feared that Anglo-Saxon women were committing "race suicide" by not having enough children, and he made his charges public after reading Bessie Van Vorst's study *The Woman Who Toils,* which was serialized in *Everybody's Magazine* in 1902. Van Vorst noted that factory women enjoyed the independence afforded them by paid labor and therefore delayed marrying. When Roosevelt left office in 1909, he became contributing editor to the *Outlook* but soon resigned to hunt big game in Africa. He returned in 1911 to write a series under the general title "Nationalism and Progress," which explored the new "Spirit of Nationalism" after the Spanish-American War. In 1912 he began his second run for the presidency by trying to secure the Republican nomination; when he failed to do so, he

Outlook, Feb. 3, 1912, 262–266.

then ran as a candidate on the third-party Progressive "Bull Moose" ticket. In 1912, the *Outlook* still enjoyed a circulation of just over 100,000.[1]

For information on the *Outlook,* see the introduction to Eleanor Tayleur's "The Negro Woman—Social and Moral Decadence" in part I.

The causes which brought about so much of dreadful failure and wrongdoing to alloy the benefits and advances which followed on the French Revolution were symbolized and foreshadowed in the action of the first revolutionary national legislature. This body passed with wild applause resolutions declaring that the people were to have all imaginable rights, and then voted down a resolution setting forth that the same people had grave and onerous duties. Much, indeed, has America owed to the fact that her two greatest men, Washington and Lincoln, though they did not neglect rights, were even more concerned with duties.

I believe in woman's rights. I believe even more earnestly in the performance of duty by both men and women; for unless the average man and the average woman live lives of duty, not only our democracy but civilization itself will perish. I heartily believe in equality of rights as between man and woman, but also in full and emphatic recognition of the fact that normally there cannot be identity of function. Indeed, there must normally be complete dissimilarity of function between them, and the effort to ignore this patent fact is silly. I believe in woman's suffrage wherever the women want it. Where they do not want it, the suffrage should not be forced upon them. I think that it would be well to let the women themselves, and only the women, vote at some special election as to whether they do or do not wish the vote as a permanent possession. In other words, this is peculiarly a case for the referendum to those most directly affected—that is, the women themselves. I believe such a referendum was held in Massachusetts, in which a majority of the women who voted, voted in favor of the ballot. But they included only about five per cent of the women who were entitled to vote, and where the vote is so light, those not voting should be held to have voted no. This was in 1895. It would be well to try the experiment again in the more doubtful States like Massachusetts or New York. I should be entirely content to abide the decision, either way; for, though I do not think that the damage prophesied from women's voting would come, or has come where it has been tried, I also think that very much less effect would be produced, one way or the other, than the enthusiasts believe. In other words, I do not regard the movement as anything like as important as either its extreme friends or extreme opponents think. It is so much less important than many other reforms that I have never been able to take a very heated interest in it.

Perhaps one reason why so many men who believe as emphatically as I do in woman's full equality with man take little interest in the suffrage movement is to be found in the very unfortunate actions of certain leaders in that movement, who seem desirous of associating it with disorderly conduct in public and with thoroughly degrading and vicious assaults upon the morality and the duty of women within and without marriage. I cordially agree with Dr. C. W. Saleeby, himself a strong advocate of woman's suffrage, when he says in his book on "Woman and Womanhood":

> Every individual case requires individual consideration, and no less than any individual case ever yet received. *But* in general those women who counsel the delay of the marriage age are opposing the facts of feminine development and psychology. They are indirectly encouraging male immorality and female prostitution, with the appalling consequence for those directly concerned, for hosts of absolutely innocent women, and for the unborn. Further, those who suppose that the granting of the vote is going to effect radical and fundamental changes in the facts of biology, the development of instinct and its significance in human action, are fools of the very blindest kind. Some of us find that it needs constant self-chastening and bracing up of the judgment to retain our belief in the cause of woman suffrage, of the justice and desirability of which we are convinced, assaulted as we almost daily are by the unnatural, unfeminine, almost inhuman blindness of many of its advocates.

Very few men in America have stood more prominently and emphatically for sound political principles than Ida M. Tarbell.[2] She is one of the few women who influence men along this line, which is ordinarily peculiarly a man's line of influence. Therefore both men and women can afford to listen to her when, in her introduction to the "Book of Woman's Power," she says (I condense):

> Men and women have always crawled or soared together. The lot of woman is hard, but the human lot is hard. The assumption that the improvement of woman's condition depends upon the vote is quite as unsound as the charge of her inferiority. The woman in industry is, after all, but a transient. A training that will lead her to apply her power with appreciation and enthusiasm to domestic and not to political life is what she needs. It is harmful and unsound to believe that woman's position in society would improve in proportion as her activities and interests become the same as those of men. This implies that man's work in society is more important and developing than woman's. But both are essential to society, and who can prove that one essential factor is inferior to another essential factor? Her aptitudes and instincts and functions are different from those of man; and her differences are her strength. She must not prove her equality by doing in his way the things the man does; but by doing the things for which she is fitted, and which the world needs from her. Life is not saved by politics, but by principles.

In his admirable book on "The College Man and the College Woman," President Hyde, of Bowdoin [College], lays their duty plainly before them both with equal fearlessness and good sense; and one hardly knows whether most to admire his scorn for the licentious man, for the cruel or callous or merely selfish and inconsiderate man, and his insistence upon the same standard of morality for the two sexes, or his insistence to the woman that her life will be worthless unless she bears on her own back her share of the world burden, and feels in her own heart her part of the world sorrow, in normal experience within the home, the shop, the market, doing first of all in her own household her every-day and vital duties, so that thereby, and only thereby, she may become "the comrade of all who labor, the sister of all who serve."

If the woman suffrage movement were to be judged only by those advocates of it who discredit themselves and their sex by disorderly antics in public, and who assail the foundations of private and public morality in their endeavor, not to raise the sense of moral duty in man, but to lower the sense of moral duty in woman, I should certainly oppose the movement. But I do not believe these undesirable apostles are in any way to be accepted as exponents of the cause, and I call attention to the fact that they are prominent, not in the region where woman suffrage does exist, but in regions where it does not exist.

I pin my faith to woman suffragists of the type of the late Julia Ward Howe. Julia Ward Howe was one of the foremost citizens of this Republic; she rendered service to the people such as few men in any generation render; and yet she did, first of all, her full duty in the intimate home relations that must ever take precedence of all other relations. There was never a better wife or mother; her children rose up to call her blessed, and the commonwealth should call her blessed for the children she bore and reared, for the character she transmitted to them, and the training she gave them in her household. We are fortunate in being able to point to such a woman as exemplifying all that we mean when we insist that the good woman's primary duties must be those of the home and the family, those of wife and mother; but that the full performance of these duties may be helped and not hindered if she also possesses a sense of duty to the public, and the power and desire to perform this duty.

In our Western States where the suffrage has been given to women I am unable to see that any great difference has been caused, as compared with neighboring States of similar social and industrial conditions where women have not the suffrage. There has been no very marked change in general political conditions, nor in the social and industrial position of woman. Yet what slight changes have occurred have been for the better, and not the worse. Moreover, I must say that, being a natural-born democrat, I do like to associate with people who possess every right that I possess. In those Western States it is a real pleasure to meet women, thoroughly womanly women, who do every duty that any woman can do, and who also are not only in fact but in theory on a level of full equality with men. I fail to see that these women are any less efficient in their households, or show any falling off in the sense of duty; I think the contrary is the case; and so far as their influence has affected political life at all it has affected it for good. I do not see much difference between Denver and the big cities of the East in those very matters where we would expect the influence of women's voting to count most; yet, after all, it is the women of Denver who have stood most stoutly behind Judge Lindsey.[3] When I passed through Seattle last spring, it had just finished an election in which a most needed bit of political house-cleaning had been performed; and the votes of the women had been a potent factor in securing decent government. The same thing was notably true in the Los Angeles election the other day. A very good citizen of Los Angeles, in a position fitting him to pass judgment, writes me as follows of this contest: "By the way, Colonel,

I used to be dead against woman's suffrage, and although I voted for it and wrote for it—because it seemed to me right and just and a necessary part of sincere democracy—still I dreaded the consequences. Of course one swallow doesn't make a summer, but up to date in this contest the women have conducted themselves in a way to excite the liveliest admiration. They are setting the men a much-needed example of rapid, thorough work, with no foolish scrapping—dignified, conscientious, and effective."

Therefore I believe in woman suffrage wherever the women wish it. I would not force it upon them where, as a body, they do not wish it. I would leave the matter to be decided by vote of the women themselves. Most of the women whom I know best are against woman suffrage, and strongly criticise me for aiding in, as they term it, "forcing" it on them. But surely both the women who oppose the suffrage and the women who demand it ought to be willing to argue the matter out with the members of their own sex. If a majority of the women of a State vote affirmatively for the suffrage, it is time to give it to them. If only a small minority vote for it, it ought not to be forced upon the hostile and indifferent majority. If benefit follows the suffrage, the suffragists will be justified. If there is weakening of moral fiber or any other evil as a result, they will be condemned, and will ultimately lose what they have gained. It is, and will ever remain, true of women as of men, that by their fruits shall ye know and judge them. Most of the women whom I know best are against woman suffrage precisely because they approach life from the standpoint of duty. They are not interested in their "rights" so much as in their obligations. They tell me that they feel that already they have as much to do as they can well attend to; that their duties are numerous and absorbing— although they are happy in doing them; and that, for the very reason that they take their duties seriously, and would accept suffrage seriously as a duty, they do not think that such a heavy additional burden should be put on their shoulders. It is, however, with me a question whether these women, with busy, happy, duty-filled lives, are really typical of those other women who are more or less defense-less. These other women, wage-earning girls for instance, and wives whose husbands are brutal or inconsiderate, would, I believe, be helped by the suffrage, if they used it wisely and honorably. I hope that if women voted we should be able to wage a more rapidly successful war against the "white slave" traffic and kindred iniquities.

But this would come about only if women remembered, what so many men forget, that social evils can be successfully assailed only if the assailants avoid hysteria as carefully as they shun lukewarmness, and are resolved to combine with their fervor cool-headed common sense and the willingness to look unpleasant facts straight in the face.

I most earnestly desire to emphasize my feeling that the question of woman suffrage is unimportant compared to the great fundamental questions that go to the root of right conduct as regards both men and women. There should be equality of rights and duties, but not identity of function; and with the man, as with the woman, the prime duties are those related to the home and the family. Selfishness, frivolity, viciousness, love of ease, shirking toil and risk, avoidance of all that is hard, fear of life—of the only kind of life worth living—all of these are as criminal in the man as in the woman. I am not speaking of exceptions among men and women, but of the average healthy citizen of either sex, of the citizen upon whose character and welfare the success of our great democratic National experiment depends. The first duty of the average citizen is to be a good father or mother, husband or wife. Heaping up money as the end of life or leading a life of vapid ease and avoidance of labor and effort, or any other form of shirking duty, means the rotting of the soul. Cynical fools who advise men against marriage are fond of saying that "to go far one must go alone." But the goal reached alone is not worth reaching! Other fools, advising women to forsake their primary duties and "go into industry" prattle about the "economic dependence" of the wife. Economic dependence, forsooth! Any husband who regards his wife as "economically dependent," or who fails to recognize her as a full partner, needs severe handling by society or the State. The service of the good mother to society is the most valuable economic asset that the entire commonwealth can show, and is of infinitely more worth to society than any possible service the woman could render by any other, and necessarily inferior, form of industry.

Motherhood must be protected; and the State should make the security of the mothers its first concern. Dr. Saleeby, in his book already quoted, utters the soundest common sense on this subject. Mothers (and children) should not be allowed to work in any way that interferes with the home duties; and widowed mothers with children and deserted mothers with children must be cared for. *But the care must not be given in such way as to encourage the man to shirk his duty*. His prime duty is to provide for his wife and his children; if he fails to do so, the law should instantly seize him and force him to do so. It should be even more severe in thus forcing him to care for his children if he has not married their mother. In such case the man has not merely grievously sinned against another human being, but has grievously sinned against society, against the commonwealth. There must be common parental care for children by both father and mother. Marriage buttresses motherhood by fatherhood. Just as it is the duty of the mother to bear and rear the children, so it is the duty of the father to support the mother and children, and if he fails in this duty the State should actively interfere and force him to perform it. We should not, in a spirit of sentimentality or false humanity, permit the State to relieve him of this duty or encourage him to escape the responsibility by having the State assume it; he is the one on whom the responsibility should fall, and he should be rigidly held to the performance of his duty. *"The last way in which to secure the rights of women is to abrogate the duties of men."* In the future it may well be that unmarried men will have to pay, as they ought to pay, a far heavier share of taxation than at present; but under no circumstances should fathers be permitted to shirk their duty of providing for their children, and the so-called reformers who advocate schemes towards this end are working for the corruption and. dissolution of the entire social fabric. Our aim must be the healthy economic interdependence of the sexes, based on equality of rights and of obligations, including the obligation of sexual and domestic morality; any attempt to bring about the kind of "economic independence" which means a false identity of economic function spells mere ruin. The home, based on the love of one man for one woman and the performance in common of their duty to their children, is the finest product of Christianity and civilization. Our consistent effort must be to strengthen it, and any movement to destroy it marks the nadir of folly and wickedness.

Much can be done by law, and whatever can thus be done should be done. But much more can be done by a vigorous, enlightened, and effectively aroused public opinion. Not only easy divorce, but the shameful shirking of duty by men and women which leads to such divorce and to all kinds of domestic unhappiness, and all unhealthy love of ease and vapid excitement, and inability to prize the really highest things in life, should be unsparingly condemned, not only in theory but in practice. It should be a subject of just indignation wherever a duty is shirked; and we should hold in unmeasured scorn the empty laughter of the fool who sees in such shirking of duty only matter for mirth. In one of the magazines a month or two ago, in what purported to be the "funny" column, was a story of a man proposing marriage to a woman who hesitated to accept him, and he was represented as holding out inducements, saying: "I am willing that we should have no children, so that you will be able to go to Europe whenever you want to, entertain your friends, and not be tied down," to which she answers, "Good!" Foolish and brutal jesting about infamy, about the profanation of what should be holiest in life, is the mark of revolting depravity; for public opinion to tolerate such jests and stories is as if we should tolerate an ape capering over an altar. Woe to us as a Nation if our men and women, our young men and maidens, fail to face life with the brave and solemn purpose to lead it on the plane of high endeavor, and to find their supreme satisfaction in the full performance, and not the avoidance, of duty. "Mother," by Kathleen Norris, is a charmingly told story; and therefore it is a most effective tract which should teach this profound and lofty truth to many, many people who cannot be reached by the preacher or essayist. . . .

"Movie of a Woman on Election Day"

With the exception of the *Philadelphia Tribune* founded in 1884, the *Baltimore Afro-American* has been in print longer than any other black newspaper in the United States. It was founded in 1892 by the Reverend William Alexander and bought in 1897 by a former slave, John H. Murphy Sr., who ran the paper until his death in 1922. In 1905 the *Afro-American* defined its mission as "first to present to the world that side of the Afro-American [people] that can be had in no other way, and in the second place to as far as possible assist in the great uplift of the people it represents." With that mission in mind, it walked a fine line of praising the efforts of both Booker T. Washington and W.E.B. Du Bois, and even initially Marcus Garvey and his Black Star Line. In 1907, the paper was incorporated as the Afro-American Company. Although Baltimore, as a liminal city between the North and South, didn't host Jim Crow abuses as egregious as those in many southern cities, its many black residents, in the words of historian Hayward Farrar, suffered from both "Northern ghettoization and poverty and Southern Jim Crow," degradations which the newspaper routinely exposed and challenged. Initially, the *Afro-American* focused on Christian moral uplift, education, and black politics, especially efforts to gain employment and housing rights, and Murphy relied on his influence in the black church, black Masons, and the Shriners to expand readership. By 1917, however, with the departure of editor George Bragg, the paper took on more aspects of yellow journalism by emphasizing crime, sex, and corruption while offering readers more vivid illustrations and bold headlines. Murphy Sr.'s son Carl Murphy took over editorship in 1918. In the two months preceding publication of the cartoon reprinted here, the *Afro-American* had given extensive positive coverage to women's new right to vote. Augusta T. Chissell, a member of the Colored Women's Suffrage Club of Maryland,

Editorial page, *Baltimore Afro-American*, Oct. 29, 1920, 9.

for example, answered readers' questions about how they should best exercise that right. In 1923, the *Afro-American* had a sworn circulation of 17,632, far behind that of the *Chicago Defender* but still the largest of a black newspaper on the East Coast.[1]

W. Ashbie Hawkins, the candidate mentioned in "Movie of a Woman on Election Day," was a prominent black attorney in Baltimore; he contributed articles to the newspaper and was one of seven directors in the Afro-American Company. According to legal historian J. Clay Smith, Hawkins "participated in almost every major civil rights case in Maryland during the first quarter of the twentieth century, including the litigation of civil rights claims before the Interstate Commerce Commission." As a Baltimore leader in the Niagara Movement—which called for black civil and political rights and whose founders included W.E.B. Du Bois and William Monroe Trotter—Hawkins spoke out against Marcus Garvey. As a lawyer for the Defense League, a local black civic group, he argued cases demanding pay equality. Working for the NAACP in the mid-1910s, Hawkins proved instrumental in legal victories against housing segregation. In 1919, the black community's growing frustration with Republican mayor William Broening over his refusal to appoint a black representative to the school board and his vacillation over appointing black doctors and nurses to serve in black schools prompted Hawkins to run as an independent Republican for the U.S. Senate. The *Afro-American*'s Carl Murphy served on the executive committee of the Independent Voters' League, which sponsored Hawkins's candidacy. Although the newspaper gave extensive coverage to incumbent Republican U.S. senator Ovington Eugene Weller's failure to serve the needs of black voters, it did endorse Republican Warren G. Harding's candidacy for president. In the November election, Hawkins received 5,770 votes. Democrat John Walter Smith also lost to Weller, who served as U.S. senator until 1927.[2]

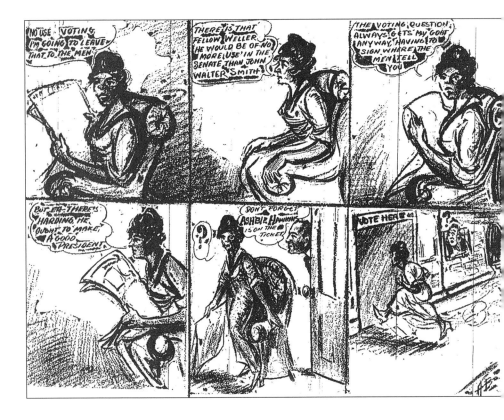

PANEL 1: No use voting. I'm going to leave that to the men.

PANEL 2: There is that fellow Weller. He would be of no more use in the Senate than John Walter Smith.

PANEL 3: The voting question always gets my goat anyway, having to sign where the men tell you to.

PANEL 4: But, er, there's Harding. He ought to make a good president.

PANEL 5: Don't forget Ashbie Hawkins is on the ticket.

PANEL 6: Vote Here.

"Squaws Demand 'Rights':

PENOBSCOT INDIAN WOMEN
WANT VOTE: PRIVILEGE IN
TRIBAL ELECTIONS"

In 1877 Stilson Hutchins founded the *Washington Post* in the nation's capital as a Democratic daily paper. In 1889, Frank Hatton and Beriah Wilkins purchased the paper and made it officially nonpartisan; under their leadership, the *Post* grew steadily more influential and successful. World War I provided a boost to the paper when thousands flocked to the capital to work in jobs related to the war effort, so that by 1919, then owner Ned McLean was enjoying profits of more than $180,000 annually and a Sunday circulation of close to 75,000. In July 1917, several months after the United States entered World War I, police arrested National Woman's Party members who were picketing the White House in support of suffrage. When they were sent to the Occoquan Workhouse in Virginia, the suffragists staged a hunger strike and were force-fed. Although President Wilson tried to limit coverage of the suffragists' protests and their subsequent treatment, the *Post* featured the arrests in front-page headlines and editorialized, "By all means pass the suffrage amendment and get on with the war." On June 4, 1919, the suffrage amendment finally passed and was ratified the following year.[1]

For additional information about the *Washington Post*, see the introduction to Kate Masterson's "The Campaign Girl" in part I.

Old Town, Me., Feb. 26.—Indian women of the Penobscot tribe today started on the warpath to obtain the right to vote in the tribal elections and share in the conduct of reservation affairs. Some of the squaws have nailed the suffrage colors to the

---

Washington Post, Feb. 27, 1921, 6.

totem pole with the assertion that a grandlady sachem would make a wiser chief than any brave that ever wove a basket or built a canoe.

Last night the new women of an ancient people began rejoicing when they received a ruling from Attorney General Shaw that they could go as far as the tribe allowed for the State would remain neutral.

"The New Woman:

WHAT SHE WANTED AND WHAT SHE GOT"

Frederick L. Collins

A "dynamo who never seemed to tire," Frederick Lewis Collins (1882–1950) was a leading voice in magazine publishing and editing in the early twentieth century. From 1906 to 1911, Collins edited the *Woman's Home Companion*. From 1911 to 1921, he served as president of McClure Publications, and from 1915 to 1920 he worked as managing editor of *McClure's Magazine,* a journal famous for its muckraking of Progressive-era scandals.[1] From 1920 to 1921 he served as the president of the Periodical Publishers Association of America and later devoted much of his time to writing book-length works.[2]

Collins's "The New Woman" was originally published by *Woman's Home Companion* and illustrated by George Illian. Begun in 1873 in Cleveland by brothers S. L. and Frederick Thorpe, the *Home* evolved into the *Ladies' Home Companion* in 1886, and finally became the *Woman's Home Companion* in 1897, partly to differentiate itself from the *Ladies' Home Journal.* Geared toward a middle-class family audience, the magazine in its first decade featured serialized stories, muckraking and reform-centered articles, household tips, travel writing, and well-printed halftone illustrations by some of the nation's leading artists. During this period the *Companion* also supported women's right to higher education, business pursuits, and athletic training. When Gertrude Battles Lane began editing the magazine in 1911, she moved it away from muckraking to feature some of the most widely read fiction writers of the period, including F. Scott Fitzgerald, Willa Cather, Edith Wharton, and, especially, Edna Ferber. Lane's editing direction proved so successful

Woman's Home Companion, June 1929, 12, 70.

that by 1929, on the eve of the Depression, the ten-cent *Companion* had reached a circulation of 2.5 million and would soon be recognized as having "the largest circulation of any magazine in its niche." Although Lane did not support the Equal Rights Amendment, she urged readers to elect women to public office who would repeal laws denying women equal treatment.[3]

Ten years ago this month the Suffrage Amendment was adopted by the Senate of the United States. The event was hailed on all sides as the dawn of the woman's power in America. Nine years and nine months later Herbert Hoover was inaugurated President of the United States. And now this second event is being hailed as the day which has been so long in following the dawn.

How much faith can we put in either of these hailings?

Was the passage of the Suffrage Amendment the significant occurrence which we then believed it to be? Is the inauguration of President Hoover the significant woman's victory we now assume it to be?

Is there any real relationship between what the New Woman wanted ten years ago and what she has today? . . .

In ten years there have been two women governors; and at the end of the ninth year there were four women representatives in the Congress. But unfortunately for the feminists' pride of office, both governors and three out of four of the congresswomen were elected to carry on the policies of their husbands. To this list must now be added Ruth Bryan Owen of Florida, Ruth Hanna McCormick of Illinois and Ruth Baker Pratt of New York—three exceedingly able women but all of them projected into public life partly by the momentum of their "men-folks'" achievements. Mrs. Owen is the daughter of William Jennings Bryan. Mrs. McCormick is the daughter of Senator Mark Hanna and the widow of Senator Medill McCormick.

Incidentally the only woman ever seriously mentioned for Vice President was the widow of a former President, Mrs. Woodrow Wilson. And Mrs. Pratt is the widow of an immensely wealthy official of Standard Oil.

As for the important field of party management, the New Woman's accomplishments are still mostly before her. To be sure, the leaders have thrown a few sops to the woman voter: a few associate memberships in political bodies, a few vice-chairmanships of political committees. But in last year's presidential campaign, the only woman who exercised any dominant influence on either side was a personal friend of one of the candidates, Mrs. Henry Moskowitz,[4] who has never been politically prominent and who did not appear in any high-sounding political rôle at any time during the campaign.

What was true of the leaders was true—up to the last weeks of the campaign—of the voting rank and file. But as registration days approached, the situation changed. Women who had never taken any interest in politics became suddenly curious about the candidates and the issues. Perhaps it was due to the fact that both presidential nominees were more than usually appealing to the feminine mind. The issues too were of the direct kind easily grasped by the newer voters: food, drink, religion, prosperity, and the campaign which was fought on them brought out for the first time a really impressive woman's vote.

To be sure, when the ballots were counted it was found that the greatly increased number of voters did not appreciably affect the result. Mr. Hoover received many more votes than any previous candidate of his party had ever received. But so did [his opponent] Mr. Smith. The woman vote seemed to have split just as the man vote regularly splits—in the usual party proportions. Maybe this failure of the woman electorate to cohere is a healthy sign. There is little to be secured by pitting sex against sex. The important point is that at last, after more than nine years of virtual inactivity, women did take an interest and did vote.

When we have said that, we have said about all that can be said for the first suffrage decade. If the period is to be judged solely by the number of political offices and the amount of political leadership, it must be set down as wholly unexciting and largely disappointing.

But should it be judged that way?

For the answer to that question I have gone scuttling back to pre-suffrage days to find out if it really was political influence that women were fighting for in those robustious times. I have searched the feminist books. One was called *What Women Want*. I defy any earnest student to read that book or any others of that crop and find the answer there. The pros were vague. The antis were worse than vague, they were funny. One Reverend Knox-Little, after denouncing the straywardness of some of his church women from their home duties, exhorted as follows: "Think of the blessedness of having children. I am the father many, and there have been those who where inclined to pity me, 'Keep your pity for yourself,' I have replied. 'They never cost me a single pang.' "

The slogans of the suffrage campaigns were equally unenlightening as to what the New Woman really did want. Between hunger strikes in a Washington prison the famous White House pickets composed what afterward became the official anthem of the Woman's Party. It began:

> Shout the Revolution
> Of women, of women,
> Shout the Revolution
> Of Liberty.

But surely, the thousands of women who marched up Fifth Avenue in a monster parade didn't want any part of a revolution. They were well dressed, frequently well husbanded, and except on parade days well fed. Such people never want revolutions.

I am equally sure that the anti-suffragists did not believe in their hearts the libelous taunts with which they assailed the paraders at every street corner. I kept some of the leaflets which were distributed among the crowd. For instance:

> Here's to the Woman of days Gone By,
> May we meet HER kind Above!
> The Woman for whom a man would die,

The Woman who ruled by Love:
Who DIDN'T PARADE and
        DIDN'T HARANGUE,
    In whose Home it was sweet to dwell,
Who believed in raising Children
    And not in raising Hell.

In the end, I found the clearest statement of what women wanted in the place I least expected to find it: in the beginning.

"The history of mankind," thundered the first woman's rights convention way back in 1848, "is a history of repeated injuries and usurpations on the part of man toward woman.

"He has never permitted her to exercise her inalienable right to the elective franchise.

"He has compelled her to submit to laws in the formation of which she has had no voice.

"He has withheld from her rights which are given to the most ignorant and degraded men.

"He has made her, if married, in the eye of the law civilly dead.

"He has taken from her all right in property, even in the wages she earns.

"He has denied her the facilities for obtaining a thorough education, all colleges being closed against her."

And, inclusively:

"He has usurped the prerogative of Jehovah himself."

Obviously what the New Woman wanted was a New Man.

And that, in the last analysis, is what she got.

It was natural, however, that this new daily contact on the campus with girls who knew their Greek and Latin better than he did or in the office with girls who knew his business better than he did should increase man's respect for womankind. And it was inevitable that this same daily contact should soften and enrich the relationship between the sexes to a point where equal suffrage, or equal anything else that women might want, would be the inevitable result.

This process was going on before the war. It moved with lightning speed once men and women began serving on an equal basis in the world struggle. The suffrage was not wrung from the male electorate by agitation and violence. It was granted—perhaps "shared" would be a better word—by that electorate out of well-earned appreciation and respect.

In this country at the present time there are over five hundred equal rights bills pending in the legislatures of the various States. And the only vigorous masculine protest against any of them has come from the Alimony Payers' Protective Association!

In the presidential campaign of last fall New Woman leadership was negligible; almost microscopic. But the individuals who made the race for the presidency were conspicuously of the New Man type. It is doubtful if either of them, ten or twenty years ago, would have been seriously considered by the politicians. Last year the very newness of their attitudes dictated their nominations.

No one stopped to think whether Governor Smith had been for suffrage or against it ten years ago. His record on legislation designed to better the condition of women and children in the home and in industry was the way he had showed his newness. The case for his distinguished opponent was even more obvious. No one cared whether Mr. Hoover, busy sinking mines in China and South Africa, had expressed any opinion on suffrage. His wartime record of counsel and coöperation was his best recommendation to women, New or Old. And it may not be too much to hope, as a result of the first ten years of woman suffrage, that no man will ever again be nominated for high office in the American republic who does not meet the New Woman's New Man test.

There is plenty left for the New Woman to achieve. Getting the vote—even getting the New Man—is only the first step. Getting high offices for herself may be the next. But in the meantime, she should be heartened by one significant thought:

She no longer treads the path alone!

"La Mujer Nueva"
[The New Woman]

Clotilde Betances Jaeger

Clotilde Betances Jaeger (1890–197?), grandniece of Puerto Rico's foremost nine-teenth-century independence leader Ramón Emeterio Betances, wrote articles on a wide range of issues, including the Puerto Rican independence movement, fem-inism, music, literature, and socialism. Born in San Sebastián, Puerto Rico, she moved to the United States in 1912 to attend Cornell University, from which she graduated with a degree in natural sciences in 1916. In 1923 she moved to New York and served as a teacher at the Beth Jacob Teachers' Seminary of America. She earned a master's degree from Butler University in Indiana and studied at the Sorbonne in Paris and the University of Salamanca in Spain. Betances Jaeger wrote for a number of periodicals in Puerto Rico, New York, and various Latin American countries. She was a member of the Asociación de Escritores y Periodistas Puertorriqueños (Association of Puerto Rican Writers and Journalists) and reportedly left several unpublished works, including a biogra-phical profile of her famous granduncle, a novel, and several plays.[1]

María Mas Pozo, whom Betances Jaeger refers to as M. M. Pozo in the essay that follows, was Puerto Rican and wrote for a number of other Hispanic papers in New York in addition to *Gráfico*. In 1936, she married the Puerto Rican inde-pendence leader José Enamorado Cuesta, and in 1973 she published *El camino de la violencia* (The road to violence), in which she criticized what she saw as the oppressive nature of Christianity and Catholicism as well as American imperial-ist ventures in Puerto Rico and around the world.[2]

Gráfico, June 15, 1929, 10–15.

The weekly *Gráfico* (1926–1931), in which Betances Jaeger's article appeared, was published by a collective of tobacco workers, writers, and theater artists. It marketed itself to Spanish-language speakers in New York, especially Puerto Ricans, but also Cubans and Dominicans. The magazine promoted a pan-Hispanic worldview and urged its readers to both fight ethnic oppression and claim their rights as American citizens. (With the Jones Act of 1917, Puerto Ricans had been granted citizenship.) A 1927 editorial (written in both Spanish and English) offered the magazine's mission: "the masses of the American people do believe that the countries South to the Rio Grande are inhabited by Toltecs and Mayas, Cholos and Gauchos, living in savage conditions and incapable of civilized life. These masses forget, or never learned, that there is a distinctive type of culture latent and vivid in Latin America, and that no matter what course the national institutions of North America shall follow regarding our relations, this culture will never perish. . . . GRÁFICO will labor to clarify all misunderstandings that may lead to serious consequences in the public life." Edited at first by Alberto O'Farrill, an Afro-Cuban actor and playwright, popular for playing in blackface a Cuban named Negrito (Blackie), *Gráfico* included in its first year many O'Farrill cartoons, which satirized the flapper sometimes through the use of risqué double entendres. In 1929, the magazine—which now included reports of international and national news affecting Spanish-speaking peoples, full pages of photographs, a women's column, fashion advice, popular culture updates, cartoons, and classified ads—sold for five cents.[3]

The Puerto Rican economy between 1917 and 1933 suffered from many problems. Among other things, it relied too heavily on too few agricultural products—sugar, coffee, and tobacco. It was dominated economically by absentee American and other corporations, and by 1920, 1.2 percent of the island's farms controlled 36 percent of the cultivated land. It suffered from increasing unemployment made more acute by increases in population. And the hurricane of 1928 was especially devastating. As a result, many Puerto Ricans came to northern cities in search of greater economic opportunity. By 1930, the mainland United States was home to 50,000 Puerto Ricans, 81 percent of whom lived in New York City. Nearly half were women.[4]

The following essay is the third installment in a four-part series that Betances Jaeger wrote on the New Woman.

Manufacturers and traders in the United States, who are the only ones who will benefit from the protectionist tariff, think that the higher tariff will prevent people from buying foreign products, and that money will thus stay home and the country will get rich.[5] This is obviously wrong because a surplus of exports over imports always hurts consumers, as restricting imports automatically causes a corresponding decrease in a country's exports. As with everything, this has advantages and disadvantages. For example, products are not imported unless they are paid for, cost plus shipping. It is clear that when exports exceed imports, the tariff leaves in its wake a permanent increase in money and prices. This is why many favor the tariff, because they view it as a source of prosperity. But this is not so, because it is obvious that the tariff raises the prices of protected products as well as unprotected products.

Women, who in the last elections tipped the balance in Hoover's favor for two sentimental reasons, religion and prohibition, now must interest themselves in a practical reason, the tariff, because their economic situation is in grave danger, and along with it the happiness of home. They must show that, as new women, they know what concerns them.

M. M. Pozo, women have responsibilities, you have said. Huge responsibilities. Blessed responsibilities!

Woman of heart, women of mind, new woman, the economy is your imminent problem and you must solve it. The economy of households is under your domain; the economy of the world is your inheritance.

Senator William E. Borah states that posterity has the right to make itself heard. Puerto Rican women have serious responsibilities.[6] Puerto Rico now must remake itself economically if it ever wants to attain its political freedom. We'll see if those women who showed themselves to be so dogged in the dark days of the Revolution of Lares, those women who are so brave in the storm, will resolve the economic problem in Puerto Rico. To do so they must forget about trifling matters, social conventions, and rotten prejudices. May Puerto Rican women prove that they are the salt of the earth. It does not matter that they cannot read; they still have a voice and vote in public affairs.[7] The amorphous masses in a country are not the ones who deprive. Only a few rule the world.

Women of reason, of heart, of good will, you have the floor. Send your comments c/ GRÁFICO, 83 Pear Street, New York City.

Translated by Paul Coltrin.

PART III

Temperance, Social Purity, and Maternalism

"At Home with the Editor"

Edward Bok

Born in the Netherlands in 1863, Edward Bok immigrated to the United States with his family in 1870. In 1886 he syndicated a weekly gossip column directed to women in the *New York Star* called "Bab's Babble," and later he expanded it to include commentary from the famous poet and New Thought advocate Ella Wheeler Wilcox. In 1889 Bok became editor of the *Ladies' Home Journal*, and like many other late-nineteenth-century ministers, politicians, and physicians, he wrote didactic columns for its pages in which he urged women to eschew most behavior associated with women's "progress." Bok and his magazine's contributors generally only sanctioned modern culture for women if it meant the use of labor-saving devices, better management of family finances, or enhanced shopping skills—in other words, if it improved woman's role within the domestic sphere. If their moral influence were needed, however, women might have a "legitimate" reason to enter the public domain.[1]

The *Ladies' Home Journal*, founded by Cyrus Curtis and Louisa Knapp Curtis in 1883, quickly became the best-selling magazine in the United States, in large part because of its aggressive advertising and cheap price. As an early leader in the battle of "ten-cent monthlies," the magazine was priced at five cents from 1883 to 1889; in 1899 it raised its price to ten cents, and then in 1904 to fifteen cents. When Edward Bok took over the editorship in 1889, he helped develop its defining characteristics: female-oriented material, personal tone, far-ranging advice, and a commodity-culture focus. Under Bok's leadership, more male writers wrote feature articles, whereas "female experts" wrote the more standard service columns. Aimed primarily at moderate middle-class families, but with some attention to those earning higher incomes, the *Journal* earned the distinction in

Ladies' Home Journal, Oct. 1894, 14.

1903 of being the first magazine to surpass a million in paid circulation. Between
1900 and 1910, the *Journal* expressed frequent opposition to women's suffrage,
although it supported women's higher education. By 1910 the editors could boast
that one in five American women were reading their publication, as well as
increasing numbers of men.[2]

. . . We are told that we have developed "a new woman." I have not been able to find
out exactly in what respect this woman is "new," unless it be that her newness lies in
her being unwomanly, or different from what God intended a woman should
be. . . . Measured by the standards set by these advocates of the new type of woman,
a woman's life is successful just in proportion as she robs it of its privacy and lays it
bare to the public. In short, she must *do* something, and do it in a public way so that
people will know about it. A life simply spent within the confines of four walls,
given over to some tyrant of a man—that is what the husband is usually called, I
believe—is a life simply wasted. If such a woman has children—although the latest
edict tells us that motherhood is the great stumbling-block in the path of woman's
progress—she must not train or educate her offspring. She must go out into the
world and tell other women how to train their children. She must do one of two
things: she must either write for the public or speak to it. She must write, even though
she fairly annihilates the Queen's English with every stroke of her pen. She must
speak, although with every sentence she utters she defies all the laws of rhetorical
grammar. She must get herself into a dissatisfied state of mind. She must school
herself, for instance, into the belief that she is defrauded of "her rights"—just what
rights it doesn't matter so much. She hasn't all her rights: that's enough. And she
wants them. This fact she must shriek forth to a patient and long-suffering public.
And when she does this, the women who listen to her will clap their gloved—pardon me, I believe the new woman is not to wear gloves—well, then, they will just
clap their bare, everyday, strong hands at her sallies of wit. One or two "cause" papers
will report what she says. Then, when she dies, some woman, whom she didn't like
when she was alive and who didn't like her, will pronounce a eulogy upon her, while
another woman, whom she never met and who never saw her, will "write a nice
notice" about her. And she will have lived a successful life!

I must not be misunderstood as belittling the value of public services rendered
by woman. Some women are born to be heard of just as some men are destined to
lead. History is thickly dotted with achievements by women who have benefited the
world just in proportion as they have been heard or read. But these are the few. To
the average woman it is given to lead a secluded home life, removed from the glare
of the public. It is given to her to mould one or two lives. But if she does this effec-
tually, her life is equally as successful as that of the woman who sways the thoughts
of a whole nation of lives. The woman who gives one true man to the world has
lived in every respect a successful life. If from the moment of the beginning of that
life until its final development into manhood she influences its destiny for good,
she has attained the highest success possible. It must not be forgotten that if every

woman fulfilled her highest duties to the lives given into her keeping, the world would be a very different sort of a place. The women who lead the many must exist as a counteracting influence to the women who are negligent of their opportunities. It is this endeavor to belittle the influence of the woman in her home which is becoming so general nowadays among a certain set that I would cry out against. It is in the home, and principally in the home, that woman's influence is most potent, and where her greatest success is possible. It is there that she moulds the inner life; it is there where men are made or unmade. It is from the portals of the home that woman's greatest achievements can come in the fashioning of the lives within it. It is there where woman's greatest arena of success has always lain; it is there where it will always be. As the homes of a nation are, so are the morals of its people, and as its women are, so will its homes be. It is woman's influence that has made the best of American institutions what they are to-day, and it is woman's success as woman which will make our American life even greater than it is. And each individual woman, no matter how humble her lot, is a distinct factor in that successful achievement. . . .

———∞∞———

"The New Woman"

Rev. Ella E. Bartlett

Ella E. Bartlett (1849–?), an ordained minister in the Universalist society, was born in Connecticut and lectured throughout the East Coast and upper Midwest promoting women's suffrage, prohibition, and labor reform. Bartlett's article "The New Woman," reprinted here, originally was illustrated with line drawings of journalist and lecturer Kate Field, Jane Addams, Frances Willard, and Susan B. Anthony.[1]

The periodical in which Bartlett's "New Woman" was published, the *American Jewess*, was the only English-language, nineteenth-century publication of Jewish women's thought. It was also the only nationally circulating Jewish publication in America at the time. Begun in April 1895 under the editorship of Rosa Sonneschein, the *American Jewess*, "a Monthly Magazine of Social, Religious and Literary Subjects," was directed primarily at an upper-middle-class audience and included sections on science and medicine, youth entertainment, music and the arts, and fashion. Although it featured articles on domestic science and fashion, the magazine also supported a wide range of progressive causes including suffrage and settlement work. Even as writers urged their readers not to lose their femininity, they condoned bicycle riding and bloomers. Writers profiled "Successful Business Women" and figures such as Hannah Greenbaum Solomon, founder and president of the National Council of Jewish Women (NCJW). *American Jewess* also advocated greater equality in Jewish religious life. At a time when women were relegated to a clearly subordinate role in Jewish religious traditions—they were excluded from playing any significant role in religious leadership, their names were not included in synagogue membership lists, and they could not attend synagogue meetings or vote—the *American Jewess* advocated greater

American Jewess, July 1895, 169–171.

religious equality. Although the magazine ceased publication in 1899, it appears to have done fairly well, boasting a circulation of nearly 31,000 in 1898.[2]

The adjective "new" has been applied to women with startling frequency of late. Almost every printed page bears evidence of her ubiquity as well as "newness" of the average contributor: What the new woman has done, is doing, or will do, is so persistently set forth that one is led to think that a new order of the "genus homo" has been discovered; yet a little study and research shows that the discovery is, after all, only the finding of eyes to see and ears to hear, on the part of the discoverer, and not a very new order of women.

Does the new woman manifest, with voice and pen, an interest in questions of national importance? Did not Miriam the prophetess, the sister of Moses, do the same as well as the other women in the days of Saul and David, and in still later days?

Does the new woman compose songs of praise and thanksgiving? Is not her prototype found in Hannah, the mother of Samuel, and is not the literature of all subsequent time enriched with the contributions of women?

Does the new woman ask for equal rights in the guardianship of her own children? The mothers of Israel had this right or Moses had not been saved to be the deliverer of Israel from Egyptian bondage, or Samuel have been given to the service of the temple and fitted for the prophetic office.

Does the new woman ask for more just property rights? So did the daughters of Zelophehad and other women, and the Lord commanded that their claim be heeded, and the necessary legislation be made to insure the same rights to all other women.

Is the new woman suspected of a desire to wear the judicial ermine? Did not Deborah judge Israel for forty years, during which time, the land had peace because of her just and beneficent rule? Would the new women lead armies to victory over evil? Did not Deborah lead the army of Israel to victory over the hosts of Sisera, and did not Sisera fall by the hand of Jael, whose deed is celebrated in song composed by a woman, and preserved for over four thousand years as a source of instruction and inspiration to others?

Does the new woman preach the word? She is by no means new on that account. In David's time it is said that "The Lord gave the word and great was the company of the women that published [preached or proclaimed] it."

Does the new woman engage in trade or commerce, does she manage real estate transactions, is she an importer and jobber in fine merchandise, does she manage a grocery or deal in textile manufacturing? The women so highly commended by Solomon did all these things, and the writer deplored the fact that there were not more of them. Does the new woman plan broadly for the help of the needy, is she a counselor to those in trouble? So was she in the days of Solomon, and then, as now, "the heart of her husband doth safely confide in her, he is continually praising her, and her children rise up and call her blessed."

Does the new woman study and teach philosophy, mathematics, astronomy and the physical sciences; is she versed in the law and able to council with jurists? Was not Hypatia the most learned philosopher of her times and has she not had most illustrious followers?

Does the new woman exercise the right of franchise in many of the cities of our own and other lands on questions of local or general interest? So did the women of Athens, until on a question of home protection, they outvoted the men in the choice of the tutelary goddess of the city, then because of the clamor of the defeated party the supreme council took away from the women the privilege of any future exercise of this right, as the United State Supreme Court did to the women of Washington Territory in a similar case a few years ago.

Thus does history defeat itself!

Does the new woman advocate dress reform, and prepare garments similar to those worn by men? Again does history repeat itself. It is but a brief period in the life of a race since the garments worn by men and women were indistinguishable; according to the earliest information we have on the subject, the first garments were made of the same material and by the same pattern for both sexes. If distinction in dress was a matter of as much importance as some people seem to think, it is a wonder that the Lord did not make the fact apparent when he made those first coats of skin. There is, however, no evidence that he thought it a matter worth considering; therefore, we may conclude that if the new woman should appear clad as men, that she would not be more unsexed than they were at first.

Is the new woman a good housekeeper? The average discoverer of this old "new women," who is still rubbing his eyes to test the accuracy of his vision, protests that she is not. But Solomon's model woman was declared to be a most excellent housekeeper. It is fair to presume, therefore, that the discoverer will find, when the scales have entirely fallen from his eyes, that this modern new woman is the very best housekeeper ever known, because the most intelligent—and the one who brings the most intelligence to any work undertaken will secure the best results. If the discoverer of this new woman should be so fortunate as to be invited to her home, this statement would have ample verification.

Will the new woman marry? The discoverer with still imperfect vision, answers with mournful accent and long drawn sigh in a negative. The answer is quite true, unless the supply shall rapidly increase, for she is now as happily married as she can be, and she has no use for the divorce courts. Like the women of Israel in the olden days, she fills the measure of her opportunity, doing what her hands find to do, guided by the best intelligence she can command.

Will the new woman of the future marry? is the question most anxiously asked. Marriage being regarded as a burden by those who ask the question, she is prejudged as unwilling to assume its duties, and herein is the chief complaint against her. It would not be strange if the new woman should refuse to accept a position of servitude to the whims and caprices, the bad manners and worse morals of many of the so-called lords of creation, but as in the past the new woman will marry her equal in moral worth, dignity of character, high aims and noble purposes. Homes will be established and children adorn them, and the world of humanity be purer, and sweeter, and richer, because of the coming of the new woman.

"The New Woman"

Lillian W. Betts

Known for her work chronicling tenement conditions in New York City and the efforts of settlement workers to ameliorate them, Lillian W. Betts (?–1938) wrote essays and at least two books, *The Leaven in a Great City* (1902) and *The Story of an East-Side Family* (1903). From 1893 to 1900, Betts served as editor of the home department of the *Outlook*.[1]

By 1893, under the editorship of Lawrence F. Abbott, the weekly *Outlook* had moved away from its religious roots to become a broader family magazine devoted to coverage of the arts and news. In 1894 its circulation topped 30,000.[2]

For more information about the *Outlook*, see the introduction to Eleanor Tayleur's "The Negro Woman—Social and Moral Decadence" in part I.

The "new woman" has been the subject for illustration and description more or less in earnest. She is described as smoking, drinking, and demanding what she calls liberty. This seems to be not the liberty of law, but of license; the right to live without restraint. So vivid have the descriptions become, the artists, the writers, the speakers are so terribly in earnest, that we must accept the fact that they believe that they are describing, depicting, that which exists. There is a new woman, the product of evolution, the result of domestic, social, and commercial changes.

Every year the giants of science and invention have been taking out of her control the industries that had been the objects of her effort, the subjects of her control. As they were lost, the unemployed activity found for itself some new field. Before woman realized the change, she found herself in a world that needed the cultivation of new powers, and she met the demand. Her education grew broader, her range of interest larger, her field of opportunity greater, and, without intending it, the woman of to-day finds herself a different being from her grandmother. Her standards of life have changed. Health has become an object most desirable, and, beginning the struggle in behalf of her children, the new woman has reached the point where she blushes for shame if health be not the normal condition of her family. She has

Outlook, Oct. 12, 1895, 587.

learned that her child is not divided into parts that can be taught and trained sepa-
rately, and now she has her eyes opened to the relation between home and school.
She is a member of a kindergarten association. She owns several books on the
kindergarten, and knows that between the kindergarten and the college graduation
there is the unbroken link of an immortal soul being trained to live.

The new woman has learned that if she would have a clean house she must have
a clean street; she must go further and have a clean neighborhood; and perfection,
which is the aim of her life, demands a clean city, town, community. The new woman
joins an organization that has cleanliness for its object, and she sees to it that those
about her obey the written and the unwritten laws of health. She knows that she
cannot secure health for her own family unless she works to secure it for those who
have not had her training, who have not her standard.

The new woman would be ashamed not to know something of the administration of the city, the State, the Nation. She prizes good citizenship for what it gives
to her home and maintains for it. She prizes it so highly that she trains her son to
value his citizenship as the highest gift of manhood, knowing that if she gives him
a true standard he "will render unto Caesar the things that are Caesar's, and to God,
the things that are God's."

The new woman is impersonal. She sees life at that focus which subordinates the
one to the many. She knows well that much of the disturbance of life comes from
the confusion that grows out of a misguided conception of one's value to the great
world of affairs. She realizes fully that no one person is as great as the group of
which he is but one. He may be a major one if he works with the group, but is sure
to be a minor one if he works apart from it. She is calm because she does not exaggerate her own importance or that of her affairs. The new woman possesses the
instincts of the artist; she appreciates beauty, she demands harmony in her surroundings, she believes in the gospel of beauty and morals, she comprehends their
relation. Seeing this, her effort is to make the world more beautiful.

The new woman knows that a democratic government is always what the people
make it. She knows that the men elected represent the character of the people who
elected them, and she strives by direct and indirect means to raise the national character. Knowing the positive effect of education on character, she identifies herself with
some association whose aim is to secure education adapted to the conditions of a country whose prosperity is dependent on the ability and character of every family under it;
she sees the dual relation of every family. It is sovereign and subject. The new woman
rebels when she sees woman spelled with a capital or harnessed to the words "progress,"
"career," "work." She knows that the world grows only when the common good is the
common concern of men and women. She rebels when she finds herself treated as a
specimen. Only when the paragraphist, and the woman with an "ism" designed for
women, thrust themselves upon her attention does she remember herself. At other
times she is "one of God's universe," filling her place in the plan of redemption.

This is the new woman, the flower of this marvelous century, not the caricature
drawn by the would-be wit, or by the unthinking man who cannot see below the
surface nor beyond the range of his personal experience.

"Miss Willard on the 'New Woman'"

Frances Elizabeth Caroline Willard (1839–1898) was born in Churchville, New York, but grew up in the rural Midwest and graduated from North Western Female College in Evanston, Illinois, in 1860. After teaching in Methodist schools in the Midwest, Willard became dean of women at the Woman's College of Northwestern University. Shortly thereafter she resigned her post as dean and became the corresponding secretary for the newly established Woman's Christian Temperance Union (WCTU). In 1879 Willard led a campaign from Evanston to convince the Illinois legislature to grant women the right to vote in local referendums on the question of liquor. Although the effort was unsuccessful, it signaled Willard's lifelong commitment to suffrage as well as temperance and gave her the national attention that helped her win election to the presidency of the WCTU. Under Willard's twenty-year leadership, the WCTU became arguably the most powerful international women's organization of its day. Under the slogan "Do Everything," Willard and other WCTU leaders of the 1880s and 1890s advocated a wide range of progressive social causes, including the women's club movement, social purity, peace, labor reform, dress reform, public kindergartens, and settlement house work. In the final decade of her life, Willard took up bicycle riding, which she described enthusiastically in *A Wheel within a Wheel: How I Learned to Ride a Bicycle* (1895). In an interview she granted to the *New York Times* several months before "Miss Willard on the 'New Woman'" appeared, she maintained that the bicycle was "the greatest agent of . . . temperance reform" because fresh air, park paths, and sobriety were all essential for a pleasant ride. "In Chicago there is nothing so hated by the saloon keeper, the cigarette dealer, and the proprietor of the low theatre as the bicycle." Due to illness, Willard spent much of the 1890s in England.[1]

Woman's Signal, Sept. 17, 1896, 181.

The following article—an interview with Frances Willard—appeared in the *Woman's Signal*, a British one-penny paper begun in 1894 under the editorial direction of Lady Henry Somerset, who became president of the British Woman's Temperance Association in 1890, and novelist Annie E. Holdsworth. The paper's main interest was advocating temperance reform, but it also addressed other feminist issues. The well-known British journalist and editor Florence Fenwick Miller took over the magazine in 1895 and broadened its focus to include articles on "art, technical education, women in religion, notes on bills before parliament, recipes and poetry."[2]

An interesting interview with Miss Frances Willard appeared in a recent issue of the *Sunday Times*, from which we make some extracts:—

Knowing that Miss Willard is an enthusiastic cyclist, I began by inquiring for "Gladys."

"Gladys is well," was her reply. "I have forsaken her for a Beeston Humber, and now Gladys is ridden by our cook, housemaid, and other servants. I do believe 30 women have learned on my steed. Lady Henry and I encourage the servants to ride, and now they are all saving their wages to buy bikes. Anna Gordon says I have begun to demoralise all the English servants, and try to make them like those we have in America. Don't you, Anna?"

"I think I said 'democratise,'" was Miss Gordon's answer. "We shall soon be having your English servants declining situations because no bicycle is provided."

"But, seriously, we find the maids much the better for cycling—quite bright, and showing fresh interest in their work. I learned to bicycle when fifty years old," said Miss Willard, "and I think it one of the best things I ever did. What pleases me is to see other worn-out women take it up, and find a new lease of health and life thereby. The little book I wrote on the subject has been brought out by a religious publishing firm in Chicago, and has thus reached thousands of women who, perhaps, might not otherwise have looked with favour on the innovation. I like to think they have found encouragement by my example."

"I fancy, Miss Willard, you are not of those who regard the 'new woman' as a failure."

"No; neither here nor in America. We need new women because we keep having relays of new men. It is quite vain ignorant persons trying to make a sex question out of what is really a matter of temperament, intelligence, the need for companionship amongst those whose aims and tastes are similar. Dull, unsocial men, sunk in their own petty interests, can always find women like unto themselves. The demand for new women is a demand by men who want women with sunny spirits, a friendly outlook in life, with scientific knowledge of how health should be preserved, perhaps gained by means of athletics; women whose lives are enriched by literature, art, the drama; women who are an active, industrial, and educational factor in the world's work. We can't go back on the fact that a section, and I am glad to think a very large section, of men want women of this pattern, call them 'new' or what you like."

"America's great gain," observed the interviewer, "is that she has so many women of this kind, and England's loss is that, as yet, she has comparatively so few."

"You think so? I, on the other hand, and probably because I am an outsider, am struck by the great movement among women on this side. Reactionaries may shriek, but your women are becoming more important individuals; they will deserve and receive more consideration. What I always deprecate is the notion that a greater share of life for women is a sex question, and that men will lose by the new movement. On the contrary, it is men who have begun it, and are all through its convinced and steady adherents. Look at Wyoming, where thirty years ago men granted women the suffrage. Wyoming was then a territory. It became a question whether it should not become a state, and thus obtain rank and privilege in the Federal Government. It was mooted that woman suffrage should be dropped. The men absolutely declined to enter on this condition. 'Either we bring in the women with us, or we remain outside,' said they. I need scarcely say that they federated on their own terms. And it is the only state where there exists an educational test for the suffrage for both sexes. On voting-day they have a copy of the American Constitution within reach, and doubtful voters have to read out of it, and afford evidence that they can write the language. In Wyoming no man can be nominated to a public post unless his life is clean, his family relations blameless. It is said of doubtful candidates, 'The women would vote him down.' The development of science, the extension of educational advantages, are the seed; the crop will be new men and new women. Man has been the universal Czar, and has owned the world in fee simple. He is becoming sublimated; he perceives the finer forces of the world; his sense of justice requires him to open wide the doors. There is not a diploma conferring university degrees upon women in arts, science, law, medicine, theology, but men have signed it. Why, I own one myself," said Miss Willard in grateful tones, "and some dear, bald-headed, religious, deaconian trustees gave me it. There are no separate interests for women. One laboratory of brain, one battery of heart, one river of blood unites the sexes, and they cannot be separated by any foolish chatter."

"The Chinese Woman in America"

Sui Seen Far [Edith Eaton]

Born in Cheshire, England, to an English father, Edward Eaton, and a Chinese mother, Grace Trepesis (or Trefusious), Edith Maud Eaton (1865–1914) wrote for the Canadian *Montreal Star* and *Dominion Illustrated*, and briefly for the Kingston, Jamaica, *Gall's Daily News Letter*, before moving to a series of cities, primarily on the West Coast of the United States, in search of work. Adopting a number of pseudonyms during her career, including Fire Fly, Sui Seen Far, Sui Sin Far, and even a male persona Wing Sing, she crafted essays and stories that often challenged the prevailing "yellow peril" rhetoric in the white press, even as they perpetuated Asian stereotypes.

The New Woman is a prominent theme in much of Eaton's work. In "The Story of Iso," written in 1896 for the Kansas City–based journal the *Lotus*, Sui Seen Far depicts a rebellious Chinese daughter who criticizes male privilege and, after speaking to a mysterious "red-headed stranger," rejects ancestor worship and arranged marriages. Writing for the *Gall's Daily News Letter* in Jamaica in 1897, society columnist Fire Fly offered a defense of the female bicyclist, the divided skirt, and the bicycle generally as "the greatest temperance reformer of the present day, for no man can drink and bicycle." And in a number of her stories collected in *Mrs. Spring Fragrance* (1912), she endorsed some aspects of the New Woman even as she criticized what she saw as the unacknowledged class bias and selfish individualism of American men and women advocating New Woman causes.[1]

Sui Seen Far's "The Chinese Woman in America" was published in the *Land of Sunshine: An Illustrated Monthly of Southern California*, which originally was

---

Land of Sunshine (Los Angeles), Jan. 1897, 59–64.

conceived as a magazine to promote southern California; it received significant backing from the Los Angeles Chamber of Commerce. When in 1895 Charles F. Lummis accepted the offer to edit the magazine, however, he envisioned it as more than a vehicle for regional boosterism. Characterizing the magazine as "exclusively Western in text, unswervingly American in spirit," Lummis believed the West's often maligned ethnic populations could temper the fervent entrepreneurial spirit of Anglo-Saxons by adding "to them something of the charm of a less anxious and more contented spirit." Lummis advocated miscegenation, Indian rights, and historic preservation and decried lynching, the Indian industrial school movement, anti-Chinese prejudice, and U.S. imperialism. The heavily illustrated magazine sold for ten cents an issue or a dollar a year, and although Lummis claimed in 1899 that the magazine had 50,000 readers, the actual circulation that year was closer to 10,000.[2]

The photographs that accompanied Sui Seen Far's essay emphasized the exotic nature of her subject. One depicted a Chinese bride, and the other two showed Chinese mothers seated with their children; in these last two photographs the women were wearing traditional Chinese dress, their expressions remote. Yet even though Sui Seen Far makes the Chinese woman in America seem an exotic ethnic Other, she refutes the popular conception of the Chinese woman as prostitute; by dressing for herself alone, the Chinese woman eschews the corruptive potential of the male and female gaze alike. With her commitment to her family, the Chinese "New Woman" promises none of the social divisiveness of her American counterpart.[3]

With her quaint manners and old-fashioned mode of life, she carries our minds back to times almost as ancient as the earth we live on. She is a bit of olden Oriental coloring amidst our modern Western lights and shades; and though her years be few, she is yet a relic of antiquity. Even the dress she wears is cut in a fashion designed centuries ago, and is the same today as when the first nonfabulous Empress of China begged her husband to buy her a new dress—of a tunic, a pair of trousers and a divided skirt, all of finest silk and embroidered in many colors. A Chinese woman in a remote age invented the divided skirt, so it is not a "New Woman" invention.

The Chinese woman in America differs from all others who come to live their lives here, in that she seeks not our companionship, makes no attempt to know us, adopts not our ways and heeds not our customs. She lives among us, but is as isolated as if she and the few Chinese relations who may happen to live near were the only human beings in the world.

So if you wish to become acquainted with her, if you wish to glean some knowledge of a type of which very little is known, you must seek her out. She will be pleased with your advances and welcome you with demure politeness, but you might wait for all eternity and she would not come to you.

Having broken the ice, you find that her former reserve was due to her training, and that she is not nearly so shy as report makes her. You also find, despite the popular idea that the Chinese are a phlegmatic people, that she is brimful of feelings and impressions and has sensibilities as acute as a child's. That she is content to live narrowly, restricted to the society of one man and perhaps a couple of females, does not prove lack of imagination; but merely that she is ignorant of any other life.

She was born in China, probably in Canton or near that city. When a little girl, she played Shuttlecock, Guessing Pennies and Blind Man's Bluff with childish playfellows, boys and girls; and grandfather and uncles kept her awake, when her mother put her to bed, by telling her stories of hobgoblins and ghosts. Amongst her memories of home are little pagodas before which she and her brothers and sisters were taught to burn incense, and an image of a goddess called "Mother," to whom she used to kneel till her little knees ached.

Until about twelve years old, she enjoyed almost as much healthful liberty as an American child; but in China it is not deemed proper for girls beyond that age to have boy playmates.

Then she learned to sew and embroider, to do light cooking and sing simple ballads. She was taught that whilst with them, her first duty was obedience to her father and mother; and after marriage, to her husband and his parents. She never had a sweetheart, but with girl friends would pass the hours in describing the beauties and virtues of future husbands.

In spite of these restraints, her years slipped away happily until time came for her to become an American bride—for the Chinese woman who comes to America generally comes as a bride, having been sent for by some Chinaman who has been some years in the States or in Canada and has prospered in business.

She has never seen her future husband, she has never perhaps ventured outside her native village; yet upon being apprised that for good and valuable consideration— for the expectant bridegroom, like Isaac of old when courting Rebecca, sends presents of silver and presents of gold to the parents or guardians of his chosen—she must leave home and friends and native land, she cheerfully sets about preparing for her journey. She may shed a few tears upon her mother's breast and surreptitiously hug her little sisters; but on the whole, she is pleased. . . .

The bride comes from a respectable middle-class Chinese family. Aristocratic or wealthy people would not give a daughter to a man living in exile; and Wah Ling, being a big enough man to keep a wife in America, feels himself too big to take a girl from the laboring classes. He wishes his friends to think that he marries well; if he were to choose a girl of mean condition he might he ridiculed. The Chinaman knows little of natural selection; though in his youth he had a sweetheart, when he wants a wife he sends for a stranger.

In China it is deemed altogether wrong for girls "in society" to have men acquaintances; but very poor girls choose their associates as they please without causing remark. Now and then a poverty stricken or outcast maid wins the heart of a Chinaman brave enough to marry her in spite of what his world may say; but such cases are rare. Very few Chinamen are introduced to their wives until after marriage.

The Chinese woman in America lives generally in the upstairs apartments of her husband's dwelling. He looks well after her comfort and provides all her little mind can wish. Her apartments are furnished in American style; but many Chinese ornaments decorate the tables and walls, and on the sides of the room are hung long bamboo panels covered with paper or silk on which are painted Chinese good-luck characters. In a curtained alcove of an inner room can be discerned an incense vase, an ancestral tablet, a kneeling stool, a pair of candlesticks—my lady-from-China's private chapel. She will show you all her pretty ornaments, her jewelry and fine clothing, but never invite you near her private chapel. There she burns incense to her favorite goddess and prays that a son may be born to her, that her husband may be kind, and that she may live to die in China—the country which heaven loves. . . .

While there are some truly pleasant to behold, with their little soft faces, oval eyes, small round months and raven hair, the ordinary Chinese woman does not strike an observer as lovely. She is, however, always odd and interesting.

Needless to say she is vain. Vanity is almost as much part of a woman's nature as of a man's; but the Chinese woman's vanity is not that of an American woman. The ordinary American dresses for the eyes of her friends and enemies—particularly the latter—and derives small pleasure from her prettiest things unless they are seen by others. A Chinese woman paints and powders, dresses and bejewels herself for her own pleasure; puts rings on her fingers and bracelets on her arms—and carefully hides herself from the gaze of strangers. If she has Golden Lily feet (Chinese small feet) she is proudly conscious of it; but should she become aware that a stranger is trying to obtain a glimpse of them, they quickly disappear under her skirt.[4]

She is deeply interested in all matters of dress; and, if an American woman calls on her, will politely examine the visitor's clothing, with many an expression of admiration. She will even acknowledge the American dress prettier than her own, but you could not persuade her to adopt it. She is interested in all you may tell her about America and Americans; she has a certain admiration for the ways of the foreigner; but nothing can change her reverence for the manners and customs of her own country.

"Why do you do that in such a way?" she is asked, and her answer is, "Oh, because that is Chinese way."

"Do it like this," she is told. She shakes her head smilingly: "No, that not Chinese way."

As a mother, she resembles any other young mother—a trifle more childish, perhaps, than young American matrons, but just as devoted. When the baby seems well, she is all smiles and Chinese baby-talk; when he is ill, or she fancies so, she weeps copiously and cannot be comforted. She dresses him in Chinese dress, shaves his head and strings amulets on his neck, wrists and ankles.

She is very superstitious with regard to her child, and should you happen to know the date and hour of his birth, she begs with tears that you will not tell, for should some enemy know, he or she may cast a horoscope which would make the child's life unfortunate.

Do not imagine for an instant that she is dull of comprehension and unable to distinguish friendly visitors from those who merely call to amuse themselves at her expense. I have seen a little Chinese woman deliberately turn her back on persons so ignorant as to whisper about her and exchange knowing smiles in her presence. She is very loyal, however, to those she believes to be her real friends, and is always seeking to please them by some little token of affection.

More constant than sentimental is the Chinese woman. She has a true affection for her husband; no other man shares any of her personal thoughts. She loves him because she has been given to him to be his wife. No question of "woman's rights" perplexes her. She takes no responsibility upon herself and wishes none. She has perfect confidence in her man.

She lives in the hope of returning some day to China. She feels none of the bitterness of exile—she was glad to come to this country—but she would not be a daughter of the Flowery Land were she content to die among strangers.

Not all the Chinese women in America are brides. Some were born here; others are merely secondary wives, the first consorts of their husbands being left in China; and there are a few elderly women who were married long before leaving home. The majority, however, are brides; or as the Chinese call young married females, "New Women."

"The New Woman"

Elizabeth Cady Stanton

In 1848 Elizabeth Cady Stanton (1815–1902) along with Lucretia Mott and several others met in Seneca Falls, New York, to draft the first public protest against women's political, social, and economic oppression. Included in this "Declaration of Sentiments" was the demand for the right to vote, a cause to which Stanton would devote her life, becoming the first president of the National American Woman's Suffrage Association (NAWSA) in 1890 at the age of seventy-five. But Stanton went further than fighting for the franchise. She denounced the Bible and most clergymen for fostering contempt for women and, with a women's committee, published feminist biblical commentaries. *The Woman's Bible* appeared in 1895. [1]

The Stanton article reprinted here originally appeared in the November 30, 1899, issue of the *Independent* (New York) as a reply to former Kansas senator John J. Ingalls's attack on women's claims to equal rights. The article was later published by the *Woman's Standard* (1886–1911), the monthly newspaper of the Iowa Woman Suffrage Association, based in Des Moines. Mary Jane Whitely Coggeshall, whom Carrie Chapman Catt called "the Mother of Woman Suffrage in Iowa," served as its first editor. [2]

The masculine and feminine forces in social life are like the positive and negative electricity, the centripetal and centrifugal forces in the material world.

Now suppose it were possible for us to suspend the equilibrium of these forces for one-half hour; the result would be material chaos.

Oceans and lands, planets, suns, moons and stars, leaving their boundaries and elliptics, would rush into one conglomerate mass. Fortunately, no man has the power to precipitate such a collapse.

Woman's Standard, Jan. 1901.

The present confusion in our social life, the corruption in politics, the dissensions in the church, the divisions in the home, the antagonisms in the world of work, are all the result of the masculine and feminine forces being thrown out of their equilibrium. The uprising of woman is nature's effort to restore this equilibrium of sex, which, for a true civilization, must ultimately be attained.

Churchmen and statesmen, presidents and professors, may all sharpen up their pens for their pronounciamentos against the "new woman"; they may denounce her on the platform, and in legislative halls, but nature, in her onward march, will leave them all as helpless as Dame Partington in beating back the Atlantic Ocean.[3]

There cannot be, in the nature of things, any real rivalry and antagonism between men and women. Fathers and mothers, husbands and wives, brothers and sisters are bound together by the most tender sentiment, in most cases.

The great moving passion in the world is love, and mother-love in freedom binds all humanity together.

You might as well talk of rivalry between positive and negative electricity as between the masculine and feminine elements. Senator Ingalls complains that we are not alike! It is a blessed thing for the race that we are not: in our differences we supplement each other. And because the sexes are different, one is not necessarily inferior to the other.

Is woman necessarily inferior to man because she could not give the world a Socrates, a Plato, a La Place, a Shakespeare, and Goethe and Scott? Or is the mother necessarily inferior to her sons because she has not produced a system of philosophy, of mathematics and astronomy, great tragedies and comedies, or the Waverly novels?

Are the brave deeds and courage of the soldier on the battle field more admirable than the tender ministrations of woman to the wounded and dying, supporting the weary head, and penning the last messages of love to the dear ones far away?

Difference does not argue disability. Nature knew what she was about when she made man and woman to differ: if the masculine and feminine elements, the positive and negative electricity, the centripetal and centrifugal forces, were alike, in the order of creation, they would have been of no use whatever.

"The New Womanhood"

Charlotte Perkins Gilman

Charlotte Perkins Gilman (1860–1935), née Charlotte Anna Perkins, was the most influential feminist intellectual at the beginning of the twentieth century. In her best-known work, *Women and Economics: The Economic Relation between Men and Women as a Factor in Social Evolution* (1898), Gilman argued that traditional marriage (for Anglo-Saxon middle-class women) was akin to prostitution because a woman was dependent on a man for her economic livelihood and therefore felt compelled to develop her sexual attractiveness at the expense of her productive skills. The man, then, chose his mate based on superficial reasons, which, according to Gilman, undercut racial progress. In *The Home: Its Work and Influence* (1903), Gilman argued for collectivist solutions to child rearing and for the professionalization of housework to help women realize their fullest human potential. In developing her feminist theories, Gilman was influenced by a number of leading economic, sociological, and evolutionary theorists, particularly Lester Ward, whose "gynaecocentric theory"—the view that organically the female sex is primary and the male secondary—proved a central component of her treatise on androcentric culture, *The Man-Made World* (1911).[1]

Even though Gilman's essays were published in a wide range of American magazines, including *Collier's, Good Housekeeping,* and the *Delineator,* she felt increasingly constrained by the ideological imperatives of these publications: "as time passed there was less and less market for what I had to say, more and more of my stuff was declined. Think I must and write I must, the manuscripts accumulated far faster than I could sell them, some of the best, almost all." From 1909 to 1916, Gilman published the *Forerunner, a* thirty-two-page monthly of fiction, editorials, poetry, book reviews, and essays written entirely by herself. The Rand

---

Forerunner 1 (Dec 1910): 17–18.

School of Social Science, the Women's Political Union, the National Woman Suffrage Association, and the Socialist Literature Co. distributed the magazine, but it never achieved a circulation greater than 1,500, including international subscribers. Gilman only accepted advertising in the *Forerunner* for items or projects she used or approved, and she reserved to the right to edit advertisements; within a year she no longer accepted them. Gilman published three of her novels serially in the *Forerunner*, including her feminist utopian novel *Herland* (1915).[2]

I have been reading Ellen Key's "Century of the Child," reviewed in this number, and am moved to add, in connection with that review, a "brief" for the New Motherhood.

Agreeing with almost all of that noble book and with the spirit of the whole of it, I disagree with its persistence in the demand for primitive motherhood—for the entire devotion of each and every mother to her own children—and disagree on the ground that this method is not the best for child service.

Among animals, where one is as good as another, "the mother"—each one of them—can teach her young all that they need to know. Her love, care and instruction are all-sufficient. In early stages of human life, but slightly differentiated, each mother was still able to give to her children all the advantages then known, and to teach them the few arts and crafts necessary of attainment. Still later, when apprenticeship taught trades, the individual mother was still able to give all the stimulus and instruction needed for early race culture—and did so, cheerfully.

But we have now reached a stage of social development when this grade of nurture is no longer sufficient, and no longer found satisfying either by mother or child. On the one hand, women are differentiating as human beings: they are no longer all one thing—females, mothers, and NOTHING ELSE. They are still females, and will remain so; still mothers, and will remain so: but they are also Persons of widely varying sorts, with interests and capacities which fit them for social service in many lines.

On the other hand, our dawning knowledge of child culture leads us to require a standard of ability in this work based on talent, love, natural inclination, long training and wide experience. It is no longer possible for the average woman, differentiated or undifferentiated, to fulfill the work of right training for babies and little children, unassisted. Moreover, the New Motherhood is belying to-day the dogma of the high cultural value of "the home" as a place of education for young children—an old world assumption which Miss Key accepts without question and intensifies.

The standards of the New Motherhood are these:

First: The fullest development of the woman, in all her powers, that she may be the better qualified for her duties of transmission by inheritance.

Second: The fullest education of the woman in all plain truths concerning her great office, and in her absolute duty of right selection—measuring the man who would marry her by his fitness for fatherhood; and holding him to the highest standards in his duty thereto.

Third: Intelligent recognition that child culture is the greatest of arts, that it requires high specialization and life service, and the glad entrance upon this service of those women naturally fitted for it.

Such standards as these recognize the individual woman's place as a human being, her economic independence, her special social service; and hold her a far more valuable mother for such development, able to give her children a richer gift by inheritance than the mothers of the past—all too much in femininity and too little in humanity.

A mother who is something more—who is also a social servant—is a nobler being for a child to love and follow than a mother who is nothing more—except a home servant. She is wiser, stronger, happier, jollier, a better comrade, a more satisfying and contented wife; the whole atmosphere around the child at home is improved by a fully human mother.

On the second demand, that of a full conscious knowledge of the primal conditions of her business, the New Motherhood can cleanse the world of most of its diseases, and incidentally of many of its sins. A girl old enough to marry, is old enough to understand thoroughly what lies before her and why.

Especially why. The real cause and purpose of the marriage relation, parentage, she has but the vaguest ideas about—an ignorance not only absurd but really criminal in the light of its consequences. Women should recognize not only the personal joy of motherhood, which they share with so many female creatures, but the social duty of motherhood and its unmeasured powers. By right motherhood they can build the world: by wrong motherhood they keep the world as it is—weak, diseased, wicked.

The average quality of the human stock today is no personal credit to the Old Motherhood, and will be held a social disgrace by the New. But beyond a right motherhood and a right fatherhood comes the whole field of social parentage, one phase of which we call education. The effect of the environment on the child from birth is what demands the attention of the New Motherhood here: How can we provide right conditions for our children from babyhood? That is the education problem. And here arises the insistent question: "Is a small, isolated building, consecrated as a restaurant and dormitory for one family, the best cultural environment for the babyhood of the race?"

To this question the New Motherhood, slowly and timidly, is beginning to answer, "No." It is becoming more and more visible, in this deeper, higher demand for race improvement, that we might provide better educational conditions for the young of the human species. For the all-engrossing importance of the first years of childhood, it is time that we prepared a place. This is as real a need as the need of a college or school. We need A PLACE FOR BABIES—and our homes arranged in relation to such places.

A specially prepared environment, a special service of those best fitted for the task, the accumulated knowledge which we can never have until such places and such service are given—these are demanded by the New Motherhood.

For each child, the healthy body and mind; the warm, deep love and protecting care of its own personal mother: and for all children, the best provision possible from the united love and wisdom of our social parentage. This is not to love our children less, but more. It is not to rob them of the life-long devotion of one well-meaning average woman, but to give them the immortal, continued devotion of age after age of growing love and wisdom from the best among us who will give successive lives to the service of children because they love them better even than their mothers!

"Alte und Neue Frauen"
[Of Old and New Women]

Frau Anna

Founded in 1834 by Adolph Neumann, the upper-middle-class *New Yorker Staats-Zeitung* was the oldest, most respected, and most openly pro-German of the city's German-language dailies.[1] In 1845 Neumann sold the paper to a Bavarian typesetter, Jakob Uhl, who married a women named Anna Behr a year later. Behr set type for the paper and ran it after her husband's death in 1852. Increasingly, she came to rely on the assistance of recent immigrant Oswald Ottendorfer, a veteran of Europe's failed revolutions of 1848, whom Uhl promoted to editor. In 1859 Ottendorfer and Behr married and became *Staats-Zeitung*'s co-owners. Six years after Anna died in 1884, Ottendorfer sold 10 percent of the newspaper's stock to his newly hired business manager, American-born Hermann Ridder. Ridder and his sons ran the paper into the 1920s and maintained its decidedly pro-German stance. During the 1910s, the paper sold for two cents; circulation, however, declined from more than 122,000 in 1916 to just 95,000 in 1918. As of 1910, more than 400,000 German immigrants lived in New York state; in addition, more than a half million state residents had been born in America to exclusively German-born parents.[2]

On March 22, 1891, the *New Yorker Staats-Zeitung* introduced its women's column, titled "Unter Uns Frauen" (Among us women). A week later, "Frau Anna" responded to women readers' requests for recipes, dress patterns, and general advice in a column titled "Briefkasten" (Letter box). Frau Anna's column was likely an homage to Anna Ottendorfer, of whom German American historian Otto Lohr recalled in 1914, "the spirit of the German homemaker merged with

New Yorker Staats-Zeitung, Sept. 16, 1917, D-4.

8

American business sense, and whose German soul found expression a generous disposition for American philanthropy." Viewed as the epitome of the self-sacrificing German American wife and mother, Frau Anna served as a role model for middle-class German immigrant women. Supposedly in keeping with her real-life model, Anna Ottendorfer, Frau Anna urged a range of conservative values, including spousal loyalty and maternal devotion. Appealing to German Americans' overwhelmingly antiprohibition attitudes and the fear that enfranchising women might turn prohibition sentiment into law, the *Staats-Zeitung* did not endorse suffrage until 1915, when it hoped that suffragists would advocate American neutrality at the outset of World War I. As late as 1917, Frau Anna enjoined readers to remember that motherhood remained woman's highest vocation.[3]

By the time the column "Alte und neue Frauen" appeared in 1917, Frau Anna's maternalist rhetoric had taken on a conflicted nationalist cast. With the United States' entry into World War I in 1917, American German-language papers faced tremendous pressure, which included federal monitoring of their content, to demonstrate loyalty to the U.S. government. Intense anti-German sentiment throughout the United States made the position of these newspapers even more vexed. Whereas before 1917 Frau Anna's column evoked the rhetoric of duty, patriotism, and loyalty to the Fatherland, after 1917 that rhetoric shifted to urge caution. As Peter Conolly-Smith writes, "Frau Anna now counseled women to maintain harmony within the home, endure all hardship, insults and injuries with stoicism, to keep a low profile and generally avoid being in public, and, most importantly, to steer clear of any discussion of politics—especially with Americans, and doubly so if the discussion involved the war."[4]

Often I get the nagging feeling that a former blessing has gone missing from our feminine existence—that of tranquility and contemplation! As I consider the many letters I receive, each of which spells out a different life's fate, I am struck by an overriding tone of haste and anxiety that cannot possibly be of benefit to my correspondents. Even letters from elderly ladies, of whom one might expect a more dignified tone, sometimes fill me with this sense of disquiet. Of course I know that the contemporary world's work demands the efforts of even our elder women, and that life's heightened pleasures demand ever-greater achievements. Yet it is precisely this imperative to produce and partake on so many levels that has cost woman many of her most genuine, sympathetic characteristics. All it takes is a glance at our old family pictures to see just how different we contemporary women have become.

Only once in a while do we encounter a woman who has not been seduced by the pressing zeitgeist of our times. Usually, it will be lady of advanced years, a serene and friendly granny who still possesses enough discerning taste to reject colors and fashions that don't suit her. Women of this type do not resist the advance of old age, which they know lies in store for all young blossoms; they would find it undignified to mask their age beneath makeup. This old-fashioned lady still places a lace cap with lilac ribbons upon her graying head, while the more modern woman dyes her hair or covers it with a wig. Her clothing hardly differs from that of her daughter, and she is unaware of the ridicule this earns her.

They are becoming ever more rare, these undemanding, sympathetic beings who, even in this day and age, still find time to perform their grandmotherly duties. And yet they are as needed in our world as a cool evening breeze after a hot summer day. This is not to belittle the achievements of those of our ladies who lead our social efforts, but they themselves know well just how little their hearts are sometimes in their work. Undoubtedly, today's ladies have organized most effectively and achieved many great things for the public good. Still, in doing so they delegate to others tasks they could otherwise perform themselves, and for all their ability to solicit charity for those less fortunate, still they feel not the satisfaction of true compassion. The calm words of elderly ladies who, without offending anyone, smile at all this silliness, are to me as a haven: a shadowy spot to rest following the exertions of the day. Many of these tired, friendly, elderly correspondents have endured much in life for their husbands and children, and have seen many of their peers depart. One pities them for their work, which was never done, and which limited them to the household. And yet their activities were always accompanied by blessings. Before me lies another such heartwarming letter recounting the modest daily routine of a loyal old reader in the twilight of her life. Here's how it begins:

My dear Frau Anna! I would so like to send you a few lines in my old age, but I know you have more to read than the ramblings of an old woman. I'm eighty-seven years and two months old now, and hoping for an end soon, because it is not good, nor happy, to get too old to find pleasure in life. But of course I have my many grandchildren, some of whom I helped raise, and whose love brings me joy. And then there is the Sunday edition, which always makes me happy, for I can still read a little despite my waning eyesight. When the *Staats-Zeitung* arrives at our house on Monday mornings at ten, I always turn to the women's section first to read your column, with its reliably wise counsel dispensed to even the most peculiar questions. And there are other features: articles about child rearing, the household, etc., and of course the society pages. All those rich families, with their summer residences! The cooking recipes are also of interest to me, and novel, and I follow them closely, although here we still prepare food in the old-fashioned way. I pay less attention to fashion, and to cars or real estate, but I avidly read the musical reviews. First and foremost, I follow the advice columns on how to economize in the household. The news of the war agitates me and I regret having to witness such misery in my old age! Is there to be yet another winter campaign? One thing that frightens me is my eyesight! Every time I renew my subscription to the *Staats-Zeitung* I tell myself, this is the last time, but then I'm so happy each time I begin receiving it for another six months. Today I too enclose a loving gift for your needy; I wish it could be one hundred times the sum. If only I knew how much longer I have to live; it could be another few years, and I don't want to be a burden to anyone! Please use my modest contribution for an orphan, or for two elderly people who no are no longer able to work.

I hope that you will remain active in your job, which is to the benefit of our sisters, for many more years. In the end, we will all find peace, but happy is she who knows the serenity of a clean conscience in her own lifetime! I wonder if you can even follow my meanderings. Please pardon my lengthy ramblings; writing doesn't come as easily to me as it once did.

Many best wishes, your loyal

Marie R., Conn[ecticut].

How much these few short lines tell us of the sufferings and pleasures of life! This old woman was surely a good partner to her husband, in whose shadow she stood, and when her children had families of their own, she withdrew quietly; she resigned. That is what the contemporary women does not do; she insists on partaking both of the work of our times and its pleasures, and she will not easily settle. Yet it is not just a hollow phrase to claim, as I do, that a domestic woman saves many a downward-going one from doom. It is she who brightens man's life by the light of the stove, who draws him to the family. A difficult and sacred task! More difficult than many a course of academic study. She can perform this work in her role as mother, sister, wife, even as aging grandmother; just so long as she has a merciful heart!

Whether modern woman will find herself enriched in happiness or spirit by this "more" she desires of life, who can tell? The fact remains that the maternal element still constitutes the basis of our nature, and the more it penetrates our civic and communal lives, the more dignified our lives will be as women.

Translated by Peter Conolly-Smith.

PART IV

The Women's Club Movement and Women's Education

"Women's Department"

Edited by Pauline E. Hopkins

In 1900, four Virginians—Harper S. Fortune, Jessie Watkins, Walter Alexander Johnson, and Walter W. Wallace—moved to Boston to form the Co-operative publishing firm and issue the first "general purpose" magazine to serve black Americans, the *Colored American Magazine*. In its early years, the *Colored American* offered biblical stories, fiction, and articles on a range of topics, including health, the social elite, travel, fashion, and especially education. Pauline Hopkins (1859–1930) began her service to the magazine as a frequent contributor and editor of the women's department, and in 1903 she was listed as the magazine's literary editor. In an effort presumably to mask the full extent of her contributions, she also published under the pseudonyms Sarah Allen and J. Shirley Shadrach. Hopkins wrote numerous biographical essays and short stories and published three of her four novels serially in the magazine. As a professional writer who was single, African American, female, and increasingly anti–Booker T. Washington in her insistence on publicly condemning white racism, Hopkins faced mounting pressure to defer to male pro-Washington members of the black elite with whom she worked. Hopkins apparently had little faith in the aesthetic judgment of founding editor Walter Wallace and "resented bitterly" white publisher Robert Elliott's "veiled authority." Pressure to adopt a pro-Washington stance only intensified, and Hopkins later revealed that a white adviser to and financial supporter of the magazine, John C. Freund, was a Bookerite who insisted that "there must not be a word on lynching, no mention of our wrongs as a race, nothing that would be offensive to the South." By September 1904 Hopkins was ousted from the magazine, reportedly for "an attitude [that] was not conciliatory enough" to Washingtonian policies. After she left, Hopkins described what

---

Colored American Magazine, June 1900, 118–123.

had been continuing pressure from Booker T. Washington supporters: "my rights are ignored in my own property, and I am persistently hedged about by the revengeful tactics of Mr. Washington's men." Sexism compounded her feelings of frustration. In a letter written to black nationalist John E. Bruce in 1906, Hopkins maintained that despite having argued for the union of the "Negro with labor for a number of years . . . being only a woman [I] have received very small notice."[1]

Walter Wallace reported that out of a total circulation of 15,000–16,000 issues a month, approximately a third were purchased by whites. Under pressure from John Freund, the magazine reduced its price in 1904 from fifteen to ten cents.[2]

The following article appeared one month after the *Colored American Magazine*, in its inaugural issue, began a two-part parody of the New Woman by the Young Men's Congressional Club. (Hopkins was vice president of the women's branch.) The parody included the proceedings of a mock divorce trial, during which the attorney accused his client's spouse of being "one o'dese hear '*New* Women'" who "just because he didn't think as she *thunk*—she was chasing him around de room wid a *red hot* poker." To my knowledge, Hopkins never used the term New Woman or New Negro Woman, although she frequently created characters who had New Woman attributes.[3]

Editor's Note: We bring to this column an enthusiastic desire to do good and pleasing work for our lady patrons, and to that end would be pleased to receive suggestions from all our friends. We would be glad to correspond with all women's clubs in relation to club matters, to insert club notices, etc. Send in the name of your club and its officers for enrollment in the Record. . . .

One of the most remarkable movements of the twentieth century has been the ramification of women in all directions where she has seen the slightest chance for business or intellectual progression. Judge Grant in his latest novel, "Unleavened Bread," has painted in Selima [*sic*] White a satire on ambitious club women, and through her, on all women engaged in public life.[4] There are, unhappily, many Selima Whites among us; but is this all? Is there anything behind the outward veneer of fuss, feathers, fine dress, and posing for public admiration? Surely it is not justice to consider the women's movement from this point of view. We believe it to be the club women's task to "little by little turn the desire of the world from things of the flesh to things of the spirit. She must make world want to do things that raise it higher and higher. She must set all high ideas and maintain it bravely in the face all opposition." The more sublime the character of the women developed by this movement, the larger the percentage of women we shall find strutting about in the borrowed plumes of the truly great ones. No one loses confidence in the soundness of Uncle Sam's currency because counterfeit greenbacks are constantly in circulation.

In all these great and good things the colored women must share. She moves with the world, it may be slowly, but as times and customs change and advance, the colored woman changes and advances with them. For all the women of color who are seeking new avenues of work and an outlet for thoughts that breathe, there is a blessing if they persevere in the name of God and humanity—if they elect to live for others.

> For the cause that lacks assistance,
> For the wrong that needs resistance,
> For the future in the distance,
> And the good that they can do.

There is quite a ripple among women just now in favor of woman suffrage. We believe it to be a good thing if limited in some degree. It is right that women vote on such questions as property rights, the wife's personal rights and rights in her children, and in all that pertains to the public school; but it seems to us that the franchise in its fullest sense is not desirable. Physically, women are not fitted for the politician's life; morally, we should deplore seeing woman fall from her honorable position as wife and mother to that of the common ward heeler hustling for the crumbs meted out to the "faithful" of any party in the way of appointments to office. There are, indeed, many reasons why it is not desirable for women to enter the political arena. Let us consider the matter as part of the race problem, and ask ourselves these questions:

Is it desirable for us as a race to place the ballot in woman's hand?

Is the aspect of woman in certain sections such as to inspire us with confidence in the honor of the white woman toward her black sister?

If we are not the "moral lepers" that the white woman of Georgia accuses us of being, then we ought to hesitate before we affiliate too happily in any project that will give them greater power than they now possess to crush the weak and helpless.

Let us study this question and prove it a good thing for our race before we rush in blindly even to please those who have been [of] material benefit to us.

Massachusetts sets the pace in all advanced ideas. Massachusetts has been swaped in some degree by the pitiful appeals of Georgia. Colored women in Massachusetts look to it!

"A Girl's College Life"

Lavinia Hart

In addition to writing for *Cosmopolitan, Collier's Weekly,* and the *New York World,* Lavinia Hart authored *When a Maid Marries: Being a Discussion of Certain Vital Problems in the Home* (1904). Even as Hart celebrated motherhood as the "supreme moment in the life of woman," she published articles focusing on women's career achievements.[1]

Hart's article "A Girl's College Life" was published by *Cosmopolitan,* a magazine begun in 1888 by Paul J. Schlicht. *Cosmopolitan* was intended as a "first-class family magazine," but over time it became more literary than general. Elizabeth Cady Stanton, Mary E. Wilkins, and Harriet Prescott Spofford all published there. By 1892, *Cosmopolitan* had found a formula for success by incorporating many illustrations (Edward Kemble, Charles Dana Gibson, and Frederic Remington all contributed), less fiction, and more public and foreign affairs articles, and adopting aggressive advertising strategies, including premiums, scholarships, and contests. At one point, editor and publisher John Brisbane Walker offered to give away a thousand college scholarships to successful salespeople. In 1895, *Cosmopolitan* joined *McClure's* and *Munsey's Magazine* and lowered its price to ten cents, and by the end of Walker's tenure in 1905, circulation had reached over 500,000. Education was a favorite topic of Walker's magazine; in 1897 he even created a free correspondence school, Cosmopolitan University, to be supported by the proceeds of the magazine. "A Girl's College life" includes photos of women playing basketball, fencing, parading a daisy chain, and swinging on the parallel bars.[2]

The difference between the life at girls' and at men's colleges is just the difference between girls and young men.

Cosmopolitan, June 1901, 188–195.

It is not the difference in curriculum, or lecture-room, or gymnasium, or team and track athletics. It is a difference in tone, and this tone is the effect of two causes:—

First. The seriousness with which the college girl regards her course.

Second. The thoroughly feminine consideration with which she regards her fellows.

Regarding the former, nine-tenths of the girls at college are there for the purpose of fitting themselves to earn a livelihood. They are aiming to become professors, tutors, lawyers, doctors, littérateurs. They are not, generally, the daughters of wealthy parents. These go to a finishing school, and study the limitations, rather than the possibilities, of society. The female college students are mostly drawn from those medium walks of life wherein ambition is given impetus by necessity.

The college girl does not give up four or five years of her life for the purpose of being called "college-bred," as many of her brothers do; nor to gain admittance to an exclusive university club, or those circles to which a college education is the open sesame; nor "to humor the governor," at a large cost per annum for indulging his whim.

The college girl takes up her course because she loves it, and because it is the means to a much-desired end.

The spirit of restlessness prevalent in men's colleges is noticeably absent. There is no case on record where students from a girls' college have spent the night in the town lockup, as the result of reckless misbehavior. They have never been known playfully to smash mirrors in restaurants, make bonfires of farmhouse gates, steal the signs from the village shops or swap the tombstones in the near-by churchyards. This sort of reckless divertisement is the result of dissatisfaction with the legitimate advantages offered in college life. It is the result, not of sex and the more boisterous nature of the male, but of choosing the college course for some reason less pertinent than the desire to acquire knowledge.

Neither do we find the students of a girls' college verging on riot over athletic victory. Yet the triumph of their class and colors is just as dear to them; "gym" and field events are just as much a part of their lives. But it is rather the beaten ones who cheer, and applaud their victors' grit and superiority. The winners argue it is sweet enough to win; crowing over the defeated ones will add nothing to their glory, but greatly increase the disappointment of the losers.

It is this consideration for the feelings of others that gives to the girls' colleges their distinctly feminine tone. . . .

Hazing is unknown. The lower classman at a girls' college has no bad dreams of midnight duckings through the ice of the lake, or rides downhill in barrels, or straw hats in winter, or sandwich boards on the main street, or handsprings, or eagles, or tabasco refreshment. On the contrary, she isn't allowed even to get homesick. . . .

Some day, let us hope, the trustees of our female colleges will wake to the crying need of a course on House- and Husband-Keeping. A chair of Gastronomical Ethics will then be provided, training the female minds to the dignity of cooking, educating them in the science of it, and revealing to them the beauties of eating and catering as a fine art, affecting every other art, science, profession and trade in the whole human system. If engineers must be tutored in mathematics, chemists in chemistry, lawyers in codes and physicians in medical lore, why should not women, whose ultimate profession is the establishment and continuance of homes, be tutored in every branch of art and science that will help to make their life-work a success?

The "higher education" has done much for women; not only in the new spheres that have latterly opened for them, but as wives and mothers. However, it is not the "higher education" girls should seek so much as the "better education." Every girl who enjoys the privilege of education should select her courses with a perfect knowledge of her individual requirements and capabilities, and with a view to strengthening herself for whatever line of work her future is to cover. And while mathematics will be a very good thing for giving balance to her mind and poise to her conceptions generally, she can't feed them to the baby; and she can't talk Greek to the cook. The curriculum in girls' colleges is not complete; but the "higher education" is still in its infancy.

Meanwhile, the natural womanly instinct asserts itself, and the chafing-dish holds sway over all small entertainments. No book-shelf is complete without a cook-book, and the natural rivalry between hostesses encourages experiment. Vassar has gone so far as to build a kitchen with splendid equipments for the use of its students, but it is too large and too public to become popular. The cozy dormitory quarters give an added flavor to fudge, rarebits, newburgs and afternoon teas, the last being the most popular. There is little work during the late afternoon hours. Between four and five-thirty the dormitories hum with gossip, and the tea-kettles make a lively tune. It is the general hour for relaxation, for the college girl arises early. The usual hour for the first bell is six-thirty, with breakfast from seven to eight. At Mt. Holyoke the girls care for their own rooms, and in several of the dormitories at Smith and Wellesley the girls devote an hour each day to this sort of work in part payment for their board. At eight-thirty recitations begin, and the mornings are invariably busy. The day is divided in eight "hours," and engagements made for the first, second, third hour, et cetera, the time never being mentioned.

Luncheon is usually from twelve to one-thirty, after which the tension relaxes.

During the afternoons the upper classmen find plenty of time for recreation. All the girls' colleges have splendid gymnasiums, but they are not popular. Open-air athletics are greatly preferred, and there is no time in the year when some outdoor sport is not available. During the winter there are skating, tobogganing and long tramps, with basket-ball practice necessarily confined to the gymnasium. As soon as the frost is off the ground, however, the basket-ball teams revel in field practice, the rowing-machines are forsaken and the shells launched with a glad hurrah, and running records are broken and made on good turf track.

College girls are very enthusiastic athletes. Basket-ball is the universal favorite sport, and there is a general struggle to get on the teams.

This game takes the place of football at the men's colleges. Two baskets are hung on poles about eight feet high, forming goals. The girls wear bloomers and loose blouses, or sweaters, with their class year across the front. The costume is not an aid to beauty, but it is indicative of sense and comfort, and proves a wholesome lack of vanity. Basket-ball is approved by physical-culture experts as the best possible all-around development for girls. Besides improving their physical strength, it gives them poise, self-confidence, and self-control. For no matter how high excitement may run, with the calls of their class spurring them on to victory, physical culture never blots out ethical culture, and the stranger is surprised, in the midst of the excited fray, by an anxious "Oh, pardon me, did I hurt you?" or "Excuse me, I think that's our ball."

Some years ago, several of the colleges started baseball nines; but they never became popular, and did not last the season out. That was before the divided skirt was accepted as a matter of fact; and the nines announced that it was an utter impossibility to "play ball" and attend to the train. No one has ever been heartless enough to probe deeper into the facts; but if all were known, the impossibility of finding a girl who could pitch might have a bearing on the case. . . .

Then come class day and commencement exercises, with their attendant excitement and pleasure—the receiving of degrees, with a justifiable flush of pride and satisfaction; the parting with chums and familiar landmarks, with the inevitable gulp and struggle for self-control; and then—

Stern reality! Back to the old place, to take up the threads of life where departure interrupted them.

Has it paid? Has the college education better fitted them to accomplish their life's purposes? Perhaps not in all cases; but at least it cannot have hindered them. Some will go out into the arts and professions, and their college educations will be the foundations for fame and fortune; others will go out, and they will return, humbled by failure and bruised by the short, decisive battle. But the experience will do good; it will set them back in the right groove.

And others will not go out at all. They will have no ambition to conquer the world, or to carve their names on marble tablets in the Hall of Fame. These will be busy helping to make great another's name, and rearing sons to bear it. They will forget their Greek, and "trig," and the ways they took to reach the Q.E.D., and institute for themselves, within the confines of home, a postgraduate course on "The Science of House-and Husband-Keeping," which their alma mater omitted.

"The Typical Woman of the New South"

Julia Magruder

Born in Charlottesville, Virginia, Julia Magruder (1854–1907) claimed an illustrious southern heritage as the niece of Confederate general John Bankhead Magruder. In addition to writing essays and short stories for a number of magazines, she wrote novels, including *Across the Chasm* (1885), in which the love between a northerner and a southerner brings national harmony, and *Princess Sonia* (1895), which was illustrated by Charles Dana Gibson.[1]

Magruder's "Typical Woman of the New South" was published by *Harper's Bazar* (as the periodical's name was then spelled) in 1900 and illustrated with a portrait of this "typical woman" by Howard Chandler Christy. The magazine, with the subtitle *A Repository of Fashion, Pleasure, and Instruction*, first appeared in 1867, and along with articles on domestic economy, fashion, interior design, and later gardening, it featured fiction and reviews, such as William Dean Howells's "Heroines of Fiction" series. Historian and translator Mary L. Booth began as editor and is credited with making the magazine a phenomenal success. In addition to the focus on fashion, *Harper's Bazar* included a gossip section, cartoons, woodcuts and etchings from Winslow Homer and Thomas Nast, and articles on women's rights. Margaret Sangster, widely known for her work in general interest, Christian, and children's magazines, served as editor of the weekly magazine during the 1890s until Elizabeth Jordan, a reporter for the *New York World*, took control in 1899 and changed the magazine to a monthly in 1901. In 1895, circulation exceeded 75,000; in 1900, the magazine sold for ten cents a copy or four dollars a year.[2]

Harper's Bazar, Nov. 3, 1900.

164

Perhaps it will be a surprise to many when the present writer pronounces one of the prominent characteristics of the women of the new South to be industry. It has so long been an accepted conclusion that Southern women of the higher class are indolent and lacking in energy, that perhaps nothing but a visible object-lesson will do away with this idea. Such an object-lesson is not far to seek, if a spirit of fairness is brought to the question. Indeed, would not the employment of that spirit modify, if it did not quite reverse, the same dictum concerning the women of the old South? When we remember the exquisite specimens of needle-work handed down from our grandmothers, and consider that all those tiny tucks and delicate ruffles were done before the invention of sewing-machines; when we see the beautiful examples of embroidery and netting and darned work and crocheting, to say nothing of the charming old patch-work quilts, etc.—do we not feel that the present generation is shamed by the past? Besides this, every Southern girl knows how her grandmother's pickles and preserves and cake and pastry are held up to her as an ideal, as well as the careful housekeeping, the cultivation of flowers, and many other such expenditures of time and energy.

It has often been maintained that the possession of slaves made the Southern women lazy, but it was oftener the case that this fact demanded an extraordinary degree of energy and industry, for to meet the needs of a hundred men, women, and children. who depended on their owners for everything, was, in itself, so great an exaction that it is no unusual thing to hear former slave-owners say that they never knew what freedom was themselves until their slaves were freed.

All this may seem irrelevant to the question under consideration, but when we reflect that the broadened and strengthened activities of the Southern woman of the present are the outcome of the habits and customs of her ancestors, it is directly to the point.

The difference between the two types is vast. As to which has the advantage, that must depend upon the ideal in each individual's mind. Some would argue that the loss of the delicate reserve, the quaint propriety, the exacting self-respect, etc., that characterized our grandmothers was not compensated for by the energy and achievement, in more public walks of life, which characterize the Southern woman of to-day. Those who are familiar with *A Southern Planter* (the book written some years ago by a Southern woman, which so delighted Mr. Gladstone that he wrote to the author asking her permission to edit and have it republished in England), will recall how the writer, in describing her father's courtship of her mother, recounted the fact that he came about twice a month to call on his *fiancée,* and in the intervals wrote to her. These letters, however, were never answered by the young lady, it being considered honor enough that she consented to receive them!

Absurd as this would be to-day, and as much better as it is to have the more wholesome and useful customs which have taken the place of the old ones, it cannot be denied that there was a certain charm in such a point of view, ineffable and delicate as the odor of lavender or the sound of an old-fashioned melody. Such a type of womanhood served its purpose and had its day. It is now, however, a thing of the past. The question before us is, what have we to take its place?

The typical woman of the new South is, or is supposed to be, the very opposite of her ancestress in this point of her attitude toward the other sex. She is accused, and with some show of justice, of being entirely too offhand in her manners with men, and, judged by conventional standards, she is perhaps so. It is a pity, because it gives what is often a wrong impression. The very freedom and naturalness of her bearing give evidence of the unspoken fact that she has been brought up to believe that a gentleman and the son of a gentleman will never misconstrue a woman's actions.

It must be admitted that the woman of the new South is proud, a trait which she also inherited from her ancestors in the female line, but this pride is less positive than relative. It is when she compares herself with her Northern sisters that it specially comes out. As a rule, it proceeds from inexperience in worldly ways, necessitated by a very insulated life, and sometimes it is speedily corrected by a little travel, and an enforced consideration of the many points in which the women she has looked down upon are her superiors. An *acknowledgment* of this fact, however, is not in her—either in the past or in the present. That will have to be left to the Southern woman of the future.

Now that women have become self-supporting members of society, there is far less inclination toward marriage, especially early marriage, than formerly, and this very fact has made her more easy of access to men, as a comrade, though more difficult as a sweetheart.

With regard to the older women of the new South, there is a marked contrast to those of the past. In no section, of course, has the new—woman movement gained ground so slowly as in the South. But, in a modified form, its gain has been decided and evident. A desire for wider intellectual development is widespread through the South. In almost every small town there are two or three book clubs, which have their meetings, in regular rotation, at the houses of the different members. At first, the only books that were bought and discussed at these clubs were novels, but, in almost all cases, a swift evolution to more solid reading has been observable, and soon Shakespearean classes and discussions of public questions followed. The good effect of these clubs is truly remarkable in the change of tone which they quickly bring about in their communities.

In contrast to the rule of the past, which left the question of politics to the men, the Southern women of to-day are great politicians, though it must be admitted that the range of their interest and partisanship is rather local than national.

In religion, the woman of the South adheres much to her traditions, and looks upon freedom of inquiry and criticism with a stern disapproval. It is a very rare thing to see a Southern woman who is not, both in faith and in practice, strictly orthodox. There may be, and is, a certain amount of jealousy and criticism among the different Christian dominations, but they amalgamate as one in the presence of any talk or teaching that is opposed to orthodox Christianity.

In the first years after the civil war, if a girl or woman of good birth and breeding was compelled to make her own living, it was always some sheltered and retired position that was sought for her, and although she filled it with dignity, it was with an air of yielding to bitter necessity, that made a certain strong self-consciousness apparent in her attitude, as well as that of her relations. Now all this is changed. To-day some of the best of Southern women are employed as not only teachers and trained nurses, but as stenographers, type-writers, and bookkeepers, and they go about their work with a straightforward simplicity that is admirable.

To sum up: The Southern woman of to-day is an evolution of the past—an upward growth, a higher development; but as nothing is gained without some form of loss, it may be conceded that she has lost, perhaps, some of the finer delicacy that belonged to the lady, though she has acquired in its place the nobler, better, and more serviceable qualities which make the ideal of womanhood.

Above all, she has learned, or is fast learning, that to grow is the noblest thing in life, while her ancestresses, in the past, too often acted on the theory that they could do no better than to be what their mothers and grandmothers had been before them.

"Rough Sketches:

A STUDY OF THE FEATURES OF THE NEW NEGRO WOMAN"

John H. Adams Jr.

In the early twentieth century, John Henry Adams Jr. (1880–?) served as an art instructor at Morris Brown College in Atlanta. He illustrated extensively first for the *Voice of the Negro* and later in the 1910s, 1920s, and 1930s for the *Crisis*. "Rough Sketches: A Study of the Features of the New Negro Woman" appeared in the August 1904 *Voice of the Negro*, an issue devoted to the St. Louis World's Fair. According to cultural historian Laura Wexler, the Fair, with its numerous ethnographic exhibits showcasing the world's "primitive" races benefiting from the influence of the "advanced" races, "was addressing the greatest anxieties of its day, to indicate where and how white Americans could and would prevail."[1] Adams's drawing of Gussie included here was one of seven female portraits he drew for this article.

At the turn of the century, Atlanta, home to the largest number of private black colleges and prep schools in the nation, emerged as a focal point of black politics, education, and religion. In 1903, officials of the Atlanta branch of the Illinois-based Hertel, Jenkins, and Company Publishing Houses developed plans with local black citizens to begin publishing the *Voice of the Negro*. Jesse Max Barber, a graduate of Virginia Union University in Richmond, became the managing editor of what would soon be regarded as a prestigious black periodical on race relations, state and national politics, and education. Although Barber published both accommodationist and radical perspectives in the journal, he became increasingly hostile to Booker T. Washington's policy of public conciliation of white racism and sided decisively with W.E.B. Du Bois and the "radicals," agitating for

Voice of the Negro, Aug. 1904, 323–326.

full voting rights, access to higher education, and an end to lynching. *Voice of the Negro,* however, would be short-lived. After the 1906 Atlanta race riot, when the *New York World* claimed the riot had been precipitated by "'a carnival of rapes' in and around Atlanta by Negro men against white women," Barber vehemently objected and called the stories a "carnival of lies." A member of Atlanta's Board of Police Commissioners told Barber to retract his statement or leave town, so he fled to Chicago, and publication ceased in October 1907. The *Voice of the Negro* sold for ten cents in 1904, and at its height it had a circulation of 15,000.[2]

One day while standing in the centre of the business section of Atlanta, there approached me, a bright eyed, full-minded youth of some nine years of respectable rearing. Both of us looked with eyes and soul upon the passing mixed panorama of men and women and children, and horses, and vehicles, and up to the modern ten and fourteen stories of stone, brick and steel structures out of whose windows, here and there, poked curious heads peering tamely upon the seeming confusion below. I saw an uncommon life picture pass slowly through the gang-way of humming electric cars, and rattling drays and of shifting humanity. Alford Emerson Clark, my innocent companion saw it also; and the throng of hurrying black and white folks paused in contemptible curiosity as the rubber-tired wheels of the open carriage rolled silently along the Peachtree thorough-fare. In the carriage sat two ladies, one white, one colored, engaged in a happy, spirited conversation all the while unconscious, of the Southern social monster which argues the inferiority of the Negro to the white folk.

Two opposing worlds riding happily, peacefully, aye, lovingly together in the worst of Negro hating cities. Is it real? Is it natural? Is it right? What a healthy breath passed over me; and I smiled and went on with my jolly companion to the outer South end of the city.

The picture continued to press upon young Alford's mind, and with the peculiar vigor of youth, he had stopped to quander over the outward aspect of the situation. Said he, "which one is the better looking, the colored lady or the white?" Expressing my inability to decide pending a closer scrutiny of the two, I asked which did he think is the better in appearance. "The colored woman of course," he replied, as though he were greatly surprised at my not having a reason to say the same thing. Asking him for his reason, Alford looking me straight in the face said, "why the other woman is white." White? Well, what has that to do with a woman's real physical charm, either adding to or detracting from her? thought I to myself. To the black man a white face means little or nothing. To the white man it means his tradition, his civilization, his bond and recognition in the present age, and his safe guard in the future. Alford saw beneath the first skin surface down to the last layer of race greatness—the preserving and honoring of race identity and distinction. He saw in that colored woman that which he could not see in the white woman so long as "white" in America stands for hope and black for despair.

The white woman's beauty was real, pure, substantial, but it came to thoughtful Alfred with no meaning. The black woman's beauty was real, pure, substantial, but

"An admirer of Fine Art, a performer on
the violin and the piano, a sweet singer,
a writer—mostly given to essays, a lover
of good books, and a home making girl,
is Gussie."

it came with a life, a soul, which had touched his and which he not only understood
but which inspired him to love.

I looked into his rich brown eyes, into his sun-lit smiling face and caught the
gilded thread wire that, from his heart, followed the trail of Negro womanhood
into all the ends of the earth. I fixed tight hand on it, I felt the fast beating of over
nine million human hearts, as but the beating of one woman's heart when all hope
seems lost, as they struggle with an inspiration which has too many times found its
bed in the bosom of American prejudice. Still holding on to the gilded wire and
placing my head close against his throbbing breast, there was something within,
with the silence of maddened power which seemed to say: Ye gods of the earth! this
woman—mine, whom you have fettered with the chains of caste, whom you have
branded with the red iron of infamy, whom you have degraded with the finger of
your own lustful body, shall be free. God made it fast and eternal. This beauty
which you have used to tame your generations shall be yours no more, and this person that has served your rawest purposes shall not enter again into your halls.

Some day however these Negro restrictive laws, these phantasms and prejudices
shall be beat and bent and tuned to the music of a more perfect civilization in
which men shall love to do honor to all women for the sake of their sacred mission
and meaning in the shaping of human destiny. There is an inseparable linking

between mother and mother, be one white and one black; and the final triumph of civilization shall be when womanhood is a unit in all things for good and when manhood is a common factor in her defence.

We present the colored woman today as she impresses herself in the world as a growing factor for good and in her beauty, intelligence and character for better social recognition. Here she is in characteristic pose, full of vigor, tender in affection, sweet in emotion, and strong in every attribution of mind and soul.

Look upon her, ye worlds! and, since there is none better, swear by her. If there is none purer, none nobler, which have stamped pre-eminence in the very countenance of man, woman and child, cast your glittering swords, and sheaths, and armor, at her untarnished feet and pledge the very life that you enjoy to the defense of her life. Look upon her, ye nations! Measure her by all the standards of human perfection. Weigh her upon the scales that were employed in the weighing of queens, and noble-men's wives and daughters. And, if, after the test has been exhausted in the finding her real merits, she is found to have not only the physical beauty, not only the intellectual graces but also the moral stamina, the purity of heart, the loftiness of purpose and the sober consciousness of true womanhood the same as her white or red or olive sisters, then let all men whose blood finds eternal unity in the brotherhood of America's proscribed, whose traditions reach back into two-hundred and fifty years of mean slavery, and worse—of enforced ignorance;—I say, let all men, even they that be not of us, who love woman for woman's sake fling their full lives to the uncertain wind when her honor is at stake.

"The Modern Indian Girl"

Published in 1909 in the *Indian Craftsman*, "The Modern Indian Girl" was written during a period when the federal government and private organizations were
attempting to assimilate Native Americans into mainstream, white American
society. Many progressives saw assimilation as the only way of saving Indians
from extinction, which seemed imminent. Predictions of a "Vanishing American"
led to the creation of a network of missionary- and government-sponsored
industrial schools in which students were compelled to speak English, follow
strict discipline, perform manual labor, and disavow their tribal allegiance. The
U.S. Indian Industrial School at Carlisle, Pennsylvania, under the direction of
Richard Henry Pratt, became famous for transforming "old" tribal Indians into
"new" English-speaking, Christian Americans. In an 1883 address before a group
of missionary Baptists, Pratt declared, "In Indian civilization I am a Baptist,
because I believe in immersing the Indians in our civilization and when we get
them under holding them there until they are thoroughly soaked." Even as Native
American students experienced tremendous cultural loss and personal trauma in
off-reservation boarding schools, they became intermediaries between Indian
and white society. In addition, as off-reservation schools tended to break down
intertribal barriers, they facilitated the creation of an Indian rather than a tribal
identity and laid the foundation of a pan-Indian rights movement.[1]

Advertising itself as a "magazine not only *about* Indians but mainly by
Indians," the *Indian Craftsman* served as an outlet for the art-craft printing
department at the Carlisle school. Edgar K. Miller directed the press on the model
of Gustav Stickley's *Craftsman,* and Moses Friedman, the superintendent of the
Carlisle school, edited the journal. Articles were written about historical or contemporary Indian affairs; Indian legends, stories, or traditions; campus events;
former students; and changes in Indian Service employees. Most articles focused
on aspects of Indian life, including education, sanitation, health, and disease,

Sunday Magazine, in the *Indian Craftsman*, Sept. 1909.

especially tuberculosis. The magazine became so successful that publishers of Stickley's magazine demanded that it change its name, which it did 1910 to the *Red Man*.[2]

There is no more interesting or remarkable development in American life today than the evolution of the squaw of reservation and ranch into the modern Indian girl. The average American knows little or nothing of the Indian girl, what she is, and what she is doing, simply because in point of numbers she is but one in ten thousand among her pale-face sisters. The popular conception of the Indian woman, formed by reservation pictures and Wild West shows, is a primitive creature garbed in a drab, blanket-like cloak with a sort of hood falling down the back—the head of a papoose protruding from the hood. The weight of centuries of servitude bows her head to the earth that she has tilled for warrior bold since the arrow and the bow came into existence. We began to think this way of the Indian woman in childhood, and our ideas have not changed to this day. An illustration of this fact was noted recently in Western Pennsylvania.

A certain rural household was all a-flutter over the expected arrival of a twelve-year-old Indian girl who was coming to spend the summer under the supervision of the "outing agents" of the great Indian school at Carlisle. Most interested of all was the youngest member of the family, a lad of ten.

In due time the little girl arrived. She proved to be a quiet, demure creature, with large, dark eyes and glossy black hair that hung down her back in a neat plait. His eyes beaming, the little boy gave her a rapid inspection. Then a look of keen disappointment spread over his face.

"Is she a real Indian, mamma?" he asked doubtingly.

"Yes, Bobbie," replied his mother, "she's a real Indian—a nice little Indian girl."

For a moment Bobbie was silent, and then in incredulous tones he asked: "Well, if she is an Indian, where are her feathers?"

Bobbie's idea of what an Indian should be is not greatly at variance with that of several million Americans who never have seen one outside a circus tent. But, as a matter of fact, the clear-eyed, intelligent, clean-limbed, progressive, and talented Indian woman of today is as different from the humble, plodding, dull-eyed squaw of the Western plains in days agone as is the "finishing school" graduate from the women who followed the Forty-Niners to California.

This unique evolution of the "real American girl" has been due to the educational advantages offered her by the Government in its non-reservation schools. The largest of these is at Carlisle, Pa. Here the Indian woman is seen at her best. From the study halls of Carlisle are going out girls who are taking their places beside their white sisters as nurses in the hospitals, as music teachers, and as teachers going back to the reservations to light the tapers of hope for those who remain there.

The Indian girl enters Carlisle when a child—before she has become a part of reservation life, with its constant tendency to shiftlessness. At once she comes into contact with Indian women of the nobler mold—women who see in their own energy and development the hope of the Indian race in America—and she begins a regular course under the instruction of teachers whose patience is matched only by their earnestness of purpose.

She is taught to make her own clothing, and in this work her talents for sewing and weaving, inherited from far generations, find ready expression. Soon she is an adept with the needle, and finally she can "build" a gown that would become any princess in a royal court. The bead-work she has learned on the reservation is continued, and the tasteful pictures and plaques that adorn her rooms are all the products of her own skillful fingers and her ability to blend colors effectively. One building at Carlisle is given over almost entirely to an exhibition of useful and ornamental household articles that were made by students.

When the school term is over, the Indian girl is placed in some well recommended household in one of the Eastern States. There she associates with the children of the family, receives religious instruction, and is given plenty of time to enjoy picnics and other excursions into the country.

In the last few years hundreds of homes in Pennsylvania, New Jersey, Delaware, Maryland, and New York have opened their doors to Indian girls, giving them every advantage enjoyed by the children in these families. Invariably they have proved obedient, energetic, and grateful for instruction and kindnesses. Sometimes a girl remains with a family throughout the winter, attending school and enjoying the social events that enliven country life.

The Indian girl studies music, for she is a musician born. Photography she learns, too, for she appreciates the beauties of nature. She trains as a nurse, and she takes a course in pedagogy. In "amateur theatricals" she makes a delightful heroine. The Indian male, as every schoolboys knows, is an orator by inheritance. In the same way almost every Indian girl is an elocutionist.

Her physical development is not neglected. While her brother is winning honors on the gridiron against the "Big Four," she is displaying her skill in basketball and tennis. A basketball game at Carlisle is a sight to make the pulse beat faster. Quick as a deer, with eye sure and arm strong, the Indian girl can pitch the ball with surprising accuracy. The teams play a fast game in which skill and strength are perfectly blended.

This "blending" process is the secret of success in the development of the Indian girl. When she doffs her graduation gown and steps forth to face the world she is a woman in every sense. Her mental training has been along sure lines, and her manual and physical training has been commensurate to her accomplishments in the literary branches.

Besides, she has reached a high state socially. She has been in constant association since girlhood with the best families that can be found by the outing agents, and her school associates have been her teachers and Indian men of the highest type.

With an eye single to the complete civilization of the race, Carlisle encourages sociability between its young men and young women. There is complete freedom between the sexes, and be it said to the credit of the big Government school, that nothing but good has come of this.

Returning to the reservation she will at once begin to prepare the children around her for entrance at Carlisle or other Government schools. If she marry and remain in the East, she will help the outing agents in placing Indian children in the best homes.

When she leaves school she will become, very likely, a designer of dresses, a school teacher, a nurse, or a music teacher. When she leaves the class-rooms at nineteen or twenty she still possess[es] in the fullest degree that greatest inheritance of her race—patience. Her patience and her forbearance make the Indian woman the finest trained nurse. In any hospital she is a treasure, and from year to year more and more nurses' aprons are being worn by her. The sight of blood and suffering does not throw the Indian girl into hysterics, not because there is any inborn cruelty in her nature, as might be supposed, but because her nerves are always under control. The skilled surgeon wants no better assistant in an operation, the patient needs no better attendant. She never complains and she is never flurried or worried. Always and under all circumstances she is tender, painstaking, and patient.

If she becomes a teacher, her patience counts as in the hospital.

In the last year or two there have gone out from Carlisle, into the several vocations mentioned, girls from the following tribes: Mohawk, Oneida, Pueblo, Sioux, Cherokee, Chippewa, Ottawa, Cheyenne, Nez Perce, Apache, Seneca, Crow, Piegan, Mission, Sac and Fox, Shoshone, Winnebago, Tuscarora, Porto Rican, Simme, Osage, Cayuga, Assiniboine, Menomonee, Delaware, Alaskan, Shawnee, Miami, Wyandotte, Omaha, Pawnee, Comanche, Puyallup, Siletz, Stockbridge, Quapaw, Coeur d'Alene, Kaw, Klamath, Elnek, Caddo, Ponca, and others.

But while she is so highly thought of as teacher, designer, and nurse, the Indian girl herself believes that her greatest work is in elevating her own people. Clearvisioned, she sees that his indolence and his innate desire to resist the encroachment of civilization have resulted almost in the annihilation [of] the Red Man.

It is her function to arouse him from his lethargy, and to show him the preservation of the race lies not only in accepting the "inevitable" but in reaching out and grasping it; in taking up the "white man's burden" and carrying it along in the march of progress.

It is she who must teach him to be energetic, to take advantage of the opportunities for educating his children, to forget the days of campfire and war feathers, and to build homes and establish within them the aims and ideals of the pale-face.

To accomplish these things is the ambition of the modern Indian girl, the most remarkable woman in some respects on this continent.

"Lo! The New Indian. Mohawk Belle"

Founded in 1871 as a politically independent newspaper, the *Los Angeles Express* (also the *Los Angeles Evening Express*) was in 1903 the city's oldest daily newspaper and a fierce rival of the *Los Angeles Times*. Purchased in 1901 by Edwin Earl, the *Express* became known for endorsing progressive initiatives and for its owner's legendary animosity toward the *Times*'s anti–trade union Harrison Gray Otis.[1]

Los Angeles Express, Oct. 3, 1903, 2.

"The Sacrifice"

Founded in May 1905 by Robert Abbott, the *Chicago Defender* would become the most important black newspaper in the United States. Across its masthead ran the motto "American Race Prejudice Must Be Destroyed." From an initial circulation of 300 copies distributed in Chicago, the paper grew steadily. In 1910, demand surged after the paper adopted many of Hearst's sensational writing techniques, banner headlines, and human-interest content. By 1915 the *Defender* had opened branch offices in New York and London, offered news items from more than twenty-five cities across the country, and boasted a circulation of 16,000; the following year that figure jumped to 50,000. Rather than relying exclusively on the postal service, Abbott depended on porters, waiters, and "stage folk," who picked up the magazine in the railroad hub of Chicago to distribute it nationwide. At the same time, these railroad workers picked up copies of newspapers from other cities that had been left on the trains and dropped them off in the *Defender*'s Chicago offices. Entertainers on tour collected news items and also helped circulate and distribute the paper. According to Fay Young, the *Defender*'s sports editor, "many people helped Mr. Abbott because they felt they were somehow helping their race." By 1918, circulation had increased to 100,000, and the price, which had begun at two cents, was ten cents by 1921. The *Defender* played a crucial role in exposing the effects of southern Jim Crow laws and in spurring the Great Migration. Between 1910 and 1920 the African American population of Chicago rose from 44,000 to 109,000.[1]

The *Defender*'s response to demands for greater rights for women was ambivalent. Abbott saw the New Woman as an affront to romance and nature: "But the new woman flies in the face of Great Nature and in her emancipation into the fields of trade and endeavor, demands the very pound of flesh that

---

Chicago Defender, Sept. 9, 1916, n. p.

Shylock did until the poetry of loving seems a lost chord in Elysian fields." He maintained that a married woman's place was in the home and initially opposed women's suffrage, fearing that the woman who "dabbles in politics must needs neglect her home and children." But after Illinois granted women some voting privileges in 1913, Abbott endorsed the measure: "The right of the ballot is the sign and safeguard of our liberty. . . . Women should have a hand in making the laws by which they are governed as well as the men, and the south by opposing woman suffrage is simply following its usual trend to place obstructions in the way of every movement that tends for the betterment of mankind."[2]

"Remember, son and daughter, that your dear old mother and father have sacrificed many necessities in life that you might be able to go away to school and gain an education to be fit to wage life's battle against the world. Your appreciation can be easily shown by hard study, good deportment, and as a reward for your earnestness you will meet with success, which will gladden the hearts of the 'folks at home.' Keep ever before you your MOTHER and FATHER."

"Professional Training"

Begun in 1921, *College Humor* was one of the most popular of the college humor magazines. In 1923 it charged thirty-five cents. It offered collections of quips, short articles, and illustrations from college magazines across the country. The following illustration originally appeared in the University of Washington's *Sun Dodger*.

"Say I wisht I had a college education like you. Mr. Gest pays you $20 a week more'n us just cause you can dance so naughty and drink whiskey in the big scene realistically."

College Humor, Summer 1923, 18.

PART V

Work and the Labor Movement

"The New Woman"

Born in Cork, Ireland, Mary Harris Jones (1837–1930), better known as Mother Jones, emigrated to the United States as a child but was raised in Toronto, Canada. As an adult she worked in Memphis, Tennessee, where she met and married her husband, a member of the International Iron Molder's Union, and bore four children. In 1867 she lost her husband and children to a yellow fever epidemic in Memphis, and in 1871, after moving to Chicago, she lost all of her possessions in the great fire when she was thirty-four. According to her autobiography, in the turmoil that followed she became converted to the cause of labor, including workers' fight for better treatment, adequate pay, and reasonable hours, and thereafter devoted her life to it. She likely joined the Knights of Labor in the mid-1880s. During a period when few workers could depend on safety measures, child labor was commonplace, miners were often paid in company scrip, and most employees worked ten hours a day, six days a week, while many others endured twelve-hour days, Jones traveled throughout the United States rallying workers: coal miners in western Pennsylvania, West Virginia, and Colorado; copper miners in Michigan's Upper Peninsula; and garment workers in Chicago. Even as Jones worked for socialist organizations, she grew disaffected with the movement for what she saw as its growing middle-class distance from the plight of American laborers. Likewise, she tended to see middle-class reformers as patronizing, and disapproved of prohibitionists, settlement house workers, and birth control advocates. Although initially supportive of women's suffrage, she later argued that the movement diverted women's attention from the far more important class struggle.[1]

In November 1873, a consortium of blacklisted printers in Pittsburgh founded the *National Labor Tribune,* in which the following article about Mother Jones was published. Issues sold for a penny a copy. In 1877, the paper became the official organ of the Miners' National Association, and by 1897 it was the official

National Labor Tribune, Aug. 26, 1897, n.p.

organ of the Amalgamated Association of Iron, Steel, and Tin Workers of the
United States and the American Federation of Labor.

Of all the subjects that have been discussed the "new woman" has received more
severe raps than any that have been discussed in the newspapers for many a day.
While we do not approve of the "new woman" that makes a show of herself bicy-
cling up and down the principal thoroughfares of a city in bloomers, but we do
approve of the "new women" in affairs that they are more than any one else directly
interested. The latest in this line is the women as labor agitators. But it is not a nineteenth century wonder that women have at this late day taken an interest in the
affairs of their husband's wage and the interests of the land that they think as much
of as any one, even if they have no say in electing men to make laws to which they
are amenable as the male population. Who done more gallant service than Mollie
Pitcher, the hero of a battle during the American revolution, who, when her husband fell mortally wounded at his post, and the gun was ordered to the rear for
want of men to man it, jumped into the breach and done as well, if not better than
her helpmeet? Who that has read history has not read of Dido, who fled from Tyre
and founded Carthage in 800 B.C., who cut up a bull's hide, some as fine as a hair,
and acquired as much land as she could cover with it? Then we have Joan of Arc, the
little French heroine, who turned ignominious defeat into a glorious victory?

But the woman that we wish to speak of in this article is Mrs. Mary Jones, of
Chicago. She has done more missionary work for the miners of the Pittsburg district than any two of the officials, and done it better. She seems to have the gift of
talking in that forcible manner that interests you the moment she enters into a conversation with you. To her, more than any one else, the miners owe much of their
success in this unpleasantness. She has "roughed" it in this district for the last four
weeks, and in all kinds of weather she is ready to take the field and use her persua-
sive powers on the men that are, in a measure, cutting their own throats. To[o]
much credit cannot be given to this "new woman," and her name will go down in
history as one of the martyrs to the cause of oppressed humanity, and in years to
come Mary Jones will be as much of a hero as Dido and Mollie Pitcher. Oh that we
only had a few more Mary Jones to lead the men out of the slough of despond that
they seem to have fallen into.

"The New Woman and Her Ways:

THE WOMAN FARMER"

Maude Radford Warren

After earning a Ph.B. and Ph.M. from the University of Chicago, Canadian-born Maude Lavinia Radford Warren (1875–1934) taught literature and composition there from 1893 to 1907 before beginning a successful career as a professional writer, primarily as a journalist and writer of children's books. During World War I, she served as a war correspondent, and many of her articles on Russia and the threat of bolshevism appeared in the *New York Times Magazine*. In November 1910, the *Saturday Evening Post* published an article by Warren titled "Petticoat Professions: New Women in Old Fields" in which she noted the barriers women face in newspaper journalism: "The authorities seem to think that women lack the news instinct and often fail in the luck of being on the spot when something happens. In the newspaper world man's prejudice against the woman worker is injurious. . . . It is hard for her to get hold of political, financial, military or waterfront news." Magazine writing, however, proved more hospitable: "The woman who writes for the magazines enjoys something as near to professional equality with men as is possible in this world where all the laws and all the important customs are made by men."[1]

Warren's "The New Woman and Her Ways" was also published by the *Saturday Evening Post*. The periodical had been bought in 1897, when it was nearly bankrupt, by Cyrus Curtis, who had intended the *Post* to be the male analogue to its successful female-centered predecessor. The magazine faltered at first, but after George Horace Lorimer was hired as editor-in-chief in 1899, it slowly grew successful by appealing to middle- and lower-level businessmen specifically and middle-class men generally. Articles on business, biographical sketches of political and military

Saturday Evening Post, July 30, 1910, 8–9, 38–40.

figures, stories, and advice columns appeared regularly. After the first few years, the *Post* gradually expanded its audience to include women by, in part, endorsing women's suffrage and white women's increasing presence in the paid labor force. At the same time, the magazine clearly positioned men as the breadwinners and women as consumers. Indeed, between 1900 and 1910 it ran a series of articles on how businesses could best persuade women to buy their products. By 1910, half of the *Post*'s pages were devoted to advertisements. In 1909, at five cents a copy, it boasted a circulation of over "a million a week."[2]

Although the period 1894–1930 witnessed a surge in the number of people living in American urban centers, the rural population in the United States also increased, from 44 million in 1900 to almost 50 million by 1910. For the first time in history, the number of farms in the United States surpassed six million. At the same time, agriculture was rapidly professionalizing. By 1908, there were 89 schools of agriculture and 458 agriculture periodicals with a combined circulation of 15 million.[3]

The article reprinted here originally included numerous illustrations by Charlotte Weber-Ditzler.

There is an increasing number of women in this country to whom spring is no longer the season of romance, the time when the blood tingles for a score of inexplicable reasons easily grouped under a general yearning for green and balminess, and when the mind turns to flowery hats and muslin gowns. To these women, numbering almost a million, spring is a hard practical business season when they put on short skirts and rubber boots, and scrutinize the green with an appraising and critical eye, and watch for the balminess with calculating mind rather than with poetical soul. They are farmers, even more anxious to get their money out of the ground than as if it came from a school board or a business office. The pay envelope does not change its character, but the face of the earth does; some little whim of Nature will blacken the wheat crop of will bring an unexpected shower of gold from the melon field.

"Why did I become a farmer?" one of these women replied to a questioner. "When I heard that the earth yielded seven billions in dividends; when I was told that the eggs sold in this country in one year were more valuable than the products of the gold and silver mines; when I read that five million square feet of glass are devoted to the growing of vegetables alone, and when I realized that no trust and no hideous barrier labeled 'Large Capital' stood in the way of my getting a share of the spoil—then I didn't see why some of those dividends shouldn't be mine. Common-sense, a liking for details, magnificent health and nine hundred dollars—that is what I began with. I had no experience or training; I got both as I went along, paying much more in losses than a training would have cost me at an agricultural college, and finding out, too, that if I had had five thousand instead of nine hundred dollars, my returns would have been much more in keeping with the hard work I have done." . . .

All women who make headway, whether they follow farming because it was the occupation of husband or father, or whether they come into it from other occupations, are of the same practical tailor-made type—women usually past their first youth, no longer eager for the life of the city with its crowds and amusements, and, above all, no longer just working at something or other till they can get married, but looking for something that will suit their particular needs and provide for their unmarried middle and old age. If they are young, they are of those who do not make marriage their preëminent aim. They are all of the nature that could never be content to be cogs in a wheel, and so they choose a self-directing life—and there is none more individual. They are alert, resourceful and tactful, the sort to master the soil, but also the sort that could anywhere master a difficult situation.

---∞∞∞---

"Debemos Trabajar"
[We Must Work]

Astrea

As a borderland city, Laredo, Texas, consisted primarily of Mexican residents, many of whom had lived in the area long before the 1848 Treaty of Guadalupe Hidalgo created the U.S.-Mexican border at the Rio Grande River. When the Mexican Revolution began in 1910, Laredo's population rose sharply as Mexicans fled their home country to find work and political refuge in the United States. *La Crónica* (1909–?) was one of the most influential newspapers along the border.[1] Written and published by Nicasio Idar and his eight children, *La Crónica* promoted the rights of Mexicans in Texas while protesting segregation and a host of other racist abuses. For Idar, a former railroad worker and one of the organizers of a union of Mexican railroad workers, the Mexican Revolution represented an opportunity for Chicanos to organize and fight for civil and economic rights. Idar held the First Mexican Congress in 1911, out of which arose the Liga Femenil Mexicana (League of Mexican Women), devoted to improving the status of women. Although many of the articles in *La Crónica* advocated that women submit to their husbands, the newspaper, with the advent of the Mexican Revolution, called on Mexican women to take on a greater role in society.[2]

The modern woman, aware of and acknowledging the need to do her part to aid in the enlightenment of all peoples, is courageously venturing into all areas and segments of the economy, with no fear or lethargy. She turns her back on leisure and inaction, because now, at a time when she is so full of life opportunities, so full of energy and hope, there is no place for idle bums in society.

La Crónica (Laredo, Texas), Nov. 23, 1911, 2

Inaction and indolence are viewed today as disgraceful traits, and as such are shunned by those who consider themselves factors in the development and progress of all peoples.

Modern women do not spend their days settled in the comfort of an armchair. Not even rich women do so; even those blessed with wealth devote themselves to charity or philanthropy by organizing charitable or recreational clubs, out of a desire to do something useful for themselves or their peers.

Working women, fully aware of their rights, proudly hold their heads high and step into the struggle. Their era of degradation has passed. They are no longer slaves sold for mere coins. They are no longer men's servants, but rather their partners, as men are their natural protectors, not their lords and owners.

Despite all that has been said and written in opposition to the feminist movement, women in California may now serve on juries and hold public office.

Sorely mistaken are those discontent, superficial spirits who are unworthy of good deeds and criticize women who brush aside social convention to devote their energy to gainful or charitable purposes. Such people ignore the moral stakes involved, as a person devoted to work or activity has no time for anything futile or harmful. A woman worker sitting at a sewing machine or performing clerical duties is more relevant than a young woman with idle time on her hands who merely visits others or hops from one commercial establishment to another, serving as a mouthpiece for gossip or idle chatter.

A dignified and hard-working single woman does not ask to live at the expense of the head of the family, be he the father, a brother, or a relative. No. A healthy, brave, strong woman devotes her energy and talent to helping her family, or at least to supporting herself.

Just as upstanding, hard-working men feel contempt for drifters and idlers, so too do working women not appreciate useless, idle women.

Translated by Paul Coltrin.

⸺⟨ΩΩΩ⟩⸺

"New Jobs for New Women"

Virginia Roderick

Stella Virginia Roderick (1880?–1965) completed a master's thesis in English at Columbia University in 1903 and thereafter spent much of her professional career in New York. After contributing to *Everybody's Magazine* for a number of years, she served as its managing editor from 1919 to 1921, where she was known as S. V. Roderick. Afterward she became editor of the *Woman Citizen* (begun in 1917, it became the *Woman's Journal* in 1928), a periodical committed to "plead as ever for the removal of discriminations against women in law and custom." In the 1920s it opposed child labor and lynching, and supported Prohibition and international peace. Roderick was then hired to write the biography of Nettie Fowler McCormick, who, after the death of her husband, played a crucial role in managing the McCormick agricultural manufacturing company.[1]

    Everybody's Magazine was begun by John Wanamaker, the famous Philadelphia founder of Wanamaker department stores. The magazine was purchased in 1903 by Erman Jesse Ridgway, who had formerly been part of the Munsey organization. Ridgway made the advertising professional John Adams Thayer an active partner. When the magazine published Thomas William Lawson's famous, long-running (1904–1907) muckraking exposé "Frenzied Finance," about the corrupt business dealings of Standard Oil, Amalgamated Copper, and large corporations, circulation soared to 750,000. Lawson authored another financial exposé for *Everybody's* in 1912–1913, but it was less successful, and Ridgway conceded that muckraking could no longer spur sales as it once had. By 1911, with a circulation of approximately 500,000, *Everybody's* could boast of being America's leading general-interest monthly. Although circulation held at half a million for several years thereafter, advertising and circulation gradually declined. John O'Hara

———

Everybody's Magazine, Mar. 1914, 324–325.

0

Cosgrave, who served as editor in 1900–1903 and 1906–1911, was followed by Trumbull White, who maintained the attractive look of the magazine. He published the work of leading illustrators—N. C. Wyeth, May Wilson Preston, James Montgomery Flagg, and others—fiction by leading writers, news analysis, theater reviews, and, beginning in 1913, a financial section. In 1914, it sold for fifteen cents. *Everybody's* saw itself as offering more serious fare than its chief competitor, *Cosmopolitan,* which at the time combined salacious "sex in society" serials with other more serious literary content.[2]

"Is she going to stay at home, or teach?"

Twenty years ago that was a common question about a college girl-graduate. "To work" practically meant "to teach."

Nowadays New York, Chicago, Philadelphia, and Boston each has an occupation agency for trained women which handles almost anything *except* teaching. All specialize in work for college women, and cooperate with college clubs, as well as with each other. The first three are managed and maintained by the alumnae associations of various colleges. And in the first report of the Intercollegiate Bureau of New York, as well as in the Boston Appointment Bureau's lists, about sixty types of non-teaching position are registered.

Many of these are comparatively new kinds of "jobs," springing out of new conditions and new knowledge: dietitians and visiting housekeepers, for instance; publicity secretaries; playground directors; the more modern forms of social work—executive secretaries for societies of sex hygiene or vice commissions, and vocational assistants; expert cooperative buyers.

Others, like that of farm manager and chaffeuse, are "men's jobs" newly opened to women; so is that of the women employed by an electric company to organize electrical demonstrations and to wire houses where timid housewives might refuse admittance to men.

Not only these but also a number of positions traditionally feminine show a breaking down of false social distinctions between "professional" and "non-professional work"—an increase in democratic feeling on the part of educated women. Out of the 422 positions filled by the New York Bureau in nineteen months, 189 went to stenographers and secretaries, and the next largest number to clerks, proof-readers, and office assistants, while matrons and house-keepers—many of them college women, mind you!—had a fair proportion.

The reason for excluding teaching is that it is a known country, well-lighted, well-mapped; also densely peopled. These agencies aim to save women from teaching *merely* because they have gone to college and are obliged to work. They are helping to put sign-boards and lamp-posts in the region of "non-teaching occupations," and definitely to enlarge the scope of women's work. So, although algebra and Latin are not within their limits, the lists of these Bureaus include teachers of manual arts in sanitariums for nervous disorders, a woman engaged to train cripples in hand-work for self-support, and another to organize industrial work for cardiac patients.

It is interesting that out of 960 applicants in the New York Agency, 201 were academic teachers anxious to change their work. . . .

That technical training is usually essential is the easiest conclusion from the experience of these Bureaus with college women. To determine when and where it should be given, is one of the hardest problems of education. On this point the Bureau chiefs are wide-open-minded, and have the honesty to admit "No final conclusions" on the merits of vocational training in college as compared with a supplementary technical course. But they are very clear on the proposition that a general college education does not turn out settlement experts, trained investigators, or tea-room managers.

Men don't expect it. Why should women?

This special training is not a very formidable consideration, however. Even if one has not chosen vocational courses in college, the technique of secretarial work, social service, or horticulture, farming, bee-raising, domestic management, can be sandwiched into vacations or acquired in a comparatively short period of post-college work. And it is to the old-line, cultural college that employers are paying tribute in their endorsement of the college-trained-candidates. Again and again they say "We like the type of women you send us," and repeatedly, after having had one college-trained employee, they come back for more. In secretarial work, indeed, a woman sometimes suffers through an employer's tendency to keep her on mechanical duties, because of the luxury of having a stenographer who "knows something." . . .

"A New Woman?"

Dorothy Weil

Born in New York, Dorothy Weil (1894–1949) moved to Chicago sometime before 1910. She earned a master's degree in English from the University of Chicago in 1923, became a junior college teacher, and served as president of Chicago's Federation of Woman High School Teachers. In a letter to the *New Republic* in August 1916, she appears to have renounced her association with the *Masses* by calling it an ineffectual outlet for women who didn't want the "tiresome routine" of a real job: "What daughter really wants is to dabble in rebellion without sacrificing her chances of the same kind of shelterdom which has been her mother's. To embrace Emma Goldman and *The Masses*—however excellent—is not rebellion. It is the mere childish beginning, the 'stagey' part of it."[1]

The *Masses* was founded as an illustrated monthly magazine in 1911 by Piet Vlag, the Dutch manager of a cooperative restaurant in the basement of New York's Rand School of Social Science, which had been established since 1906 as a center for socialist education. The publication would became, according to literary historian Walter Rideout, "the most gifted, the most varied, and the most iconoclastic" of the more than three hundred socialist periodicals published in the United States at the time. Throughout its relatively short life, the magazine functioned as a cooperative, where the artists, writers—including John Sloan, Art Young, Louis Untermeyer, and Mary Heaton Vorse—and office workers maintained full control but no pay. Because of the magazine's disinterest in profits, it needed a financial backer, which it found in the socialist Rufus Weeks, a vice president of the New York Life Insurance Company. Under the editorship of Max Eastman, the *Masses* became a major socialist literary and political magazine, although it published a range of socialist, anarchist, and syndicalist perspectives.

Masses, Jan. 1916, 17–18.

At its peak it reached a circulation of approximately 15,000 to 25,000, but on average its monthly circulation was 14,000. And although when the magazine began in 1911 it charged five cents, by 1912 it charged ten cents. In December 1912, Eastman declared his intention to make the magazine an antidogmatic, popular socialist periodical: "A revolutionary and not a reform magazine; a magazine with a sense of humor and no respect for the respectable; frank, arrogant, impertinent, searching for true causes; a magazine directed against rigidity and dogma wherever it is found; printing what is too naked or true for money-making press; a magazine whose final policy is to do as it pleases and conciliate nobody, not even its readers." Indeed, the magazine never became an official publication of the Socialist Party, nor were contributors paid, and it heralded anarchists, the Industrial Workers of the World, Freudians, birth-control advocates, free love proponents, and feminists. In its feminist articles, the magazine concentrated on those social evils that would be ameliorated by socialism and feminism—prostitution, outmoded divorce laws, and a belief in male exceptionalism. Particularly known for its artwork, the *Masses* gave center stage to its cartoons and drawings.[2]

Believing World War I to be an imperialist "bankers' war" contrary to the needs of the working class, the magazine published a number of antiwar articles and cartoons. As a result, under the Espionage Act of 1917 the *Masses* was denied use of the mails. To appease the U.S. Post Office, the magazine was reorganized, took a pro-Wilsonian stance, and called itself the *Liberator*.[3]

Mrs. Knox is my cleaning woman. For six years and more now she's been coming to me every Wednesday regular, and never missed a day. And there never was a woman like her to clean straight through from top to bottom.

Wednesday morning, three or four weeks ago, when I was expecting her as usual, she called me up.

"I can't come this morning, Mis' Bullock," she said.

"Why, what's the trouble, Mrs. Knox? Are you sick?"

"Well," she answered kind of slow, "I'm going to the hospital."

"To the hospital! Whatever is the matter with you?"

"It's—it's—well, it's another child comin'," she said, so low I could just barely get it. I almost let the telephone drop bang out of my hand.

"W-what?" I managed at last. "Why, how can it? Your husband—

Her husband's a good-for-nothing that she's had to get away from; though she, being a Catholic, couldn't divorce him once for all.

"Oh, yes, my husband right enough," she came back, with a bitter tone in her voice. "I told you he'd been givin' me money this last year. Well, no man ain't givin' no woman money for nothin' in this world!"

"Why didn't you tell me about it sooner?" I asked.

"Why, you didn't seem to notice, ma'am, and somehow I couldn't bring myself to be a' tellin of it. I'd it all fixed for someone else to call you up, if things hadn't been kind of sudden."

Well, what could I say? "There, there, Mrs. Knox, I hope it's all for the best," I said. And then I told her to send over one of the boys for some things I had around.

Of course Henry had to know about it. He talked about the "senseless follies of the working classes," which didn't have anything to do with it so far as I could see. I told him straight that Knox was her husband right enough, if he had been off like a vagabond for six years and more.

"See here, Henry Bullock," I said, "who're you and I, I'd like to know, that we should set up as the Lord Almighty to judge his creatures? I've an idea that we can't criticize a woman who slaves every day cleaning people's houses and every night scrubbing out office buildings, to feed her family. It appears to me that most anything she does after that deserves forgiveness even if it were a lot worse that bearing her own husband's children."

Well, I had to have a new cleaning woman. That was how Jennie Brill [?] came to me. A pleasant young thing, but frail and consumptive looking. She couldn't come up to Mrs. Knox, but she was awfully willing. She seemed just terribly anxious to please me.

The second week she had just got in and was drinking some hot coffee to warm her, when in came Mrs. Knox, ready to go to work again. I hadn't the heart to send either one of them off without her day's work in that kind of weather, so I told them I'd keep them both and clean down the attic. Jennie looked so grateful, I was glad I'd thought of it. But they'd been working less than two hours when Mrs. Knox came to me all hot and excited.

"Mrs. Bullock," she says, "you'll have to get that critter out of here, I'm a respectable woman, Mrs. Bullock, and the honest mother of a family, and I'll not be working next a woman unmarried who has a child."

For a minute I just stared at her. "How—how do you know?" I asked.

"She told me herself!"—and Mrs. Knox was so triumphant that, Lord forgive me, I couldn't resist saying,

"Well, what of it?"

The minute it was out, of course, I felt as wicked as need be, but I wasn't going back on it for all that. "Wait a minute till I call her down," I said, "and we'll see what she's got to say for herself."

When she came in, "Jennie," I said, "what's this Mrs. Knox is telling me?"

"Yes'm," says Jennie, looking from one of us to the other and trying to see how to take us.

"You *have* a baby?" I asked nervous.

Jennie's face crinkled up, loving—you know how I mean, if you've every watched a woman talking about her child. "Oh yes'm, I've got him right enough, bless his heart. I just couldn't keep quiet about him any longer when Mrs. Knox here told me all about her new one."

"Why *should* you keep quiet?" broke in Mrs. Knox cannily.

"I don't know. I can't say as I *feel* anything wrong. But everywhere, every job I get—as soon as they find out about the child, off I go. It appears like a woman trying to earn a living for her child ought to hold a job better than if she's only got herself to work for." Jennie's big eyes were all troubled-looking.

"Yes, but the father? You're not married," I couldn't help saying, and Jennie came back with my own words to Mrs. Knox.

"Well," she said, "what of it?"

It was the vengeance of the Lord upon me and I couldn't answer a word; but that didn't stop Mrs. Knox.

"What of it?" she cries. "What *of* it? If you haven't got no religion to keep you straight, Miss Jennie, you might consider us respectable women that has, and *our* children. It's only to keep my children from the likes of yours that I've put up with a drunken beast all these years. It's only for that I've slaved through the days and nights. I won't work side by side with your kind. I know ye."

"Well," says Jennie, "my work's honest and I don't see as anything else matters. I'm willing as another to work for my child. I'm working myself to the grave for him as it is," she said, and she coughed, stirred up as she was with excitement.

"Yes, but Jennie," I said, "there are other things that matter. How could you *have* the child? How could you do it? You look like a good girl, Jennie—"

"How could I?" Jennie caught me up. "Well, I didn't do it for money from nobody, ma'am, whether he calls himself my husband or something else. I suppose you'll not think me so good, ma'am, but I did it because I wanted to. Well, look at me! It ain't folks like you in your comfort that can judge me. It's only the women that works day and night and year in and year out, and stands beatings and starvings and freezings like mine that might have a word to say. That was why it seemed to me just natural to be telling Mrs. Knox here. I thought she'd understand. But I guess"—with a mean laugh—"if a woman's got the intellec' to understand the Catholic religion she ain't got none left for ordinary things."

I broke in quick at that. "Jennie, don't you dare to say anything about anyone's religion. That's her business. I think you'd be the better for a little of it yourself. I feel as though I ought to call in my minister right away. I'm sure I don't know what to do with you, girl."

"Oh please, ma'am," says Jennie at that, "I don't want none of your ministers. He'll call me a 'case' and send me to Denver or some place and put the child in a Home. It's only to keep the child, ma'am, that I'm living and standing all this, I tell you. You don't know what it is to earn for two of us, or you'd see I was dead in earnest to try it. This out-by-the-day stuff's terrible irregular, and people are always afraid they'll catch your disease, or that you'll die on their hands or something. And for anything else you need decent clothes, and then they don't want you either if you cough."

"Well, don't you see from that," I broke out (I haven't been a Willing Worker all these years without being equal to *some* arguments)—"don't you see you're putting the thing off? You'll have to be separated from the child sooner or later."

"Not as long as I can help it I won't," said Jennie, and at that Mrs. Knox broke in again.

"Oh, put the hussy out, ma'am," she said. "She's naught but a brazen thing, and we'll never get the attic done at this rate."

"Mrs. Knox," I said, "be quiet. This is more important than the attic!" Whatever had got into me to say things like that I don't know. But that stopped Mrs. Knox, so I hurried right back at Jennie.

"There's the authorities, my girl," I said. "I'm sure the authorities could take the child away from you on account of its health."

"Oh please, Mis' Bullock," said Jennie, looking scared, "they can't if they don't know about me, and they won't if you don't tell them, ma'am. I ain't asked no odds of no one yet, so they ain't no one has got a right to butt into my private affairs. You won't tell 'em, Mis' Bullock; oh please, don't tell 'em. The boy'd be lots worse off than if I cared for him. I *love* the boy, Mis' Bullock, ma'am."

Was ever a woman in such a fix? Those big eyes of hers were running over with tears and I felt myself choking. And then Mrs. Knox, who has so many children I guess she'd as soon be rid of a few, gave a snort. "Mrs. Knox," I said, "if you'd rather be doin' the attic you can go along. I don't know what to do, girl. I think you'd ought to tell me a bit more so's that I'd see clearer. How—how *did* you come to do it?"

I don't suppose I would have dared to ask a second time that way if I had been a real good woman, and remembered that the whole thing was taking place in Henry Bullock's bedroom, but I never gave Henry or his strict opinions one single thought!

"I'll tell you all I can, ma'am," said Jennie. And Mrs. Knox, seeing a story coming, sat down to listen.

"Well ma'am," Jennie began, "I was the oldest girl and my father had ten kids besides my oldest brother, who was always a regular tough and bum and is serving his six years now. And I've been taking care of babies and doing housework and washing and scrubbing always, so you can see I'm used to it, ma'am. From before I was twelve I been working a dozen hours a day in a box factory or a clothes shop or a hat factory or something else, depending on where we lived near, and I seen a lot of things that made me swear a promise to myself I'd never in this world get married. Oh, don't think me a silly, ma'am; all that was only a sort of bitterness and working hard, I guess, because when Jim come along I forgot it quick enough and was right ready to marry him. But it was while we was going together, Jim and me, that I got took with coughing so bad, and I knew then that if him and me got married we'd not be able to go into the world and make good like we'd planned. I'd be sick all the time and not able to help him, you see, and the doctors would cost, and Jim would never get ahead like he should. So we fixed it up that he was to go alone, and you see, ma'am, before he left, I—I done it, ma'am—because I wanted to."

Jennie's large eyes looked into mine so steady I couldn't so much as breathe before the girl. Even Mrs. Knox kept quiet. "But the child?" I said at last, my voice all squeaky and rusty.

At first Jennie didn't understand, but after a minute, thinking she said, "Oh, of course we didn't think of that, ma'am. How many people in their goings on do you suppose there is that do? But I was just as glad anyhow when I knew it, because, you see, ma'am, he's a child of love anyway. It was along of the child too, ma'am, that I got away from my father and my stepmother and the whole brood of little ones. So afeared they was of me causing 'em a bit more trouble, that they threw me out *right*, and I only got myself and the boy to shift for since."

"And Jim?"

"Oh, he's doing fine out West, ma'am. Been married a year now to a big strong woman as'll help him. He sends me a bit of money now and then when he can, ma'am, and I know he'll take little Jim when I'm—gone."

"The beast!" broke in Mrs. Knox. "Does he know about the boy then? All these men are like, I tell you. Good-for-nothin's!"

"Nothing of the sort," came back Jennie. "He had a hard tussle of his own, Jim did, and when he heard about little Jim he was for giving it all up to come back and fetch me. But I told him sure as he did I'd kill myself right off, and he knew I meant it. That's why he went and married, like I told him."

So certain solemn she said it that I had an idea I'd a done what she told me, too; yes, even if I'd a been Jim. She looked such a person, somehow. It didn't matter she was weak and worn and shabby a bit; I envied her knowing her own mind like that. I felt that I must say something, but goodness knows I don't think what. I couldn't talk religion to the girl like I ought, because it didn't seem to mean anything. "Jennie," I said honestly, "I don't know what'll help you, girl. I can't even tell you to come back here next week, because Mrs. Knox as been with me pretty nearly seven years now, and besides she's got six children while you've only got the one."

"So I supposed, ma'am," said Jennie, quietly. "I'll be going then." And she folded up her apron and put on her poor-looking coat and hat while Mrs. Knox and I, who had both gone downstairs with her, looked on without saying a word. Finally I just couldn't stand the stillness no longer. I had to say something and I couldn't think of anything except, "I'm afraid I can't recommend you to friends, either, Jennie, because they feel just like everybody else."

"Oh I know, ma'am," answered Jennie. And after a minute, "You was real good to listen to me."

I couldn't say another word but at least Mrs. Knox, after coughing a bit, says, "I'll tell you Jennie, if you'll keep quiet about the kid, and are up to scrubbin' a bit, I'll see if I can't get a night job for you in the Rush Building where I work. Can you be down by five-thirty to-night?"

Jennie looked at her grateful. "I'll be there," she said. But I had such trouble making her take the dollar and sixty cents for her day that I was glad Henry keeps me kind of close I hadn't enough to give her more, like I first thought I would.

"Take it Jennie," I says at last, trying to joke, "and I promise I'll not tell my minister about you."

"Oh you couldn't, ma'am," she answered calm, "because you don't know where I live or nothing."

And the girl had me there. I didn't even know where Mrs. Knox lived, for all she'd been working with me these six years and more.

"Well," I said, "take it anyhow, Jennie."

She looked at me long and steady with those big eyes. "Mis' Bullock, I will, because I think you mean it!" And she went out, givin' me a wisp of a kiss.

"The Negro Woman Teacher and the Negro Student"

Elise Johnson Mcdougald

The daughter of Mary Whittle Johnson, a white Englishwoman, and Peter Johnson, the third African American physician to practice in New York City and one of the founders of the National Urban League, Gertrude Elise Johnson Mcdougald (1885–1971) became in 1924 the first African American full principal of a public school in New York City. She began teaching in the New York public schools in 1905, married Cornelius McDougald in 1911, served as head of the Women's Department of the U.S. Employment Bureau, a social worker with the Henry Street Settlement, and a vocational training expert. As a member of the Women's Trade Union League and the YWCA, she joined a YWCA-sponsored committee in 1918 to study the employment conditions and job opportunities of black female workers in Manhattan and Brooklyn. The results of her research became part of the volume *A New Day for the Colored Woman Worker* (1919). She wrote for a number of New Negro publications, including the *Crisis, Opportunity,* and *Survey Graphic,* and for Alain Locke's famous *New Negro* anthology published in 1925.[1]

The *Messenger,* the periodical that published the following article by McDougald, was begun in November 1917 by A. Philip Randolph and Chandler Owen as "the Only Radical Negro Magazine in America." Accordingly, Randolph and Owen criticized W.E.B. Du Bois, T. Thomas Fortune, and Fred R. Moore (of the *New York Age*) as members of the "Old Crowd" and too conservative generally, especially on matters of class, and promoted the careers of those they considered members of the "New Crowd," including Harlem Renaissance writers Claude McKay, Langston Hughes, and Wallace Thurman. In 1920, Randolph and Owen founded the Friends of Negro Freedom to promote civil rights and to organize

Messenger, July 1923, 771–772.

black workers. By 1922 the Friends of Negro Freedom and the *Messenger* editors opposed Marcus Garvey vehemently, and in January 1923 the editors urged the U.S. Department of Justice to prosecute him as a "menace to harmonious race relationships." By 1923, however, the magazine was struggling (with its monthly readership down to 5,000), so when Chandler Owen left the magazine to become managing editor of Chicago's *Bee,* the *Messenger* dampened much of its radicalism. Like the *Chicago Defender,* it circulated well beyond New York to all the major northern and midwestern cities to which blacks migrated and claimed that two-thirds of its readers were black and one-third white. The paper ceased publication in 1928 due to lack of funds.[2]

For further information on the *Messenger,* see the introduction to the *Messenger*'s editorial statement, titled "The New Negro Woman," in part I.

. . . The present day Negro teacher faces problems equally difficult. Modern life has become so complex and indirect that much that was taught formerly in even the humblest home is now within the scope of teacher's duty. This is true of teachers of all groups, but expecially so of the Negro teacher. Because the Negro mother must work outside of the home to supplement the Negro father's earnings, the Negro woman teacher must needs to [be] mother and guide, as well as class-room instructor.

Throughout the North and the South, urban and rural teachers form an earnest and forward-looking body of women. They are endeavoring to hold for the future the progress that has been made in the past. She finds that, figuratively speaking, she must stand on her top-toes to do it, for educational standards are no longer what they were. The great upheaval of the World War has quickened the public insight into the need for better and more education for all groups. The Negro woman's qualifications for, and the standards of the work expected of her, have been elevated to keep pace with the times. Her salary has in most places lagged behind, and is often unbelievably low. The satisfaction of giving service has to constitute half the pay received by these women. Were it not for such funds as the Jeanes–Slater, and for such men as Julius Rosenwald, the situation in many localities would be intolerable.[3]

On the other hand, her inspiration is the belief that the hope of the race is in the New Negro student. More vital than what he is compelled to be today, is what he is determined to make of himself tomorrow. As he is trained to think, so will he gradually make his world. Among interested adults there is a well-grounded dissatisfaction with the quality of thought emanating from the general student body of American colleges. An element of real tragedy will enter if the Negro youth falls prey to the malady of sterility of vigorous thought which is attacking other student groups. It is the high duty of the Negro woman teacher to teach the Negro youth to maintain a critical attitude toward what he learns, rather than to lay emphasis on stuffing and inflating him only with the thoughts of others. Surrounded by forces which persistently work to establish the myth of his inferiority the Negro youth must learn to think vigorously, to hold his spiritual and mental balance. Lacking this power, forging ahead will be impossible for him. In a brief summary, of this nature, it is possible to indicate only a few of the outstanding contributions which the Negro woman teacher is hopeful of making. Hers is the task of knowing well her race's history and of finding time to impart it in addition to all other standard facts required, and to impart it in such a way that the adolescent student will realize: 1. That, in fundamentals he is essentially the same as other humans. 2. That, being different in some ways does not mean that he is inferior. 3. That, he has a contribution to make to his group. 4. That, his group has a contribution to make to his nation 5. That he has a part in his nation's work in the world. To stimulate this spirit is the most lasting and far-reaching phase of the Negro teacher's work.

She must be ever on her guard to recognize the most progressive steps in education and to analyze deeply their meaning to her group. Comparisons and unfounded generalizations about mental ability and school achievement of various races, for instance, are but a recurring fad of pseudo-scientists. The truly scientific psychologists are searching carefully for the basic reasons for any apparent inferiorities. They and the sociologists show that the roots of the trouble run deep into the social fabric and feed upon such conditions as the low wages of the Negro man, the outside work of the Negro mother, health hazards, spiritual exhaustion and general mal-adjustment. Confronting the results of these forces in the class-room, the Negro teacher, throughout the country meets each individual case with the best of her skill and judgment. She brings to the situation the most that a sympathetic heart can give. But more and more she is becoming convinced that over and above her class-room duties, she must work in a larger way outside the classroom to aid all movements for general betterment.

Above all she must keep before her the highest ideals. In her special field she will do well to find courage to "carry on" by sharing with Professor Follett of Brown University his conception of the aims of education. He says: "It means deliberately to prepare the individual for a better world."

"Pin-Money Slaves"

Poppy Cannon

In 1930, after the stock market crash of November 1929, 4.5 million people were listed as unemployed; by 1931 the figure was almost double. The Depression resulted in a profound readjustment in women's work roles. Even as some women were being pushed into wage work by dire necessity, others were being urged to avoid or quit paid work, in the interest of making more jobs available to men. Women's magazines published articles with titles such as "You Can Have My Job: A Feminist Discovers Her Home." At the same time, to justify paying women lower wages, many argued that the majority of women had someone to support them so they were only working for "pin money."[1]

Poppy Cannon (1905–1975), author of "Pin-Money Slaves," was best known as an authority on food and a writer of cookbooks. Born in South Africa but raised in Pennsylvania, she earned a bachelor's degree from Vassar and studied at Columbia University. She married her fourth husband, Walter White, secretary of the NAACP, in 1949. During her career, she was an advertising executive and later a food editor at the *Ladies' Home Journal*, the *Los Angeles Times*, *Town and Country*, *House Beautiful*, and *Mademoiselle*, and she wrote prolifically on a number of topics, including fashion, race relations, and travel.[2]

The *Forum and Century* published Cannon's article in 1930, soon after the distinguished monthly *Forum* merged with the even more venerable *Century*, in July 1930, to stave off financial pressure after the stock market crash. In 1929, under the able leadership of Henry Goddard Leach, the *Forum* had enjoyed a peak circulation of 92,000. "Pin-Money Slaves" was illustrated with drawings by Johan Bull.[3]

For additional information about the *Forum*, see the introduction to Ella W. Winston's "Foibles of the New Woman" in part II.

Forum and Century, Aug. 1930, 98–103.

If they can't have a covered wagon, America's pioneer women resort to jobs and the subway. They are congenital frontiersmen and there is no restraining them. They will do anything, anywhere, any time to harass and discommode themselves and everybody around them. Their atavistic pioneerism (if one may be permitted an ism so soon) crops up in the most unlikely places—in effete metropolitan centers like New York and in progressive colleges where they teach euthenics and the fine art of living with one small voice and, at the same time, bellow forth tirades of contempt for the jobless woman.

If you are inclined to be dubious at this point, you ought to attend a reunion of recent graduates at an Eastern woman's college and notice the shamefaced attitude of the young women who are forced to admit that they are "not doing anything—just staying at home." By their shame you shall know them—the women who confess themselves guilty of the new sin none the less heinous because of its recent origin. A sin, moreover, which could have been invented only in America or in Soviet Russia—the new sin of leisure for women.

Why is it that women always trail along behind, gleaning the vices which men discard? At the beginning of the century drunkenness was losing caste and sexual immorality and wild oats were being frowned upon as diversions for promising young men. Then suddenly these sins were resuscitated and appropriated by young men's younger sisters. The same phenomenon has occurred in respect to leisure. American men had been accused so often and so loudly of materialism and business preoccupation that they were just about ready to admit grudgingly that all men need not labor at wage-earning all the days of their lives. Masculine public opinion had progressed so far as to permit rich men's sons to indulge without stigma in such unremunerative pursuits as exploration, art, and scholarship; and even captains of industry were retiring before they dropped dead of heart failure at the exchange and were devoting a good many years of their lives to golf or book collecting.

But just when Father is almost persuaded to sit down by the roadside and roll life under his tongue to get some savor of it—just about that time, Mother is infected by his old Busyness Germ and cannot be happy without an interior decorating shop, economic independence, recognition as a worker in the world, etc., etc. There is something touching about her eagerness and energy, and something pathetic, too, in the inner and outer compulsion to be worth while in a great, big way.

Not long ago I had a letter which embodied this pathos. It came from a college friend who is married and living near Chicago. She said, "If I were not continually oppressed by a feeling of guilt and worthlessness, I should be very happy. For, after all, I have a beautiful life. Ed is a dear and the house is amusing to fuss about. Then I have a Garden Club and time for books, music, pictures—not to mention etchings and the Graphic Arts Society, which I have just joined. But I can't let myself go on like this. I shall have to get a job—maybe a part-time job—anything. I keep thinking about the rest of the crowd—busy every minute, all *doing* something, pay envelopes getting more and more bulgy. And I am ashamed of myself for just living and consuming. I feel sinful. My friends have a good-humored contempt for me and even my husband seems to have caught the spirit. He calls me his sweet, old-fashioned, lazy girl. I know where I can work afternoons as a file clerk. . . ."

JOB-BENT WOMEN

That letter is a fair sample of what public opinion is doing to America's demileisured women; and there are hundreds of thousands of them—a favored class, indigenous to our nation and our times—who have been freed by mechanical appliances and prosperity from household drudgery and ought to be dedicated to the furtherance of the civilized graces. Instead, they are being shamed into becoming petty robots for Big Business, and Big Business does not really need or even want them.

The changeling values of our age are such that it seems desirable to a woman far above the average in intelligence to give up a pretty, well-kept house, gardens, books, and art to become a file clerk—and a part-time file clerk at that. Because business activity is regarded as the highest good, part-time business activity no doubt partakes of its sanctity as the next best thing. Probably this is the ethical origin of our part-time wives—the scourge of present-day domesticity.

Thousands of women who have some household and family duties, but not enough of either to fill every shining moment, feel impelled by conscience to take part-time jobs which bring in far less than they cost in car fare, restaurant meals, and household breakage, not to mention doctor bills and sanitarium expenses. At this point I shall be howled down by all the ardent feminists who insist that there will be no physical or nervous casualties, because women are just as healthy and capable as men. This may be true, but men are proverbially unfitted to serve two masters. Is there any reason why the normal, average woman should be expected to serve three or four—just to prove that she is emancipated?

Of course, there are superwomen who can handle a home, a husband, children, a corporation, and a couple of kennels without feeling any strain, but these women are rare enough to be dismissed. Human beings and the modern world are so constituted that there are few *really* part-time jobs, and when a woman presumes to have half a job and half a home, there is likely to be rather more job and little home or not much job and rather more home. In any case, any woman with a job will tell you that she has to give up a great many social amenities at home—so many, in fact, that one wonders whether the struggle is worth keeping up and whether society wouldn't be better off with more leisured charm and grace, fewer frazzled-nerved wage earners, and fewer grimy curtains hung askew by careless helpers from Harlem whose main interest—like that of their mistress—is "fifty cents an hour and car fare."

Offhand, all of this may appear to be a tempest in a teapot; one might imagine that the women affected by the fad for work are still negligible in number and radical in tendency. It is true that the pioneer worship of labor for labor's sake and for the good of the soul is most noticeable among intellectual women in cities and colleges; but the fad and its accompanying sense of guilt has spread so that pin-money workers—women who are driven into industry by other than economic reasons—have become a serious social menace.

Frances Perkins, Industrial Commissioner of New York State, remarked in a recent interview that the women pin-money workers who compete with necessity workers are selfish, short-sighted creatures who have no reason to be proud of themselves and plenty of reason to be ashamed. She points out that thousands of well-dressed, college-bred women, backed by a monthly allowance from father or husband, seek jobs in our large cities every year. They work as stenographers, sales girls, clerks, waitresses, and willingly accept eighteen or twenty dollars a week. This flimsy pay envelope acts as a sop to the fashion which dictates that women should be wage earners and maintain the pose of economic independence even if it drains the pockets of their male relatives and forces out of a job another unskilled woman who needs to work in order to live.

Neither Dr. Perkins nor anybody else denies that a woman should have ample opportunities to earn money whenever she needs or wants it. Woman's place in professional, business, and artistic pursuits has been established. What has not been established—or has been overthrown in the scuffle—is her right to lead a life of gracious leisure without laying herself open to a charge of parasitism, and her right to do work which does not bring in money. For our latest *mores* require not only that woman should labor, but that she should receive wages for her labor—or else remain abashed and shamefaced among her energetic sisters.

There is the case of a post-débutante who used to work at the Presbyterian Hospital in New York. Her work required considerable psychological knowledge, as well as tact and an ability to handle people. It was a real job, but it paid her a salary of exactly nothing per week. Other post-débutantes in her set were brandishing pay envelopes which labeled them as good citizens, but she had nothing but the consciousness of good works.

Since personal philanthropy was no longer fashionable, she got herself a routine clerical job at twenty-five dollars a week. She now awaits her pay days with quiet pride and insists that there is a certain something about twenty-five dollars which you earn yourself that makes it entirely different from an equal amount bestowed upon you by your family, and that work without money is no thrill at all. In other words, good and interesting works are less satisfying than good moneys; our enthusiasms are so weak and lame that they must constantly be whipped up by the clink of nickels.

THE LOST ARTS

Part of the trouble is that jobs, freedom, and independence have been press-agented and, nationally advertised like a new skin cleanser or a certain shape of dirty pink. All modern heroines in fiction or on the stage have their "work" to salve lacerations of the emotions of the soul. Every door slammed in literature since Ibsen's Nora has opened a year or two later to reveal the lady in question wearing, in addition to tweeds by Paquin, gloves by Régny, marcel by Charles of the Ritz, an air of assurance which implies not a penny less than eight thousand a year and the vice-presidency of a growing concern. No matter how old or how young, how inexperienced or how badly equipped the heroine may be, she invariably makes good in business nowadays, starts a chain of chicken and waffle restaurants, or founds a cannery based on her famous strawberry jam recipe. Moreover, this inspiring fantasy, known among blurb writers as "a woman's fight for freedom," is accepted as progressive and significant by sophisticated readers who would hoot at a similar success story formula applied to a male protagonist. . . .

Housekeeping, even now, is not so dull as it is considered, but efficiency methods carried over from factories and offices are introducing dullness, and standardization has a way of making homes depressing. A great many people have lost interest in homes; and those who retain their interest have been striving, by the introduction of mechanical appliances and efficiency methods, to make houses into so many little factory outlets, with the result that they have become equally exhilarating as places in which to live and work.

After the furniture has been installed and the draperies hung, all the creativeness is gone out of the average modern household. Canned food and hand-me-down baked stuffs are partly to blame. With everything in the way of nourishment obtainable at the chain stores, what will prevent us from forgetting the miracle of metamorphosing pallid flour, baking powder, and a couple of runny eggs into a tray of golden brioche? It is a thrill which ought to be preserved for posterity—more of a thrill in brioche than in regular biscuits, incidentally, because more time and patient care is required, three or four risings and cuttings, not to mention mixing and shaping.

Nobody except a fanatic will continue to make brioche, however, when it can be purchased at the corner and reheated in the oven. Perhaps the bought variety is just as good or even better. These are immaterial considerations compared to the fact that the adventure of cooking with raw materials is going out of housework along with the excitement of periodic cleaning.

Modern housekeeping ethics demand that homes should always be tidy. Consequently they are never glistening-clean or comfortably and gloriously tousled. Most of us can remember how old-fashioned households were allowed to slide along during washing, ironing, and baking days and then "got at and cleaned up." Now we are denied all that variety of experience, and even spring and holiday cleanings are no longer considered good form. Despite the comic strip jibes, spring cleanings had much to be said for them. It was good to turn one's world upside down once in a while, to reduce it to the bare essentials of uncovered floors, bare walls, stark windows, to have all the accumulated stuffiness dragged out into the sunlight of the backyard to be beaten, aired, and wind-whipped. And then after it was all over—the clean, clean smell! Houses which stay neat all the time like hotels never smell so clean as ours did when the windows were all gleaming at once, the newly-starched curtains billowing, the rugs shining, and the whole house with such a hushed and dewy, newborn expression that you wanted to walk tiptoe.

Even among women who are definitely committed to the new cult, one hears occasionally the whispered suspicion that the job-home combination is not an open sesame to bliss. One of my friends is a successful commercial artist. She has as much work as she can do, and a husband and studio apartment thrown into the bargain. All this excites enthusiastic comment about her "full life." But, strangely enough, she is philosophical rather than ecstatic when she discusses the arrangement. She says, "I really haven't a husband, a job, and a home, as they say. I have a husband and a job—and if I don't stop working at queer hours, I'll probably have just a job."

Unfortunately this particular case has no alternative. Some peculiarity in her mental make-up forces her to go on working until her nerves are so frayed that it is almost impossible for her to achieve a civil word. Her free hours are spent dabbing bits of cotton on her eyes in order to relieve the strain. She has a real mania for drawing—one of those obsessions (not invented by the New Woman) which is as old as the hills and as incurable. There are, happily, few women so genuinely attached to a job, but even she is not too busy or too blinded by artistic temperament to see that her antique mahogany secretary grows dingier and dingier for want of a long and loving rubdown, or that her floors are grimy under a film of oil and that her new yellow linen sheets come back from the laundry cotton (white and frayed at that) because she has not time for tapes or laundry lists and can't think of her household and her drawing at the same time. Yet she yearns for a linen closet like that of her German grandmother—towels, pillowcases, and sheets all tied into neat piles with embroidered bands and scented with lavender.

"They must have let me chew drawing pencils when I was young," she once remarked with a sigh, "and now I can't get over it. Too bad, isn't it? There are so many better artists, and I can make beautiful *bunt kutchen*."

WAKE UP AND DREAM!

The psychoanalysts revived the notion that work is a therapeutic measure when they propounded their theory of sublimation—that psychological alchemy by which they professed to change lust into labor and make libido laniferous. At this juncture it is unnecessary to consider the merit of their claims. Because of their eloquence, the public came to look upon work not only as a medicine but as a panacea calculated to cure all ills, whether physical or mental, and to remedy all evils. When we hear talk of cure-alls, it is time to be careful.

Excessive work may be, after all, nothing more or less than a spiritual drug. No doubt there are more people in America stupefied, stultified, and cut away from the normal joys of life by overdoses of work than by any other narcotic. And one cannot be sure that work addiction is not just as much a symptom of spiritual bankruptcy as drug addiction. These mothers who come to Greenwich Village at the age of fifty (I know two such) and start tea rooms when they do not need money—and the Villagers, heaven knows, do not need tea rooms—aren't they confessing their own emptiness and lack of resource just as much as those pitiable business men whose death occurs within a few months after their retirement because of mental and emotional vacuity?

The work fetish in our times is an atavistic revival. We get it from our Pilgrim fathers, who were afraid to live except under the influence of labor. But the Pilgrims had reason for their attitude. In a pioneer community one had to work constantly in order to live; and furthermore, their religion taught that the Devil would find work for idle hands. When people are convinced of the inherent wickedness of human nature, they will, of course, find some way of bludgeoning their vile yearnings into senselessness. The monks resorted to fasts, the Puritans to labor. . . .

With the return of lace mitts and the new humanism in literature, why not the revival of the lady who does not need a pay envelope to justify her existence? Even so, millions of women would continue to work outside the home, in as much as our economic structure requires their participation in other than domestic affairs. But perhaps the women who need not take the first job that offers might come to regard work as an accomplishment rather than a bribe to the gods and a prop for their wavering self-importance.

PART VI

World War I and Its Aftermath

Cover of *Hearst's Magazine*

Hearst's Magazine began in Chicago in 1901 as the home-study periodical *Current Encyclopedia* and then during 1902–1912 became the public affairs–centered *World To-Day*. Finally, William Randolph Hearst acquired the magazine in 1911, moved it to New York, and in 1912 changed its name to *Hearst's*. To boost circulation, Hearst reduced the magazine's page size to compete with the *Saturday Evening Post* and changed its content to that of an entertainment magazine featuring fiction by famous writers, especially European ones. A vocal opponent of the United States' entry into World War I, Hearst seemed to relish the negative publicity his stance generated. Even before America's entrance into the conflict in April 1917, Hearst was under government surveillance for suspected ties to the German government, and once the United States entered the war, he and his newspapers were publicly accused of having "labored in the German cause." Sentiment against Hearst papers grew, and in several cities crowds burned his effigy or his newspapers in bonfires. With his papers losing money, Hearst wrote to the head of his magazine division in January 1918 insisting that revenue from his magazines had to compensate.[1]

Hearst's Magazine, Feb. 1918, cover.

Hearst's

For February 20 Cents

"A Farewell Letter to the Kaiser from Every Woman"

Helen Rowland

Born in Washington, D.C., but of Virginia parentage, Helen Rowland (1876–1950) was a popular journalist and humorist famous for her satirical epigrams on the topic of marriage. She began writing "verse, dialogues, and short interviews with authors" for the *Washington Post* after her father died and she needed a job. Thereafter she wrote for a number of newspapers, including the Sunday newspaper the *New York Press* and the *New York Evening World*, and magazines, including the *Critic* and *Life*. After prodding by a publisher to write a funny article about men rather than women, she developed her column "Reflections of a Bachelor Girl" (circa 1908), which proved immediately popular. Later Rowland reminisced that "feminism was rife in the land, the suffragettes were battling for the vote— and the column was an instantaneous success!" From these articles, she compiled the book *Reflections of a Bachelor Girl* (1909) and later wrote *"If"; also, the White Woman's Burden* (1927). Rowland served as vice president of the New York Newspaper Women's Club and wrote for the *New York Journal and American* and Hearst's King Features Syndicate, which featured her column titled "The Marry-Go-Round."[1]

The *Washington Post*, in which Rowland's "Farewell Letter to the Kaiser" was published, had long been an adamant supporter of U.S. neutrality in World War I. The *Post* changed course dramatically, however, after an intercepted telegram revealed that Germany hoped to make an alliance with Japan and Mexico against the United States. On April 2, 1917, President Wilson stood before Congress to make his case for U.S. intervention to make the world "safe for democracy." In the wake of the October 1917 Russian Revolution, the *Post* became virulently anti-Bolshevik.

Washington Post, Nov. 12, 1918.

During 1918, the population of Washington, D.C. grew from 395,000 to 525,000, and demand for government workers surged. Women began working for the post office delivering mail. Retail stores and banks actively recruited female employees. The *Post* flourished during the war, and by 1919 circulation neared 75,000.[2]

For further information on the *Washington Post*, see the introduction to Kate Masterson's "The Campaign Girl" in part I.

KAISER WILHELM.

. . .

I thank you

For having given me back my faith in Humanity, and in the ultimate triumph of the good and the right and human justice.

You have restored and strengthened my faith in Divinity, and in a Divine Providence, which allows NOTHING to happen in vain!

You have shown me, in all their fairest colors.

The soul of the American MAN, and the spirit of American WOMANHOOD!

Into the dull round of my tight, little, commonplace life you have sent tragedy and sorrow.

But WITH it a new and vital spark, a glorifying flame.

Which has burned out all the old materialism and smug cynicism.

And awakened all my dormant ideals, all my old romanticism, all my sleeping visions of beauty and nobility and heroism!

You have aroused and strengthened my love of my Country, and stirred in me a glowing patriotism which shall never die!

You have starred my horizon with HEROES.

Until a dull world glitters with their deeds of valor, and shines in the reflection of their undying glory.

(And, to a woman, what is a world without heroes and hero-worship?)

You have torn the veil of materialism from a commercial age,

And shown me that great souls, and great men DO exist.

And that "there are GIANTS," even in these days—great men, like Woodrow Wilson, and Lloyd George, and Clemenceau, and Foch, and Diaz!

Super-statesmen, with a broad vision, and a selfless devotion to humanity!

You have given me the ballot and the rights of citizenship.

But, best of all, you have stirred me out of my selfish lethargy, strengthened my brain and soul, and muscles, and taught me the usefulness of WOMAN!

You have given me a deep and vast respect for my own sex

And an admiration and respect for MEN, which nothing shall ever shake.

In short, you have made of me a NEW WOMAN, in a brand NEW WORLD!

A finer, stronger, wiser, sweeter, broader, tenderer, happier woman!

Yes. YOU have done all this—unconsciously and quite unintentionally, of course—and you didn't MEAN to do it.

But, you see, it sometimes takes the greatest forces of EVIL.
To awaken and stir up the greatest and most powerful forces for GOOD.
And so, to meet all the EVIL which you started.
All the BEST in all the hearts of men and women, all over the world.
Have ARISEN!
And "God is still in His Heaven."
And Peace shall reign on all the earth—at last!
Thank you—and farewell!

  EVERY WOMAN.

---⊗⊗⊗---

"The New America, the American Jewish Woman:

A SYMPOSIUM"

Mrs. Caesar Misch

Born in Allentown, Pennsylvania (although some sources list her birthplace as Newark, New Jersey), Marion Simon Misch (1869–1941) studied with Rabbi de Sola Mendes and at age fourteen organized the first Jewish Sabbath school in Pittsfield, Pennsylvania. In 1900 (some sources say 1890), she married Caesar Misch and had one son. After marrying, the couple moved to Providence, Rhode Island, and opened a department store, which Marion Misch operated after her husband's death in 1921, making her at the time the only female department store owner in New England. She served on the Providence school board for fifteen years and became the first Jewish woman to become president of the Rhode Island Federation of Women's Clubs. Among other philanthropic efforts, she was founder of the Providence Plantation Club, director of the Providence Society for Organizing Charity, and director of the Providence District Nursing Association. She served as president of the National Council of Jewish Women from 1908 to 1913 and served on the executive board of the National Federation of Temple Sisterhoods (NFTS). Initially the NFTS devoted itself to supporting the synagogue and other institutions of Reform Judaism (including religious education and museums), to awarding scholarships, and to performing public relations functions. Within a few years, however, it became more vocal in national and international affairs, and passed a resolution protesting literacy requirements for new immigrants. In the aftermath of World War I, the group also worked for world peace and justice.[1]

American Hebrew, Sept. 26, 1919, 462, 466.

The *American Hebrew*, the periodical that published Misch's "The New America, the American Jewish Woman,"[2] was begun in 1879 in New York City by Philip Cowen and favored Orthodox over Reform Judaism. Devoting itself to maintaining high literary standards and covering international Jewish news, the *American Hebrew* published fiction, poetry, including the work of Emma Lazarus, and essays on a wide range of topics, among them anti-Semitism and immigrant rights. In 1906, Cowen sold his controlling interest to leading New York Jews including Isaac Seligman, Oscar S. Straus, Cyrus L. Sulzberger, Nathan Bijur, and Adolph Lewisohn. Joseph Jacobs assumed editorship for the next ten years, followed by Herman Bernstein. During 1918–1937, when Rabbi Isaac Landman edited the paper, the *American Hebrew* often took anti-Zionist positions and emphasized the importance of fostering Jewish-Christian understanding. It ceased publication in 1956.[3]

How can one write with finality of such kaleidoscopes? America today is in a stage of evolution, of indecision, of groping upward to higher ideals, of downward plunges under undisciplined passions and class-antagonism. If we continue our present class and race riots, our bitterness and greed, we must pass through a period of darkness, of blood-shed and of shattered ideals before we emerge purified by our trials and chastened by the cost of our experience.

As with the New American so with the New American Woman. She also is in a chaos of bewilderment. Under war conditions the complacent dowagers, and the card-playing, matinee-attending, window-shopping contingents found that this suddenly opsy-urvy [sic] world had no use for Qutens [Queens?] or drones—it needed workers. All women of worth had but the one watchword—"America," and every-where stlf [self] was routed by the Spirit of Nobility which War, the most cruel of school masters, yet instills into his pupils.

And now that his lash is laid aside, the American Jewess is like the American Protestant or the American Catholic. Americanism knows no creed. We are all American women, now led upwards by patriotic or religious fervor, now depressed to the depths by War's aftermath of sorrow and suffering. The sudden cessation of war-work, dread of the jobbery which threatens us with civil war, the determination to put into helpful channels our new-found energy and initiative, the uncertainty as to the immediate future and the firm confidence in the ultimate future—all these are moulding the American woman. And whatever her Spirit of Religion, for this also does War give his pupils. In the midst of our Job-like questionings come also his flashes of faith. We may say with him "The earth is given into the hand of the wicked," but we also say with him "God is excellent in power and in judgment and in plenty of justice."

What then is the future of the New America and the New American? I see first a strong feeling that though we cannot now fathom God's purposes, in the fullness of time that knowledge will be granted us. I see America one great patriotic family with the present fomenters of trouble slinking into the background. I see business conducted on high ideals, adequate schools in every hamlet, the minimum working age raised to 16, widowed mothers pensioned, no more Child Labor to swell the bank accounts of Capital, no more strikes to coerce Capital, no more "combines" to coerce Labor; but a brotherly feeling of co-operation driving out distrust and mis-understanding. I see orphans no longer in rule-ridden institutions, but in cottages with the pettings and scolding and individuality in dress and thought which make the normal home. I see the old and helpless no longer living on bitter poor-house charity, but cared for by Old-Age Pensions as a matter of justice. I see a rapid spread of better housing, public recreation parks, free concerts, higher education of the Denver Public Opportunity School type, and the school-houses open every evening in the year for public use. I see taxation laws radically reformed and more equitably administered. I see the country so contented and prosperous that we shall not need [the] strong coercive measures against alien workmen now being advocated, for every newcomer will eagerly seek citizenship. A Utppian [Utopian] dream? Yes, but better than that of the Bolshevist which hovers over us today like a vulture cloud.

And our women? We have shown our mettle in time of need—we can never again be drones. We, too, have been purified by suffering, for every woman of us has suf-fered vicariously with every mother who wears the gold star. The altruistic spirit which has dominated us, making the wife of the millionaire and the wife of the day-laborer sisters in communal work can never entirely leave us. We have learned to know and to respect each other. We have learned that religious, social or educational differences are no differences, and that for equality we need only similar standards of honor and a fulfilled desire to be of service.

And to what better service can we dedicate ourselves than to true Americani-zation? Perhaps you think Americanization is only for the alien and means only learning English and being naturalized. No, my friends, many of our native-born citizens need also to be Americanized. True Americanization means a full and sym-pathetic understanding of and devotion to the principles symbolized by our flag, and an individual feeling of responsibility for the affairs of State. It means an amal-gamation of all races and the appreciation of the contribution of each. When we are truly Americanized there will be no race-hatred, creed-hatred or class-hatred for we shall be Americans all, and there will be no slackers, military or civil, for all will be equally ready for the duties as well as the privileges of the New America.

Much there is in this program for which women are peculiarly fitted. Their war-time training fits them for advisory places on [the] Food and Fuel Commission while their sympathetic nature brings close to them the appeal of reconstruction work. Whether the work be great or small, national or local, extensive or intensive, the American woman will be found ready and competent.

So I see the New America a proud, peaceful Ship of State and the New American Woman better, nobler, kinder, with prejudices softened, with a new conception of her neighbors, with increased desire for altruistic work, and above all, within her heart "the knowledge of God which passeth all understanding."

"What the Newest New Woman Is"

Harriet Abbott

Under the longtime editorship of Edward Bok, the *Ladies' Home Journal* had over many years opposed women's suffrage. But when Bok retired from the magazine in 1919 and suffrage became law, the *Journal* accepted in part women's new role and offered articles on how women's votes might change politics. At the same time, however, the magazine did not endorse the Equal Rights Amendment. In 1919, the *Journal* had a circulation of more than 1.8 million, and in 1920 it raised its price from fifteen to twenty cents.[1]

The same month that women's suffrage became law (the amendment was ratified by the requisite number of states on August 18, 1920), *Ladies' Home Journal* published Harriet Abbott's article "What the Newest New Woman Is." According to journalism historian Jennifer Scanlon, Abbott's credo, which appears as an insert in the article, flanked by two line drawings of women, one looking pensive, the other holding an infant, reflects the attitude of the *Journal* in the twenties toward the New Woman:

I believe in woman's rights; but I believe in woman's sacrifices also.

I believe in woman's freedom; but I believe it should be within the restrictions of the Ten Commandments.

I believe in woman's suffrage; but I believe many other things are vastly more important.

I believe in woman's brains; but I believe still more in her emotions.

I believe in woman's assertion of self; but I believe also in her obligation of service to her family, her neighbors, her nation and her God.

Ladies' Home Journal, Aug. 19, 1920, 154.

Following that faith we have the most modern expression of feminism. The newest new woman deifies not herself, but through her new freedom elects to serve others.

The preceding month the *Journal* published Abbott's "Doctor? Lawyer? Merchant? Chief? What Shall She Be? Woman's New Leadership in Business." In it, Abbott argues that women have a unique capacity to be advertising executives because of their greater intuitive powers.[2]

For more information about the *Journal*, see the introduction to Edward Bok's "At Home with the Editor" in part III.

. . . Relearning World-Old Values

Each woman enjoys the creative world of business, but to each the creative work of child-rearing is the greater obligation and opportunity. . . .

Guarding Woman's New Freedom

Every woman among us to-day has had her sense of values so shaken that sometimes she stands bewildered on the edge of revolt. Nora slammed the door of revolution, and Havelock Ellis and Ellen Key and Olive Schreiner have jerked us from the blind leading strings of traditional obedience to customs just because they were customs.[3] We have eaten the apple and never again shall we be good in a pre-Adamite, pre-woman-movement sense. Now, our conduct shall be the result of intelligent choice, and when we elect to live according to the older doctrines it shall be because we recognize truth even when it comes to us in some of the shackles of platitudes.

But although we shall be acting according to those platitudes, it will be because we have seen their real contents, their real meanings, not merely obeying them with the unquestioning unintelligence of the mediaeval or Victorian woman. In the full flood-light of understanding and free will we shall choose the better way.

The goodness of the flower has no virtue; nor has the flowerlike goodness of the woman who lives according to a rule handed down from her mother and her grandmother any virtue. Real virtue in woman is the result of visualizing clearly the wrong and the right and then, with free woman will, electing to do the right.

Many of the woman commandments grow deep and far back into the centuries. Indeed they grow back almost to the beginning of time itself. They grow in the soil of biology and of sex psychology and of the divine purposes of human development and evolution. We dare not hack away at such a centuries-old tree without realizing whence it draws its sustenance and what we may be destroying.

Every girl who shirks marriage because its homely duties are irksome, every woman who refuses to have children, every mother who needlessly delivers her home and her children into the care of a servant is using her saw-toothed ax on progress. And in selfishly seeking her own comfort or satisfying her personal ambitions, she smothers her womanhood.

The Red element, the Bolshevist party, as it may well be called, in the woman movement, is sparring to-day as openly for the destruction of womanhood as the Soviet element in industry is shaking the pillars of organized economics.

It is that element at which thinking women begin to look with caution. For more than a decade its message has been seeping to us through popular magazines, current fiction and the works of certain psychologists and biologists.

We who believe that women are out of swaddling clothes, we who believe in the fullness of their powers in business or the professions, if their life points up properly in either field, or in the home if Life places them there, we who honor and reverence the new powers, the new freedom of women, begin to be jealous of those powers and that freedom.

A TYPICAL NEW-WOMAN FAITH

We dare not permit it to be prostituted by exaggeration, to be destroyed by being so apotheosized and extended that it will topple to its ruin.

We must save it from the threat of Bolshevist invasion.

To-day we are building steadily and surely, brick by brick, a new philosophy that grows from, yet is not consubstantial with, the postulates of the woman movement so called. We are creating a new-woman faith typical of the newest new-woman movement.

This is an after-war movement, a resumption of some of the old axioms that have persisted, like Homeric classics, through the centuries, and an idea that persists is like religion or a classic in art or literature; it cannot endure unless it has reality. It is an eclectic choosing of all that is sanest in the sweep of the last century toward a new freedom for women, combined with the persisting older ideas.

It is a philosophy that stands on the foundation stones of old, tested, true experiences, so it is stable; but it is not made up of superstition and tradition; it couples to itself the best of what is new and so it is flexible. It is the expression of our maturity as women, the advance from the "teen age" of our woman development.

PART VII

Prohibition and Sexuality

"What Shall We Do with Jazz?"

Martha Lee

In 1868, in the midst of Reconstruction and with Georgia still under federal military rule, Atlanta lawyer and businessman Carey Wentworth Styles started the *Atlanta Constitution*. Evan P. Howell bought into the paper in 1876 and became its president and editor-in-chief until his death in 1897. In the 1880s, during Howell's tenure, the paper became a leading voice for economic development in the New South. Howell's son Clark became managing editor in 1897 and editor-in-chief after his father's death, in addition to serving as director of the Associated Press's news-gathering service. Within the context of Georgia politics, the *Constitution* was considered moderate on race because it supported some measure of black economic advancement while endorsing segregation. Howell, in fact, reportedly helped persuade Booker T. Washington to speak at the 1895 Atlanta Exposition. In 1921, at an annual subscription price of a dollar, the paper's circulation was close to 110,000. In 1922 the paper purchased a radio station, which a year later Clark Howell gave to Georgia Tech as a gift.[1]

The article that follows was the first in a series written by Martha Lee (in the later articles she is identified as Mrs. Martha Lee) for the *Atlanta Constitution*'s weekly Sunday magazine on the evils of jazz. Like the other articles in the series, which ran through March 1922, this one was extensively illustrated. In addition to numerous black-and-white cartoon figures, a picture of Mrs. Oberndorfer, national music chairman of the General Federation of Women's Clubs, appeared with the caption that she "is campaigning strenuously to keep jazz out of the homes and out of the hearts of the new generation."

Sunday Constitution Magazine, in the *Atlanta Constitution*, Jan. 15, 1922, 1–2.

"They were playing the jazz. The lights were down. I didn't fall much for the fellow, judge, but—oh, the jazz got me! I closed my eyes and let myself go—. That's the way it started, judge. The music done it."

A weepy story like this it is that Judge Lindsay, of Denver, says unfortunate girls, their young lives wrecked by the jazz fire that is consuming the minds and morals of at least part of this generation, narrate to him these days.

Doctors are even going further than judges in their condemnation of the jazz fever. "If jazz is not stopped we will have no more clean-minded children. Even our babies are being sullied and ennervated by the jazz music, the shimmying and the general looseness of actions they see about them," doctors proclaim.

"Danger! Stop!" Mrs. Oberndorfer,[2] national music chairman of the General Federation of Women's Clubs, cries. "Think. What instincts are being vicariously aroused by this jazz?"

Any adult who has attended recently a dance of young people in their teens and early twenties, at public dance hall, at country club, even at a private home—who has witnessed corsetless girls, clamped tightly to over-heated partners, eyes closed as if asleep, but lips humming suggestively with raggy rhythm and the blatant cacophony of the orchestra, "You'll Have to Put a Nightie on Aphrodite to Keep the Married Men Home"—need not think long before answering this question.

"We didn't check our corsets when we waltzed to Strauss and two-stepped to Sousa in the days before we were poisoned by jazz gas," Mrs. Oberndorfer points out.

With jazz to the right of us and jazz to the wrong of us, until the children of today are actually imagining the angels in heaven as a wriggling, gyrating jazz orchestra instead of peacefully playing psalms on the harp, where are the young folks bound for? Some say, Inferno. Others, the dangerous ward in the insane asylum. Others, the reformatory or the home for the erring. And some are confident that—common-sense to the rescue—they're coming through it all not much besmirched than their elders, as human beings have succeeded in surviving lax periods in past history.

As long as we are in this whirlwind of jazz, it is just as well to understand what the jazz atmosphere it is living in, is doing to Young America.

"Jazz music sends temperature up. It produces a fevered physical condition. It atrophies the fine nerve control balance. It has the same effect as alcohol," says Mrs. Oberndorfer, leader of the club women's crusade against the evil. "The human organism responds physically and emotionally to musical vibrations. Scientists who have been experimenting in music-therapy with the insane have no hesitation in saying that even on the normal brain, jazz produces an atrophied condition of certain cells. Under constant syncopation, combined with inharmonic partial tones, the brain becomes so disorganized that it is actually incapable of distinguishing between right and wrong, of making right judgements."

After jazz music had been played to them, girls in cigar factories could not work, Mrs. Oberndorfer declares. They were too much worked up emotionally and physically to pay close attention to what they were doing.

In many factories, dancing to jazz music during lunch hour has had to be done away with because the girls had so many accidents as the result of the nervous excitation.

In hospitals experiments with jazz music sent the temperature of convalescents up three degrees. Shell-shocked men, on the contrary, were gradually cured by means of good music—brought back to normal health and state of mind.

Stand on any busy city street and watch the jazz faces among the young people who pass. The sophisticated faces of fifteen-year-olds. Faces over which all the emotions of maturity have passed. Artificial intensity, the result of living and especially "emoting" at high pressure, is mirrored there. A super-strenuosity, nervous, almost hysterical, shows itself in walk, gestures, in voice, in all actions.

The passion to be always on the go, the desire to be always in a high-keyed excitement, to be keenly alive even though falsely stimulated, and to live much, even though indiscriminately, is the mental world in which many are now living.

The jazz music starts it, they say. And then comes the desire for other kinds of excitement. It's a speedy life that the "jazz baby" lives. A life empty mentally but riotously crowded emotionally.

Many American households are inhabited by jazz babies of both sexes, old and young, though most of them are between the ages of sixteen and twenty-five. Professor Burges Johnson, of Vassar college, says the loss of mental stability in them is due to "the wave of individual freedom that has swept over the world in the last few years," and the consequent relaxing in family discipline.

"Enjoy life" is the jazz motto. Dancing intimately in the dark, carrying a hip flask, going "bumming" in the motor, unchaperoned, scorning the conventions in every way, vulgarizing the emotions that should be kept most sacred, eating, drinking, camel-walking, living in the material and sensual and forgetting the spiritual—such is "enjoying life."

It's a retrogression. Back to the monkey. That's individual freedom.

The Home Brew Mothers

When grandma shimmies the Chicago, or convulses the camel, or rolls the scandal walk more adeptly than her granddaughter, when father and mother brew their own and hold their own at anti-prohibition revels with all the other tipplers rebelling against the blue laws, how can they chide eighteen-year-old Tommy or fifteen-year-old Anne?

Haven't Tommy and Anne just as good a right to their jazzy times as dad and mother? It would be heresy, of course, to suggest that the fall of the modern parents from that higher plane of ideals and inspiration from which most children view them, preceded and is responsible for the jazz-wallowing of the off-spring.

Even in the churches jazz music is now heard. . . .

Monkey music in the churches.

Some ministers even advertise their sermons suggestively. Adam and the apple—yoo-hoo—you know. . . .

It is in reality musical anarchy. Syncopated music is said to be found mostly among races of people that have suffered from political tyranny and need an outlet for their pent-up emotions. It is the reaction of the slave, of the person who cannot find means of expressing himself in normal action.

Syncopation is exhilarating. It buoys up drooping spirits. It stimulates nerve energy. It breaks down reserve and self-control, just as liquor does. It leads to the breaking of social customs, the overlooking of conventions that have been found necessary as civilization has advanced. As witness, the apparent collapse of the "hands off" rule that all girls of good breeding formerly held to in their friendship

R. Seon, "In the Grip of Jazz, many a young person is losing self-control. Primitive passions run wild."

with boys. "It's quite the clever thing to 'mush up' now," the young folks say. "All the popular girls do it."

Some Choice Bits of Jazz

Spooning while dancing is seven-eighths of the thrill. And no wonder when jazz songs are written to words like the following, taken at random from popular dance songs:

> I'm beside him,
> Mercy, let his conscience guide him.
> Ma, I'm meeting with resistance,
> I shall holler for assistance.
> Ma! He's kissing me.

> Them that love and run away
> Live to love another day.

> Now I ain't handsome, I ain't sweet,
> But I've got a brand of lovin' that can't be beat.
> When I wanna, you no wanna;
> But I wanna what I wanna when I wanna.

As for emotional excitement generated by jazz, imagine the syncopated clang and batter, the barbaric clatter and rhythm that accompany these words:

> Get hot, shake your shoulder,
> Get hot, shake a little bolder.
>   You will have your way
>   If you make him follow and say,
> Get hot, step right on 'em,
> It's hot, step right on 'em.
>   Don't be slow,
>   Just go get a beau
> And yell, "Get hot."

And here's another song, "Spread Your Stuff," that music store men declare sells quickly to the jazz crowd:

> First knock yo' knees, Hon, with me,
> Then float aroun' like a ship that's lost at sea;
> Get busy, Hon, don't make a bluff,
> Because you, I can't get enough,
> Oh, Honey, come on, spread your stuff.

. . . The "blues"—that's another type of jazz. Mrs. Oberndorfer classifies these as ennervators, as atrophiers of the rational balance.

"The softer you play the 'bine' pieces, the funnier the crowd gets," a member of a dance orchestra informs me. "In my opinion, it isn't the loud, boisterous dance music that makes people lose their reserve, it's the slow, soft, nasty syncopation; the whining, the slurring and the crying of the saxophone seems to get the dancers.

"You can see them tightening up. The fellows draw the girls closer and the girls close their eyes and pretend to be in an ecstasy of sensual pleasure. The languor and the faintly whispering syncopation of the music, the faint lights, and all—say, it's actually awful to witness the sights on some ballroom floors nowadays."

CHECKING THE CORSETS

This summer were heard many outcries because the girls who attended the tea and dinner dances at the country clubs checked their corsets, preferring to dance corset-less. This winter they are leaving their stays at home so they won't have to bother to check them when the orchestra plays the slinking, sinking, sliding "Dangerous Blues." The less clothes, the more successful the dance from the jazz hound's point of view. . . .

There are jazz manners. There is jazz slang. Jazz love, which is another way of saying free-and-easy love. There are jazz parties that break up at "half pash stew" and are characterized by drinking, smoking, dancing to jazz music and the craziest of actions. There is jazz art and jazz literature and much jazz advertising, charac-terized by its appeal to the primitive impulses.

The petting parties that Wellesley girls and Brown boys have been warned against, which in past were rarely seen except perhaps on an excursion boat, now take place in the smaller hours at affairs that begin the evening formally enough. A frankness concerning this form of "entertainment" exists such as never existed before.

THE EMANCIPATED GIRL

The war did it? Maybe so. Many a hitherto protected girl in her teens appeared upon the street corners and in lobbies of public buildings selling tags and boosting cam-paigns until she became a pushing little politician—in some cases a brazen little trifler.

She became emancipated from the chaperone, from adult control.

The young person is going it on her own hook now, and she's taking it on high speed that frightens her older and less energetic relatives.

If mamma had dared in her salad days to slip off from a dance and visit a man's room, her name would have been "mud" and her social career wrecked. Today the debs do it with impunity, because they're only going after a drink.

"Exodo de Una Flapper" [Exodus of a Flapper]

Jorge Ulica

Julio G. Arce (1870–1926), son of a respected physician in Guadalajara, started his first newspaper when he was fourteen. Eventually he would become one of the most important journalists in the Mexican American community of the southwestern United States. In Cuilican, Sinaloa, he cofounded his first magazine and the city's first daily newspaper, earned an appointment as a professor of Spanish, and served in a number of political positions. After his criticism of the Maderist revolution, he fled with his family in 1911 to Guadalajara. There, in 1915, Carranza's army found and imprisoned him. After fellow journalists freed him, he immigrated to San Francisco and soon began his connection with *La Crónica*. In 1919, he bought the newspaper, which was now called *Hispano América*, becoming its only publisher and owner.

Arce first began using the pseudonym Jorge Ulica in 1918. His "Crónicas diabólicas" (Diabolical chronicles), from which the following essay is taken, became the most widely syndicated column in the Southwest. For Arce, as for most of the Hispanic journalists during this period, one of the primary goals was to create a cohesive, Mexican-identified community. According to journalism scholar Nicolas Kanellos, these journalists urged their readers to "to maintain the Spanish language, keep the Catholic faith and insulate their children from what community leaders perceived as the deleterious example of low moral standards practiced by Anglo-Americans." Indeed, Arce's short weekly columns, coming out of a long tradition of the *crónica* in Mexico, functioned primarily to promote a distinct Mexican culture and identity. The favorite target of Arce's satire was the poor Mexican woman who learns immediately upon arrival in the United States that

Hispano América, Nov. 21, 1925, 2–3.

233

here she is in charge. In one of his satiric *crónicas,* a Mrs. Blackberry divorces her husband and marries an Anglo because he refuses to wash his face in gasoline in order to whiten it: "I left him, because he was dark, old and his teeth didn't smell nice like those refined Americans."

In 1914 Spaniard J. C. Castro began *La Crónica* in San Francisco as an immigrant newspaper. In 1919, after Julio G. Arce bought the newspaper, he emphasized its political independence and made it into the most important Hispanic paper of the Bay area.[1]

One of the most "significant" flappers, as they say nowadays, kicked the bucket. That is, she passed away without a peep, the victim of a fearsome case of alcohol poisoning aggravated by the use of chewing tobacco. In this there is nothing odd, as flappers are not immortal, and when they come down with tobacco-aggravated lung disease they are as good as gone.

This merry young woman, because she was young and merry, came before the judge who reviews people's lives. As she was still somewhat hung over and smelled strongly of tobacco, she was sent straight to the teeming infernos, to the circle of Hell where drunkards and smokers are burnt alive.

There she found many supporters. In bringing them the latest news from Earth, she told them about the Charleston, that new dance so popular in dance halls and parlors. To help them understand it better, she started dancing in front of the sinners, all of them burning in the same cauldron, and moments later all you could see were feet flying, as horrifying screams rang out from the many condemned souls dancing at the flapper's expert direction. All of Hell was abuzz, and as late as midnight one could hear the disquieting refrain of the dancers:

Hay foot, straw foot,
Your foot, my foot,
Charleston, Charleston.

The Devil himself, forever sensible and fond of tranquility, reported these goings-on to Heaven, saying that the young woman had caused such a commotion throughout the infernal legions that mutiny was imminent. Hence the flapper was ordered to be escorted to Limbo, where her Charlestonian propaganda would be useless among the small children.

Now it was her turn to be annoyed, as the small children, with no mothers to care for them, cried so much that the poor girl couldn't sleep. But, expert in flapperism that she was, she went to her trunk, took out some opium, and mixed it into the food of the young innocents. Soon they were sleeping like logs, and later they showed signs of intoxication. Once the cause was discovered, the offender was cast into Purgatory, where she found old acquaintances so burnt they smelled like barbecue.

There, with boundless charity, she began giving cocaine injections to those who were roasting, thereby nullifying their punishment. The head of the department reported what had happened, and in the big celestial mansion it was agreed that she be taken there, under tight watch, to find a place for her where she couldn't do harm.

As soon as she heard the strumming of the harps from the archangelic militias, she broke into classical-style dance, causing the chaste, modest people who abound in such places to blush. She tried to sneak in, but an angel wielding a sword of fire ordered her to stop. She quickly removed a hypodermic needle from her sock and gave the angel a sharp prick. The angel performed a somersault, brandishing his flaming sword. But upon feeling the delightful effects of the morphine solution, he approached the flapper for another shot. The winged guard fell into a comatose state and was replaced by another, who met the same fate. The same thing happened to each and every replacement until the entire corps guarding the gates of Heaven was incapacitated. At that point, the flapper tried to go and dance the Charleston at the foot of the throne, and for such brazen disrespect she was sent back to Hell, with explicit orders that her belongings be taken out of commission and that she be thoroughly searched for any hidden drugs or intoxicating substances.

Back in the realm of the Devil, the young woman went and found an old sergeant friend she had met in her worldly adventures, and she gave him several packages to hold for her.

When she was searched, the flapper lost an immeasurable amount of narcotics, whisky, tequila, brandy, and dynamite.

Everything seemed to be going smoothly, and the vamp seemed to have left her activities behind, when one fine day the condemned and many of the devils watching over them awoke in a semi-crazed state. The situation has not improved. Instead, the number of dazed demons is growing, and the sinners are drunk day and night.

The packages that the flapper had given the sergeant contained marijuana seeds, *Cannabis sativa*. The grass was planted widely and is now growing in abundance in the very ground that was previously paved with good intentions. Now there is not a devil or condemned soul who, aside from to being a true demon, is not a marijuana addict. This leads us to believe that the flapper won't last long there and will be sent back to Earth, the only place where she can be withstood, though not stood.

Translated by Paul Coltrin.

"Sweet Sexteen"

John Held Jr.

Whether dancing the Charleston, rolling dice, or crashing the car, the gangly and independent flappers as drawn by John Held Jr. epitomized the restlessness of the Jazz Age and made Held the most famous and highest-paid graphic artist of the 1920s. Born in Salt Lake City in 1889, he moved to New York in 1910 and began illustrating for *Vanity Fair, Puck, Life,* and *Judge,* while freelancing for *College Humor* and many other magazines and newspapers. Although Held frequently depicted her as a college student known as Betty Co-Ed, studying was never primarily on his flapper's mind. Indeed, one of Held's contemporaries described her as a "girl [with] fingers snapping, feet jumping, troubled by nothing very much except yesterday's hangover and tomorrow's heavy date." Held illustrated F. Scott Fitzgerald's *Tales of the Jazz Age* (1922) and drew the cover for Fitzgerald's comic drama *The Vegetable* (1923). His most popular series, "Oh! Margy!" ran from 1924 to 1927 in papers across the country, and when William Randolph Hearst syndicated its sequel, "Merely Margy," in over seventy daily and Sunday editions of his newspapers, Held earned $2,500 a week from Hearst alone. He earned even more for his cartoons in *Life* and *Judge,* his *New Yorker* block prints, and his advertising art for Packard automobiles, Planter's Peanuts, Timken roller bearings, Tintex dyes, and Van Heusen shirts.[1]

Circulation for the humor magazine *Life,* on whose cover the following Held illustration appeared, reached a high point of nearly 500,000 in 1920 and then declined abruptly to just over 124,000 by 1925.[2] For more information about *Life,* see the introduction to Edward Kemble's "Ise Gwine ter Give You Gals What Straddle" in part I.

Life, Sept. 30, 1926, cover.

—⊶⊷—

"The 'Outrageous' Younger Set:

A YOUNG GIRL ATTEMPTS TO EXPLAIN SOME OF THE FORCES THAT BROUGHT IT INTO BEING"

Elizabeth Benson

Elizabeth Benson was a child prodigy who at the age of twelve scored 214 on a Binet-Simon IQ test—at the time the highest score recorded in the United States. She wrote the essay that follows for *Vanity Fair* when she was a thirteen-year-old sophomore at Barnard College. Benson's *Vanity Fair* essays were later collected and published as *The Younger Generation* (1927).[1]

In 1913 Condé Nast, a leading publisher of elite magazines, launched *Dress & Vanity Fair*, a magazine with the subtitle *Fashions, Stage, Society, Sports, the Fine Arts*. When Frank Crowninshield became editor in 1914, he moved the magazine away from fashion—dropping the "Dress" from the subtitle in the process—to focus on the theater, arts, and humor. Under his guidance, the magazine entered its most illustrious period. Crowninshield had supported the 1913 Armory show in New York, the first major public display of modern art in the United States, and later he had helped found the Museum of Modern Art in New York City; in *Vanity Fair* Crowninshield wanted to create a similar modern spirit. Throughout the 1910s and 1920s, *Vanity Fair* published the work of the world's leading avant-garde artists and writers, including Aldous Huxley, D. H. Lawrence, Collette, T. S. Eliot, e. e. cummings, Dorothy Parker, Gordon Conway, and Robert Benchley. Under Crowninshield, *Vanity Fair* also embraced the new modern ideal of feminism. In his first editorial, he announced that for women he would offer in *Vanity Fair* something that had "never been done for them by an American magazine.

———
Vanity Fair, Sept. 1927, 68, 104.

We mean to make frequent appeals to their intellect." A year later, in the pages of the *New York Times,* he announced his conversion to the cause of women's suffrage, a conversion motivated in part by the fact that so many women had proven their mettle in the trenches of clerical work. At the same time, however, he capitalized on the frustration many housewives must have felt with their daily lives. Magazine advertising pages, according to Crowninshield, "are magical carpets on which they ride out to love, the secret gardens into which they wander in order to escape the monotony of their work-a-day world and the banality of their well-meaning husbands." Throughout the 1920s, *Vanity Fair* sold for thirty-five cents, and by the end of the decade, circulation hovered around 85,000.[2]

. . . The younger American generation of which I am writing will go down to history as our post-war generation. . . .

. . . But I am not going to recite all the old arguments of middle-aged novelists who have been erudite enough to point out that cocktail drinking and sex freedom and wild parties were a means of forgetting and escaping the strain of the war. Those arguments are so well known, so fresh in the reader's mind, that I will make no mention of them all.

But it was not the war alone which was responsible for the wave of freedom upon which the younger generation of today is riding high, and for which it is so universally condemned. It had a much more respectable genesis than war hysteria. It was mothered by a brood of reformers such as good old, ridiculous old, crusading old Carrie Nation.[3] That doughty female has passed into the limbo of history, to be unearthed only as a subject of humorous analysis in the ideal-destroying pages of *The American Mercury,* and so, too, is poor Emmeline Pankhurst now little more than a memory to be smiled at, but the forces which they and their brood helped to bring into being have been largely instrumental in moulding the character of the wild young sex radicals of today.

The Nineteenth Amendment was passed while the present younger generation was just entering adolescence. The shout of "Equality of the Sexes" mingled in our alert young ears with the rattle of broken windows and the clanging of axes upon election booths. We cut our second teeth on "Women's Rights," "The double versus the single standard of morality," and "Birth control." Margaret Sanger was one of our first memories. "Sex," which had been a word to whisper and blush at, was flung at us on banners carried by our crusading mothers. The wrappings were removed from the piano legs in Victorian homes and such unmentionable words as "male" and "female" mingled with "personal freedom," "sex equality" and "prohibition" in arguments between our parents around the dinner table. We didn't wholly shut our ears.

Under such a bombardment of sex talk, and drink talk, and equal rights talk, and double standard talk did we enter upon our adolescence. We saw women don men's clothes and men's personalities and force their way into business. We saw them snatch the ballot from unwilling hands and turn municipal government, throughout the country, topsy turvy. We read of women who retained their own names when they married.

Then, as soon as American women began to yell for sex equality, a vast flood of sex literature was let loose upon the land. As soon as sex was admitted into American literature—at first by way of translations of Continental classics—we were not slow to seize our opportunities for knowledge. It was with no regret that we laid aside the Elsie books and the Alger series and fell upon Anatole France, Voltaire, Flaubert, Maupassant, Boccaccio, Rabelais, and Gautier.

And there was, of course, no restraining our joy when the delightful pastime of psychoanalysis was presented to our eager young minds. We did not invent psychoanalysis, and we can scarcely be blamed for having profited by it. We studied Freud, argued Jung, checked our dreams by Havelock Ellis, and toyed lightly with Adler. And all these authorities warned us of the danger in repressing our normal instincts and desires. Most of us have felt very virtuous in making up our minds not to invite mental and physical ill-health by suppressing our natural tendencies, but (to give away a secret of the sacred and honorable order of the younger generation) most of us talk big—and step pretty carefully.

As one of my own friends puts it, "I certainly don't want to be a victim of repressed desires, but I'll be hanged if I want to make a mess of my life."

At any rate we don't lock ourselves in our bedrooms and experience vicarious thrills over Robert W. Chambers' *The Common Law* or Elinor Glyn's *Three Weeks*[4]— as our parents did.

We, the younger generation of today, are the children of crusaders. Our parents were always in a terrific stew over something. If it wasn't "women's rights" it was the war; if it wasn't war, it was prohibition; if it wasn't prohibition, it was a crusade against fundamentalism in religion.

The crusade for prohibition was such a worthy one! How nobly our parents fought and bled for it! And we have come along to bear the brunt of it. It is scarcely necessary to point out that the younger generation does not gaze with uplifted, adoring eyes upon the spectacle of its elders taxing themselves billions of dollars for a prohibition law which does not prohibit. We can have little respect for a law which its own makers, the older generation, show no respect for. If the older generation had only made its laws with honesty and common sense, we would not have grown up to be rebels against the law. We bid you look to the mote in your own eye and the quality of liquor in your own cellar.

We do not charge, as our anti-Volsteadian elders do, that prohibition has made us drink. History shows that young men have always drunk and that they drink in other countries where liquor flows freely and legally. It is safe to conclude that people will always drink, no matter what law says that they shall not. As for the liquor consumed by young girls today no one seriously contends that prohibition has caused them to drink, or has prevented them from doing it. Girls smoke now; their mothers did not; they wear knee-high dresses now instead of the sweeping skirts which once saved the street cleaners so much unpleasant work. Drinking by the girl members of the younger generation is an expression of the feminism which we inherited from our crusading mothers, if the "boy friend" has a *right* to take a drink, we naturally ask ourselves: why haven't we?

But what we *do* charge against prohibition is that the inability to get good liquor and to consume it openly has kept many of us—of course I mean the boys, particularly—from learning to drink with moderation and discrimination, and has made many of us drink when we did not really wish to, out of sheer, exuberant revolt against an absurd law.

Then those crusading parents of ours started something else which we, their children, are left to finish—and be blamed for. I refer to the crusade against fundamentalism in religion. Our parents decided that there was no hell of brimstone and forked-tailed devils, no method of frying erring souls on red-hot coals. Fine! Our elders were too set in their ways to get much good out of that happy discovery, but we, of the plastic age, have not been slow to seize upon the freedom of action which comes to people when fear of eternal damnation is removed. They can't scare us any more by telling us that we will burn in hell forever and ever, amen, if we aren't good little girls and boys, and at home and in bed by ten o'clock.

So we have learned to prefer an automobile trip to the country to being bored and antagonized by the Elmer Gantrys of our churches,[5] or even to listening to our more enlightened preachers. I feel safe in saying that the automobile has done more to reduce the number of church-going persons of all ages than any other single factor. But it was not the younger generation which invented the automobile. That, too, we inherited from the older generation. The automobile differentiates the youth of this generation from its parents' youth by many centuries, by the difference between the beast of burden age and the machine age.

Don't forget that we are not the only people living our own lives. Our parents are also having a fairly good time. They are living too much the same sort of lives as we are to cast the first stone. Hence it is left to the professional noise-makers, in the older generation, to grow alarmed about us—teachers, preachers, editorial writers.

There is still another factor in the fashioning of the present younger generation—physical education and biological instruction in schools, colleges and magazines. When it was discovered that a girl's body was a machine which could stand exercise as well as a boy's a stride toward freedom and sanity was taken—a stride leading directly toward the present younger generation.

Women began to go in violently for athletics. The wasp waist emerged from the harness of steel and whalebone, and a normal twenty-six inch waist came into fashion. Skirts were lifted permanently from the rank of sidewalk sweepers and elevated to a discreet position halfway between the ankle and the knee—all in the interest of athletics and hygiene. Our mothers had begun to study and to take care of their bodies before we were born, and we have but carried on the good work by becoming good golf players, channel swimmers and winners of tennis tournaments.

Nature, and war, and prohibition, and feminism, and psychoanalysis and new fashions in dress; a tottering religion, imitation of our elders, automobiles, radios and free money, the industrial era, indulgent parents and a new physical education—these forces have had their hand in baking the pie out of which, like the four and twenty blackbirds, has sprung the younger generation of today.

It may not be a dainty dish to set before a king, or upon the altar of civilization; but the waiter has certainly set it there, and there it sits.

So, we feel justified in calling upon all those who have denounced and reviled us, and bidding them look upon us, not as individuals who have chosen their destiny, but as the inevitable products of that destiny. If we are not what we should be, we are not wholly to blame and, so far as we can see, there is very little that can be done about us.

"Fumando Espero" [Smoking I Wait]

Alberto O'Farrill

Alberto O'Farrill, the original editor of *Gráfico* (1926–1931), drew most of the illustrations for the magazine during its first two years. Most of O'Farrill's cartoons satirized the flapper, sometimes with risqué double entendres. In addition, *Gráfico* contributing editor and writer Jesús Colón, one of the most influential Hispanic columnists in the New York community during his day, frequently criticized Hispanic American women who imitated what he viewed as decadent American customs. In a poem for a September 1927 issue of *Gráfico,* for example, Colón writes:

> Like a chole girl who would be a New Yorker,
> the "flapper" agitates the air with her affectatious struts. . . .
> Expert queen of the latest dangerous dance jump,
> make-up streaked, superficial, fickle girl,
> like a liberated slave entering a new life.
> In contrast, they make me remember my grandmother,
> who as she sewed told me of flying giants,
> in a voice as shaky as a lost prayer.[1]

"Fumando espero," the *Gráfico* cover reprinted here, however, seems to offer an endorsement of the sexualized flapper, which is especially intriguing in that the artistic style of the drawing strongly points to O'Farrill as the illustrator. The title comes from a tango made popular in Argentina in the late 1920s, in part through a recording by Rosita Quiroga for the Victor label in 1927. Juan V. Masanas's lyrics

---

Gráfico, June 5, 1927, cover.

to the song portray a woman's smoking of a cigarette as a sensual prelude to an
erotic interlude:

> To smoke is a pleasure, brilliant, sensual . . .
> Smoking I wait the man I want,
> behind the crystals of happy large windows.
> . . . .
> For when my darling is in
> my smoking is an eden.
> Give me the smoke from your mouth
> Give me that in me,
> provokes passion
> Run that I want
> to go crazy with pleasure.[2]

For further information about *Gráfico,* see the introduction to Clotilde Betances
Jaeger's "La mujer nueva" of June 15, 1929, in part II of this volume.

Gráfico

SEMANARIO DEFENSOR DE LA RAZA

Año 1   NEW YORK, N. Y., DOMINGO 5 DE JUNIO DE 1927.   Núm. 15

Fumando espero....

PART VIII

Consumer Culture, Leisure Culture, and Technology

——— ⊸⊗⊗⊸ ———

"The Eternal Feminine"

Jas. H. Collins

Born in Detroit, James Hiram Collins (1873–?) enjoyed a successful career as an advertising agent and writer for periodicals, including *Printers' Ink*, the *Saturday Evening Post*, *McClure's Magazine*, the *New York Times*, and the *Ladies' Home Journal*. Sometimes using a pseudonym, John Mappelbeck, and sometimes his own name, he contributed numerous articles throughout the first three decades of the twentieth century to the *Saturday Evening Post* on business topics as varied as Bible selling, taxation, hotel management, marketing, vocational education, and immigrant labor. His book-length works include *Human Nature in Selling Goods* (1909), *The Art of Handling Men* (1910), *The Story of Condensed Milk* (1922), and *The Story of Canned Foods* (1924). In 1917, Collins's article for the *Mother's Magazine*, "She Spends $20,000 Every Minute," was entered into the *Congressional Record*. In this essay, Collins argues that women, who now served a new function as "purchasing agents" of the home, had an obligation to support their neighborhood stores rather than being lured downtown by bargain retailers.[1]

    Advertising, one of Collins's most frequent topics, had a bad reputation in the nineteenth century in that it had long been associated with the guile of the confidence man and the carnival hype of P. T. Barnum's freak shows. The Boston advertising-agent pioneer George Presbury Rowell founded two landmarks in advertising history that elevated the industry's standing. In 1869, he began *Rowell's American Newspaper Directory*, which attempted to provide advertisers with more accurate estimates of newspaper circulation to counter papers' often trumped-up figures. And in 1888 he founded *Printers' Ink*, which became the most influential periodical on advertising in a rapidly professionalizing industry. Under editor John Irving Romer, who served from 1890 to 1933, the trade

Printers' Ink, June 1901.

journal published some of the first articles on the psychology of purchasing. Nicknamed "the Little Schoolmaster in the Art of Advertising," *Printers' Ink* offered advice on writing advertising copy, developing marketing strategies, and analyzing prospective advertising venues.[2]

By the complex phrases of philosophy and metaphysics one may clearly prove that woman is a secondary factor in human affairs. By the simple and altogether incontrovertible facts of everyday life, however—cash balance and grocer's bill, the latest novel's sales and the new floor for the parlor—it is not possible to prove that she occupies any other than foremost place. Woman undoubtedly has—in scientific books, at least—less brain than man, yet she rules him; she has no single grain of the faculty called reason, yet she takes his reasoning into hand; she has none of the sterling qualities called common sense, yet she manages his home, his children, his comings in and his goings out and his estate after he has done with it; she has neither thrift, nor foresight, nor generalship, nor ability to work simple sums, yet she does all of his buying and the whole world is built pretty much to her tastes, whims and prejudices. The advertiser talks vaguely of a creature which he calls, variously, "he," "it," "clientele" and "the public"; yet this creature is woman, pure and simple, and though he may safely call her general, indefinite names in his theories, he would better take her into strict account when he deals with her in space and dollars and cents.

In a recent number of a ten-cent magazine which carries the largest amount of advertising accorded any monthly publication, there were very nearly three hundred separate ads, ranging in size from the four-line announcement of a school for girls to the double page insert of the biscuit trust. In all these three hundred carefully gotten up bids for business there were just twenty-one that would not be likely to appeal to women. These were ads of pipes, razors, machinery, card systems and office helps, guns, band instruments, cigars and tobacco. About twenty more fell into a class that was a sort of borderland—typewriters, naphtha launches, ads of financial houses and the like—ads that made appeal to men, but which might, by a freak of advertising, bring a limited amount of trade from feminine intermeddlers.

But, of the remaining two hundred and fifty, there was no ad that did not frankly address the "lady of the house," either as a helpmate of the lord thereof, or as the one and only factor in it. Things there were that belonged to men of right—cameras, pianos, horse and auto carriages, railroad and sea trips, fishing tackle, phonographs and biographs, floor paints, shingle stains, things to work with and play with, things to eat and wear, things with which to decorate homes and persons— things that man had made for his own uses and proved philosophical ownership to. Yet here were their makers and keepers printing ads with pictures of women, and catchlines addressed to women, and treating the economy, uses and advantages of their wares from the standpoint of the woman who keeps a home and rears children and bosses some lord of creation. From the baby food ad to that of marble monuments—from the cradle to the grave, as it were—but twenty-one ads were addressed directly and solely to men.

Now, gallantry is a beautiful human quality in a novel or in some phases of life, but in an ad it is worth nothing at all—means nothing at all. These two hundred and fifty advertisers were, mainly, men and firms who have filled space often enough to know that the dollar is the ultimate end of publicity, however sordid a principle that may be. Yet they ignored or snubbed the lord of creation and offered things of his own devising to the creature made of his rib. Nay, these very advertisers who offered him pipe and tobacco and shaving brushes in this issue of the magazine had at Christmas-tide appealed to the woman who had the spending of his money, telling her that their wares were "for him," and urging her to take into her hands the buying of his very cocktails.

From a philosopher's standpoint it was all wrong—should not exist and should be ignored if discovered in the act of existing. But as it did exist, and promise to grow as well, it was thought best to pry into the reasons that had brought it about. These were found in the daily life of the average man. The average man swinks and swelters six days in the week, making as much money as he can and considerable hubbub beside. It would seem a logical conclusion that the average man, having made the money, should spend it. As a matter of fact he does no such thing. From the time of his rising at dawn unto the time of his returning to bed the average man spends about one-twentieth of the money that goes out of his income for housing and subsistence. He is entrusted with the purchase of some of his clothing, his smoking material, the tools and appliances he uses in his office or at his work, and—generally under protest—a greater or lesser amount of strong drink. Within that narrow circle he ranges, and when he tries to go beyond it his tether brings him up roundly. Neither his bed nor his bedchamber are furnished with a single article of his own choosing; he may have a penchant for wheat breakfast food rather than for oats, yet he never selects the brand; no bit of tin or copper or china ware is of his selection, and when he goes away to office or work the machinery of the household that is put in operation has no cog or lever of his devising. He may be called upon for his opinion of a carpet sweeper or a pillow-sham holder or a parlor lamp, but he is rather in the plight of the comic weekly missionary who is to give his choice of being roasted, boiled or fricasseed. Though he gain his very livelihood in the making of or trafficking in these things, yet will he starve unless he keeps his eye upon the ultimate buyer and user of them all—the woman.

If he goes out in the evening to ball or lecture or theater he is more than apt to go under orders. His wife wears thrice the value of his evening or business suit—wear, wearer and wearing being alike a mystery beyond his solving. If he stays home and reads he will be driven to one of her novels after he has surrendered the evening paper, while, when his little pause for summer rest comes round, he goes to a place that she has selected. If, by some accident, there should be money enough ahead to warrant a trip to Europe or a visit to some one's "folks," there is seldom any dispute as to who is to go. Or if there be—

Woman spends nineteen-twentieths of her husband's money in every community, whether her lord be a millionaire or a ditch digger, and in the spending she sets the laws of the markets of the world. There is, to a woman, no such coin as a dollar.

Her calculations deal with eighteen nickels and ten pennies. Man is so lax and unthinking in his spending that no one takes him into consideration when prices are fixed. He is a perpetual good fellow, and can always be brought to pay a dollar for something worth but ninety-eight cents. This basic trait of his character has brought into being a class of people who prey upon him. The cigar man knows that when he comes in with a friend he will be ashamed to buy a five-cent cigar; the saloon man thrives off his weakness for ordering "the best in the house"; deprecatory mention of the word "cheap" is the open sesame to his pocket at the tailor's. And when he is sent to the grocer's or butcher's he is practically a treasure ship, to be looted of coin of the realm and ballasted with goods that have been on the shelves untold ages.

Woman, however, is a natural spender. Early in life her mother or her grandmother or her elder sisters take her out on expeditions and initiate her in the mysteries and wiles of those who stand in the market place. She has no false shame. When she and the woman who lives next door go into the ice cream parlor they make sure that their dissipation is to cost no more than five cents. She will beat the butcher down three cents and throw his meat in his face if it does not come up to her standard. She buys only after she has had a sample and made comparisons with all other samples she can gather. With her, purchases are a matter of estimates; he who would have her patronage would better enter into figures at once. She will stand an hour in Smith's grocery, taste and pinch and delve into the very vitals of his ware, and then, for the matter of a penny, go away to Brown's and spend her eight cents. She lives according to a schedule of prices and is continually comparing that schedule with every other woman's, just as men compare watches, or sea captains exchange longitude and latitude.

In view of this real purchasing power there is little food for wonder in the fact that two hundred and fifty ten-cent magazine ads should be deliberately aimed at women. Long ago the whole publishing world learned her true status in society and trimmed sail accordingly. The newspaper is made for her, and the magazine and the novel. Man has his financial news and sporting page crowded over into the latter half of the daily, while the murders and accidents, the deaths, weddings and society news are played up under red heads. Fortunes have been made in the invention of trifles, but they were all trifles for her. A patent unbreakable hairpin brings in a round million; an ever-present pants button does well if it pays for its patent and making. From the philosopher's standpoint woman is an incidental helpmeet to man; from the standpoint of the wise advertiser she is queen of the nether world, mistress of the privy purse, keeper of the rolls, the hounds and the exchequer. Man is but a scullion at her court.

"Battle Ax Plug"

Almost from her inception, the New Woman was featured in advertising and used to sell a wide range of products. Even in the *Ladies' Home Journal*, where the editorial policy under Edward W. Bok was anti–New Woman, ads appeared using her image to sell goods. Patent medicines marketed to women faced a quandary when telling their customers that they would feel like a "new woman" after using the product. Peruna, a general antipain remedy, even went to the trouble to reassure readers that, despite the controversial nature of the phrase, they could exclaim "I feel like a new woman."[1]

Established in 1890, the American Tobacco Company, which had already gained a virtual monopoly in the cigarette industry, began in 1894 an aggressive, predatory pricing campaign to control the plug or chewing tobacco business. The chief brand name used in this effort was "Battle Ax."[2]

The *Santa Fe New Mexican*, publisher of the following advertisement, was the oldest paper in New Mexico and maintained a circulation of about 2,000. By 1900 there were only five daily newspapers in the state.[3]

Advertisement in the *Santa Fe New Mexican*, Sept. 8, 1896, 2.

"The New Woman."

BattleAx
PLUG

The "new woman" favors economy, and she always buys "Battle Ax" for her sweetheart. She knows that a 5-cent piece of "Battle Ax" is nearly twice as large as a 10-cent piece of other high grade brands. Try it yourself and you will see why "Battle Ax" is such a popular favorite all over the United States.

"The Athletic Woman"

Anna de Koven

Born in Chicago to U.S. Senator Charles B. Farwell and Mary E. Smith Farwell, Anna Farwell (1860–1953) married Reginald de Koven in 1884. Reginald became a successful composer of comic operas and a music critic, and the couple socialized in New York's most elite circles. Anna de Koven distinguished herself with her translations of French fiction, her novels, and biographies, in addition to numerous essays and poems for mainstream periodicals. Even as she cautioned women against forgetting their "natural duties" of homemaking and child rearing, de Koven, an accomplished amateur golfer, advocated physical activity for women. Writing for *Cosmopolitan* in 1896, she celebrated golf as an ideal sport for the New Woman: "What the bicycle has left undone toward the transformation of the life of American women, the game of golf bids fair to complete." The article reprinted here was published at a time when *Good Housekeeping* had been devoting more attention to women's work outside the home. It was heavily illustrated with photographs of women enjoying a wide range of outdoor activities: flying, riding on horseback, fishing, mountain climbing, golfing, playing tennis, and pumping an automobile tire.[1]

Good Housekeeping was begun in 1885 by Clark Bryan as "A Family Journal Conducted in the Interests of the Higher Life of the Household"; it offered advice on housekeeping, dressmaking, and home decorating, and published poetry and short stories for primarily a lower middle-class audience. From its beginnings, the magazine solicited a significant portion of its content from readers and prided itself on its connection to them. In 1900 it started the Good Housekeeping Experiment Station (later to become the Testing Institute), which conducted tests on new products and reported the results, and in 1909 it began issuing the Good

Housekeeping Seal of Approval to recognize those products in its magazine. By 1911 editor James Eaton Tower had expanded the magazine to 125 pages, lowered its cost $1.25 a year, featured in its pages some of the most popular writers of the day, and offered more and higher-quality colored illustrations. *Good Housekeeping*'s circulation rose to over 300,000 and was purchased in 1911 by the Hearst interests.[2]

. . .

ATHLETICS AND EFFICIENCY OF WOMEN

Signs are not wanting in the rising generation of American women of a high development of the reasoning faculties and a great efficiency in civic activity.

The highest development of the American woman cannot be attained without due regard to the preservation of physical activity, and for that reason the practice of athletics is an essential for all ages.

The arguments of physicians and educators in favor of athletics for women were only partially successful until fashion set the stamp of approval. The hoydenish tomboy, who was the despair of the mother of the past generation, is today just the normal girl whose keen love for outdoor sports is the pride of the family. This development in athletics for girls and women has been very rapid the past ten years, and the effect is clearly discernible in the schools and colleges, as well as in the homes. The old-time gymnasiums are now considered too artificial for present needs and are being replaced by outdoor contests and folk dancing.

The result naturally is a new type of American girl, new not only physically, but mentally and morally. Dr. Thomas Wood, the physical director of Barnard College, who has had plenty of opportunity to study the effect of this athletic development of women, says that "one of its benefits is to teach self-control. Wholesome play, suitable games, selected gymnastics, though these have no direct utilitarian end," he explains, "give to young women, as well as to young men, a part of the best preparation for the more serious work of later life. Women, as well as men, need to learn through practical experience the rules of fair play, generous treatment of rivals and opponents, merging self into cooperative effort, concentration of power, and the blending of all energies toward an impersonal goal."

He quoted a woman of experience who had said: "There is no training which girls need so much as that which develops a sense of honor and loyalty to each other, and games will do more to make these living qualities than the ethical system taught in a college curriculum. It takes the finest kind of courage to be fair, to be honest and to be loyal, and these are absolutely necessary in good team work."

Some eminent authorities, on the other hand, are opposed to the more strenuous forms of exercise indulged in to-day. They contend that the publicity and excitement resulting from competitive athletic events are not good in their influence, and that over-exercise is apt to lead to degeneracy of muscle, once the sports are abandoned, as is so often the case with men athletes who have suffered physical decline. . . .

WOMEN NOW EXPERT AT POLO

But the women contestants are far more interested in wresting honors from their male competitors than in the ethics of the movement. No sport is too reckless, too daring, or too strenuous for the more experienced among athletic American women. . . .

Whether the sport is mountain-climbing or any of the many other athletic pursuits mentioned in this article, the spirit of contest is keen, and it is in friendly contest that the American woman will develop the finer qualities of loyalty, courage, justice and good *camaraderie* which has made the American sportsman a much-admired individual.

—⊶⊷⊶—

"The Woman of the Future"

Thomas A. Edison

As recorded in an interview by Edward Marshall

Thomas Alva Edison (1847–1931), the "wizard of Menlo Park" and author of the
following article, patented over a thousand inventions, including the phonograph, the incandescent light bulb, and the motion picture. In 1911, Edison con-
solidated his business ventures into Thomas A. Edison, Inc., a larger, more
diversified and streamlined company, with the goal of sustaining a market for his
inventions rather than making new ones. Edison wrote for a number of periodicals, including the *Scientific Review*, the *North American Review*, the
Independent, and *Forum*. In 1913, the readers of the *Independent* voted Edison the
"most useful" man in the United States.[1]

Rodney F. Thomson (1878–1941), the illustrator of this article, was born in San
Francisco, where he studied art; he later moved to New York City.[2]

See the introduction to the previous section, Anna de Koven's "The Athletic
Woman," for information about *Good Housekeeping*.

*"She will in no sense be a drudge, but will be a household engineer, super-
intending wonderfully simplified electrical appliances in the conduct of her home.
She will finally be able to 'think straight,' will achieve new capabilities, will take
the place selfish man has for centuries denied her, and will become the mother
of a race of mental prodigies." That is the prophecy of Thomas A. Edison.*

"The housewife of the future will be neither a slave to servants nor herself a drudge.
She will give less attention to the home, because the home will need less; she will be

Good Housekeeping, Oct. 1912, 438–439, 436–444.

rather a domestic engineer than a domestic laborer, with the greatest of all hand-maidens, electricity, at her service. This and other mechanical forces will so revolutionize the woman's world that a large portion of the aggregate of woman's energy will be conserved for use in broader, more constructive fields."

As we talked, Thomas A. Edison, doubtless the greatest inventor of all time, said some things which may offend the woman of now, but he said others so appreciative and inspiring that they surely will wipe offense away. He declared, without reserve, his concord with the suffrage workers; he explained that woman as she is, and speaking generally, is an undeveloped creature and—here is where the women's wrath will rise at first—vastly man's inferior. But he went on to say that anatomical investigation of the female brain has shown it to be finer and more capable of ultimate aesthetic development than man's, and he explained that that development is undoubtedly, at last, well under way.

"It may be a perfectly natural detail of the development of the race that the modern woman not only does not wish to be, but will not be, a servant," Mr. Edison declared. "This has had its really unfortunate effect in that it has led, of late years, to general neglect of woman's work, and has resulted in the refusal, or, at least, the failure, of many mothers to rightly teach their daughters. But good will ultimately come of it, for the necessities arising out of womankind's unwillingness, have turned the minds of the inventors toward creation of mechanical devices to perform that work which woman used to do. The first requisite of such machinery was a power which could be easily and economically subdivided into small units. Such a power has been found in electricity, which is now not only available in the cities, where it can be obtained from the great electrical supply concerns, but is becoming constantly more easily available in the rural districts, through the development of the small dynamo and of the gasoline engine and the appreciation and utilization of small water-powers which are becoming general even on our farms."

Electricity in the Home of the Future

"Electricity will do practically all of the manual work about the home. Just as it has largely supplanted the broom and dustpan, and even the carpet sweeper, by being harnessed to the vacuum cleaner, it will be applied to the hundreds of other littler drudgeries in the house and in the yard. Attached to various simple but entirely effective mechanical contrivances now everywhere upon the market, and many others soon to be there, it will eliminate the task of maintaining cleanliness in other ways as well as in cleaning up dirt. No labor is much worse than sweeping. It has killed many women. Did you ever stop to think what a boon to women the vacuum cleaner really has been?

"Electricity will not only, as now, wash the clothes when turned on in a laundry and plugged into any one of dozens of existent patent washers, but will dry them, gather them and iron them without the use of the little manual labor even now required in ironing by electrically heated individual irons and by the application of electricity to the other parts of the process. Electricity already dries clothes, after washing, quickly and with great economy of fabric, in easily equipped and inexpensive

Rodney Thomson, "Woman Presses the Button, and the Wizard Electricity Does Her Bidding."

drying-rooms, electrically heated, free from the dust of coal-fires and from the winds which tore grandmother's wash to tatters when it was hung upon the out-door lines of the old days. These electric laundries have already been reduced to what approaches absolute perfection in the larger establishments, such as commercial laundries, hotels and the more luxurious apartment buildings, but it will not be long before they will be made possible for the small home in the cities or on farms.

"By supplying light through bulbs containing neither wicks to trim nor reservoirs to be filled with dust-accumulating oil, and involving no lamp chimneys to be cleaned of soot, electricity is constantly eliminating one large detail of the old-time household drudgery.

"As improved methods of production are developed, especially as water-power comes into use for its creation, the electric current is becoming cheaper, so that it is now available, even in the kitchen, as a substitute for coal or oil, or gas in cooking. A vast advantage which comes from it, lies in the fact that it does not heat up a kitchen and that, with nominal expenditure for additional current, ventilators can be arranged and operated which will keep the kitchen absolutely free of fumes. Many a woman's life in old days was shortened; many a woman's life in these days is being shortened, by her presence for long hours each day in an overheated atmosphere above a cook-stove. The application of electricity to domestic work will do away with this."

Advantages in Electric Cooking

"A kitchen in which the cooking is electrically done and in which a ventilation system electrically operated is installed, cannot become unduly heated even in the worst days of our terrific American summers. Electricity will cool the room as readily as it will cook the food. The kitchen of the future will be all electric, and the electric kitchen will be as comfortable as any room in the house.

"And the electric cooking of the future will, in many instances, improve the food. It will permit the preparation of many dishes literally on the dining-table, by means of the electric chafing-dish, and more complete utensils, and so reduce the labor of food preparation that there will be no temptation to prepare it in large quantities and put parts of it aside for future use, a system which results frequently in sad deterioration of the food involved.

"And not only will it make cooking simple and economical, but it will make it better, for electric heat can be locally applied as no other heat can be. The electrically-cooked roast will be the perfect roast. No part of it need be under-done, no part of it need be burned in the oven. The housewife's great problem of imperfectly adjusted draughts and dampers will be solved—indeed, it has been solved—in many kitchens, for electric cooking is already widely practiced."

Future Housewife an Engineer

"The housewife's work, in days to come, will amount to little more than superintendence, not of Norah, fresh from Ireland, or Gretchen, fresh from Germany, but

CONSUMER CULTURE, LEISURE CULTURE, TECHNOLOGY

of simplified electrical appliances; and that is why I said, to start with, that electricity will change the housewives of the future from drudges into engineers.

"Electricity has already cheapened very greatly; it is getting cheaper every day. It used to cost ten cents a kilowatt hour, but the price has been reduced to five cents, four cents, even three cents to large consumers of power. An element in the cost is the time at which the current is consumed. If it is not used at the times known as 'peak hours,' that is, at hours when it is most in demand for lighting and for power, it can be manufactured and served very cheaply."

Electricity to Be Cheapest of All Power

"The problem of the storage of electricity must enter our calculations when we endeavor to make predictions of its future cost, and that is, perhaps, too complicated to go into here; but I do not hesitate to say that in the not far distant future electricity will be sold in New York City at fifty per cent of its present cost. In cities where water-power is available for its manufacture, the rate already is much lower than it is in New York City, and it will continue to decrease until electricity becomes the cheapest power which man has ever known.

"Even as things are now, all sorts of minor mechanical appliances such as brushes to clear the hair from dust in barber shops, factories and homes, vacuum cleaners and a hundred other things operated through air condensed by electricity are in daily and growing use—a use which must be economical or it would not exist. There are lawn mowers which are chargeable 'off the line,' and indeed if I were to attempt to make a catalogue of all the minor uses to which electricity is already put, the list would fill a good part of an issue of GOOD HOUSEKEEPING. Here is a distinct advance, for everything performing labor without requiring power from human muscles must be regarded as real progress.

"To diminish the necessity for utilizing man himself, or woman herself, as the motor-furnishing force for this life's mechanical tasks, is to increase the potentiality of humanity's brain power. When all our mental energy can be devoted to the highest tasks of which it may be capable, then shall we have made the greatest forward step in this world's history. To so conserve our energy as to trend toward this eventuality is the tendency of the age.

"It is there that electricity will play its greatest part in the development of womankind. It will not only permit women to more generally exercise their mental force, but will compel this exercise, and thus insure a brain development in them such as has been prevented in the past."

Women to Be Able to Think Straight

"It will develop woman to that point where she can think straight. Direct thought is not at present an attribute of femininity. In this woman is now centuries, ages, even epochs behind man. That it is true is not her fault, but her misfortune, and the misfortune of the race. Man must accept responsibility for it, for it has been through his superior physical strength that he has held his dominance over woman and delayed her growth. For ages woman was man's chattel, and in such condition progress for her was impossible; now she is emerging into real sex independence, and the resulting outlook is a dazzling one. This must be credited very largely to progression in mechanics; more especially to progression in electrical mechanics.

"Under these new influences woman's brain will change and achieve new capabilities, both of effort and accomplishment. Woman will grow more involved cross fibers and that will mean a new race of mankind.

"Man is at present little, if any, more than half what he might be. The child may be considered the mean between his father and his mother—between the undeveloped female and the developed male. The male has had his full of mental exercise since society first organized; it has been denied the female. To growth, exercise is an essential. An arm which never has been used will show weak muscles. A blacksmith's arm is mighty because it lifts great weights, strikes heavy blows. Development of brain is not so very different from muscular development. The idle brain will atrophy, as will the idle arm."

CHILDREN OF FUTURE TO BE WONDERS

"The brain of woman in the past has been, to an extent, an idle brain. She has been occupied with petty tasks which, while holding her attention closely, have not given her brain exercise; such thinking as she has had time for, she has very largely found unnecessary because the stronger sex has done it for her. Through exercise men's brains have developed from the low standard of the aborigine to the high standard of the modern man, and if, in the new era which is dawning, woman's mental power increases with as great rapidity as that with which man's has grown, the children of the future—the children of the exercised, developed man, and of the exercised, developed woman—will be of mental power incredible to us today.

"The evolution of the brain of the male human has been the most wonderful of all the various phenomena of nature. When, in the new era of emancipation from the thraldom of the everyday mechanical task, the brain of woman undergoes a similar development, then, and only then, will the race begin to reach its ultimate. Yes, the mental power of the child born in the future will be marvelous, for to it women will make a contribution as great as that of man.

"There never was any need for woman's retardation. Man's selfishness, his lust for ownership, must be held responsible for it. He was not willing to make woman equal partner in his various activities, and so he held her back from an ability to fill an equal partnership.

"Less of this is evident in the development of the Jewish than in that of any other race. The almost supernatural business instinct of the Jew maybe, I think, attributed to the fact that the various persecutions of the race have forced it to develop all its strength—its strength of women as well as that of men. Women have, from the beginning, taken part in Jewish councils; Jewish women have shared, always, in the pursuits of Jewish men; especially have they been permitted to play their part in business management. The result is that the Jewish child receives commercial acumen not only from the father's but from the mother's side. This may be taken as an evidence of what may come in future when womankind in general is equally developed with men along all lines.

"This development of woman through the evolution of mechanics will, by means of those mechanics, probably be the quickest which the world has ever seen. The refinements of life in the future will be carried to a point not dreamed of now. I think the time has just arrived when the menial phases of existence may be said to be upon the verge of disappearing. This undoubtedly accounts for the great difficulty we experience now in hiring men, and more especially in hiring women, to do menial labor. The servant girl performs her tasks unwillingly in these days, and when she sees an opportunity, deserts them for the factory, where, through mechanical appliances, her potentiality as a human being finds new effectiveness."

LIFE TO BE MORE REFINED

"The drudgery of life will, by and by, entirely disappear. In days to come, through a small outlay of money, both men and women will be gratified by an infinite variety of delightful sights, sounds, and experiences that today are unknown and unimagined.

"An illustration of what may eventually be accomplished has arisen recently in my own experience. I have been once more working on the phonograph, endeavoring to bring it to perfection, and, within a few months, have succeeded in so doing. Here at my laboratory we now know not only that we can make records of and reproduce the finest music which humanity has yet created, but through our work we have discovered imperfections in the music of the past which, now that they have been found out, will be corrected. In a short time it will be possible to produce within the humblest home the best music of the world, and to produce it there as perfectly as it was in its first form. The reproduction will be presented so that any individual listening to it will hear the music to far better advantage than could any individual listening to the original production, unless his seat, while listening, were located in a scientifically determined spot in the, auditorium wherein the music was produced. At concerts, now, the listener on one side of the hall hears too much brass. On the other side wood instruments or the strings are dominant. . . .

"Science has, by this advance, removed one more of the great time-eaters which have so oppressed all women. With the home picture machine, now well developed, taking moving pictures into the family circle, it will be possible to furnish, quickly and concretely, such knowledge of the wonders of the nature which surrounds us as was impossible for our forefathers to obtain through any means of study. The revelations are illimitable. We could start at eight each morning, and watch films till eight each night for a period of a thousand years, and see new things each moment, without more than slightly touching on the surface of the facts which are available. The moving picture is developing the circumstance that we live in an environment of which we know practically nothing, and of which we even surmise little.

"All these things will do more for the development of women than they will for the development of men, and they are but a few of many influences which now are working toward that end. They occur to me because they are involved in those things which most engage my thought. They will help develop those cells in a woman's mind which have not in the past had opportunity or encouragement to grow. Give them opportunity and encouragement, and they will grow with great rapidity. They are very smart—these little cells! I have not much muscle, because I never have had reason to develop muscle. If I had had to do hard manual labor in the past, my little cells would have built muscle for me."

Woman Now Getting Her First Fair Start

"The exercise of women's brains will build for them new fibers, new involutions, and new folds. If women had had the same struggle for existence which has confronted men, they would have been physically as strong, as capable of mind. But in the past they were protected, or, if not protected, forced to drudgery. These days are the days of woman's start upon the race—her first fair start.

"More and more she must be pushed, and more and more she will advance herself. It is lack of those brain-folds which has made her so illogical. Now, as they begin to come to her she will gain in logic. When she has to meet, in future, the same crises which men in the past have had to meet, the conservation of her time, which modern science has made possible, will have armed her for the encounter. This will make Earth a splendid planet to live upon."

Better Marriage, Better Births

"The development of women will solve many problems which we now deem quite insoluble. When women progress side by side with men, matrimony will became the perfect partnership. This perfect partnership will produce a childhood made up of individuals who would now be thought not only mental, but physical and moral prodigies. There will be no drawbacks to life. We shall stop the cry for more births and raise instead a cry for better births. We shall wake up presently to the dire fact that this world is getting settled at a rate which presently will occupy its total space. The less of that space which is occupied by the unfit and the imperfect, certainly the better for the race. The development of women which has now begun and is progressing with such startling speed, will do more to solve this problem than any other thing could do. What we want now is quality, not quantity. The woman of the future—the domestic engineer, not the domestic drudge—the wife, not the dependent; not alone the mother, but the teacher and developer, will help to bring this quality about."

"The Woman's Magazine"

Jeannette Eaton

Born in Columbus, Ohio, Jeannette Eaton (1886–1968) earned a bachelor's degree
from Vassar and, in 1910, a master's degree from Ohio State University. It appears
that she first spoke publicly in support of women's suffrage after college. In 1915,
working as a "vocational investigator" under the auspices of the Co-operative
Employment Bureau for Girls in Cleveland, she co-authored *Commercial Work
and Training for Girls*, which examined the working conditions of a thousand
women office workers. In August of that year, in *Harper's Weekly*, she argued that
neither suffrage nor education was the "best friend" of women's freedom but
rather modern inventions—electricity, washing machines, ready-made clothes,
typewriters—spurred women's liberation. By the late 1920s, she had become well
known as an author of biographies for young adults, writing about such well-
known figures as Gandhi, Louis Armstrong, and Eleanor Roosevelt. She also
served as an editor for the children's magazine *Story Parade*. In the 1930s, she
wrote for the feminist periodicals *AWA [American Woman's Association] Bulletin*
and *Woman's Journal*, edited by Virginia Roderick.[1]

    The Eaton article reprinted here was first published in the *Masses*, an illus-
trated monthly magazine founded by Piet Vlag in 1911. Throughout its relatively
short life, the magazine was a cooperative, with artists and office workers maintaining full control but receiving no pay. Under the editorship of Max Eastman,
the *Masses* became a major socialist literary and political magazine, although it
published a range of socialist, anarchist, and syndicalist perspectives. With an
average monthly circulation of 14,000, the ten-cent magazine heralded anarchists, the Industrial Workers of the World, Freudians, birth-control advocates,
free love proponents, and feminists.[2]

Masses, Nov. 1915, 19.

For additional information about the *Masses*, see the introduction to Dorothy Weil's "A New Woman?" in part V.

It has glorified the work-basket and the egg-beater and has infinitely stretched woman's belief in the miracles which may be wrought with them. It has taught her what to do for the baby, what is the right way to puff her hair and why she should win her daughter's confidence.

Think of the old tomato cans made into pretty pincushions, the thread lace collars, the embroidered scarfs, the hand-painted match receivers, the linen pin-trays, the discarded boxes converted into "what-nots"! If not for this perennial adviser, it would be hard to imagine how a woman could get up a dinner party, mind her manners, keep her beauty or her husband's love.

While, on the other hand, if she were not thus usefully absorbed, a chivalrous man dreads to think how often a woman might nowadays be tempted to engage in activities outside the home.

It is a great service that these widely-circulated publications are performing for America to-day, whether they are sent to the great apartment building or to the old farm-house. It is a service to men, a fundamental service to the established order. For their message to women is one of domesticity and contentment.

Confess now!!

Which kind of woman would you rather have pour out your morning coffee for you—a complacent or an eager-minded woman? Do you not feel uneasy in the presence of a woman who is filled with turbulent desires for experience, life, work—self expression, power, responsibility, independence, and freedom? Once the impulse in woman to be a personality is let loose, the comfort of man is doomed.

The woman's magazine is the savior of society, man's best friend, the final hope of our chivalric civilization. Woman's ambitious, her independence, the assertion of her own free personality are gradually but certainly inhibited by a few years of such reading.

It is the one sure antidote to feminism.

"Famous Bobbed-Hair Beauties"

To many African Americans who faced continued bigotry despite their migration north, and violence despite service to their country during World War I, Jamaican-born Marcus Garvey was a "Black Moses" who offered a message of self-help, black separatism, race pride, and the promise of returning to Africa on black-financed ships. Garvey founded the Universal Negro Improvement Association (UNIA), which, beginning in 1918, published the *Negro World*. In the early 1920s the paper's circulation was over 200,000, and it was the most widely distributed black newspaper of its kind.[1]

Even though Marcus Garvey condemned face bleaches and hair straightening, the *Negro World* included advertisements for such products by November 1923. The paper's editors likely didn't realize, however, that Madame Mamie Hightower's Golden Brown Beauty Preparations was the brainchild of a white-owned company. Although white advertisers tended to ignore the growing purchasing power of African Americans in the 1920s, some exploited it. Hoping to capitalize on the success of black-owned beauty-product business enterprises like the Madame C. J. Walker Manufacturing Company, the white-owned, Memphis-based, wholesale drug company Hessig-Ellis registered the Golden Brown trade name and "set up a 'dummy' organization that employed thirty-five black workers and sold only to black customers." Hessig-Ellis produced an ad campaign featuring the invented African American company founder, Madame Mamie Hightower, who in actuality was the little-known wife of Zack Hightower, a porter for the company. Whereas Madame C. J. Walker became renowned for her rags-to-riches success, philanthropic support of a number of black institutions, and for the fact that hundreds of African American female sales agents had gained economic

Negro World, Nov. 22, 1924, 3.

independence by selling her products, the Golden Brown Hair Company duped its customers not only by inventing a black female company founder but also by giving her an elaborate fictional story of uplift and race pride. Few customers knew the true origin of Golden Brown products.[2]

The "Famous Bobbed-Hair Beauties" ad reprinted here features a number of cast members from the black musical hit *Shuffle Along*. Created by Noble Sissle and Eubie Blake in 1921, the musical played in Harlem first before becoming a sensation in Manhattan. In addition to providing many black performers with well-paid work and wide recognition, *Shuffle Along* marked the beginning of black musicals on Broadway and desegregation in New York theaters. Most of the black women who appeared in black musicals like *Shuffle Along*, however, were chosen in part for their light skin and European features, and the musical perpetuated stereotypes of black Americans as comical buffoons.[3]

For additional information about the *Negro World*, see the introduction to Saydee E. Parham's "The New Woman" in part IX.

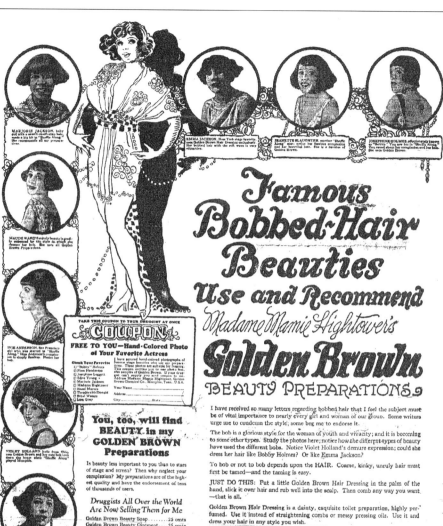

"From Ping Pong to Pants"

Photoplay Magazine, the "queen of the fan magazines," began in Chicago in 1911 as a ten-cent motion picture magazine for movie enthusiasts and quickly became successful. The publication focused on the films of independent studios rather than those of larger film companies and featured profiles of actors and actresses, illustrated stories about movies, and a few departments, including "Answers to Inquiries." James R. Quirk, who edited the magazine from 1920 to 1932, sought to change the image of movie fans from that of bubble-gum-chewing schoolgirls to middle-class devotees who were primarily female consumers with plenty of disposable income and a love for the genre. In *Photoplay*, as Quirk defended moviegoers against the criticism of conservatives, he urged his readers to appreciate cinematic aesthetics. At the same time, he advised the business community to realize that movies had created "perfect consumers" in that moviegoers were dependent on motion pictures to create their desires, be they for new cars or the latest fashions. He commissioned features such as Terry Ramsaye's history of American film, *A Million and One Nights*, in 1920. In 1927, *Photoplay* had a circulation of almost 519,000 and sold for an annual subscription rate of $2.50.[1]

The page from *Photoplay* reprinted here features three actresses from Paramount's 1927 silent-film comedy *Casey at the Bat*, in which Ann Sheridan and Doris Hill play Floradora (also spelled Florodora) girls and Rosalind Byrne plays Lotus Thompson, a chorine or chorus girl.

The stage musical *Florodora*, which premiered in London in 1899 and New York the following year, had made the working-class chorus girl both respectable and an icon of female rags-to-riches success. The musical would have been a flop except for six fashionable, parasol-carrying women, chosen for their beauty rather than any acting or singing talent, who waltzed around the stage with their handsome male partners and became a sensation. Photographers and reporters followed them everywhere; wealthy men showered them with gifts, and all six of the original sextet married millionaires.

Photoplay, Apr. 1927, 106.

By the 1920s, working as a chorus girl provided the single greatest opportunity for steady employment for women in the entertainment industry. Often positioned on stage bare-legged and bare-breasted, these women were characterized in the press as both enviably beautiful icons and dangerously wicked vamps and gold diggers.[2]

From Ping Pong to Pants

And all in 25 years!

The Floradora girl had an angel's face and a teamster's appetite. Rosalind Byrne, the chorine of today, only gets a lamb chop, a pineapple and a calory chart

Miss 1927 (Doris Hill) romps in the gym. Miss 1902 (Ann Sheridan) considered ping pong hectic sport

"There's no kick to that," says Rosalind Byrne of Ann Sheridan's Floradora step. Twenty-five years ago it brought blushes to the bald-headed row. Today it would bring snores. And that billowy, trailing skirt!

"Daughters of the Sky"

Vera L. Connolly

American journalist Vera L. Connolly (1888–1964) wrote articles on juvenile delinquency, drug addiction, sweatshops, and American Indians. Her work appeared in magazines such as *Good Housekeeping, Colliers,* and *Woman's Home Companion.*[1]

The Connolly article that follows was published in *Delineator,* a periodical founded in 1873 as a fashion magazine, which went on to become one of the most popular women's magazines of its day. By 1903, the *Delineator* included essays on fashionable society, articles full of domestic advice, and fiction. When Theodore Dreiser became editor in 1907, he introduced more controversial material, including essays on divorce, "race suicide," and women's suffrage, as well as work by more famous writers. In 1926, after Oscar Graeve took over the editorship, the nature of the magazine changed yet again. Under Graeve, "an air of piquancy, . . . sophistication and exclusiveness characterized" the *Delineator.* Now, instead of reform topics, articles about Hollywood or the theater, celebrity profiles combined with illustrations by leading artists—Ralph Barton, Rose O'Neill, and Rockwell Kent—and fiction writers—Edith Wharton, John Galsworthy, and Hugh Walpole—enticed readers. In 1929 the magazine lowered its price to ten cents and circulation surpassed two million.[2]

"Daughters of the Sky" was heavily illustrated with drawings by Dynevor Rhys and photos of Amelia Earhart, Elinor Smith, Ruth Nichols, and Bobby Trout.

Flying talk! The air is full of it! Motors. Propellers. Three-point landings. Stalls. Skids. Banks. Wing-overs. Barrel-rolls. Dead-sticks.

A preposterous jargon, really. Senseless to older ears. But it is certainly electric with meaning to modern youth.

Delineator, Aug. 1929, 9, 81–83.

There is no escaping it!

It has replaced the polite conversation at our dinner tables. It is the center of interest at dances and teas. It has spoiled many a good bridge game. It even has "It" backed off the map at fraternity parties and on motor rides.

All good motor roads, today, lead in just one direction: to the nearest flying field. Seek air-minded youth under the parental roof on a Saturday or Sunday afternoon, and you will hunt in vain.

Instead—find the flying field! There a colorful sight will rejoice your eyes. You will behold a great meadow lined with hangars, its runways alive with sparkling, colorful, man-made birds. Yellow, brown, red, green and silver birds. Birds perched, throbbing, on the ground, or soaring up into the blue, or, with a white streamer attached (which means some trembling new student is making his or her first landing), spiraling down gracefully out of the sky.

And all around the field, lined two-deep, you will find the family autos from the nearby towns, filled with rabid young enthusiasts and middle-aged doubters engaged in violent argument.

For as surely as middle age is resisting aviation today, youth is rushing into it, living it and loving it.

Middle age once resisted bathtubs, history reminds us. The Philadelphia city fathers denounced the first ones as "dangerous, extravagant, and impious." Sermons were preached against them.

Our first railroad trains were similarly decried. "Providence never intended," breathed a fervent writer of that time, "that man should rush through space at so wicked a speed."

Then came the auto. For years it was a "dangerous contraption."

"I'll never get into one!" women would exclaim.

But they did, finally—in garb so funny that we would ripple into laughter now if it should appear on our comic stage. Long dusters, boots, huge hats swathed like Easter rose-bushes in voluminous veils, and goggles. Always goggles. The theory being that if the speed of the creature did not kill outright, it most certainly would blind.

We smile, comparing those "horseless wagons" with the high-powered cars purring along our roads today. Now every second car is driven by a girl—veil-less, goggle-less, fearless. The auto is a commonplace.

What has all this to do with flying? A great deal. For along has come the aeroplane! And the youth of the race is about to climb into it, bodily. Oh yes, it is. Resisting will do no good. The aeroplane is here, and here to stay. And it is youth's very own.

We cannot banish it any more than we could bathtubs or locomotives or autos. Into the air youth is going, with or without our sympathy and protective aid. How much better for us to sympathize and protect! Youth needs us sorely, just now, in its air-adventurings. Its need is rather desperate. For the whole relation of eager youth to the aviation industry is chaos at present. . . .

How did the successful women in aviation get their start? Had they wealthy, parents who paid for their training? I determined to put that question to some of them, and also ask what openings there are for other eager girls in the aviation industry today. . . . [I put] my query to an extremely pretty girl in an orchid sweater-suit, a girl with a background of college, Junior League, society and polo. She is the holder of the first international hydroaeroplane license issued to an American woman, and was the second woman in the United States to obtain a transport license. I am speaking of Miss Ruth Nichols.

"Is there a future for girls in aviation? Certainly!" she replied spiritedly. "Why not? Girls and women are holding down almost every sort of job today in aviation. Everything except the job of commercial pilot. Piloting isn't suitable for a girl, any more than taxi-driving. Tell girls to discriminate between flying and aviation. I don't think many girls can earn a living at flying. Flying should be a sport, to women—that and a quick, convenient means of getting about. The woman who has a car today will have a plane tomorrow. A number of women own planes now; some use them for pleasure, some for business trips. I believe that will increase until almost every one can fly a plane. The woman who does not learn to fly now will be laughed at as old-fogeyish by her children, before many years. Flying will be an essential part of her children's lives."

"Then flying training is of no use at all?"

"Oh, don't misunderstand me!" said Miss Nichols. "Knowing how to fly is of great value to a girl breaking into aviation. It is part of the background she should have. But—it is not as important as a good, technical training, without which she will stay in a subordinate position. If a girl planning to enter aviation can afford college, she should specialize in the physical sciences, navigation, meteorology and so on. If unable to afford college, she must attend night classes at some good flying school, buy all the maps and books she can, and read, read, read! Then she should get a salaried job with some aeroplane company. But—" Miss Nichols made a forceful gesture—"warn her to keep climbing and *not* get stuck there for life as a stenographer. Tell her to remind herself daily that she is out for a big job."

"How do you account, Miss Nichols," I asked, "for the fact that most men in aviation strongly discourage women from getting into it?"

"It is a vestige of medievalism," was her smiling retort. "Tell women to ignore it." . . .

PART IX

Evolution, Birth Control, and Eugenics

"Effeminate Men and Masculine Women"

William Lee Howard, M.D.

The usually sober *Dictionary of American Medical Biography* (1928) provides an unusual entry for Dr. William Lee Howard (1860–1918). Howard A. Kelly, joint author of the *Dictionary*, describes Howard as "an eccentric, irresponsible character whose native ability was wasted in a desultory, rambling life, and in neglect of those codes which society has erected as safeguards to the perpetuity of the race. A writer of books on sex subjects, and a pamphleteer . . . [he] was held to more esteem by the laity than by the profession." Born in Hartford, Connecticut, Howard was educated in Europe and the United States and received his M.D. from the University of Vermont in 1890. For most of his professional life he practiced in Baltimore, specializing in "nervous diseases and laying stress on hypnotic suggestion." Howard was a prolific writer who published in a number of general-interest magazines, including the *Ladies' Home Journal* and *Arena*, as well as medical periodicals. His longer works include *The Perverts* (1901), *Plain Facts on Sex Hygiene* (1910), *Facts for the Married* (1912), *Sex Structure of Society* (1914), *Sex Problems in Worry and Work* (1915), and *How to Live Long* (1917).[1]

Howard's article "Effeminate Men and Masculine Women" was published by the *New York Medical Journal,* which had been founded during the Civil War by a group of physicians led by William Alexander Hammond. With the war had come a great demand for hospitals, physicians, and educational material for the growing profession, and the *New York Medical Journal* was established in part to help meet this need. First published in New York City in 1865, the journal primarily served New York City physicians and struggled as a "rather anaemic monthly" until Frank Pierce Foster, a specialist in gynecology and dermatology, took over editorship in

New York Medical Journal, May 5, 1900, 686–687.

1880. When the A. R. Elliott Publishing Company combined it with the *Philadelphia Medical Journal* in 1903 and the *Medical News* in 1905, circulation increased dramatically. Foster served as editor of the journal until his death in 1911. Transformed into a successful and respected weekly under Foster's leadership, the *New York Medical Journal* was, according to his son, "one of the most important medical weeklies of the world . . . and its circulation was second only to that of *The Journal of the American Medical Association*." *JAMA* described Foster as the "dean of the medical journalistic profession."[2]

Weak physiological traits, like moral traits, can be increased or decreased by education, training, and example. Environment plays a most active and powerful role in this development. The child born of parents in the prime of physiological life, each one having strong sex characteristics, is apt to show these characteristics in its development and growth, regardless of environment and education. But not so the unfortunate child born of unstable parents; of those who have assumed the responsibility of parentage when life is on the wane, or whose physical or mental activities have been in channels far removed from anticipation and thoughts of married life. Such parents belong to the physiologically degenerate class. They forget that the tendency is, in all animal life, to degenerate rather than improve. This goes on, generation after generation, unless care is exercised to introduce improved blood on one side or the other.

When a child demonstrates in its acts and tastes an indifference to the natural preference and inclination of its sex, it should be strictly confined to the companionship of that sex. Its education should be along the same lines, and every encouragement given it to develop its normal attributes. An indifferent boy who grows up an effeminate man should be allowed to share the ridicule and contempt thrust upon him with his parents, the mother being given the major part. This same mother, who shields her son from physical harm, will bring him up in the nursery with embroidery; take the poor creature, dressed up in linens and velvet, to exhibit him to female admirers; shift him off to the nursery of her hostess, where he is left to dress dolls and have his hair curled by the female attendants, and sit down to a make-believe tea party with his little girl playmates.

He grows up psychically unsexed, detested by the vigorous male, utilized as a willing servitor by the society woman, and sternly admonished by a true father if he finds him dancing attendance with all his mincing manners upon a daughter. The female with masculine ambition is always amusing and often pitiable; but the attenuated, weak-voiced neuter, the effeminate male: pity him, but blame his mother for the false training, and give scorn to the father for his indifference. Even the woman, when she meets such a man, should passionately and involuntarily exclaim: "*O! surgit amari aliquid*" [Oh! Something bitter arises].

The female possessed of masculine ideas of independence; the viragint who would sit in the public highways and lift up her pseudo-virile voice, proclaiming her sole right to decide questions of war or religion, or the value of celibacy and the curse of woman's impurity, and that disgusting antisocial being, the female sexual pervert, are simply different degrees of the same class—degenerates. These unsightly and subnormal beings are the victims of poor mating. When a woman neglects her maternal instincts, when her sentiment and dainty feminine characteristics are boldly and ostentatiously kept submerged, we can see an antisocial creature more amusing than dangerous. When such a woman marries, which she often does for the privileges derived from attaching Mrs. to her name, the husband is certain to be one she can rule, govern, and cause to follow her in voice and action. Should this female be unfortunate enough to become a mother, she ceases to be merely amusing, and is an antisocial being. She is then a menace to civilization, a producer of nonentities, the mother of mental and physical monstrosities who exist as a class of true degenerates until disgusted Nature, no longer tolerant of the woman who would be a man, or the man who would be a woman, allows them to shrink unto death.

The female who prefers the laboratory to the nursery; the mother quick with child who spends her mornings at the club, discussing "social statics," visiting the saloons and tenements in the afternoon, distributing, with an innocence in strange contrast to her assumptions, political tracts asking the denizens to vote her ticket, is a sad form of degeneracy. Such females are true degenerates, because they are unphysiological in their physical incompleteness. The progeny of such human misfits are perverts, moral or psychical. Their prenatal life has been influenced by the very antithesis of what the real woman would surround her expected child with. The child born of the "new woman" is to be pitied. If it could be taken away from its environments, kept from the misguidance of an unwilling mother, nurtured, tutored, and directed along the sex line Nature has struggled to give it, often would the child be true to its latent normal instincts and grow to respected womanhood or manhood. Unfortunate it is that this development does not take place. The weak, plastic, developing cells of the brain are twisted, distorted, and a perverted psychic growth promoted by the false examples and teachings of a discontented mother. These are the conditions which have been prolific in producing the antisocial "new woman" and the disgusting effeminate male, both typical examples of the physiological degenerate.

It is this class that clamors for "higher education" for the woman; that crowds public halls, shouting for the freedom of woman and demanding all the prerogative of the man. It is these female androids who are insulated in the dark umbrage of ignorance and delusion regarding their negative nature, who are faddist, "ism"-ites, and mental roamers. Ideally mobile, they go from the laboratory to the convent, ever restless, continuously discontented, morbidly majestic at periods, hysterically forcible at times. They form sects and societies regardless of sense or science.

They demonstrate their early perverted mental growth by their present lack of reasoning powers. They form the victims of shrewder degenerates. They claim to know more about the science of medicine without study than the men who have devoted their lives to that science. They walk broadcast, superciliously flaunting our health laws and hygienic regulations in the faces of the assumed intelligent masses, and shout their incomprehensible jargon and blasphemous voicings from the portals of their money-making mosques.

—⊗⊗⊗—

"The Evolution of Sex in Mind"

Henry T. Finck

Henry Theophilus Finck (1854–1926) served as music critic for the *New York Evening Post* (formerly the *Nation*) for forty-three years. Finck also wrote about philosophy, psychology, and travel in addition to music and was credited with being the first to argue that romantic love and personal beauty were modern products of civilization and unknown to the "lower races." He published a number of books, including *Romantic Love and Personal Beauty* (1887), *Chopin and Other Musical Essays* (1889), *Wagner and His Works* (1893), and *Primitive Love and Love Stories* (1899).[1]

Finck's article "The Evolution of Sex in Mind" was published in the *Independent*, which had begun in 1848 as a weekly Congregationalist newspaper and became by the 1880s one of the most important American interdenominational newspapers to include opinions by leading writers. When in 1896 William Hayes Ward took over editorship, he made the publication more secular by including discussions of world affairs and currently debated issues, some fiction, and illustrations. The *Independent* endorsed the "new knowledge" of Darwinian evolution, U.S. expansion overseas (as a means of "taking up the white man's burden"), and the League of Nations. Although the periodical had been staunchly Republican, after 1900 it made a point of including position statements by all political candidates before elections. In 1900, its annual subscription rate was two dollars, and although the circulation of the magazine was never large, it prided itself on attracting a learned audience.[2]

Talk of a true woman needing the ballot as an accessory of power, when she rules the world by a glance of the eye!

—*Horace Greeley*

Independent, Dec. 1901, 3059–3064.

A woman impudent and mannish grown
Is not more loath'd than an effeminate man
In time of action.

—*Shakespeare*

. . . The assertion made by me in *The Independent* of Jan. 31, 1901, that if women continue to ape men, "their thoughts and feelings, their tastes and manners, and even their features and figures, will approximate those of the men," was violently resented by the suffragists. They pointed to the existence of women who have held their doctrines and who have, nevertheless, remained indisputably feminine. As a matter of fact, I have the honor of knowing a few such women myself. But that has nothing to do with the question. What I assert is, not that the mere holding of such opinions makes women unwomanly, but that if they persist in doing the work which makes men manly they will in the course of a lifetime, and more still in a few generations, become mannish—that is, unsexed.

What biologists call the primary sexual qualities are, of course, unalterable. But some of the secondary and all of the tertiary qualities of sex, including sex in mind, can be effaced. The traits of pugnacious lawyers, boisterous brokers, unemotional scholars, fighting politicians can be easily substituted for the gentle, domestic, sympathetic qualities we admire in women. As for the corresponding physical traits, there are countless warning examples, especially in the Old World, showing how the doing of men's work, such as mining, building railways and houses, plowing, harvesting, unsexes women, making them unpleasantly mannish in appearance, coarse in morals and rough in manners.

When Dr. Heber Newton declared the other day that "there is no danger of anything unsexing a woman," he had not, I fear, given this subject so much thought as he has those topics on which he speaks as an authority.[3] I call his attention to a particularly instructive instance of the lamentable potency of masculine activity in unsexing women—the case of the Dahoman Amazons. "The warlike instinct, as the annals of the four quarters of the globe prove, is," as R. H. Burton wrote in his book on Dahomey, "easily bred in the opposite sex." Ever since 1728 the rulers of that region of Africa have surrounded themselves, as J. R. Sketchly remarks, "with an armed body of viragos, who, like every bluestocking among civilized nations, were conceitedly vain of their manly qualities." There have been many thousands at a time of these spinster soldieresses. They are divided into different classes—blunderbusseers, elephant huntresses, musketeers, and the "razor women," whose gentle work consists in chopping off heads. These Amazons have a great reputation for valor, and surrounding nations look on them with special dread because, as Sketchly adds, "whenever a woman becomes unsexed, either by the force of circumstances or depravity, she invariably exhibits a superlativeness of evil." Commander Forbes testified that the Dahoman Amazons "indulge in the excitement of the most fearful cruelties"; and Burton adds that "they are savage as wounded gorillas, more cruel far than their brethren in arms." Which shows once more that women can never be quite the equals of men; they are either better or worse: "For men at most differ as heaven and earth; But women, worst and best, as heaven and hell."

It is by order of the king that these Dahoman women are thus unsexed by assuming the activities of men. In other parts of Africa bands of women have become warriors of their own accord; as in the Soudan, where, Professor Bastian informs us, "the power of the women banded together for protection is so great that men are often put under ban and obliged to emigrate."

This calls attention to another suggestive fact: that, wherever women become abnormally mannish, we must expect the men to degenerate in the opposite direction, into equally loathsome and unnatural effeminacy. Among the Beni-Amer, for instance, Munzinger found that "the sexes seem to have exchanged *rôles*," the women being aggressively masculine and the men timid and henpecked. Chapman commented on "the passive and effeminate disposition" of the Bushmen as compared with their pugnacious wives; Barrow noted the "timid and pusillanimous minds" of the Hottentot men; and so on.

On the American continent we find the same state of affairs. Professor Agassiz and his wife noted in their book on Brazil that "the Indian woman has a very masculine air, extending, indeed, more or less to her whole bearing; for even her features have rarely the feminine delicacy of higher womanhood."

The Jesuit missionaries in Canada often commented on the difficulty of distinguishing the squaws from the men except by certain articles of dress; and in the minds of these Indians, too, the sexual traits were little differentiated. Parkman relates that in the Huron villages there were squaws who "in vindictiveness, ferocity and cruelty far excelled the men." Before marriage, he says, they were wantons, after marriage drudges. In the words of Champlain, "their women were their mules." It is needless to add that neither as wantons nor as drudges did they represent real womanliness—that womanliness which we sum up in the word "lady."

Three important truths are established by the foregoing facts and considerations: (1) that there is sex in mind; (2) that sexual distinctions can be weakened or altogether eliminated by making women do the work of men or men that of women; (3) the truth—the most important truth in the whole suffrage controversy—that the state in which the sexes most resemble each other—that is, in which there is least sex in face and mind—is the state of savagery. Anthropology, the youngest and the most suggestive and delightful of all sciences proves that the tendency of civilization has been to make men and women more and more unlike, both in body and mind; that it has strengthened the manly qualities in men, the womanly qualities in women.

Comparatively, however, man has changed less than woman. He has acquired more muscle in body and mind (compare a Newton with a savage who cannot count ten without feeling tired!), he has become more truly courageous (Indians fight from ambush only) and he has gradually acquired noble virtues, like the chivalrous impulse to protect women and release them from the hardest labor. But, on the whole, there was less occasion for a radical change in man than in woman, because the conditions of savage life were always much more favorable to the development of manly than of womanly traits. The men fought and hunted; the women did the rest.

Fighting and hunting bring out at least some of the traits peculiar to men; but being a man's "mule" does not give a woman much chance to be womanly. The barbarian ideal of woman is, indeed, purely muscular—that is, manly. An Indian once told Hearne that "Women were made for labor; one of them can carry as much as two men can do." Similar conditions prevail even now in European countries, where men have not yet emerged from the barbarous habit of compelling or permitting women to do hard work. Professor Mantegazza points out that, whereas, under the normal conditions of modern civilization, man's strength is to woman's as 9 to 5, in Northern Italy and Switzerland women often carry heavier burdens than the men. "To the present day," wrote Burton, "the woman of the Scotch fishing islands is the man of the family, who does not marry till she can support what she produces; and the times are not long passed since she was, among the Southrons, a barber, a mason, and a day laborer."

If the so-called New Woman, who is so eager to support herself and to be a barber and a day laborer and everything that man is, had any sense of humor, she would see in the mirror of these anthropologic and historic facts that she is in reality a very old-fashioned, primitive and crab-like sort of a woman. Like the squaw and the peasant woman, she has taken to smoking again, and, in some respects she is even more mannish than the savage woman, for that woman in most cases leaves at least hunting and politics to the men. The "New Woman," who has a periodical ironically called *Progress*, really represents ideals which the world outgrew more and more as civilization progressed. It was in the days of savagery that woman had the "right" to support not only herself with hard labor, but her husband, too. O, for the good old times! . . .

In the early barbarous ages utility, not beauty, was considered woman's cardinal virtue. . . . In proportion as men acquired the esthetic sense they saw that beauty was woman's real sphere, and they, therefore, began to treat her in such a way that it became possible for her to unfold her charms of body and mind and make them her specialty, for her own sake as well as for man's. This was the first and most important of "woman's rights" granted to her by man. But before he could grant this boon deliberately he had to make the discovery that she could not compete with him in trials of strength and be beautiful at the same time. And thus, in course of time, was established the real antithesis between the sexes—strength in man, beauty in woman. It was the most important discovery ever made, for it brought a new sex into the world—the fair sex.

All Europe and civilized America had accepted this antithesis between fair women and strong men when, about half a century ago, a small band of American women (most of them not conspicuously of the fair sex) came together, concluded that the world was out of joint, and proceeded in an attempt to swim up the Niagara Falls, to make the clock of time move backward, and change the laws of nature. Far from recognizing beauty as woman's special prerogative, they promptly began a war of extermination against it. In the years 1851–52 about a hundred of them, "as a matter of principle," adopted the Bloomer costume—the most hideous parody on dress ever conceived by human brain. Nor was that all. As Ida Husted Harper informs us in her biography of Susan B. Anthony, "In order to be entirely relieved from the care of personal ornament, they also cut off their hair." Precisely what the Dahoman Amazons did!

How did the American public receive this campaign against womanly dress and womanly beauty? The same biographer tells us:

"The outcry against it extended from one end of the country to the other; the press howled in derision, the pulpit hurled its anathemas, and the rabble took up the refrain. On the streets of the larger cities the women were followed by mobs of men and boys, who jeered and yelled. . . . Their husbands and children refused to be seen with them in public, and they were wholly ostracized by the other sex."

What was the meaning of these extraordinary demonstrations and protests? Was it simply the ugliness of the Bloomers as clothes? Obviously not, for various freaks of fashion, almost equally ugly—the hoop skirts, for instance—have always been accepted meekly and adopted universally. The real meaning of the demonstrations is hinted at in the lines from Shakespeare prefixed to this article. A woman bold and mannish grown is loathed no less than a man who is effeminate and cowardly in time of danger.

In other words, the question of sex in mind came into play here. It was not so much the Bloomers on the bodies of these would-be "reformers" that excited indignation, as *the Bloomers in their minds*. The garb of their minds, as of their bodies, was half trousers, half skirts—a most unlovely combination. And many who saw and heard these "reformers" were doubtless tempted to ask, with the poet,

Sir, or madame, choose you whether
You are one or both together.

The public had gradually accepted as its ideal of womanhood a lady, refined, modest, gentle, sympathetic, shrinking, if possible, from rough conflict of any sort, and blessed with a voice "ever soft, gentle and low—an excellent thing in woman." It had learned instinctively that these qualities represented *beauty of mind*, and that beauty of body and mind—or at least of mind, the more important of the two—is the *sine qua non* of true womanliness. It knew that as the pen is mightier than the sword, so beauty is mightier than manly muscle; that beauty needs no strong cords, because it "draws us with a single hair," and woman has whole tresses with which to govern "man's imperial race." Yet here were a handful of persons clamoring that women should throw overboard all these advantages, and once more enter into competition and conflict with man in his own realm of muscle, strength, strife and struggle for existence! . . .

If the evolution of sex in mind—that grandest achievement of civilization—is to continue; if we are unwilling to go to Dahomey for our ideals of womanhood; if we are to have two sexes instead of one, or one and a half, then our women must be saved at all costs from what President Roosevelt in his recent message called "the bitter animosities incident to public life." Politics is too rough a game for them. It is essentially a perpetual fight against unscrupulous adversaries, and women were not meant to be fighters any more than they were meant to be hod-carriers, stokers, or football players. . . .

"The New Woman Monkey" and "Evolution"

The artist of "The New Woman Monkey" was Rudolph E. Leppert (1872–1949), who began his career on the art staff of the *New York Herald* and served for many years as the art director of the *Literary Digest*.[1]

Born in Springfield, Ohio, Walter Earnest Tittle (1883–1966), the illustrator of "Evolution," studied art under William M. Chase, Robert Henri, and Kenneth Hays Milier. Tittle was most famous for his etchings and drypoints of leading British literary figures and American statesmen. He also illustrated for *Harper's Magazine, Scribner's, Century*, and *Life*.[2]

The illustrations reprinted here were originally published in *Life*, a humor magazine that offered Americans more genteel comic fare than could be found in either *Puck* or *Judge*, both of which were larger, color-filled, raucous magazines of the period. Despite a shaky beginning in 1883, John Ames Mitchell's *Life* became "the most influential cartoon and literary humor magazine of its time," largely because of the popularity of its black-and-white illustrations by Charles Dana Gibson as well as work by prominent illustrators, including Art Young, James Montgomery Flagg, and Tittle. Corruption, populists, monopolies, immigrants, Jews, imperialism, Booker T. Washington, and women's suffrage were all subjects for *Life*'s satire. During Roosevelt's tenure as president (1901–1909), when muckraking was the rage, *Life* concentrated on trusts and urban problems. *Life*'s advertising, which by the 1910s included many ads for automobiles, cameras, and liquor—reflected its upper-middle-class audience. Throughout this period, it still charged ten cents a copy, and by 1916 its circulation had reached 160,000.[3]

For additional information about *Life*, see the introduction to Edward Kemble's "Ise Gwine ter Give You Gals What Straddle" in part I.

Life, Jan. 18, 1906, 94; *Life*, Apr. 10, 1913, cover.

THE NEW WOMAN MONKEY.

Life

PRICE 10 CENTS

Vol. 61, No. 1589.   April 10, 1913

"Flapper Americana Novissima"

G. Stanley Hall

Granville Stanley Hall (1844–1924), one of the founding fathers of American psychology, focused his analysis on the lives of children, "primitives," and women. Along with a belief that acquired characteristics could be inherited, Hall adopted German Darwinian Ernst Haeckle's famous "recapitulation" argument, in which "every individual organism repeats in its own life history the life history of its race." For Hall, childhood and adolescence contained the secret ancestry of man. So the tendency of children to clutch men's beards reflected "the necessity for anthropoids of arboreal habits to cling to the shaggy sides of their parents." Women likewise represented the continuous elements in the race, especially the emotional warmth of perpetual youth. Because a woman's heart dominated her head, she must be protected from too vigorous intellectual training and must realize that her true vocation lay in motherhood. In her pursuit of education, modern woman risked undermining that primary maternal function.[1]

Hall's "Flapper Americana Novissima" was published in the *Atlantic Monthly,* which, from its inception in Boston in 1857, was considered the United States' most distinguished literary magazine. Its founders, however, led by Francis Underwood and including James Russell Lowell, Oliver Wendell Holmes, and Ralph Waldo Emerson, also sought to influence political debates, especially that on abolition. When Ellery Sedgwick became owner and editor of the magazine in 1909, he changed the focus of the magazine, albeit gradually, to reflect his own experience in the competitive world of New York journalism. He included essays on current and controversial economic, social, and political changes affecting Americans. Science and religious topics also became more frequent, and in 1922 the *New York Times Book Review* reported that the *Atlantic Monthly* was no

---

Atlantic Monthly, June 1922, 771–780.

longer a "staid" magazine, for "it has moved with the times and, finely enough, yet retained that dignified composure that is associated with it." Under Sedgwick, the *Atlantic*'s circulation passed 100,000 in 1921, while the annual subscription price remained four dollars.[2]

I

When, years ago, I first heard the picturesque word "Flapper" applied to a girl, I thought of a loose sail flapping in whatever wind may blow, and liable to upset the craft it is meant to impel. There was also in my mind the flitting and yet cruder mental imagery of a wash, just hung out to dry in the light and breeze, before it is starched and ironed for use. I was a little ashamed of this when the dictionary set me right by defining the word as a fledgling, yet in the nest, and vainly attempting to fly while its wings have only pinfeathers; and I recognized that thus the genius of "slanguage" had made the squab the symbol of budding girlhood. This, too, had the advantage of a moral, implying what would happen if the young bird really ventured to trust itself to its pinions prematurely. . . .

We must, then, admit at the outset that the world has not yet found the right designation for this unique product of civilization, the girl in the early teens, who is just now undergoing such a marvelous development. But why bother about names?

As a lifelong student of human nature, I long ago realized that of all the stages of human life this was *terra incognita*. We now know much of children, of adults, and of old age, while the pubescent boy has become an open book. So I began months ago to forage in libraries, and was surprised to find how sentimental, imaginative, and altogether unscientific most of the few books, and the scores of articles, about girls in the early teens really were. Very persistent is the tendency to treat this grave and serious theme flippantly—to invoke Puck, Ariel, or Momus as the only muses who can help us in threading the labyrinthine mazes of feminine pubescence. Moreover, since the war, the kind of girl whom most ante-bellum authors depict has become as extinct as the dodo, if indeed she ever existed at all. So we must turn from literature, and come down from the roseate heights, whereon we thought she dwelt, to the street and home, and be as objective and concrete as possible.

II

First, the street. The other day I found myself walking a few rods behind a girl who must have been approaching sweet sixteen. She held to the middle of the broad sidewalk. . . . her gait was swagger and superior. "Howdy, Billy," she called to a youth whom I fancied a classmate; and "Hello, boys," was her greeting to three more a little later.

. . . She wore a knitted hat, with hardly any brim, of a flame or bonfire hue; a henna scarf; two strings of Betty beads, of different colors, twisted together; an open short coat, with ample pockets; a skirt with vertical stripes so pleated that, at the waist, it seemed very dark, but the alternate stripes of white showed progressively downward, so that, as she walked, it gave something of what physiological psychologists call a flicker effect. On her right wrist were several bangles; on her left, of course, a wrist watch. Her shoes were oxfords, with a low broad heel. Her stockings were woolen and of brilliant hue. But most noticeable of all were her high overshoes, or galoshes. One seemed to be turned down at the top and entirely unbuckled, while the other was fastened below and flapped about her trim ankle in a way that compelled attention. This was in January, 1922, as should be particularly noted because, by the time this screed meets the reader's eye, flapperdom, to be really *chic* and up-to-date, will be quite different in some of these details. She was out to see the world and, incidentally, to be seen of it; and as I lingered at the campus block to see the students frolic, she passed me three times, still on her devious way home, I presume, from school.

Sheer accident had thus brought me within the range of the very specimen I sought, and perhaps a rare and extreme hope; therefore, all the more interesting.

But a deep instinct told me that I could never by any possible means hope to get into any kind of personal *rapport* with her or even with her like. I might have been her grandfather, and in all the world of man there is no wider and more unbridgeable gulf than that which yawns between me and those of my granddaughter's age. If I should try to cultivate her, she would draw back into her shell; and to cultivate me would be the very last of all her desires. Hence, as was only fair to her, I turned to a third source of information about her, namely, her teachers.

They told me a large notebook full—far more than I can, and, alas! some that I would not, repeat; so that it is puzzling to know what to omit, or even where to begin, in the tangle of incidents, traits, and judgments.

III

Let us start at random, with dancing, on which the flapper dotes as probably never before, in all the history of the terpsichorean art, made up of crazes as it has been, has anyone begun to do.

A good dance is as near heaven as the flapper can get and live. She dances at noon and at recess in the school gymnasium; and, if not in the school, at the restaurants between courses, or in the recreation and rest-rooms in factories and stores. She knows all the latest variations of the perennial fox-trot, the ungainly contortions of the camel walk; yields with abandon to the fascination of the tango; and if the floor is crowded, there is always room for the languorous and infantile toddle; and the cheek-to-cheek close formation—which one writer ascribes to the high cost of rent nowadays, which necessitates the maximum of motion in the minimum of space—has a lure of its own, for partners must sometimes cling together in order to move at all. Verticality of motion and, at least, the vibrations of the "shimmy," are always possible. . . .

She dotes on jewelry, too, and her heart goes out to the rings, bracelets, bangles, beads, wrist watches, pendants, earrings, that she sees in shop-windows or on some friend or stranger. Her dream is of diamonds, rubies, sapphires, and gold; but imitations will go far to fill the aching void in her heart; and so in recent years she has made a great run on this market, as those who sell them testify.

The hair, which the Good Book calls a woman's "crown of glory," of which amorists in prose and poetry have had so much to say, and which, outside the Mongolian and Negroid races, has always been one of the chief marks of distinction between the sexes, is no longer always so. The old-fashioned, demure braids once so characteristic of the budding girl are gone. Nor is the hair coiled, either high or low, at the back of the head. This medullary region long so protected is now exposed to wind and weather, either by puffs on either side, or, still more, by the Dutch cut which leaves the hair shortest here. Indeed, my barber tells me that he now shaves a space below the occiput for girls more frequently than when, in Italy, he used to freshen the tonsure of young priests above it. It is now more nearly immodest, I am told, to expose an ear than a knee, and special attention is given to the ear-lock. It is very *chic* to part the hair on one side, to keep it very smooth, as if it were plastered down on top; but on all sides of the head it must be kept tousled or combed backward *à la* Hottentot, and the more disordered it is here, the better. In all such matters, as in so many others, the girl imitates, consciously or unconsciously, her favorite movie actresses.

At least half the movie films seem almost to have been made for the flapper; and her tastes and style, if not her very code of honor, are fashioned on them. Librarians report that she reads much less since the movies came. No home or other authority can keep her away; the only amelioration is to have reels more befitting her stage of life.

I even interviewed the head of a city traffic squad, who said, as nearly as I can quote him: "When a fella speeds or breaks the rules and gets pinched, it's more than a fifty-fifty proposition he had a girl alongside, and was showin' off to her or attendin' to her, and forgettin' his machine. Some of them think it's smart to step up to Judge _____, pull their roll, and peel it to pay a fine, with the girl lookin' on, or to tell her after. She sure likes joy-ridin'; and say, there was an old song about a bicycle made for two, and that's the way she wants the auto. She loves the back seat empty—no one lookin' on. They ought to have some of us out on the country roads, where they slow down and stop."

At this point the traffic became congested and took his attention, and I left him.

But I am forgetting the curriculum. In college, some subjects attract girls, and others boys, each sex sometimes monopolizing certain courses. But in high school, wherever the elective system permits choice, most girls are usually found in classes where there are most boys. Girls, too, seem fonder of cultural subjects, and less, or at least later, addicted to those that are immediately vocational. They do far better in their studies with teachers whom they like; and I have heard of an attractive unmarried male teacher who was accused by his colleagues of marking the girls in his classes too high, but whose principal had the sagacity to see that the girls did far better work for him than for any other teacher and to realize the reason why.

In the secondary school the girl finds herself the intellectual equal of her male classmate, and far more mature at the same age in all social insights. Hence coeducation at this stage has brought her some slight disillusionment. Her boy classmates are not her ideal of the other sex, and so real lasting attachments, dating from this period, are rare. Perhaps associations and surroundings here bring also some disenchantment with her home environment, and even with her parents. But docile as she is, her heart of hearts is not in her textbooks or recitations, but always in life and persons; and she learns and adjusts herself to both with a facility and rapidity that are amazing. It is things outside her studies which seem to her, if indeed they are not in fact, far more important for her life.

IV

If any or all of the above seems extravagant, let the reader remember that I am writing so far only of the *novissima* variety of the species, which fairly burst upon the world like an insect suddenly breaking from its cocoon in full imago form; so that she is more or less a product of movies, the auto, woman suffrage, and, especially, of the war. During the latter she completed her emancipation from the chaperon, and it became good patriotic form to address, give flaglets, badges, and dainties, to young men in the street and, perhaps, sometimes, to strike up acquaintance with them if they were in uniform. Her manners have grown a bit free-and-easy, and every vestige of certain old restraints is gone. In school, she treats her male classmates almost as if sex differences did not exist. Toward him she may sometimes even seem almost aggressive. She goes to shows and walks with him evenings, and in school corridors may pat him familiarly on the back, hold him by the lapel, and elbow him in a familiar and even *de-haut-en-bas* way, her teachers tell us; and they add that there is hardly a girl in the high school who does not have face-powder, comb, mirror, and perhaps rouge, in her locker, for use between sessions.

Never since civilization began has the girl in the early teens seemed so self-sufficient and sure of herself, or made such a break with the rigid traditions of propriety and convention which have hedged her in. From this, too, it follows that the tension which always exists between mothers and daughters has greatly increased, and there now sometimes seems to be almost a chasm between successive generations. If a note of loudness in dress or boisterousness in manner has crept in, and if she seems to know, or pretends to know, all that she needs, to become captain of her own soul, these are really only the gestures of shaking off old fetters. Perhaps her soul has long been ripening for such a revolt, and anxious to dissipate the mystery which seemed to others to envelop it. Let us hope that she is really more innocent and healthier in mind and body because she now knows and does earlier so much that was once admissible only later, if at all.

So it is "high time" to be serious, and to realize that all the above are only surface phenomena, and that the real girl beneath them is, after all, but little changed; or that, if she is changed, it is, on the whole, for the better. Beneath all this new self-revelation, she still remains a mystery. She is so insecure in all her new assurance that it may be shattered by a slight which others do not notice; or some uncomplimentary remark by a mate may humble her pride in the dust. The sublime selfishness, of which the flapper is so often accused, which makes her accept service and demand to be served by parents and all about her whom she can subject; her careless irresponsibilities, which render her unconscious of all the trouble she makes, or the worries which others feel for her present and future: and the fact that she never seems to realize what it means to clean up after herself, easily alternate with the extreme desire to serve, herself, and to lavish attention upon those whom she really likes. Despite her mien of independence, she is tinglingly sensitive to every breath of good- and ill-will; and if she has shattered old conventions, she has not gone wrong; and if she knows about many things of which she must still often pretend to be ignorant, she is thereby only the more fortified against temptation. . . .

V

. . . She is in the most interesting stage of the long and complex process of getting ready to love and be loved. It is already several years since all boys ceased to seem crude, oafish, and altogether inconvenient, and began—at least, one or two of them—to be interesting. She has also pretty well passed the stage of amatory fetishisms, when she was prone to dote on some single feature, trait, or act, and feel a degree of aversion for others for which nothing could compensate. She is just learning to perform her supreme selective function of passing judgment on personalities as a whole, with all their *ensemble* of qualities. A small but rather constant percentage of girls of high-school age evolve, more or less unconsciously, an ideal hero, or make one of some older youth; and this sometimes seems to serve as a defense against "falling for" even the best specimen of the other sex among her acquaintances of her own age. George Eliot rather crassly says that for some years a girl's every act may tend to provoke proposals. But, if she wants attention, she flees from it, if she detects serious signs of intention. She has no idea of marrying till she has had her innocent fling, or perhaps tried her hand at self-support. Intuition warns her of the danger of loving or being loved with abandon. . . .

Thrice happy the girl who, through these years of seething and ferment, has a father whom she can make the embodiment of her ideals; for he is, all unconsciously, the pattern to which her future lover and husband must conform. But even here there are dangers; for if her fondness for her father is too intense, or unduly prolonged, this may make it impossible for her ever to be happy if mated to a man not in the father image. She may be even a little motherly toward her parents, although her attitude toward her mother is infinitely complex. While we almost never find any of the jealously which Freudians stress, there is, especially in these days of sudden emancipation from the conventions in vogue a generation ago, an unprecedented tension between mother and daughter, which may be reinforced if the former has failed to give certain instruction in life-problems. Thus, occasionally a girl's devotion to her mother, if it is excessive, may be due to a blind instinct to compensate for thoughts and feelings toward her that she deems not truly filial; and if she has caught herself in a mood of hostility, she may overwhelm her mother with attentions that are embarrassing.

VI

. . . Thus despite the uniformitizing effect of fashions, the contagion of fads, and the intense imitativeness of this stage, individuality is being developed, and the new and ostensive assertiveness has in it the promise and potency of a new and truer womanhood. In all the long struggle for emancipation, sometimes called the war of sex against sex, woman has, and perhaps necessarily, laid aside for the time some of her most distinctive traits, and competed with man along his own lines, and has perhaps grown thereby a trifle masculine. But true progress demands that sex-distinctions be pushed to the uttermost, and that women become more feminine and men more virile. This need modern feminism has failed to recognize; but it is just this which flapperdom is now asserting. These girls not only accept, but glory in, their sex as such, and are giving free course to its native impulses. They may be the leaders in the complete emancipation of woman from the standards man has made for her. Up to this age our Binet-Simon tests can grade and mark, at least for intelligence, but here they baulk, stammer, and diverge.

The flapper's new sophistication is thus superficial. Her new self-consciousness is really naïve, and in her affectations she is simply trying out all the assortments of temperamental types, dispositions, and traits of character, as she often tries out styles of handwriting before she settles upon one. This is all because hers is the most vital and most rapidly developing psyche in all the world. The evolutionary stages of flapperdom are so many, and they succeed each other so fast, and are so telescoped together that we cannot yet determine the order of their sequence, and all my glimpses are only random snapshots of the wonderful quadrennium, the first four teens.

She accepts the confirmation, and perhaps even the conversion, that the church prescribes; but her heart is set on this world and not on the next. She conforms with more interest to the "coming-out" customs of society; but these are now much belated, for in all essentials she came out unaided, and the age of her legal majority she deems too late. Once it was commonly held that those who were precocious would become blasé later; but if there ever was danger here, it exists no longer. In fact, civilization itself, and all our hope that mankind may attain superhumanity, depends on the prolongation, enrichment, and safeguarding of the interval between pubescence and ripe nubility.

What a reversal of ancient and traditional mores it would be if the flapper, long repressed by so many taboos, were now to become the pioneer and leader of her sex to a new dispensation, and to give to the world its very best illustration of the trite but pregnant slogan, *Das ewig Weibliche sieht uns hinan* [The Eternal-Feminine draws us upward]. She has already set fashions in attire, and even in manners, some of which her elders have copied, and have found not only sensible, but rejuvenating. Underneath the mannish ways which she sometimes affects, she really vaunts her femininity, and her exuberance gives it a new charm. The new liberties she takes with life are contagious, and make us wonder anew whether we have not all been servile to precedent, and slaves to institutions that need to be refitted to human nature, and whether the flapper may not, after all, be the bud of a new and better womanhood.

"The New Woman:

IN THE POLITICAL WORLD SHE IS THE SOURCE OF ALL REFORM LEGISLATION AND THE ONE POWER THAT IS HUMANIZING THE WORLD"

Saydee E. Parham

Marcus Garvey formed the Universal Negro Improvement Association (UNIA) in his native Jamaica in 1914. Later, in 1917, he moved its headquarters to Harlem, and by the early 1920s the UNIA had thousands of chapters throughout the United States, Canada, the British Isles, Africa, the Caribbean, and Central and South America. For many African Americans who had migrated north and who had served their country during World War I yet continued to face bigotry and white violence, Marcus Garvey was a "Black Moses" who offered a kind of New Thought optimism about the possibility of success through transformative thinking. Garvey's message of self-help, black separatism, race pride, and the promise of returning to Africa on black-financed ships appealed to millions of African American men and women, especially those from working-class backgrounds. In 1923, Garvey was found guilty of using the mail to defraud investors in Black Star Line stock. One of the NAACP founders, Mary White Ovington, noted in 1927 that "among the poor and the exploited, even among those whose money he misappropriated, he is defended with an ardor that abashes the critic." But his espousal of racial purity after 1921 and his rejection of black folk culture as primitive provoked bitter recrimination from many black leaders of the Harlem Renaissance.[1]

The *Negro World*, a Saturday paper begun in 1918 and published by the UNIA, reflected the militancy of this largest of Pan-African organizations in the world at the time. In the early 1920s the *Negro World* had a circulation of over 200,000 and

---

Negro World, Feb. 2, 1924, 10.

was the most widely distributed black newspaper of its kind. After Garvey was indicted for mail fraud in 1923, T. Thomas Fortune edited the newspaper until his death in 1928, and Amy Jacques Garvey, despite objections from some male UNIA leaders, became a leading voice in the organization, serving as an associate editor for the *Negro World* and editing its woman's page from February 1924 to June 1927. In addition to a regular editorial statement and news items of UNIA activities and related items of interest from around the world, the woman's page generally included poetry, household advice, fashion advertisements, and a biblical quote of the day. Using the rhetoric of racial uplift and social purity, Jacques Garvey urged her women readers to serve as models of industry and virtue for their men in their struggle for UNIA's vision of Pan-African unity. The explicit rhetoric of the New Negro Woman also figured prominently in its pages. In an April 1924 issue, for example, Jacques Garvey included a letter from Eunice Lewis, who, according to biographer Ula Yvette Taylor, offered sentiments matching those of Jacques Garvey. For Lewis, the New Negro Woman must first be "conscious of the value of pure womanhood that has the power to win and conquer the beastly side of man." Then, to help realize the "rebirth of Africa at home and abroad," the New Negro Woman must strive to "work on par with men in the office as well as on the platform"; to practice thrift; to teach children both the "practical and constructive race doctrine" as well as the "moral dangers of social diseases"; and to "demand absolute respect from men of all races."[2]

Saydee (also spelled Saddie) E. Parham, born in New Jersey (1892?), was a contributor to the *Negro World*, a law student, a member of the Universal Negro Improvement Association, and Marcus Garvey's secretary.[3] Her article reprinted here appeared in the inaugural installment of Jacques Garvey's "Women and What They Think" page for the newspaper. On the same page as Parham's article was one by Carrie Mero Leadett in which she urged those of the "Negro race" "to produce girls who could surpass those of all other races, socially, industrially and morally." Another article spoke in favor of efforts by the National Woman's Party to repeal a law forbidding the employment of women at night in certain jobs. Another story in that issue, from the Associated Press, featured the headline "African Ladies Are Leaders in Fashion: Clothes on Egyptian Mummy 2,642 Years Old Same Style as Today." Accompanying an article on Ramsay Macdonald, Britain's first Labour prime minister, was one that described Macdonald's daughter as more interested in science, physics, and social welfare than housekeeping. Near the bottom of the page, readers saw an advertisement for *Natura*, an advice book for childless couples on how to conceive—in keeping with UNIA's eugenic mission of fighting "race suicide." In 1924, the paper sold for five cents in New York, seven cents elsewhere in the United States, and ten cents in foreign countries.[4]

All life is but a continuous process of evolution. Nothing that embodies the vitalic principle of life is static. It is by the very inherent law of nature that in the changing order of every species of life we find a higher, nobler and greater ascent of life. In the mineral kingdom with its amazing wealth of stones, we find this principle in the ever increasing change of the vast variety of the mineral life. And as we ascend the scale of elevation until we reach the mammal or the animal kingdom, we find that even here is a distinctive change in the physical, mental and biological condition of men and animals. There was a time when rough men fought the ferocious beasts of the forests with their naked hands and a mere bludgeon. Today they can silence the wildest animal with a rifle. And so, onward and upward the majestic drama of civilization is proceeding scene by scene, act by act in its glorious unfolding of the higher and nobler changes in the progress of her principal actor—woman. From the brow-beaten, dominated cave woman, cowering in fear at the mercy of her brutal mate; from the petted toy reared for the sensual indulgence of the Roman and Greek nobility, from the safely cloistered woman reared like a clinging vine, destitute of all initiative and independence—a product of the middle-ages, we find her at last rising to a pinnacle of power and glory so great, so potential that she has actually become the central figure of all modern civilization. In the business world, she is the master of the clerical detail work; in the factories she is the dynamo of production; in the theatre she is the most magnetic form of entertainment; in the political world she is the source of all reform legislation and the one power that is humanizing the world. In all great movements for the redemption of the oppressed masses, she is always ready and responsive to the great appeal, and this power generated by this great civilizer of all future civilization is the new woman!

———— ✦ ————

"The New Woman in the Making"

Leta S. Hollingworth

Leta Anna Stetter Hollingworth (1886–1939) earned a Ph.D. in educational psychology at Teachers College of Columbia University in 1916 and then joined the faculty there, where she built a distinguished career critiquing biological reasons for sex differences in achievement, analyzing the characteristics of exceptional children, and promoting eugenics. In *Functional Periodicity* (1914), Hollingworth debunked the popular belief that menstruation impaired women's mental ability. She used sociological arguments to refute the Darwinian theory that women were less variable then men and hence less capable of great intellectual achievements.[1] In the early 1910s, Hollingworth joined the New York–based Heterodoxy, a consciousness-raising feminist group that discussed topics such as psychoanalysis, socialism, and birth control. Members included socialist trade unionist Rose Pastor Stokes, the lawyer and political radical Crystal Eastman, and the Industrial Workers of the World organizer Elizabeth Gurley Flynn.[2]

During the 1920s and 1930s, Hollingworth became one of the leading experts on mentally handicapped and gifted children and a leading proponent of eugenics. As Hollingworth saw it, social or economic inequalities didn't explain the fewer numbers of gifted children born to members of the lower classes or to recent immigrants, but heredity did. Philanthropy only exacerbated the problem, according to Hollingworth, because it tried to improve what heredity had preordained: "philanthropic efforts, originally meaning love of man, [had] degenerated to mean love of stupid and vicious man."[3]

Hollingworth's "New Woman in the Making" was published in the New York Times Company's *Current History*,[4] a monthly magazine begun in 1914 and devoted to international news and war coverage. In 1923, the current events magazine charged three dollars a year for subscriptions and reported a circulation of over

---

Current History, Oct. 1927, 15–20.

38,000. The entire October 1927 issue in which Hollingworth's article appeared was given over to New Woman debates.[5]

. . . For a general understanding of the New Woman in the making it is, perhaps, enough for us to note that a puzzle or question is created whenever a craving organism is balked in the search for satisfaction; that uninformed, multiple activity is then set up; and that whatever act within the available répertoire happens to bring satisfaction will become fixed habit. . . .

First Changes in Woman's Status

We do not know how long the human species had existed before acute thinkers demonstrated the true and invariable cause of infants. At all events this was disseminated knowledge by the time records of civilization were established in Crete, Egypt and Greece. The discovery of paternity must have affected woman's then existing status variously. In the first place, men learning that they too were creators of children, must have been modified in their attitude toward procreation. In order to identify "his own flesh and blood" it was now plainly to be seen that a man must insure strict faithfulness to himself in sex relations, on the part of the mother. In the interests of such assurance special restrictions were placed upon women, under the concept of feminine virtue. By the time Hammurabi, King of Babylonia, formulated his code of social regulation, in 2250 B.C. . . . , the ideal of feminine virtue was well established, to hold for many subsequent centuries: "If the finger have been pointed at the wife of a man because of another man, . . . for her husband's sake she shall throw herself into the river." No similar arrangement is made for a husband in like circumstances.

Pair marriage was also, no doubt, definitely promoted by the discovery of paternity. The man, now understanding that the children were created by him as well as by the woman, became the husband of the latter, guaranteeing subsistence, while she stood under obligation to perform for her lord and master such labor as was consistent with the limitations of her reproductive system. In pair marriage, as anciently instituted, the man was lord and master inevitably, because in any contract between two persons for mutual gain the one who needs the other least is in position to dictate terms.

Also, the discovery of paternity made it feasible to avoid procreation. This was a long step in the evolution of the New Woman. It is very doubtful whether there were any old maids under the most primitive conditions. After the discovery of paternity the intelligent and intentional old maid became possible.

The function of the strong, intelligent old maid must have been extremely important in the making of the New Woman. We know that many of the early verbal formulations of the woman question emanated from unmarried women. They had time and energy to examine closely the puzzle in which women were involved. Their minds were free from the importunate pressures of infants' needs to state the question as they severally saw it, and to offer suggestions for solution. Also, as time went on, these childless women were free to demonstrate in their own persons that women have abilities and aspirations other than those represented by reproduction and manual work. Subsistence finally being quite generally guaranteed by the increased mastery of humankind over the earth, and for women by pair marriage, cravings other than those for food and shelter began to be major, and to be stated as such.

Only a small part of the history of woman's status is a matter of written records. The greater part of the time of mankind lies, of course, in those darker than dark ages, before the invention of the alphabet. Verbal formulation of suggestions for change and improvement did not begin to be recorded by women until recent centuries. (Wollstonecraft, Mary: *Vindication of the Rights of Women*, 1798.) These suggestions we find to have been quite various, as would be expected from knowledge of how people learn. Some thinkers declared that suffrage would solve the woman question. Others believed that motherhood insurance would give the answer. Still others suggested that dress reform would go a long way toward solution.

Not a few of these spokeswomen were inclined to blame men as intentional, malevolent trappers of women. In this they gave men too much credit for far-sighted planning, and too little credit for kindly impulse. Woman was caged not by man but by her own physiological nature, as has been pointed out. It was inevitable, and indeed fair enough, that women should wrestle with their problems for themselves. Men had and have problems of their own to engage their attention. It must be noted, nevertheless, that men have not been, in fact, indifferent to the Woman Question. They, too, offered from time to time suggestions bearing directly upon its solution. Plato (400 B.C.), Samuel Sewall (1718), John Stuart Mill (1869), President Barnard (1882), John Dewey (1886), stand as conspicuous examples of such men. On the whole, however, people want what they are used to having; so that suggestions of change were widely resisted by those not personally afflicted with unsatisfied cravings. Much censure of the advocates of "women's rights" was expressed. (Polwhale, A.: *Unsexed Females*, 1798.)

The ideas expounded by suffragists and feminist reformers during the past hundred years did not, however, primarily cause the change in woman's status, but they had a secondary value in that they hastened the change by calling attention to it. The influence of Feminism as propaganda should, therefore, not be minimized. Woman suffrage was important to women when granted, and it is important to them today, not as a *cause* of change but as a *sign* of change in status. The New Woman had already been evolved before the vote was gained. Suppose typical women to be still bearing ten to fifteen infants each and still carrying forward the industrial work of the world by manual labor in the home. How could they use the vote to effect change in their condition? True, they might "pass a law" that men must not only hunt and fight but must also tend the children half of the time. A law, however, must be enforced as well as passed. Behind it must stand police and militia. It must be sufficiently in accord with human nature to be enforceable. Suffrage can be used to modernize law, but it has very limited use as an instrument to modernize people.

The primary causes of change in woman's status originated through the efforts of persons who were, as a group, indifferent to the Woman Question. Men of science, inventors and philosophers were the real makers of the New Woman.

For many centuries preceding the conscious formulation of scientific method and the establishment of laboratories, invention had come slowly forward by the trial-and-error activities of acute thinkers. Probably about one in a hundred of human beings is capable of thinking with sufficient effect to produce new knowledge, however slight. The tool began to be known and used in the Stone Age and was improved upon constantly as time passed. New processes of obtaining greater material satisfaction were discovered, such as cooking, grinding, spinning and weaving. These, being at first manual processes, with tools fitted to the hand, made women industrial workers. All these tasks were originally carried out in complete compatibility with reproduction, since they could be done at home, near the cradle.

In the eighteenth and nineteenth centuries great advances were made in science. Printing came into use (1450). The microscope was invented (1590–1609). Steam was harnessed (1807). Electricity was studied (1800–25). Steel was made in quantity (1856). A thousand applications of physics and of chemistry were utilized, and industrial processes were made possible on a scale too large for the home. Factories arose. This exploitation of the tool, more commonly called the machine in recent years, has developed, until now scarcely any industrial work, save part of cooking, is done by hand in the home. The machine modified woman's environment tremendously and rather suddenly. (Smith, H. B.: *Industrial History*, 1926.)

INFLUENCE OF BIOLOGY

Great as was this influence of applied physics and chemistry in the making of the New Woman, the influence of biological research was more potent still. In 1827, and years following, by means of the microscope, Van Baer and others observed the organisms which unite to form the new human being. From the advancement in exact knowledge of reproduction thus initiated, scientific methods of birth control other than celibacy were invented and disseminated.

Also in the field of biology, the publication of *The Origin of Species* (1859) indirectly affected woman's status by promulgating the conviction that human beings had not been divinely ordained once for all, but had in the past undergone evolution, and therefore might in future continue to change.

The influence of invention in the realm of ethical and social attitudes, though secondary to the advancement of science, was important. Aside from the ideas bearing directly upon the Woman Question, subsumed under the concept of Feminism, there were general systems of thought abroad which set the minds of increasing numbers to favor changes in woman's lot. Liberalism, naturalism and humanitarianism were promulgated as philosophies in the seventeenth and eighteenth centuries. It is true that many of the chief exponents of these philosophies, Rousseau for instance, neglected the Woman Question, or denied it completely. Nevertheless, the spread of these points of view through the agency of print prepared men's minds to receive with sympathy verbal formulations of this question. (Mill, *The Subjection of Women.*)

Thus, to recapitulate, by the opening of the twentieth century men of science were rapidly abolishing the need for woman's industrial labor in the home. They were giving to woman control over reproduction. Liberation from the cage of her burdensome generative system was being achieved. By this time philosophy had developed points of view favorable to such liberation. Intelligent women had formulated the Woman Question in positive though somewhat various terms and had, demonstrated women's abilities by their own exceptional lives.

"New women," therefore, emerged in considerable proportion upon the scene, especially in cities. These New Women were freed from incessant maternity and from routine hand labor, so that they could set about the satisfaction of human cravings according to individuality, as men do and have done. The essential fact about the New Women is that they differ among themselves, as men do, in work, in play, in virtues, in aspirations and in rewards achieved. They are women, not woman.

Is the Woman Question now finally answered so as to disappear? No, not yet. In any social change based on science and philosophy there remains in law, in religion and in common custom what sociologists call "lag." (Ogburn, W. F.: *Social Change*, 1922.) The laws within which we live today were codified when the typical woman was a typical housewife without political entity. The creeds of churches were formulated when woman's status was that of chattel. Common custom preserves a thousand manners, which took form when women were protected or exploited in the home, according to their luck in mating. "Lag" is of special interest to the New Woman, as it pertains to advance and change in mitigating the burdens of reproduction. It is of record that the perambulator was deplored as wicked and dangerous when it was first invented. The true mother it was said, carried her child "as God intended." The physician who first used anaesthetics to lighten the pains of childbirth was set upon for a scoundrel. At present birth control is condemned in religion and in law.

There are, in fact, numerous details of the New Woman's *modus vivendi*, which still remain to be worked out through the living of many experimental lives. For instance, although she is now gaining control of procreation, she does not yet know how to use this power most advantageously in the total management of life. She does not know how many children she should have, nor, all things considered, what years of her life are most suitable for bearing them. She does not known whether the artificial feeding of infants can be developed with out detriment to the latter. She does not know how young children may best be supervised, whether in groups by experts, or in the isolated home by each mother herself. She does not know what to do about expectant motherhood. Is this a kind of illness, "a delicate condition"? Or is it a normal, healthy state?

The taboo on this state is still strong among us. In primitive times men feared that the distortion and culminating pains of this condition might be communicated to them by sympathetic magic, and so they isolated the woman from their sight. Shrinking from any physical crisis in another person is deep-seated in human psychology. No artist has painted a realistic portrait of a prospective mother. Visible signs thereof on the lecture platform, on the medical staff, in congress, behind the counter has still to achieve the respectability attained in the kitchen and the laundry.

Each woman, even now, who sets out upon a way of life different from that of the dependent housewife, is still an explorer, especially if she sets out to mate and reproduce. The results of such experimental lives are being compiled and studied by the New Woman. (Collier, Virginia M.: *Marriage and Careers*, 1926.) She is trying to chart the causes of success and failure. The New Woman of today is *consciously* experimenting with her own life to find out how women can best live. To experiment knowingly with one's own life to find the Good Life—surely this requires a courage and a genius deserving something better than blame or jeers, deserving at least open-minded toleration and assistance.

"La Mujer Nueva"
[The New Woman]

Clotilde Betances Jaeger

Clotilde Betances Jaeger (1890–197?), grandniece of Puerto Rico's foremost nineteenth-century independence leader Ramón Emeterio Betances, published essays on a wide range of topics including the Puerto Rican independence movement, feminism, music, literature, and socialism. Born in San Sebastián, Puerto Rico, she moved to the United States in 1912 to attend Cornell University, from which she graduated with a degree in natural sciences in 1916. She was a frequent contributor to *Gráfico* as well as other Spanish-language magazines.[1]

Gráfico, a weekly published by a collective of tobacco workers, writers, and theater artists from 1926 to 1931, marketed itself to Spanish-speaking people around the world but especially to those in New York City. The magazine promoted a pan-Hispanic worldview, urging readers both to fight ethnic oppression and to claim their rights as American citizens in the wake of the Jones Act of 1917, by which Puerto Ricans had been granted citizenship.[2]

During the second half of the 1920s, despite the fact that many U.S.-owned corporations reaped large profits in the Puerto Rican sugar industry, Puerto Rican workers and their families faced starvation as they struggled to cope with inflation, wage cuts, and record overall unemployment, which was 60 percent according to a 1930 colonial government report. Referring to the hunger problem on the island, then governor Theodore Roosevelt Jr. described Puerto Rican children in 1930 as "suffering more than any other children under the American flag." Hurricane San Felipe, which destroyed the sugar crop for 1928, had only exacerbated an already weak Puerto Rican "insular" economy. Despite these root causes,

---

Gráfico, May 18, 1929, 10, 15.

the most frequent reason given not only for the nation's economic crisis but also for its social problems of homelessness, prostitution, disease, and crime was over-population. And during a period when eugenic theories popularized a kind of "reproductive racism," birth control became the de facto remedy. Middle-class professional Puerto Ricans interested in modernizing the nation countered Catholic teaching and advocated birth control as a remedy to the nation's ills. This "soft eugenics" stressed "that the excessive childbearing of working-class women was involuntary, unwanted, and detrimental to the health of the mother, the children, and the nation."[3]

The following essay is an installment in a four-part series that Betances Jaeger wrote on the New Woman. For additional information about her or *Gráfico*, see the Betances Jaeger entry for June 15, 1929, in part II.

Gloss by M. M. Pozo

There are still ladies and there are still gentlemen. Woman, by virtue of her emancipation, is the true queen of the home; man, her husband, the king, her first subject; and the family, her most fiercely devoted court.

You lament the many obligations that fall to today's woman. Blessed responsibilities! They fertilize the soil. They prepare us for life outside the home, since we already know everything inside it. If you will indulge the comparison, a woman is like an ox. Patient and docile, she takes upon her shoulders the most onerous burdens and, like the gentle, noble, sweet-eyed animal, she toils and suffers, and occasionally gets a head of steam.

Are today's chores more oppressive for women than those of the past? No. Raising a family and preserving the votive flame of the lares has always been under the wife's domain. Now, the entire world of human activity presents itself to her. As Havelock Ellis says, the practical application of the scientific spirit is in women's hands, hands of iris, hands of beauty. Women are in government, qualified and determined to pass laws that will make for happier homes. Women are in everything, everywhere. The arts of life are in our hands, hands of iris, hands of strength. Men cannot conceive our strength because their eyes are still blinded by the illusion that women will always be helots, dependents, just mothers and then husbands' possessions. However, great men like G. González Beauville are able to see things as they are:[4]

> Gravely mistaken and blatantly unjust are those who maintain that political duties should be the exclusive privilege of men by alleging the superiority of our sex in such matters. Those who so believe forget that both sexes—oh, such a fundamental truth! —share a common origin, for a woman not only descends from her mother but also from her father, and a man, in turn, is not only the creation of his father's seed but also of the womb that conceived him from inside his mother.

Men are brute strength. Women have the strength of the sun, which gradually ignites to take over the world; women are like sand, with the natural sculpting strength to penetrate live rock and settle deep in the ground. The strength of women is in her violated rights. The strength of women lies in attaining what is legitimately hers, cooperation with men, not separation. If they are under a single yoke inside the home, so should they be outside it as well.

Separation of the sexes is not the issue. Equality of the sexes must be instilled in people until it becomes biological. Plato said that women are small men, but be that as it may, what greatness is in her psyche!

The woman, because of her procreative nature, is by necessity the conservative element in the family. This is imposed. She is latent power, heroic power. It is only here where the much-discussed inequality of the sexes lies.

Obviously, the issue of equality of the sexes is interpreted differently according to a person's ability to make use of their mental capacities, because mindless people who don't think don't even bother to consider it. They, of course, are not the concern of this article.

To smoke and vomit mouthfuls of smoke until God's air is rarefied, opaque, and unbreathable is subversive to nature. The manly boastings of certain women are met with amusement by both sexes. The double standard is a childish myth. Only a harlot can give herself away again and again. Even men feel repugnance when they throw themselves in the arms of any and all women. A woman might brag that she can do so nowadays, but she knows she can't because of that inescapable law governing any woman not inclined to prostitution.

What is intolerable in our day is the outrageous hypocrisy that pollutes the environment. Tolerance is preached; licentiousness prevails. Could there be any greater impudence than what is happening with prohibition in the city on the Hudson? Incorruptible (?) judges allow hostesses of New York night clubs to do as they please, and Mrs. Willebrandt has been unable to stop it.[5]

There are courageous women who feel the enticement of sex and the intense desire to be a mother. Rather than give in to insanity, neurosis, or childlessness, they raise their child without a father, yet they become healthy women, vanquishing the vice of corruption.

There are wives who under the semblance of marriage dishonor all women with their sexual abandon; reprobates, they do not go to church, and they offer votive candles at the altar of licentious love. They don't realize the importance of their actions; they are not women; they are freaks. Courage is not part of their being, and they slither.

And the men who live with them in illegal cohabitation violate constantly the laws they voted on to safeguard the morality of others; those who can only debase and drool on themselves are nothing more than degenerate fools.

Such sexual encounters do yield something on occasion. Fodder for insane asylums, leper colonies, and hospitals. Heavy burdens for the state and the taxpayers.

Today's education system is pernicious, outdated, intolerant, blind. When schools do not teach life, they are no longer part of it. Schools today are useless. The mothers of yesterday, weighted down by false concerns of an educational and moral nature, basked in the ostracism of hygiene and prophylaxis.

I know a woman who is ignorant, stupid, and prejudiced, a religious fanatic, the work of an ignorant, brutish priest in a backward village. She has made her son unhappy; she says she adores him, but if you ask me, her adoration is twisted self-ishness. She told me: "My daughters will go to their wedding bed pure. They will know nothing about the first sexual act."

This woman describes the crassest form of ignorance of the procreative act as purity. So much respectability is startling, as one of Ibsen's heroines said. I beg to differ. Sex will have no shadowy mysteries for my daughters. Their curiosity will be scientific, not stupid or sick. My children will not avert their gaze from a nude figure, because they will recognize the beauty of the line, the bold eurythmy of the artist's conception, his profound knowledge of physiology and of life in general.

What causes these cases of pregnancy among schoolgirls? Ignorance. If nothing is learned at home, schools and churches must step in. Church and school, the former calling the amorous kiss sinful, the latter forbidding and discouraging children who are brimming with curiosity from wanting to learn about their origin, their pleasures, their pain, their feelings; the church conceals the truth just as the adulterous woman conceals the fruit of her illegitimate love, and the school fears speaking the truth and settles for a criminal passivity harmful to the people.

Truth above all. The curtain must be drawn. Sincerity is of gods and geniuses. The grand fabric of humanity must be woven on the basis of the body of man. I would not send my children to today's schools or to church for fear that their souls—candid yet avid, eager to know where they were formed, how they were born, why they are alive, what their essence is—would be corrupted. This curiosity should be satisfied at all times, effectively, according to the healthiest, purest aesthetic as is the naked-ness of a star, the whiteness of dawn, the shimmer of morning dew. Herein lies the strength of women. Herein lies her boundless strength.

Ignorance is slavery. Women want to be free, like the butterfly wants to become beautiful, like the silkworm wants to be useful, like the sun wants to give light. Freedom comes submissively to those who open their eyes to the light such as the cocoon to the ephebic kiss. Tradition is the enemy of freedom. A spirit of questioning imposes itself. Truth—where is it? Search, search, question, always question. A woman must be judge, priest, teacher, mother. A woman's multiple responsibilities are no reason to be startled. She is like Hercules going to clean the Augean stables.

Translated by Paul Coltrin.

Notes

INTRODUCTION

1. Teresa Mangum, *Married, Middlebrow, and Militant: Sarah Grand and the New Woman Novel* (Ann Arbor: University of Michigan Press, 1998), 227n7. Daylanne K. English, *Unnatural Selections: Eugenics in American Modernism and the Harlem Renaissance* (Chapel Hill: University of North Carolina Press, 2004), 22.

2. Before 1914, when the Audit Bureau of Circulations was established, circulation figures, especially if only reported by the publisher, could be unreliable. Carl F. Kaestle, Helen Damon-Moore, Lawrence C. Stedman, Katherine Tinsley, and William Vance Trollinger Jr., *Literacy in the United States: Readers and Reading since 1880* (New Haven: Yale University Press, 1991), 25, 169. Frank Luther Mott, *A History of American Magazines*, 5 vols. (Cambridge: Harvard University Press, 1938–68), 3:5, 4:11. Theodore Peterson, *Magazines in the Twentieth Century* (Urbana: University of Illinois Press, 1964), 2–4. Richard Ohmann, *Selling Culture: Magazines, Markets, and Class at the Turn of the Century* (London: Verso, 1996), 21–29. John Tebbel and Mary Ellen Zuckerman, *The Magazine in America: 1741–1990* (New York: Oxford University Press, 1991), 57, 66–68. Leonard Ray Teel, *The Public Press, 1900–1945: The History of American Journalism* (Westport, CT: Praeger, 2006), 7. Frederick G. Detweiler, *The Negro Press in the United States* (College Park, MD: McGrath Publishing, 1968), 60–63. Sally M. Miller, introduction to *The Ethnic Press in the United States: A Historical Analysis and Handbook*, ed. S. Miller, xi–xxii (New York: Greenwood Press, 1987).

3. Maureen Honey, *Breaking the Ties That Bind: Popular Stories of the New Woman, 1915–1930* (Norman: University of Oklahoma Press, 1992), 5. Mott, *History of American Magazines*, 4: 6, 24–27, 410. Ohmann, *Selling Culture*, 21–29, 55. Tebbel and Zuckerman, *Magazine in America*, 66–67, 76, 79. Frank Presbey, *The History and Development of Advertising* (New York: Greenwood Press, 1968), 436–437, 487–488. Ted Curtis Smythe, *The Gilded Age Press, 1865–1900* (Westport, CT: Praeger, 2003), 182–183. W. Joseph Campbell, *Yellow Journalism: Puncturing the Myths, Defining the Legacies* (Westport, CT: Praeger, 2001), 15, 59. Teel, *Public Press*, 2, 7, 15.

4. Charlotte Perkins Gilman, *Women and Economics: A Study of the Economic Relation between Women and Men* (Amherst, NY: Prometheus Books, 1994), 148–149. Tebbel and Zuckerman, *Magazine in America*, 71, 75.

5. Agnes Hudson Young, "Very Cheap Wit," *Woman's Era* (Utica, NY), Sept. 1895, 4.

6. I don't want to suggest, however, that Held's flappers were the only New Woman images during this period. Nell Brinkley's florid, sinuous images of the New Woman working,

surfing, and hiking, for example, gained a wide following in the Hearst papers, while Gordon Conway offered the affluent readers of *Vogue, Vanity Fair,* and *Harper's Bazaar* a more sophisticated version. See Trina Robbins, *Nell Brinkley and the New Woman in the Early 20th Century* (Jefferson, NC: McFarland, 2001). Raye Virginia Allen, *Gordon Conway: Fashioning a New Woman* (Austin: University of Texas Press, 1997). As quoted in Angela J. Latham, *Posing a Threat: Flappers, Chorus Girls, and Other Brazen Performers of the American 1920s* (Hanover, NH: University Press of New England for Wesleyan University Press, 2000), 21, 30, 38. See Ann Douglas, *Terrible Honesty: Mongrel Manhattan in the 1920s* (New York: Farrar, Straus and Giroux, 1995), 135–136. Carolyn Kitch, *The Girl on the Magazine Cover: The Origins of Visual Stereotypes in American Mass Media* (Chapel Hill: University of North Carolina Press, 2001), 132–133.

7. Recent scholarship on the New Woman reflects this international dimension. See, e.g., Ann Heilmann, ed., *Feminist Forerunners: New Womanism and Feminism in the Early Twentieth Century* (London: Pandora, 2003) and Ann Heilmann and Margaret Beetham, eds., *New Woman Hybridities: Femininity, Feminism and International Consumer Culture, 1880–1930* (New York: Routledge, 2004). Linda Gordon, *The Moral Property of Women: A History of Birth Control Politics in America* (Urbana: University of Illinois Press, 2002), 41–44. Candace Falk, ed., *Emma Goldman: A Documentary History of the American Years,* vol. 1: *Made for America, 1890–1901* (Berkeley: University of California Press, 2003), 1:66. Clara Lomas, "Transborder Discourse: The Articulation of Gender in the Borderlands in the Early Twentieth Century," *Frontiers: A Journal of Women Studies* 24 (2003): 51–74. Nancy F. Cott, *The Grounding of Modern Feminism* (New Haven: Yale University Press, 1987), 13–16. Liz Conor, *The Spectacular Modern Woman: Feminine Visibility in the 1920s* (Bloomington: Indiana University Press, 2004), 7.

8. Amy Kaplan, *The Anarchy of Empire in the Making of U.S. Culture* (Cambridge: Harvard University Press, 2002), 95–120. Martha Banta, *Imaging American Women: Idea and Ideals in Cultural History* (New York: Columbia University Press, 1987), 555–558. Thomas G. Paterson, J. Garry Clifford, Shane J. Maddock, Deborah Kisatsky, and Kenneth J. Hagan, *American Foreign Relations: A History to 1920* (Boston: Houghton Mifflin, 2005), 198–299. Howard Chandler Christy, *The American Girl* (New York: Moffat, Yard, 1906), 16. Charles Dana Gibson, "These Foreign Relations: Do I Want to Go in with That Crowd?" *Life,* Aug. 25, 1898.

9. Aileen S. Kraditor, *The Ideas of the Woman Suffrage Movement, 1890–1920* (New York: W. W. Norton, 1981), 7, 48–50, 65–73, 123–131, 168–169. Cott, *Grounding,* 53–54. Douglas, *Terrible Honesty,* 257. See W.E.B. Du Bois, *The Correspondence of W.E.B. Du Bois: Selections, 1877–1934,* ed. Herbert Aptheker (Amherst: University of Massachusetts Press, 1973), 127; and Paula Giddings, *When and Where I Enter: The Impact of Black Women on Race and Sex in America* (New York: William Morrow, 1984), 126–128.

10. Rosalyn Terborg-Penn, *African American Women in the Struggle for the Vote, 1850–1920* (Bloomington: Indiana University Press, 1998), 9. Mary Jo Buhle, *Women and American Socialism, 1870–1920* (Urbana: University of Illinois Press, 1981), 240. Kraditor, *Ideas,* 142–143.

11. Dorothy Brown, *Setting a Course: American Women in the 1920s* (Boston: Twayne, 1987), 60–74.

12. Crystal Eastman, *Nation,* Nov. 2, 1924, 523.

13. Brown, *Setting a Course,* 67–74.

14. Catherine Gilbert Murdock, *Domesticating Drink: Women, Men, and Alcohol in America, 1870–1940* (Baltimore: Johns Hopkins University Press, 1998), 9. Ruth Bordin, *Woman and Temperance: The Quest for Power and Liberty, 1873–1900* (New Brunswick, NJ: Rutgers University Press, 1990), xxiv. Frances E. Willard, "Address before the Second

Biennial Convention of the World's Woman's Christian Temperance Union, and the Twentieth Annual Convention of the National Women's Christian Temperance Union" (London: White Ribbon Publishing, 1893); Library of Congress, American Memory, Votes for Women: Selections from the National American Woman Suffrage Association Collection, 1848–1921, http://memory.loc.gov/ammem/index.html.

15. Beryl Satter, *Each Mind a Kingdom: American Women, Sexual Purity, and the New Thought Movement, 1875–1920* (Berkeley: University of California Press, 1999), 1–22, 112.

16. Ibid., 22, 44. Molly Ladd-Taylor, *Mother-Work: Women, Child Welfare, and State, 1890–1930* (Urbana: University of Illinois Press, 1994), 43–44, 74–76. Alice Kessler-Harris, *In Pursuit of Equity: Women, Men, and the Quest for Economic Citizenship in 20th-Century America* (New York: Oxford University Press, 2001), 33.

17. Ladd-Taylor, *Mother-Work*, 104–108. Gilman, *Women and Economics*, 86–110, 120–121. Charlotte Perkins Gilman, "The New Motherhood," *Forerunner* 1 (Dec. 1910): 17–18.

18. Anne Ruggles Gere, *Intimate Practices: Literacy and Cultural Work in U.S. Women's Clubs, 1880–1920* (Urbana: University of Illinois Press, 1997), 5. Mary White Ovington, *Black and White Sat Down Together: The Reminiscences of an NAACP Founder* (New York: Feminist Press, 1995), 97. Gere, *Intimate Practices*, 5, 67. Anne Meis Knupfer, *Toward a Tenderer Humanity and a Nobler Womanhood: African American Women's Clubs in Turn-of-the-Century Chicago* (New York: New York University Press, 1996), 11–29.

19. Estelle Freedman, "Separatism as Strategy: Female Institution Building and American Feminism, 1870–1930," *Feminist Studies* 5 (1979): 514. Ovington, *Black and White*, 97. As quoted in Deborah Gray White, *Too Heavy a Load: Black Women in Defense of Themselves, 1894–1994* (New York: W. W. Norton, 1999), 124–141.

20. Giddings, *When and Where*, 203.

21. Cott, *Grounding*, 148. Herbert Spencer, *The Principles of Biology* (London: Williams and Norgate, 1899), 2:512–513. Barbara Miller Solomon, *In the Company of Educated Women: A History of Women and Higher Education in America* (New Haven: Yale University Press, 1985), 60–63, 115–140, 75–77.

22. Mary Antin, *The Promised Land* (Boston: Houghton Mifflin, 1912), 33–34.

23. Dexter Fisher, foreword to *American Indian Stories*, by Zitkala-Ša (Lincoln: University of Nebraska Press, 1985), 12. Zitkala-Ša, *American Indian Stories*, 79–80.

24. Alice Kessler-Harris, *Out to Work: A History of Wage-Earning Women in the United States* (New York: Oxford University Press, 2003), 122–123, 141, 229. Karen Manners Smith, "New Paths to Power, 1890–1920," in *No Small Courage: A History of Women in the United States*, ed. Nancy F. Cott (New York: Oxford University Press, 2000), 359, 377. David M. Katzman, *Seven Days a Week: Women and Domestic Service in Industrializing America* (New York: Oxford University Press, 1978), 81–82; and Jacqueline Jones, *Labor of Love, Labor of Sorrow: Black Women, Work, and the Family, from Slavery to the Present* (New York: Vintage Books, 1985), 164, 178–180. Sarah Jane Deutsch, "From Ballots to Breadlines, 1920–1940," in Cott, *No Small Courage*, 427, 429.

25. Kessler-Harris, *Out to Work*, 152–160. Joan M. Jensen, "The Great Uprisings: 1900–1920" and "The Great Uprising in Rochester," both in *A Needle, a Bobbin, a Strike: Women Needleworkers in America*, ed. Joan M. Jensen and Sue Davidson (Philadelphia: Temple University Press, 1984), 83, 101. As quoted in Ann Schofield, "The Uprising of the 20,000: The Making of a Labor Legend," in Jensen and Davidson, *Needle, Bobbin, Strike*, 167–169. Victoria Bissell Brown, *The Education of Jane Addams* (Philadelphia: University of Pennsylvania Press, 2004), 251–252.

26. Buhle, *Women and American Socialism*, xvi. Peter Conolly-Smith, *Translating America: An Immigrant Press Visualizes American Popular Culture, 1895–1918* (Washington, DC: Smithsonian Books, 2004), 117–118.

27. See Harriet Hyman Alonso, *Peace as a Women's Issue: A History of the U.S. Movement for World Peace and Women's Rights* (Syracuse: Syracuse University Press, 1993), 56–84. Susan Zeiger, "She Didn't Raise Her Boy to Be a Slacker: Motherhood, Conscription, and the Culture of the First World War," *Feminist Studies* (Spring 1996): 6–39. Susan R. Grayzel, *Women and the First World War* (London: Pearson, 2002), 85.

28. Susan Zeiger, *In Uncle Sam's Service: Women Workers with the American Expeditionary Force, 1917–1919* (Philadelphia: University of Pennsylvania Press, 2004), 4–5, 137, 21–22, 26–30. Cott, *Grounding*, 63. As quoted in Lettie Gavin, *American Women in World War I: They Also Served* (Niwot: University Press of Colorado, 1997), x–xi.

29. Gere, *Intimate Practices*, 254–255. John Higham, *Strangers in the Land: Patterns of American Nativism, 1860–1925* (New Brunswick, NJ: Rutgers University Press, 1992), 225–228, 310–311, 324. Nancy Cott, however, makes the point that when a first-generation club declined, often a next-generation club took its place. What began as the National Congress of Mothers in 1897 became the Parent-Teachers Association in 1908 and grew rapidly, reaching a membership of nearly a million and a half by the 1920s. Its goals were similar to those of the earlier club movement: to fund playgrounds, libraries, and health clinics, and on the national level, to set film standards and support international peace. The National Colored Parent-Teachers Association, founded in 1926, shared a similar emphasis on child welfare and grew rapidly (Cott, *Grounding*, 87).

30. Andrew Sinclair, *Era of Excess: A Social History of the Prohibition Movement* (New York: Harper and Row, 1962), 233. Paula S. Fass, *The Damned and the Beautiful: American Youth in the 1920's* (New York: Oxford University Press, 1977), 319. Lois Long, "Tables for Two," *New Yorker*, Sept. 12, 1925, 32. Harrison Kinney, *James Thurber: His Life and Times* (New York: Henry Holt, 1995), 378–379.

31. Angela Davis, *Blues Legacies and Black Feminism: Gertrude "Ma" Rainey, Bessie Smith, and Billie Holiday* (New York: Vintage, 1998), 213, 310.

32. Allison Davis, "College Girl," *Crisis*, Mar. 1928, 87.

33. "Girls Seek Risque, Thrive on Thrills but Believe Situation Unalarming," *Ohio State Lantern*, Jan. 10, 1922, 1. Kinney, *James Thurber*, 379. David M. Kennedy, *Birth Control in America: The Career of Margaret Sanger* (New Haven: Yale University Press, 1970), 57. Linda Gordon, *Woman's Body, Woman's Right: A Social History of Birth Control in America* (New York: Penguin, 1977), 187. Mabel Dodge Luhan, *Movers and Shakers* (Albuquerque: University of New Mexico Press, 1985), 71.

34. William O'Neill, *Divorce in the Progressive Era* (New York: New Viewpoints, 1973), 20–32, 159. Cott, *Grounding*, 149, 156–157.

35. Edward Carpenter, *Love's Coming of Age* (New York: Modern Library, 1911), 72. Richard von Krafft-Ebing, *Psychopathia Sexualis: A Medico-Forensic Study* (New York: G. P. Putnam's, 1965), 418–419. Carroll Smith-Rosenberg, *Disorderly Conduct: Visions of Gender in Victorian America* (New York: Oxford University Press, 1985), 272. Havelock Ellis, "Sexual Inversion in Women," *Alienist and Neurologist: A Quarterly Journal of Scientific, Clinical, and Forensic Psychiatry and Neurology* 16 (1896): 141–158. Cott, *Grounding*, 160.

36. Chris Albertson, *Bessie* (New Haven: Yale University Press, 2003), 134–136. Lillian Faderman, *To Believe in Women: What Lesbians Have Done for America: A History* (New York: Houghton Mifflin, 1999), 6, 62–78, 291–302.

37. James H. Collins, "The Eternal Feminine," *Printers' Ink*, June 26, 1901, 3. See William Leach, *Land of Desire: Merchants, Power, and the Rise of a New American Culture* (New York: Pantheon Books, 1993), esp. 50, 73, 104–106.

38. Roland Marchand, *Advertising the American Dream: Making Way for Modernity, 1920–1940* (Berkeley: University of California Press, 1985), 4, 7–24, 156–160.

39. Claude S. Fisher, "Gender and the Residential Telephone, 1890–1940," *Sociological Forum* (Spring 1988): 211–233. David E. Nye, *Electrifying America: Social Meanings of a New Technology* (Cambridge, MA: MIT Press, 1991), 114–115. "The New Power and Woman," *Independent*, Feb. 6, 1902, 357. Thomas A. Edison, "The Woman of the Future," *Good Housekeeping Magazine*, Oct. 1912, 436, 440, 444.

40. Nye, *Electrifying America*, 156–157. Lynn Dumenil, *The Modern Temper: American Culture and Society in the 1920s* (New York: Hill and Wang, 1995), 77. Virginia Scharff, *Taking the Wheel: Women and the Coming of the Motor Age* (Albuquerque: University of New Mexico Press, 1991), 67–68, 141–142. Christine McGaffey Frederick, "The Commuter's Wife and the Motorcar," *Suburban Life*, July 1912, 13.

41. Joseph J. Corn, "Making Flying 'Thinkable': Women Pilots and the Selling of Aviation, 1927–1940," *American Quarterly*, Autumn 1979, 556–571.

42. Kessler-Harris, *Out to Work*, 146–147.

43. Fass, *Damned and Beautiful*, 122, 134. Beth L. Bailey, *From Front Porch to Back Seat: Courtship in Twentieth-Century America* (Baltimore: Johns Hopkins University Press, 1988), 13–24. Kathy Peiss, *Cheap Amusements: Working Women and Leisure in Turn-of-the-Century New York* (Philadelphia: Temple University Press, 1986), 6.

44. Tom Lewis, "'A Godlike Presence': The Impact of Radio on the 1920s and 1930s," Organization of American Historians, Spring 1992, http://www.oah.org/pubs/magazine/communication/lewis.html. Dumenil, *Modern Temper*, 77. Susan J. Douglas, *Listening In: Radio and the American Imagination* (Minneapolis: University of Minnesota Press, 1999), 84. William Pickens, "That 'Colorless' Radio Wave," *New York Amsterdam News*, Mar. 10, 1926, n.p.

45. Cynthia Eagle Russett, *Sexual Science: The Victorian Construction of Womanhood* (Cambridge: Harvard University Press, 1989), 11–12. Charles Darwin, *The Descent of Man, and Selection in Relation to Sex* (1871; repr., Princeton: Princeton University Press, 1981), 564, 565–566.

46. According to Peter J. Bowler, *The Eclipse of Darwinism: Anti-Darwinian Evolution Theories in the Decades around 1900* (Baltimore: Johns Hopkins University Press, 1992), the term "neo-Lamarckianism" was coined in 1885 by the American scientist Alpheus Packard to describe those who wished "to establish the inheritance of acquired characteristics as an alternative to Darwinism" (59). As Cynthia Eagle Russett notes in *Darwin in America: The Intellectual Response, 1865–1912* (San Francisco: W. H. Freeman, 1976), even though by 1900 American natural scientists strongly supported Darwinism, many also embraced Lamarckian theory in large part because Lamarckianism offered scientific support for the efficacy of education in improving humanity (10). Yet as Russett points out in *Sexual Science*, a Lamarckian worldview was not necessarily an optimistic one in that it emphasized the ways in which the negative traits of ancestors appeared in subsequent generations. Degeneration occurred when these negative traits, such as alcoholism or criminality, occurred in subsequent generations (200).

47. Gordon, *Moral Property*, 75–77.

48. Ibid., 22–24.

49. Fass, *Damned and Beautiful*, 63–64. Kennedy, *Birth Control in America*, 16–17, 24, 136. Gordon, *Moral Property*, 142–154. Cott, *Grounding*, 166. Margaret Sanger, *The Autobiography of Margaret Sanger* (Mineola, NY: Dover, 2004), 90–92. Gordon, *Woman's Body*, 62.

50. Margaret Sanger, *Woman and the New Race* (New York: Truth Publishing, 1929), 30–44. As quoted in Kennedy, *Birth Control in America*, 43. Gail Bederman, *Manliness and Civilization: A Cultural History of Gender and Race in the United States, 1880–1917* (Chicago: University of Chicago Press, 1995), 200–205.

51. English, *Unnatural Selections*, 1–6, 10, 111, 142, 144.
52. Kate Chopin, *The Awakening*, ed. Margaret Culley (New York: W. W. Norton, 1976), 113, 165. Allison Berg, *Mothering the Race: Women's Narratives of Reproduction, 1890–1930* (Urbana: University of Illinois Press, 2002), 72–73. See Ellen Glasgow's *Virginia* (1913) and *Life and Gabriella* (1916).
53. English, *Unnatural Selections*, 38, 59–60, 121–122, 133.
54. Louise Michele Newman, *White Women's Rights: The Racial Origins of Feminism in the United States* (New York: Oxford University Press, 1999), 157–160.

PART I: DEFINING THE NEW WOMAN IN THE PERIODICAL PRESS

Sarah Grand, "The New Aspect of the Woman Question"

1. Mangum, *Married, Middlebrow, and Militant*, 3–4.
2. Edward E. Chielens, ed., *American Literary Magazines: The Eighteenth and Nineteenth Centuries* (New York: Greenwood Press, 1986), 289–300. Mott, *History of American Magazines*, 2:254–256.
3. Grand is mocking Britain's Contagious Disease Act (1864), which allowed women suspected of venereal infection to be detained and compelled to undergo an internal medical exam. The CDA was repealed in 1886. See Roxanne Eberle, *Chastity and Transgression in Women's Writing, 1792–1897: Interrupting the Harlot's Progress* (New York: Palgrave, 2002), 203, 221.

Ouida, "The New Woman"

1. Roy B. Stokes, "Ouida," *Dictionary of Literary Biography*, vol. 18: *Victorian Novelists after 1885*, ed. Ira B. Nadel and William E. Fredeman (Detroit: Gale Group, 1983), 239–246. As quoted in Dee Garrison, "Immoral Fiction in the Late Victorian Library," *American Quarterly* (Spring 1976): 71–89. "Ramee, Louise de la," *Biographies Plus Illustrated*, Holman Library, McKendree University, http://www.mckendree.edu/academics/database_list.aspx.
2. Translation courtesy of Edward Cook, St. Louis Public Library.
3. Translation courtesy of Edward Cook, St. Louis Public Library.

Kate Masterson, "The Campaign Girl"

1. "For Women," *Atlanta Constitution*, Feb. 20, 1896, 9. "Kate Masterson's First Poem," *Fort Wayne News*, July 4, 1900. "Deaths," *New York Times*, June 9, 1927, 27. Kate Masterson, "Small Beginnings in Journalism," *Journalist* 1 (Dec. 1894): 5, col. 1.
2. Chalmers M. Roberts, *In the Shadow of Power: The Story of the Washington Post* (Washington, DC: Seven Locks Press, 1989), 26, 32–33, 42–47, 60–66, 77.
3. From its heyday in the mid-nineteenth century to the early twentieth century, Tammany Hall, a powerful and corrupt political organization within the Democratic Party in New York City, governed the city through its bosses.
4. Along with Anthony Comstock, the Protestant minister Charles Parkhurst was a leading anti-vice campaigner in New York. For Parkhurst, vice flourished in the city because of rampant police corruption, and his outcries against it led to the formation of the Lexow Committee in the New York State Senate. Led by State Senator Clarence Lexow, the committee helped bring about a major political defeat for Tammany Hall politicians in the November 1894 elections. See Warren Sloat, *A Battle for the Soul of New York: Tammany Hall, Police Corruption, Vice, and Reverend Charles Parkhurst's Crusade against Them, 1892–1895* (New York: Cooper Square Press, 2002).
5. Assistant District Attorney John Goff was named chief counsel of the Lexow Committee.

"Here Is the New Woman"

1. Frank Luther Mott, *American Journalism: A History of Newspapers in the United States through 250 Years, 1690–1940* (New York: Macmillan, 1962), 350–352, 520–521. John D. Stevens, *Sensationalism and the New York Press* (New York: Columbia University Press, 1991), 67–80.
2. Renowned for urging economically depressed Kansas farmers to "Raise less corn and more hell," Mary Elizabeth Clyens Lease (1853–1933) was a firebrand lecturer and activist for the Populist Party.

"Bloomers at the Bar"

1. Mott, *History of American Magazines*, 2:325–337.
2. Guy Reel, *"The National Police Gazette" and the Making of the Modern American Man, 1879–1906* (New York: Palgrave Macmillan, 2006), 66, 112, 130, 145–158. Guy Reel, "This Wicked World: Masculinities and the Portrayals of Sex, Crime, and Sports in the *National Police Gazette*, 1879–1906," *American Journalism*, Winter 2005, 64.

"The New-Woman Santa Claus"

1. Mott, *History of American Magazines*, 3:552–555.

Mrs. Booker T. Washington, "The New Negro Woman"

1. Jacqueline Anne Rouse, "Out of the Shadow of Tuskegee: Margaret Murray Washington, Social Activism and Race Vindication," *Journal of Negro History* 81 (1996): 31–46. Frances Willard was president of the Woman's Christian Temperance Union from 1897 until her death in 1898 and cofounder of the General Federation of Women's Clubs in 1889. Ellen Henrotin was a labor organizer, social reform advocate, and prominent Chicago clubwoman. She was president of the General Federation of Women's Clubs from 1894 to 1898. Mary Dickinson was a poet and novelist and president of the National Council of Women from 1895 to 1897. Louis R. Harlan, ed., *The Booker T. Washington Papers*, 14 vols. (Urbana: University of Illinois Press, 1972–89), 4:238–239.
2. Mott, *History of American Magazines*, 4:742.

"Woman in Another New Role"

1. Matthew Schneirov, *The Dream of a New Social Order: Popular Magazines in America, 1893–1914* (New York: Columbia University Press, 1994), 11, 86, 117–120, 150–151. Mott, *History of American Magazines*, 4:606–615.

Emma Goldman, "The New Woman"

1. Falk, *Emma Goldman*, 1:20–21, 489–503, 519. Emma Goldman, *Living My Life* (New York: Dover, 1970), 2:557. Emma Goldman, *Anarchism and Other Essays* (Port Washington, NY: Kennikat Press, 1969), 217.

"Women in the Territories"

1. Michael Schudson, *Discovering the News: A Social History of American Newspapers* (New York: Basic Books, 1978), 106–120. Robert L. Duffus, "1851–1926: The Story of the *Times*," *New York Times*, Sept. 19, 1926, AN2. James H. Collins, "The *Times*' Golden Anniversary," *New York Times*, Oct. 20, 1901, A6.

"The 'New Woman' Got the Drop on Him"

1. Dennis McDougal, *Privileged Son: Otis Chandler and the Rise and Fall of the L.A. Times Dynasty* (Cambridge: Perseus Publishing, 2001), 26, 33. Robert Gottlieb and Irene Wolt, *Thinking Big:*

The Story of the Los Angeles Times, Its Publishers, and Their Influence on Southern California (New York: G. P. Putnam's, 1977), 11–16, 32–45. Jack R. Hart, *The Information Empire: The Rise of the Los Angeles Times and the Times Mirror Corporation* (Washington, DC: University Press of America, 1981), 7–29. *American Newspaper Directory* (New York: Geo. P. Rowell, 1895), 48.

Eleanor Tayleur, "The New Negro Woman—Social and Moral Decadence"

1. Mott, *History of American Magazines*, 3:422–430.
2. Mrs. Grundy is an extremely priggish character alluded to in the comedy *Speed the Plough* (1798) by British playwright Thomas Morton (1764–1838).
3. This reference is to Grant Allen's best-selling novel *The Woman Who Did* (1895), in which a university-educated New Woman protagonist, Herminia Barton, who believes that traditional marriage is oppressive, refuses to marry her lover even though she has conceived his child.

"Bicycle Number"

1. *Judge*, Apr. 30, 1898, 280. Kristin L. Hoganson, *Fighting for American Manhood* (New Haven: Yale University Press, 1998), 46.

Edward Kemble, "Ise Gwine ter Give You Gals What Straddle"

1. Richard E. Marschall, "*Life*," in *American Humor Magazines and Comic Periodicals*, ed David E. E. Sloane (New York: Greenwood Press, 1987), 141–153. Mott, *History of American Magazines*, 4:556–568. *Newspaper and Magazine Directory* (St. Louis: H. W. Kastor and Sons Advertising Co., 1902–1903), 142.

Charles Dana Gibson, "St. Valentine's Number"

1. Martha Patterson, *Beyond the Gibson Girl: Reimagining the American New Woman, 1895–1915* (Urbana: University of Illinois Press, 2005), 27–49. Fairfax Downey, *Portrait of an Era as Drawn by C. D. Gibson: A Biography* (New York: Charles Scribner's, 1936), 318. Marschall, "*Life*," 147–148.

H. L. Mencken, "The Flapper"

1. Perry J. Ashley, ed., *American Newspaper Journalists, 1926–1950* (Detroit: Gale Research Company, 1985), 225–232. Mott, *History of American Magazines*, 5:246–272. Marion Elizabeth Rodgers, *Mencken: The American Iconoclast* (New York: Oxford University Press, 2005), 124–125. Edward A. Martin, *H. L. Mencken and the Debunkers* (Athens: University of Georgia Press, 1984), 55.
2. Stuart A. Kollar "*The Smart Set*," in Sloane, *American Humor Magazines*, 259–264.
3. Actress, suffragist, and writer Elizabeth Robins (1862–1952) was born in the United States but spent most of her career in England. She is best known for her play *Votes for Women!* (1907), which subsequently was adapted into a novel, *The Convert*. Clifford G. Roe (1875–1934) authored numerous books on white slavery, including *What Women Might Do with the Ballot: The Abolition of the White Slave Traffic* (1912). During the 1910s, American socialist novelist Richard Wright Kauffman (1877–1959) was perhaps best known for his novel on the socioeconomic causes of prostitution, *The House of Bondage* (1910).
4. Twilight sleep is a term describing the state produced by the drug combination of morphine and scopolamine to alleviate the pain of childbirth. Once popular in obstetrics, twilight sleep also produced amnesia.
5. *Ladies' Home Journal* editor Edward Bok argued as early as 1906 that young people should be given sex education.

6. The Wassermann test is an antibody test for syphilis, named after August von Wassermann, who first developed it in 1906.

7. Ophthalmia neonatorum, a serious bacterial infection of a newborn's eyes, is usually transmitted via the birth canal of a mother infected with gonorrhea.

8. Militant British suffragist Christabel Pankhurst (1880–1958), together with her mother Emmeline and sister Sylvia, helped found the Women's Social and Political Union (WSPU) and led a campaign that included rallies, hunger strikes, and destruction of property. Swedish feminist Ellen Key (1849–1926) argued that women's primary role was that of mother, but she promoted the right of both men and women to feel physically and emotionally fulfilled within marriage. Among her best-known works are *The Century of the Child* (1909) and *Love and Marriage* (1911).

9. *Damaged Goods* (*Les avariés*) by Eugène Brieux, performed in the United States in 1913, was the first play on the American stage to make venereal disease a central theme and to discuss syphilis frankly. In April 1913 the *New York Times* called the play "epoch-making" because it spurred a eugenics movement aimed at curbing social diseases.

10. *Mrs. Warren's Profession*, a play written by George Bernard Shaw in 1894, dealt frankly with prostitution. It was initially banned in Britain but finally performed there in 1902.

11. The novel *Trilby*, published in 1894, was written and illustrated by George du Maurier and became a best seller in the United States. The heroine of the same name "smoked cigarettes, dressed like a man, posed in the nude with no sense of shame, enjoyed the bohemian comradeship of the Latin Quarter, delighted in dancing the can can, and was promiscuous in her sexual relationships." Lois W. Banner, *American Beauty* (New York: Knopf, 1984), 170. In 1907 Elinor Glyn published what proved to be the tremendously popular *Three Weeks*, in which an older woman, Lady Henrietta, and a handsome younger man have an affair, at one point making love on a tiger-skin rug. Elizabeth Robins's novel *My Little Sister* (1913) describes the abduction of an innocent young women into prostitution or white slavery.

"The New Negro Woman"

1. Theodore Kornweibel Jr., *"Seeing Red": Federal Campaigns against Black Militancy, 1919–1925* (Bloomington: Indiana University Press, 1998), 97–98. A. Philip Randolph, "A New Crowd—A New Negro," *Messenger*, May–June 1919, 27. Theodore Kornweibel Jr., *No Crystal Stair: Black Life and the Messenger, 1917–1928* (Westport, CT: Greenwood Press, 1975), 54–57. Walter Daniel, *Black Journals of the United States* (Westport, CT: Greenwood Press, 1982), 241–244.

Russell, "A Bit of Life"

1. Emma Lou Thornbrough, *T. Thomas Fortune, Militant Journalist* (Chicago: University of Chicago Press, 1972), 39, 95–96, 297–298. Heather Martin, "New York Age," in *Encyclopedia of the Harlem Renaissance*, ed. Cary D. Wintz and Paul Finkelman (New York: Routledge, 2004), 2:901–902. Roi Ottley and William J. Weatherby, eds., *The Negro in New York: An Informal Social History* (New York: New York Public Library, 1967), 168. Kornweibel, *Seeing Red*, 50–52, 57. Sondra Kathryn Wilson, ed., *The Selected Writings of James Weldon Johnson*, vol. 1: *The "New York Age" Editorials (1914–1923)* (New York: Oxford University Press, 1995), 5, 82, 86. "Compromises on the Suffrage Amendment," *New York Age*, Mar. 1, 1919, n.p.

PART II: WOMEN'S SUFFRAGE AND POLITICAL PARTICIPATION

Josephine K. Henry, "The New Woman of the New South"

1. Mrs. Josephine K. Henry, "Property Rights of Kentucky Wives," *Woman's Journal* (Boston), Apr. 27, 1889, 131.

2. Laura Clay, "Equal Rights Victory in Kentucky," *Woman's Journal* (Boston), Mar. 24, 1894, 92.
3. Aloma Dew, "Josephine Kirby Williamson Henry," in *Kentucky Women: Two Centuries of Indomitable Spirit and Vision*, ed. Eugenia K. Potter (Louisville, KY: Big Tree Press, 1997).
4. Mott, *History of American Magazines*, 4:401–413.

Ella W. Winston, "Foibles of the New Woman"

1. Mott, *History of American Magazines*, 4:511–523.
2. Mrs. Jellyby, a character in Charles Dickens's *Bleak House* (1852–1853), becomes so fixated on helping the African natives of Borrioboola-Gha that she neglects her hygiene, home, and children.

"In the Public Eye"

1. Schneirov, *Dream of a New Social Order*, 11, 86, 117–120, 150–151. Mott, *History of American Magazines*, 4:606–615.
2. Brooke Speer Orr, "Mary Elizabeth Lease: Nineteenth-Century Populist and Twentieth-Century Progressive" (Ph.D. diss., George Washington University, 2002), 1, 136–169.
3. "They Got Ingalls's Scalp," *New York Times*, Feb. 26, 1891, 1. Burton J. Williams, *Senator John James Ingalls: Kansas' Iridescent Republican* (Lawrence: University Press of Kansas, 1972), 111–112.

Augustus Smith Daggy, "Suffragette [to the Bearded Lady]: How Do You Manage It?"

1. Angelika Köhler, "Charged with Ambiguity: The Image of the New Woman in American Cartoons," in Heilmann and Beetham, *New Woman Hybridities*, 158–178. Laura L. Behling, *The Masculine Woman in America, 1890–1935* (Urbana: University of Illinois Press, 2001), 31–59.

Theodore Roosevelt, "Women's Rights: and the Duties of Both Men and Women"

1. Frederick Logan Paxson, "Theodore Roosevelt," in *Dictionary of American Biography* (American Council of Learned Societies, 1928–1936). Mott, *History of American Magazines*, 4:31–432. Bederman, *Manliness and Civilization*, 171, 201–202.
2. In 1894, Samuel S. McClure hired Ida Minerva Tarbell (1857–1944) as an editor, and soon she became arguably McClure's most important journalist. Tarbell's most famous serialized work, *The History of the Standard Oil Company* (1902–1904), exposed how John D. Rockefeller Sr. used unethical business practices to gain monopolistic control of the U.S. oil market. Despite her widely recognized achievements, Tarbell opposed women's suffrage in part because she thought that woman's highest contribution lay in the private sphere, an argument she made in her book *The Business of Being a Woman* (1912).
3. Judge Benjamin Barr Lindsey (1869–1943) is considered a pioneer in the development of the modern juvenile justice system. Despite intense opposition, he transformed Denver's judicial treatment of young offenders by stressing the importance of environmental influences on rather than the supposed inherent moral defects of juvenile delinquents.

"Movie of a Woman on Election Day"

1. Hayward Farrar, *The Baltimore Afro-American* (Westport, CT: Greenwood Press, 1998), 1–33, 60–61, 103, 143, 146–147. Evelyn Brooks Higginbotham, "Clubwomen and Electoral Politics in the 1920s," in *African American Women and the Vote, 1837–1965*, ed. Ann

D. Gordon, with Bettye Collier-Thomas, John H. Bracey, Arlene Voski Avakian, and Joyce Avrech Berkman (Amherst: University of Massachusetts Press, 1997), 139.

2. J. Clay Smith Jr., *From Emancipation: The Making of the Black Lawyer, 1844–1944* (Philadelphia: University of Pennsylvania Press, 1999), 147.

"Squaws Demand 'Rights'"

1. Roberts, *Shadow of Power*, 150–158.

Frederick L. Collins, "The New Woman: What She Wanted and What She Got"

1. Mott, *History of American Magazines*, 4:602–603, 768.
2. "Frederick Collins, Author and Editor," *New York Times*, July 26, 1950, 25.
3. Kathleen L. Endres, "*Woman's Home Companion*," in *Women's Periodicals of the United States: Consumer Magazines*, ed. Kathleen L. Endres and Therese L. Lueck (Westport, CT: Greenwood Press, 1995), 444–455.
4. In the 1920s, the descendant of German-Jewish immigrants Belle Moskowitz (1877–1933) became well known as the most influential woman in New York state and national progressive politics. She served as Democratic candidate Alfred E. Smith's chief campaign manager in his failed 1928 presidential bid.

Clotilde Betances Jaeger, "La Mujer Nueva" [The New Woman]

1. I am indebted to María Teresa Vera Rojas not only for helping me locate information about Clotilde Betances Jaeger but also for helping me better understand the context in which she wrote. María Teresa Vera Rojas, e-mail to author, Jan. 23, 2007. Edna Acosta-Belén, "Clotilde Betances Jaeger," in *Latinas in the United States: A Historical Encyclopedia* (Bloomington: Indiana University Press, 2006), 87–88.
2. María Teresa Vera Rojas provided the information I include on Mas Pozo. Rojas, e-mail to author, Dec. 20, 2006.
3. Nicolás Kanellos with Helvetia Martell, *Hispanic Periodicals in the United States, Origins to 1960: A Brief History and Comprehensive Bibliography* (Houston: Are Público Press, 2000), 54–57, 106–107.
4. Truman R. Clark, *Puerto Rico and the United States, 1917–1933* (Pittsburgh: University of Pittsburgh Press, 1975), 106–132. Deutsch, "From Ballots to Breadlines," 429.
5. Generally considered an extreme protectionist measure, the Hawley-Smoot Tariff raised taxes on goods imported into the United States from 33 to 40 percent and on farm products from 20 to 35 percent. On June 17, 1930, despite receiving a petition signed by 1,038 members of the American Economic Association, Hoover signed the Hawley-Smoot Tariff bill into law. Although as a colony of the United States, Puerto Rico did not have to pay the higher duties, living standards on the island continued to decline. Marian C. McKenna, *Borah* (Ann Arbor: University of Michigan Press, 1961), 265. Ellis W. Hawley, *The Great War and the Search for Modern Order: A History of the American People and Their Institutions, 1917–1933* (Prospect Heights, IL: Waveland Press, 1992), 167. Clark, *Puerto Rico*, 106–108.
6. William E. Borah, a Republican senator from Idaho, advocated farm relief, specifically an export debenture plan "whereby the government would pay a subsidy on agricultural exports equivalent to one half the American tariff rate," but he voted against the Hawley-Smoot Tariff in part because the bill raised the duties on a number of industrial products, such as pig iron, shoes, and cement, that weren't from depressed industries. McKenna, *Borah*, 261–265.
7. In April 1929, the Puerto Rican governor Horace Mann Towner signed into law a bill giving the vote to Puerto Rican women who could read and write. María de Fátima Barceló-Miller, "Half-Hearted Solidarity: Women Workers and the Women's Suffrage Movement in Puerto

Rico during the 1920s," in *Puerto Rican Women's History: New Perspectives*, ed. Felix V. Matos Rodríguez, and Linda C. Delgado (Armonk, NY: M. E. Sharpe, 1998), 136–137.

PART III: TEMPERANCE, SOCIAL PURITY, AND MATERNALISM

Edward Bok, "At Home with the Editor"

1. Helen Damon-Moore, *Magazines for the Millions: Gender and Commerce in the Ladies' Home Journal and the Saturday Evening Post, 1880–1910* (Albany: State University Press of New York, 1994), 62–63, 82–83.
2. Mott, *History of American Magazines*, 4:6–7, 16, 551. Damon-Moore, *Magazines for the Millions*, 1, 56, 73, 159–160.

Rev. Ella E. Bartlett, "The New Woman"

1. *Woman's Journal* (Boston), Aug. 1, 1891, 247. *Woman's Tribune*, Feb 25, 1888, n.p.
2. Barbara Straus Reed, "*The American Jewess*," in Endres and Lueck, *Women's Periodicals*, 11–20. See also Susan A. Glenn, *Daughters of the Shtetl: Life and Labor in the Immigrant Generation* (Ithaca, NY: Cornell University Press, 1990), 9–11.

Lillian W. Betts, "The New Woman"

1. Francesco Cordasco, *Dictionary of American Immigration History* (Metuchen, NJ: Scarecrow, 1990), 74.
2. Mott, *History of American Magazines*, 3:422–430.

"Miss Willard on the 'New Woman'"

1. Ruth Bordin, *Frances Willard: A Biography* (Chapel Hill: University of North Carolina Press, 1986). Bordin, *Women and Temperance*, 95–116. "Miss Willard Hopeful," *New York Times*, Apr. 19, 1896, 14.
2. *Woman's Signal*, Jan. 4, 1894, 1.

Sui Seen Far [Edith Eaton], "The Chinese Woman in America"

1. Annette White-Parks, *Sui Sin Far/Edith Maude Eaton: A Literary Biography* (Urbana: University of Illinois Press, 1995), 1. "Fire Fly" attributes this quote to a "Mr. R." I am indebted to Dominika Ferens for sending me copies of Eaton's work published in the *Gall's Daily News Letter*.
2. Edwin R. Bingham, *Charles F. Lummis: Editor of the Southwest* (San Marion, CA: Huntington Library, 1955), 52–53, 57, 63. Mark Thompson, *American Character: The Curious Life of Charles Fletcher Lummis and the Rediscovery of the Southwest* (New York: Arcade Publishing, 2001), 179–182.
3. Bingham, *Charles F. Lummis*, 164. Patterson, *Beyond the Gibson Girl*, 102–104.
4. The ancient Chinese practice of binding a young girl's feet lasted from the tenth century to 1911, when it was banned by the new Republic of China. At a young age, a girl had her smaller toes broken and her feet bound tightly with cloth in an attempt to create a "three-inch golden lotus."

Elizabeth Cady Stanton, "The New Woman"

1. Kraditor, *Ideas*, 1–2, 10, 78–80.
2. *History of Woman Suffrage*, vol. 4: *1883–1900* (Rochester, NY: Privately published, 1902), 628–637. "The Iowa Commission on the Status of Women: Mary Jane Whitely Coggeshall," http://www.state.ia.us/government/dhr/sw/hall_fame/iafame/iafame-cogge shall.html.

3. This reference is to "Rev. Sydney Smith's speech at Taunton, on the Lord's rejection of the Reform Bill, October, 1831": "The attempt of the Lords to stop the progress of reform, reminds me very forcibly of the great storm of Sidmouth, and of the conduct of the excellent Mrs. Partington on that occasion. . . . In the midst of this sublime and terrible storm, Dame Partington, who lived upon the beach, was seen at the door of her house . . . trundling her mop, squeezing out the sea-water, and vigorously pushing away the Atlantic Ocean. . . . The Atlantic Ocean beat Mrs. Partington. She was excellent at a slop or a puddle, but she should not have meddled with a tempest." *American Bibliopolist*, June 1869, 190.

Charlotte Perkins Gilman, "The New Womanhood"

1. Newman, *White Women's Rights*, 132–146.
2. Kathleen L. Endres, "*The Forerunner*," in Endres and Lueck, *Women's Periodicals*, 98–108.

Frau Anna, "Alte und Neue Frauen" [Of Old and New Women]

1. I am greatly indebted to Peter Conolly-Smith not only for finding and translating this article for me but for providing the invaluable historical context from which it emerged. See Conolly-Smith, *Translating America*.
2. Ibid., 56–59. Peter Conolly-Smith, e-mail to the author, Mar. 15, 2007. *N. W. Ayer & Son's American Newspaper Annual & Directory* (Philadelphia: N. W. Ayer & Son, 1917), 672. *N. W. Ayer & Son's American Newspaper Annual & Directory* (Philadelphia: N. W. Ayer & Son, 1919), 679. Historical Census Browser, Geostat Center Collections, University of Virginia Libraries, http://fisher.lib.virginia.edu/collections/stats/histcensus/.
3. Conolly-Smith, *Translating America*, 15, 56–59, 107, 114–129.
4. Ibid., 130–131. Peter Conolly-Smith, "The Translated Community: New York's German-Language Press as an Agent of Cultural Resistance and Integration" (Ph.D. diss., Yale University, 1996), 489. Peter Conolly-Smith, e-mail to the author, Mar. 15, 2007.

PART IV: THE WOMEN'S CLUB MOVEMENT AND WOMEN'S EDUCATION

Pauline E. Hopkins, "Women's Department"

1. Hanna Wallinger, "Pauline E. Hopkins as Editor and Journalist: An African American Story of Success and Failure," in *Blue Pencils and Hidden Hands: Women Editing Periodicals, 1830–1910*, ed. Sharon M. Harris and Ellen Gruber Garvey (Boston: Northeastern University Press, 2004), 147–148, 158. Patterson, *Beyond the Gibson Girl*, 66. William Stanley Braithwaite, "Negro America's First Magazine," *Negro Digest*, Dec. 1947, 21–26. John E. Bruce Papers, Schomburg Collection, New York Public Library. Patterson, *Beyond the Gibson Girl*, 66–67. Alisha R. Knight, "Furnace Blasts for the Tuskegee Wizard: Revisiting Pauline Elizabeth Hopkins, Booker T. Washington and the *Colored American Magazine*," *American Periodicals* 17, no. 1 (2007): 54–56.
2. Walter N. Wallace, "To Booker T. Washington," Aug. 6, 1901, in Harlan, *Booker T. Washington Papers*, 6:184–185. Knight, "Furnace Blasts," 56.
3. *Colored American Magazine*, May 1900, 57–59; Aug. 1900, 144–145.
4. Hopkins refers here to Robert Grant's influential and popular novel *Unleavened Bread* (1900), in which the ambitious, self-absorbed heroine Selma White climbs her way through marriage and divorce to rise from a country schoolteacher to a senator's wife. Her third husband, the senator, capitulates under her corrupting influence. For many, Grant's novel epitomized the predatory New Woman, for whom marriage was a stepping-stone and divorce an inconvenience.

Lavinia Hart, "A Girl's College Life"

1. Lavinia Hart, "Motherhood," *Cosmopolitan*, Mar. 1902, 463-475.
2. John Bekken and Lisa Beinhoff, *"Cosmopolitan,"* in Endres and Lueck, *Women's Periodicals*, 49-57. Mott, *History of American Magazines*, 4:480-505.

Julia Magruder, "The Typical Woman of the New South"

1. R.W.B., "Magruder, Julia," in *Dictionary of American Biography*, ed. Dumas Malone (New York: Charles Scribner's Sons, 1933), 206.
2. *American Newspaper Directory*, 610. Mott, *History of American Magazines*, 3:388-390. August Gribbin, *"Harper's Bazaar,"* in Endres and Lueck, *Women's Periodicals*, 137-143.

John H. Adams Jr., "Rough Sketches: A Study of the Features of the
New Negro Woman"

1. Lynn Moody Igoe, *250 Years of Afro-American Art: An Annotated Bibliography* (New York: R. R. Bowker, 1981), 402-404. Jessie Parkhurst Guzman, ed., *Negro Year Book: A Review of Events Affecting Negro Life, 1941-1946* (Tuskegee, AL: Department of Records and Research of Tuskegee Institute, 1947), 415. Laura Wexler, *Tender Violence: Domestic Visions in an Age of U.S. Imperialism* (Chapel Hill: University of North Carolina Press, 2000), 266.
2. Daniel, *Black Journals*, 369-372.

"The Modern Indian Girl"

1. Jon Reyhner and Jeanne Eder, *American Indian Education: A History* (Norman: University of Oklahoma, 2004), 3, 140-167, 199-203. Richard Henry Pratt, *Battlefield and Classroom: Four Decades with the American Indian* (New Haven: Yale University Press, 1964), 335.
2. Daniel F. Littlefield Jr. and James W. Parins, *American Indian and Alaska Native Newspapers and Periodicals, 1826-1924* (Westport, CT: Greenwood Press, 1984), 314-316.

"Lo! The New Indian. Mohawk Belle"

1. Gottlieb and Wolt, *Los Angeles Times*, 28-31.

"The Sacrifice"

1. Henry Lewis Suggs, *The Black Press in the Middle West, 1865-1985* (Westport, CT: Greenwood Press, 1996), 11, 24-26. Roi Ottley, *The Lonely Warrior: The Life and Times of Robert S. Abbott* (Chicago: Henry Regnery, 1955), 88, 105-106. Homer C. Hawkins, "Trends in Black Migration from 1863 to 1960," *Phylon* 34, no. 2 (1973): 140-152.
2. "The Cave Man," *Chicago Defender*, June 5, 1915, 8. "Woman Suffrage," *Chicago Defender*, Jan. 1, 1916, 1. Mary E. Stoval, "The *Chicago Defender* in the Progressive Era," *Illinois Historical Journal* 83 (Autumn 1990): 159-172.

PART V: WORK AND THE LABOR MOVEMENT

"The New Woman"

1. Jones proclaimed her birth date to be May 1, 1830, in honor of the Haymarket May Day demonstration for the eight-hour day, but Elliott Gorn maintains that she was actually born on August 1, 1837. Elliott Gorn, *Mother Jones: The Most Dangerous Woman in America* (New York: Hill and Wang, 2001), 9, 28-29, 33, 41-42, 44-45, 71, 76, 89-92, 101-104, 119-122, 161-163, 230-233, 284-285. Jeremy Atack and Fred Bateman, "How Long Was the Workday in 1880?" *Journal of Economic History* 52, no. 1 (Mar. 1992): 129-160.

Maude Radford Warren, "The New Woman and Her Ways: The Woman Farmer"

1. "Auto Gas Kills Maude R. Warren," *New York Times*, July 7, 1934, 11. Maude Radford Warren, "Petticoat Professions: New Women in Old Fields," *Saturday Evening Post*, Nov. 5, 1910, 33.
2. Damon-Moore, *Magazines for the Millions*, 109–124, 127–143, 151, 177–178. Mott, *History of American Magazines*, 4:692.
3. Stuart W. Shulman, "The Progressive Era Farm Press: A Primer on a Neglected Source of Journalism History," *Journalism History* 25, no. 1 (Spring 1999): 27–35.

Astrea, "Debemos Trabajar" [We Must Work]

1. Jessica Enoch, "Para la Mujer: Defining a Chicana Feminist Rhetoric at the Turn of the Century," *College English*, Sept. 2004, 20–37.
2. Kanellos and Martell, *Hispanic Periodicals*, 100–101. Enoch, "Para la Mujer," 24–25.

Virginia Roderick, "New Jobs for New Women"

1. Jennifer Comins, Archives Assistant, Columbia University, e-mail to author, Apr. 6, 2007. Kathleen L. Endres, "*The Woman Citizen*," in Endres and Lueck, *Women's Periodicals*, 429–437. The Wisconsin Historical Society offers information regarding Roderick's association with the McCormicks,http://www.wisconsinhistory.org/libraryarchives/ihc/biblio.asp.
2. Mott, *History of American Magazines*, 5:72–87.

Dorothy Weil, "A New Woman?"

1. Obituary of Dorothy Weil, *Chicago Tribune*, May 12, 1949, A6. "Either Shelter or Real Work," *New Republic*, Aug. 5, 1916, 17–18.
2. Walter B. Rideout, *The Radical Novel in the United States, 1900–1954: Some Interrelations of Literature and Society* (New York: Columbia University Press, 1992), 17, 98–99, 100–103.
3. Leslie Fishbein, *Rebels in Bohemia: The Radicals of The Masses, 1911–1917* (Chapel Hill: University of North Carolina Press, 1982), 17–29.

Elise Johnson McDougald, "The Negro Woman Teacher and the Negro Student"

1. Lorraine E. Roses and Ruth E. Randolph, eds., *Harlem's Glory: Black Women Writing: 1900–1950* (Cambridge: Harvard University Press, 1996), 519. Alain Locke, ed., *The New Negro* (New York: Atheneum, 1968), 419.
2. Kornweibel, *Seeing Red*, 97–98. Randolph, "New Crowd," 27. Kornweibel, *No Crystal Stair*, 54–57. Daniel, *Black Journals*, 241–244.
3. The Anna T. Jeanes Fund and the John F. Slater Fund were private philanthropic organizations that subsidized black education in the South. Businessman Julius Rosenwald helped transform Sears Roebuck into a major retailer and established a philanthropic fund to subsidize black education in the South.

Poppy Cannon, "Pin-Money Slaves"

1. Kessler-Harris, *Out to Work*, 250–253. "You Can Have My Job: A Feminist Discovers Her Home," *Forum*, Apr. 1932. Winifred D. Wandersee, *Women's Work and Family Values, 1920–1940* (Cambridge: Harvard University Press, 1981), 67–69.
2. Lawrence Van Gelder, "Poppy Cannon White, 69, Dead; Writer Was Authority on Food," *New York Times*, Apr. 2, 1975, 42. *Foremost Women in Communications: A Biographical*

Reference Work on Accomplished Women in Broadcasting, Publishing, Advertising, Public Relations, and Allied Professions (New York: R. R. Bowker, 1970), 102.

3. Mott, *History of American Magazines*, 4:521.

PART VI: WORLD WAR I AND ITS AFTERMATH

Cover of Hearst's Magazine

1. Mott, *History of American Magazines*, 4:499–501. David Nasaw, *The Chief: The Life and Times of William Randolph Hearst* (New York: Mariner Books, 2001), 261–266. "Asks Why Hearst Is Urging Hylan," *New York Times*, Oct. 27, 1917, 7.

Helen Rowland, "A Farewell Letter to the Kaiser from Every Woman"

1. Helen Rowland, "Double-Harness Philosophy," in *Writing up the News: Behind the Scenes of the Great Newspapers. Top Ranking Editors and Reporters Tell Their Own Inside Stories,* ed. Miriam Lundy (New York: Dodd, Mead, 1939), 139–147.

2. Roberts, *Shadow of Power*, 137–147.

Mrs. Caesar Misch, "The New America, the New American Woman: A Symposium"

1. Mary McCune, "Misch, Marion Simon," in *Jewish Women in America: An Historical Encyclopedia*, ed. Paula E. Hyman and Deborah Dash Moore (New York: Routledge, 1997), 2:930–931. "Mrs. Caesar Misch," *New York Times*, Jan. 20, 1941, 17. "An Inventory to the Women of Reform Judaism Records," American Jewish Archives, http://www.american-jewisharchives.org/aja/FindingAids/wrj.htm.

2. The *American Hebrew* identified the author as Mrs. Caeser Misch, in the process misspelling Caesar.

3. See S.D.T., "*The American Hebrew*," in *Encyclopedia Judaica* (Jerusalem: Macmillan, 1971), 2:820–821. Frank H. Vizetelly, *The Jewish Encyclopedia* (1901–1906) http://jewishencyclopedia.com.

Harriet Abbott, "What the Newest New Woman Is"

1. Kathleen L. Endres, "*Ladies' Home Journal*," in Endres and Lueck, *Women's Periodicals*, 174–175. *N. W. Ayer & Son's American Newspaper Annual & Directory* (Philadelphia: N. W. Ayer & Son, 1920), 856.

2. Jennifer Scanlon, *Inarticulate Longings: The Ladies' Home Journal, Gender, and the Promises of Consumer Culture* (New York: Routledge, 1995), 124–125.

3. Nora is the female protagonist in Henrik Ibsen's (1828–1926) play *A Doll's House*. Feeling infantilized by her conventional Victorian marriage, Nora leaves her husband and children at the end of the play, in a scene that sparked tremendous controversy at the time.

    British physician Havelock Ellis (1859–1939) analyzed what for many at the time was considered taboo sexual behavior, including homosexuality and masturbation. He also advocated sex education and some rights for women.

    Swedish feminist Ellen Key (1849–1926) drew controversy for her promotion of physical and emotional intimacy within marriage.

    Olive Schreiner (1855–1920), born in South Africa, was one of the most important feminist theorists of the twentieth century. *The Story of an African Farm* (1883) endorsed the life of Lyndall, an outspoken female character who refuses to marry despite becoming pregnant by her lover. In *Women and Labour* (1911) Schreiner charted women's descent into "sex parasitism" or economic dependence and passivity as an effect of industrialization.

PART VII: PROHIBITION AND SEXUALITY
Martha Lee, "What Shall We Do with Jazz?"

1. Chuck Perry, "*Atlanta Journal-Constitution,*" in *The New Georgia Encyclopedia* (Atlanta: Georgia Humanities Council and the University of Georgia Press, 2004), http://www.georgiaencyclopedia.org/nge/Article.jsp?id = h-1807. Wallace B. Eberhard, "Clark Howell and the Atlanta *Constitution,*" *Journalism Quarterly* (Spring 1983): 118–22. *N. W. Ayer & Son's American Newspaper Annual & Directory* (Philadelphia: N. W. Ayer & Son, 1922), 164.
2. In 1923, Mrs. Max E. Oberndorfer led a movement by the General Federation of Women's Clubs to return the "best old hymns" to church services across America. "To Popularize the Best Old Hymns of America," Ampico Recordings, Oct. 1923, n.p.

Jorge Ulica, "Exodo de Una Flapper" [Exodus of a Flapper]

1. Kanellos and Martell, *Hispanic Periodicals*, 47–51. Nicolás Kanellos, "Cronistas and Satire in Early Twentieth Century Hispanic Newspapers," *Melus*, Spring 1998, http://findarticles.com/p/articles/mi_m2278/is_1_23/ai_53501894/print.

John Held Jr., "Sweet Sixteen"

1. Shelley Armitage, *John Held, Jr.: Illustrator of the Jazz Age* (Syracuse: Syracuse University Press, 1987), xi–xv, 3, 8, 20–24, 159–161. Kitch, *Girl on the Magazine Cover*, 123. "John Held Jr., Cartoonist, Dies; Satirist of the Twenties Was 69," *New York Times*, Mar. 3, 1958, 27.
2. *N. W. Ayer & Son's American Newspaper Annual & Directory* (Philadelphia: N. W. Ayer & Son, 1926): 737.

Elizabeth Benson, "The 'Outrageous' Younger Set: A Young Girl Attempts to Explain Some of the Forces That Brought It into Being"

1. "Editor's Note," *Vanity Fair*, Sept. 1927, 68.
2. Tebbel and Zuckerman, *Magazine in America*, 298–299. Norma Green, "*Vanity Fair,*" in Endres and Lueck, *Women's Periodicals*, 398–405. Peterson, *Magazines in the Twentieth Century*, 271. Frank Crowninshield, "An Editor's Conversion," *New York Times*, Feb. 20, 1915, 26. Frank Crowninshield, "Thoughts on Sin—and Advertising," in *Vanity Fair: A Cavalcade of the 1920s and 1930s,* ed. Cleveland Amory and Frederic Bradlee (New York: Viking, 1960), 259–260.
3. Describing herself as a "bulldog running along at the feet of Jesus," Carrie Nation (1846–1911) led a fierce temperance campaign characterized by the smashing of saloons.
4. With its plot revolving around an unmarried couple who lived together, Robert W. Chambers's *The Common Law* (1911) scandalized many readers. British writer Elinor Glyn, in her shocking novel *Three Weeks* (1907), traced the seduction of a young British aristocrat by a Balkan queen.
5. Elmer Gantry, the protagonist of Sinclair Lewis's 1927 satiric novel of the same name, transforms himself into a bombastic preacher and becomes a model of crass, hypocritical American success.

Alberto O'Farrill, "Fumando Espero" [Smoking I Wait]

1. Kanellos and Martell, *Hispanic Periodicals*, 53–57.
2. Translation of "Fumando espero" by Alberto Paz, Planet Tango, http://www.planet-tango.com/lyrics/fumando.htm.

PART VIII: CONSUMER CULTURE, LEISURE CULTURE, AND TECHNOLOGY

Jas. H. Collins, "The Eternal Feminine"

1. *Who Was Who in America*, vol. 5: *1969–1973* (Chicago: Marquis Who's Who, 1973), 144. *Who Was Who among North American Authors* (Detroit: Gale Research, 1976), 337–338. U.S. House Committee on Interstate and Foreign Commerce, *Hearings on Regulation of Prices*, 64th Cong., 1917.
2. Frank Presbrey, *The History and Development of Advertising* (Garden City, NY: Doubleday, Doran, 1929), 262–269, 319–323. Jackson Lears, *Fables of Abundance: A Cultural History of Advertising in America* (New York: Basic Books, 1994), 92–93, 154, 156, 213–215.

"Battle Ax Plug"

1. *The Colored American* (Washington, DC), June 8, 1901, n.p.
2. Eliot Jones, "Is Competition in Industry Ruinous," *Quarterly Journal of Economics* (May 1920): 473–519.
3. Pablo Mitchell, *Coyote Nation: Sexuality, Race and Conquest in Modernizing New Mexico, 1880–1920* (Chicago: University of Chicago Press, 2005), 83.

Anna de Koven, "The Athletic Woman"

1. "Anna F. De Koven, Author and Poet," *New York Times*, Jan. 13, 1953, 27. Edward Marshall, "Are Our Women Either Idle or in a Frenzy," *New York Times*, Dec. 31, 1911, SM8. Mrs. Reginald de Koven, "The New Woman and Golf Playing," *Good Housekeeping*, Aug. 1912, 148–157.
2. Mott, *History of American Magazines*, 5:125–143.

Thomas A. Edison, "The Woman of the Future"

1. "Edison, Thomas Alva," *Biographies Plus Illustrated*.
2. Doris Ostrander Dawdy, *Artists of the American West: A Biographical Dictionary*, vol. 3: *Artists Born before 1900* (Athens: Ohio University Press, 1985), 429.

Jeannette Eaton, "The Woman's Magazine"

1. Christine Nasso, gen. ed., *Contemporary Authors* (Detroit: Gale Research Company, 1978), 179. "Jeanette Eaton, 82, Children's Author," *New York Times*, Feb. 21, 1968, 47. "Suffragists Get Hearing at Columbus," *Evening Telegram* (Elyria, OH), Feb. 8, 1912, 1. See, e.g., "The College Girl of 1930," *Woman's Journal*, May 1930, 5–7, 42–44. Jeannette Eaton, "The Feminist's Best Friend," *Harper's Weekly*, Aug. 7, 1915, 129.
2. Rideout, *Radical Novel*, 17, 98–99, 100–103.

"Famous Bobbed-Hair Beauties"

1. Robert A. Hill, "Vol. I: 1826–August 1919," Marcus Garvey and Universal Negro Improvement Association Papers Project, UCLA, 1995–2007, http://www.international.ucla.edu/Africa/mgpp/intr.asp (accessed June 1, 2007).
2. Robert A. Hill, ed., *The Marcus Garvey and Universal Negro Improvement Association Papers*, 10 vols. (Berkeley: University of California Press, 1983–1995), 5:228n7. Kathy Peiss, *Hope in a Jar: The Making of America's Beauty Culture* (New York: Metropolitan Books, 1998), 117–118, 90–94. Susannah Walker, *Style and Status: Selling Beauty to African American Women, 1920–1975* (Lexington: University Press of Kentucky, 2007), 25, 70–71.

3. John Bush Jones, *Our Musicals, Ourselves: A Social History of the American Musical Theatre* (Lebanon, NH: Brandeis University Press, 2003), 69–71. Walker, *Style and Status*, 70–71.

"From Ping Pong to Pants"

1. Anthony Slide, ed., *International Film, Radio, and Television Journals* (Westport, CT: Greenwood Press, 1985), 282–285. Kathryn H. Fuller, *At the Picture Show: Small-Town Audiences and the Creation of Movie Fan Culture* (Charlottesville: University Press of Virginia, 1996), 150–168. *N. W. Ayer & Son's American Newspaper Annual & Directory* (Philadelphia: N. W. Ayer & Son, 1928), 255.
2. Banner, *American Beauty*, 180–182. Latham, *Posing a Threat*, 113–114.

Vera L. Connolly, "Daughters of the Sky"

1. "Service for Vera Connolly, Writer, Will Be Tomorrow," *New York Times*, Oct. 14, 1964, 45. See also the Vera Connolly Papers, 1913–1945, Columbia University Libraries.
2. Mott, *History of American Magazines*, 3:481–490.

PART IX: EVOLUTION, BIRTH CONTROL, AND EUGENICS
William Lee Howard, M.D., "Effeminate Men and Masculine Women"

1. Howard Kelly, *A Dictionary of American Medical Biography* (Boston: Milford House, 1928), 807. Stephen Greenberg, National Library of Medicine, e-mail to author, Dec. 7, 2006.
2. Pascal James Imperato, M.D., "A History of the New York Medical Journal," *New York State Journal of Medicine* (July 1989): 403–414.

Henry T. Finck, "The Evolution of Sex in Mind"

1. "H. T. Finck Dead: Noted Music Critic," *New York Times*, Oct. 2, 1926, 19.
2. Mott, *History of American Magazines*, 2:367–377. Tebbel and Zuckerman, *Magazine in America*, 87.
3. Renowned Episcopal minister Reverend Richard Heber Newton (1840–1914) served as rector of All Souls' (Anthon Memorial) Church in New York City from 1869 until 1902. A prolific writer widely known for his liberal views, he advocated women's suffrage and equal pay for equal work.

"The New Monkey Woman" and "Evolution"

1. "Rudolph E. Leppert," *New York Times*, Oct. 5, 1949, 29.
2. "Tittle, Walter (Ernest)," *Who Was Who, 1897–2006*, http://www.xreferplus.com.ezproxy.library.tufts.edu/entry/6202385.
3. Marschall, "*Life*." Mott, *History of American Magazines*, 4:556–568. *Newspaper and Magazine Directory*, 142.

G. Stanley Hall, "Flapper Americana Novissima"

1. Russett, *Sexual Science*, 50–63.
2. Mott, *History of American Magazines*, 2:493–515. Ellery Sedgwick, "Atlantic Monthly," in Chielens, *American Literary Magazines*, 50–57. "Current Magazines," *New York Times*, Jan. 15, 1922, 49.

Saydee E. Parham, "The New Woman: In the Political World She
Is the Source of All Reform Legislation and the One
Power That Is Humanizing the World"

1. Hill, "Vol. I: 1826–August 1919," Garvey and Universal Negro Improvement Association Papers Project. E. David Cronon, *Black Moses: The Story of Marcus Garvey and the Universal Negro Improvement Association* (Madison: University of Wisconsin Press, 1969), 204.
2. Ula Yvette Taylor, *The Veiled Garvey: The Life and Times of Amy Jacques Garvey* (Chapel Hill: University of North Carolina Press, 2002), 65–68, 79. Barbara Bair, " 'Our Women and What They Think': Amy Jacques Garvey, the New Negro Woman, and the Woman's Page of the Negro World," in Heilmann, *Feminist Forerunners*, 10. Eunice Lewis, "Our Letter Box: The Black Woman's Part in Race Leadership," *Negro World*, Apr. 19, 1924, 10.
3. Taylor, *Veiled Garvey*, 79. Saydee E. Parham, "Woman's Part in Building Nationhood," *Negro World*, Nov. 22, 1924, 8. See Hill, *Garvey and Universal Negro Improvement Association Papers*, 6:406. U.S. Federal Census, 1920, http://ancestry.com.
4. Bair, "Our Women and What They Think," 110–111. Carrie Mero Leadett, "Our Girls: The Negro Girl of Today Has Become a Follower—Future Success Rests with Her Parents and Home Environment," *Negro World*, Feb. 2, 1924, 10.

Leta S. Hollingworth, "The New Woman in the Making"

1. Rosalind Rosenberg, "Leta Anna Stetter Hollingworth," *American National Biography* (New York: Oxford University Press, 1999), 2:67–68.
2. Cott, *Grounding*, 38–39.
3. Steven Selden, *Inheriting Shame: The Story of Eugenics and Racism in America* (New York: Teachers College Press, Columbia University, 1999), 100–103.
4. It appears that *Current History* misspelled Hollingworth's name; this article originally appeared under the name of Leta S. Hollingsworth.
5. Peterson, *Magazines in the Twentieth Century*, 152. *N. W. Ayer & Son's American Newspaper Annual & Directory* (Philadelphia: N. W. Ayer & Son, 1923), 699.

Clotilde Betances Jaeger, "La Mujer Nueva" [The New Woman]

1. Rojas, e-mail to author, Jan. 23, 2007. Acosta-Belén, "Clotilde Betances Jaeger," 87–88.
2. Kanellos and Martell, *Hispanic Periodicals*, 54–57, 106–107.
3. Emilio Pantojas-Garcia, "Puerto Rican Populism Revisited: The PPD during the 1940s," *Journal of Latin American Studies* (Oct. 1989): 521–557. Laura Briggs, *Reproducing Empire: Race, Sex, Science, and U.S. Imperialism in Puerto Rico* (Berkeley: University of California Press, 2002), 74–94. Harwood Hull, "Roosevelt Makes Plea for Children: Executive in Porto Rico Would Relieve Hunger Ignored Officially for 30 Years," *New York Times*, Dec. 1, 1929, 61.
4. Prominent newspaper owner and member of the Cuban House of Representatives Gustavo González Beauville purchased the island's most influential daily newspaper, *El Heraldo de Cuba*, in 1924 and turned it into the mouthpiece of the Cuban president and increasingly dictatorial General Gerardo Machado y Morales, who came to power in 1925. Charles E. Chapman, *A History of the Cuban Republic* (New York: Macmillan, 1927), 497–499, 599, 654–655.
5. Mabel Walker Willebrandt (1889–1963) served as assistant U.S. attorney general from 1921 to 1929, specializing in enforcing new income tax law and the National Prohibition Act or Volstead Act of 1919.

Index

Page numbers in italics indicate illustrations

About the Editor

Martha H. Patterson is an associate professor of English at McKendree University. Her next project explores the Harlem Renaissance through the lens of New York's major black newspapers.